Studies on Interdisc

Özer Özçelik (ed.)

Studies on Interdisciplinary Economics and Business

Volume II

PETER LANG

Bibliographic Information published by the Deutsche Nationalbibliothek
The Deutsche Nationalbibliothek lists this publication in the Deutsche Nationalbibliografie; detailed bibliographic data is available online at http://dnb.d-nb.de.

Library of Congress Cataloging-in-Publication Data
A CIP catalog record for this book has been applied for at the Library of Congress.

Cover image: monsitj / fotolia.com

ISBN 978-3-631-79729-7 (Print)
E-ISBN 978-3-631-80413-1 (E-PDF)
E-ISBN 978-3-631-80414-8 (EPUB)
E-ISBN 978-3-631-80415-5 (MOBI)
DOI 10.3726/b16227

Peter Lang – Berlin · Bern · Bruxelles · New York · Oxford · Warszawa · Wien

This publication has been peer reviewed.

www.peterlang.com

Foreword

This study was prepared as a continuation of *Interdisciplinary Economics and Business* – Volume I published in 2018. Volume II includes articles prepared by the researchers from various universities and institutions. The authors and their studies are briefly described as follows.

In their study, Odabasi and Citlak examined the causality between economic growth, electrical energy consumption and carbon emissions in the selected EU countries. Cimen examined the relationship between direct foreign investment and economic growth in BRICS countries. In his study, Ozcelik attempted to estimate the relationship between foreign direct investment and economic growth in Turkey. Yazici and Yazici analyzed the long-term relationship between economic growth and outstanding external debt in Turkey. Ozen attempted to estimate the effects of loans on macroeconomy in Turkey. Korap and Konak examined the status of the declared interest rate parity in Turkey. Al, examined the stability of demand for money in Turkey. In his study, Kilci presented the examples of emerging market economies and examined the role of fixed exchange rate regime in financial crises, excess credit growth and deposit insurances. Akbulut Yildiz and Tosun examined the effect of globalization on foreign trade in BRICS countries. Mercan and Canbay attempted to reveal the theoretical framework of the asset price channel. Oksak examined how much added value was created by the export in the industry sector in Turkey. In his study, Bozkurt evaluated Sadrettin Tosbi's perspective on Turkey's economy. Uyaniker and Apali examined the records of salary payments in the Ottoman State. In his study, Yildiz evaluated the corruption, its reasons and Broken Windows Theory approach to corruption. Arabaci, Sanal and Oguzhan examined working women's perceptions of genderbased discrimination. In his study, Saylan examined tourism in sister cities in Turkey. Taskin investigated the sustainable tourism policy of the World Tourism Organization. Tuzunturk analyzed the effect of past experiences on purchase intention in white goods. Kayakiran analyzed and compared business mergers and acquisitions transactions in Turkey and in the world. Ozturk evaluated the service quality in logistics sector by ahp and TOPSIS methods. Akar examined the sustainable production in Turkey's automotive industry. Bas, Kurnaz and Kestane performed the statistical analysis of corporate sustainability after crisis in the TRNC banking sector. Cetinoglu examined the cloud accounting which is a new concept in the accounting profession. Utku and Kaya examined the industry sector in which IFRS was accepted in Europe. Düger examined the effects of HRM applications and leadership on internal branding. Erdogan and Bilgin evaluated the statism efforts of ISIS as a terrorist organization. Gumus and Ciftci critically evaluated the development of minimum wage in Turkey.

I would like to thank the authors who contributed to the emergence of the book and hope that this study will gain a good place in the literature.

Özer Özçelik
Kutahya/Turkey

Contents

List of Contributors

Gulsah Sezen Akar
Ph.D., Assistant Professor, Aydin Adnan Menderes University, Department of International Trade and Finance, gsezen@adu.edu.tr

İbrahim Al
Ph.D., Assistant Professor, Karadeniz Technical University, Department of Economics, ibrahimal@ktu.edu.tr

Ali Apali
Ph.D., Assistant Professor, Mehmet Akif Ersoy University, aapali@mehmetakif.edu.tr

Bahar Arabaci
Lecturer, Kırklareli University, Lüleburgaz Vocational School, bahararabaci@klu.edu.tr

Metin Bas
Ph.D., Assistant Professor, Dumlupinar University, Department of Econometrics, metin.bas@dpu.edu.tr

Abdulbaki Bilgin
TKDK (Agricultural Development Agency), Communication Expert, abdulbaki.bilgin@tkdk.gov.tr

Selahattin Bozkurt
Ph.D., Assistant Professor, Kütahya Dumlupinar University, History of the Republic of Turkey, selahattin.bozkurt@dpu.edu.tr

Serif Canbay
Ph.D., Assistant Professor, Düzce University, Akçakoca Bey Faculty of Political Sciences, Department of Economics, serifcanbay@duzce.edu.tr

Tansel Cetinoglu
Ph.D., Assistant Professor, Kütahya Dumlupinar University, Departmant of Accounting, tansel.cetinoglu@dpu.edu.tr

Ayşe Nur Ciftci
Ph.D Program Student, Kırklareli University Institute of Social Sciences Department of Labor Economics and Industrial Relations

Aysegul Cimen
Ph.D., Research Assistant, Dokuz Eylul University Faculty of Economics and Administrative Sciences, aysegul.cimen@deu.edu.tr

Useyd Citlak
Master of Science

Yavuz Selim Düger
Ph.D., Assistant Professor, Kütahya Dumlupinar University, Department of International Trade and Finance, yselim.duger@dpu.edu.tr

Selami Erdogan
Ph.D., Assistant Professor, Kütahya Dumlupınar University, Faculty of Administrative and Economics Sciences, Department of Public Administration, selami.erdogan@dpu.edu.tr

İskender Gumus
Ph.D., Assistant Professor, Kırklareli University Faculty of Economics and Administrative Sciences Department of Labor Economics and Industrial Relations, igumus@gmail.com

Yusuf Kaya
Ph.D., Assistant Professor, Pamukkale University, Department of Banking and Insurance, ykaya@pau.edu.tr

Dilek Kayakiran
Ph.D., Assistant Professor, Nisantasi University, Departmant of Logistic, dilek.kayakiran@nisantasi.edu.tr.

Ali Kestane
Research Assistant, Kilis 7 Aralık University, Department of Business Administration, alikestane@kilis.edu.tr

Esra N. Kilci
Ph.D., Assistant Professor, Istanbul Arel University, Faculty of Economics and Administrative Sciences, Department of International Trade and Finance, esrakilci@arel.edu.tr,

Ali Konak
Ph.D., Assistant Professor, Karabuk University Faculty of Economics and Administrative Sciences Department of Economics, alikonak@karabuk.edu.tr

Levent Korap
Ph.D., Assistant Professor, Kastamonu University, Faculty of Economics and Administrative Sciences Department of Economics, lkorap@hotmail.com

Niyazi Kurnaz
Ph.D., Assistant Professor, Kütahya Dumlupinar University, Department of Business Administration, niyazi.kurnaz@dpu.edu.tr

Derya Mercan
Ph.D., dmercan@gmail.com

Yavuz Odabasi
Ph.D., Assistant Professor, Kutahya Dumlupinar University, Faculty of Economics and Administrative Sciences, Department of Economics, yavuz.odabasi@dpu.edu.tr

Adil Oguzhan
Ph.D., Professor, Trakya University, Faculty of Economics and Administrative Sciences, adiloguzhan@trakya.edu.tr

Yuksel Oksak
Ph.D., Assistant Professor, Bursa Uludag University, Inegöl Faculty of Business, yukseloksak@uludag.edu.tr

Özer Özçelik
Ph.D., Assistant Professor, Kütahya Dumlupinar University, Department of Economics, ozer.ozcelik@dpu.edu.tr

Eda Ozen
Ph.D., Assistant Professor, Bilecik Şeyh Edebali University, Department of Economics, eda.ozen@bilecik.edu.tr

Derya Ozturk
Ph.D., Associate Professor, Ordu University, Ünye Faculty of Economics and Administrative Sciences, Department of Business, deryaozturk@odu.edu.tr

M. Engin Sanal
Ph.D., Associate Professor, Trakya University, Faculty of Economics and Administrative Sciences, enginsanal@trakya.edu.tr

Ugur Saylan
Ph.D., Assistant Professor, Kütahya Dumlupinar University, Tourism Management, ugur.saylan@dpu.edu.tr

Figen Taskin
Ph.D., Assistant Professor, Ordu University, Department of Political Science and Public Administration, figentaskin@odu.edu.tr

Bengu Tosun
Ph.D., Student, Atatürk University, Department of Economics, bngtosun@gmail.com

Selim Tuzunturk
Ph.D., Assistant Professor, Bursa Uludağ University, Department of Econometrics, selimtuzunturk@uludag.edu.tr

Mehmet Utku
Ph.D., Assistant Professor, Pamukkale University, Department of Business Administration, mutku@pau.edu.tr

Ahmet Uyaniker
Ph.D., Assistant Professor, Ardahan University, ahmetuyaniker@ardahan.edu.tr

Ayla Yazici
Ph.D., Assistant Professor, Anadolu University, Department of Economics, Faculty of Economics and Administrative Sciences, ayazici@anadolu.edu.tr

Resul Yazici
Ph.D., Assistant Professor, Bilecik Şeyh Edebali University, Department of Economics, Faculty of Economics and Administrative Sciences, resul.yazici@bilecik.edu.tr

Gizem Akbulut Yildiz
Ph.D., Assistant Professor,
Gümüşhane University, Department of Economics, gizemakbulut@gumushane.edu.tr

Baris Yildiz
Ph.D., Assistant Professor
Gümüşhane University, Department of Public Finance, barisyildiz61@gmail.com

Yavuz Odabasi and Useyd Citlak

Causality between Economic Growth, Electrical Energy Consumption and Carbon Emission: An Analysis on Chosen EU Countries[1]

1 Introduction

Energy can be defined mostly with some examples like the gasoline put in car or the power entering the house through electric cables that made a television work. However, this term actually has a much wider meaning. In fact, energy is the essence of life in the universe, and the supply of energy is a key to mankind progress (Degunther, 2009: 25). The reason for the considerable economic growth experienced by the world in the last 200 years is the mankind's ability to generate and store energy. Asimov and White concluded that the ability to control energy, whether by making a fire or establishing a power plant, is a prerequisite for civilization (Covary, 2006: 7).

Energy can be used for different purposes and is derived from many different sources. Common types of the energy usage are doing work, heating buildings, cooking (this is a special use of heat), transportation and communication (Towler, 2014: 3). Today, none of the economies in the globalized world are able to produce goods and services without energy input. Undoubtedly, the most important nutritional source that feeds the production is electric energy. None of the mass production facilities can deliver its final good without electrical energy to their customers. Even the raw materials or the agricultural products that are produced by the most primitive methods are being delivered through the vehicles that have accumulator facilities. In these facilities, those products pass through various processes (barcoding, registration on computer, invoicing, etc.) by utilizing electrical energy and then are ready to dispatch.

As it is understood, electrical energy is one of the indispensables of production and thus of economic growth. Each one unit increase in the Gross Domestic

1 This study is derived from the master's thesis prepared and presented by Useyd Cıtlak under the supervision of Yavuz Odabasi at Dumlupinar University Institute of Social Sciences, Department of Economics. Thesis was named as "Causality between Economic Growth, Electrical Energy Consumption and Carbon Emission: An Analysis on Chosen EU Countries".

Product (GDP) of a country will bring an increase in electricity consumption evenly. This increase will be fed by electricity generation and thus one of the elements that have huge importance for sustainable economic growth will be secured.

In addition to the positive results arising from this bidirectional relationship, there are also the negative results arising to deal with. Because, the consumption and generation of energy plays a major role in some sustainability problems worldwide. For example, carbon dioxide emissions from fossil energy combustion form the main cause of anthropogenic climate change. In addition, emissions from both fossil and conventional biofuel combustion are the main cause of air pollution in regional, urban and indoor areas (Ruijven, 2008: 5).

Since approximately 1850, global use of fossil fuels (coal, oil and gas) has increased to supply the energy demand, and this action caused a rapid growth in carbon dioxide emissions (Intergovernmental Panel on Climate Change – IPCC, 2012: 7). Today, a large part of the electricity supply is still generated not via renewable energy sources, but by burning fossil fuels (oil, gas, coal, etc.) in many countries. In this circumstance, there will be an extra carbon emission value in addition to the existing carbon emission value that is caused by goods and services production, and because of this there will be a constant increase trend on carbon emission values.

It is obvious that there is a causal relationship between economic growth, electricity consumption and carbon emission parameters. Therefore, in this study, it is aimed to examine and interpret this causality relationship between economic growth, electricity consumption and carbon emission parameters by panel data analysis. For this purpose, 20 European Union member countries that generate electricity with combusting fossil fuels intensively were selected. The economic growth, electrical energy consumption and carbon emission values of these countries between 1995 and 2014 were analyzed.

In the study, a short review of the literature, description of the materials and methods used, results and discussions, conclusions and recommendations are given, respectively.

2 Literature Review

There are many local and foreign studies related to this study. It is possible to summarize some of the studies on this subject and to present some clues about it as follows.

Pao and Tsai (2011) aimed to investigate the relationship between economic growth, energy consumption, carbon emission and foreign direct investment.

For this purpose, they used the multivariate Granger causality analysis and benefited from the data between 1980 and 2007. According to their findings, there is a bidirectional causality relationship between economic growth and carbon emission, direct foreign investment and carbon emission and economic growth and energy consumption, respectively. On the other hand, they observed that there is a one-way causality relationship from economic growth to foreign direct investment, from energy consumption to foreign direct investment and carbon emission.

Durgun (2013) aimed to investigate the causality relationship between economic growth and electricity consumption for Turkey in his study. For this purpose, data between 1980 and 2010 were used. According to his results, he observed that there is a one-way causality relationship between economic growth and electricity consumption.

Polat (2014) aimed to examine the relationship between carbon emissions, economic growth and electricity consumption for the Organization for Economic Cooperation and Development (OECD) countries in his study. In this context, the data between 1980 and 2010 belonging to OECD countries and Dumitrescu-Hurlin panel causality analysis were used. On the other hand, the countries which are the members of the OECD were examined separately as seven developed countries (G7) and rest of the 23 OECD countries. Results obtained for G7 countries show that there is a bidirectional causality relationship between economic growth, and carbon emissions. Also, there is a bi-directional causality relationship between economic growth and electricity consumption. In addition, it was determined that there is a one-way causality relationship from electricity consumption to carbon emission. According to the results obtained for the remaining 23 OECD countries, it is seen that there is one-way causality relationship from carbon emission to economic growth and electricity consumption to carbon emission. On the other hand, no causality relationship between economic growth and electricity consumption could be determined.

Rufael (2014) aimed to examine the relationship between electricity consumption and economic growth for 15 transition economies in his study. In this context, data between 1975 and 2010 were selected and bootstrap panel causality analysis was used. According to the results, for some countries, one-way causality relationship is observed from electricity consumption to economic growth and for some from economic growth to electricity consumption, while for some there is no causality relationship.

Usta (2015) aimed to analyze the impact of the sectoral and regional energy consumption on economic growth of Turkey in his study. And he also aspired to determine the direction of the relationship, if there is any. In order to determine the direction of this relationship, he benefited from the annual data from the period 1970–2012 and used Toda-Yamamoto causality analysis. According to the results obtained in the study, it is concluded that there is a bi-directional causality between transportation and industrial sectors' energy consumption and economic growth. In addition, it was observed that agricultural and residential energy consumption had no effect on economic growth.

Salahuddin et al. (2016) aimed to examine the relationship between internet use, economic growth, financial development, trade openness and carbon emissions in OECD countries. For this purpose, the annual data of the OECD countries for the period 1991–2012 and Dumitrescu-Hurlin panel causality analysis were used. According to the findings, it is observed that there is no causality relationship between internet usage and carbon emission. On the other hand, there is a two-way causality relationship has been determined between financial development, economic growth and carbon emission. In addition, bidirectional causality relationship between economic growth, internet use, trade openness and financial development has been determined. Also, there is a bidirectional causality relationship between trade openness, economic growth and internet usage too. Finally, one-way causality from carbon emission to trade openness was observed, but no causality was observed between internet use and carbon emissions.

Saidmurodov (2016) aimed to investigate the relationship between economic growth, electricity consumption and foreign direct investment in Central Asian countries. For this purpose, data were used between 1992 and 2014, and three different models were established in the light of these data. The results obtained according to these models are presented and evaluated in this study. According to the first model used in the study, one-way causality relationship from economic growth to electricity consumption, and two-way causality relationship between electricity consumption and foreign direct investment was determined. In addition, no causality relationship between economic growth and foreign direct investment has been observed. In the second model, while a causality relationship between electricity consumption and economic growth and between direct foreign investment and economic growth was not reached, a one-way causality relationship from direct foreign investment to electricity consumption was determined. In the third model, one-way causality relationship from economic growth to electricity consumption was observed, while there was no causality relationship between economic growth and foreign direct investment and between electricity consumption and foreign direct investment.

3 Material and Methods

3.1 Data and Sample

In this study, it is aimed to examine the causal relationship between economic growth, electricity consumption and carbon emission. The study contains the years between 1995 and 2014. GDP (constant 2010$) variable is used as the economic growth variable. For electric energy consumption variable, total electric energy consumption (ELCON) (billion Kwh) variable is used. Finally, carbon emission (kt) variable is used for CO_2 emission. The GDP and CO_2 emission data of these variables are retrieved from the World Development Indicators (WDI) in the World Bank database. Electricity consumption data is retrieved from the U.S. Energy Information Administration (EIA) database. All variables have used with their logarithmic values. Among the countries of the European Union, which are subject to the analysis, the countries that generate electricity by using fossil fuels intensively are chosen for the purpose of the study. These countries are ranked as follows: Bulgaria, Croatia, Cyprus, Czech Republic, Denmark, Estonia, Germany, Greece, Hungary, Ireland, Italy, Latvia, Luxembourg, Malta, Netherlands, Poland, Portugal, Romania, Spain and the United Kingdom

3.2 Panel Unit Root Test

The concept of stationarity, which can be expressed as the mean, variance and autocovariance of a series over time, means that the series is approaching a value in the long term or fluctuated around an expected value. Working with non-stationary panel data models leads to a spurious regression problem as in time series (Tatoglu, 2017: 1–2). In order to determine the stationary of the series, it must be checked whether the series contains unit roots. If the series contains root, it means that it is not stationary. On the contrary, the series is stationary if it does not contain root. For this reason, as in time series, the unit root tests are also used in panel data for testing the stationary of the series. The panel unit root test type to be used for the determination of stationary is determined according to the cross-sectional dependency. First-generation panel unit root tests are used in cases where there is no cross-sectional dependency and second-generation panel unit root tests are used in cases where there is a cross-section dependency.

CIPS test, one of the second-generation panel unit root tests, was used in the study. The CIPS (Cross-Sectionally Augmented IPS) statistics is formulated as follows:

$$CIPS\,(N,T) = N^{-1}\sum_{i=1}^{N} t_i\,(N,T)$$

In the CIPS test, in addition to the hypothesis that there is no unit root in the series, an alternative hypothesis is established that there is no unit root in the series (i.e., it is stationary). The CIPS statistics value is compared to the critical table values determined by Pesaran (2007). If the CIPS test statistic values are higher than the critical table values (as absolute value), the absence hypothesis is rejected, and the panel series are considered to be all stationary.

3.3 Pedroni Panel Cointegration Test

Tests with non-stationary series cause spurious regression. Therefore, differences of the series are taken in order to ensure the stability of non-stationary series. However, in this case, the shocks in which the variables are affected by the past period are eliminated and this situation causes the long-run relationships which may be outside of the shocks to be lost. For these reasons, the concept of cointegration has developed. This concept suggests that the series of economic variables may be stationary (in some combinations) even if they are not stationary. These combinations, which are stationary, show that the variables have a long-run equilibrium relationship (Tari, 2008: 405).

When working with non-stationary panel data, spurious regression problems occur as in time series. In such a case, the statistical tests for the established regression model have deviant results and also the R^2 values give misleading results. On the other hand, despite the permanent shocks affecting the system, it is possible to have an equilibrium relationship between the variables in the long term (Tatoglu, 2017: 189). The existence of this probable relationship is tested by using panel cointegration tests.

Pedroni panel cointegration test was used in this study. Pedroni's (1999) panel cointegration test is based on a null hypothesis that assumes no cointegration between the panel series and suggests seven different tests for testing this hypothesis. Four of these tests are called intra-group and three of them are called inter-group test statistics. While a common autoregressive coefficient can be estimated in intra-group statistics, a common autoregressive coefficient is not estimated in the inter-group tests. This is the most important difference between intra-group and inter-group tests (Sak, 2015: 269).

In addition, intra-group tests are derived for homogeneous panels, and inter-group tests are for heterogeneous panels and these tests can be used in both cases. Pedroni panel cointegration test can be used in the series that are stationary in the first difference, i.e., I (1).

The model used for this test, includes mean and trend, is defined as follows:

$$Y_{it} = \alpha_i + \delta_i t + \beta_{1i} X_{1i,t} + \cdots + \beta_{ki} X_{ki,t} + \varepsilon_{it}$$

Here, the variables Y_{it} and $X_{ki,t}$ are I (1), i.e., the first-order stationary series. On the other hand, α_i refers to the mean, δ_i is the trend for each unit, β_{ki} refers to the coefficients of the independent variables and ε_{it} is the error term. The hypotheses tested in both cases with this model are as follows:
For intra-group tests:

$$H_0 : \rho = 1, \quad H_0 : \rho < 0$$

For inter-group tests:

$$H_0 : \rho_i = 1, \quad H_0 : \rho_i < 0$$

In these hypotheses given for both groups, the null hypothesis refers to 'there isn't any cointegration' and the alternative hypothesis refers to 'there is a co-integration'.

3.4 Dumitrescu-Hurlin Panel Causality Test

The concept of causality was first derived in 1969 by Granger to determine the causal relationship between variables. Because determining the direction of the relationship between the variables will provide more economic information than the existing relationship.

In this context, the definition of causality proposed by Granger is expressed as "when predicting the value of a dependent variable, if the independent variables' past values are more successful than the present values, this independent variable is the Granger cause of the dependent variable" (Emirmahmutoglu, 2011: 84). In this way, the independent variable becomes the cause while the dependent variable is becoming the result and the direction of the relationship between the variables can be determined.

This causality approach, which was first proposed by Granger for time series, was examined by many researchers from different perspectives and different methods were developed. In these methods developed within the panel data, the first developed tests are presented under the assumption that the parameters in the panel data model are same for each unit. However, the researches show that the results are not reliable when the parameters are not homogeneous. For this purpose, a test was developed by Dumitrescu and Hurlin (2012), which considers the heterogeneity of the parameters (i.e., the parameters are not the same for each unit) in the panel data model and the cross-sectional dependency.

Dumitrescu and Hurlin (2012) model for panel causality testing is formulated as follows:

$$Y_{it} = \alpha_i + \sum_{k=1}^{K} \gamma_i^{(k)} Y_{i,t-k} + \sum_{k=1}^{K} \beta_i^{(k)} X_{i,t-k} + \varepsilon_{it}$$

k, γ, β and ε show, respectively, the lag length, autoregressive parameter, slope coefficient and the error term in this formula. In addition, the autoregressive parameter and the slope coefficient differ from unit to unit.

In this test, the null hypothesis is established as 'there is no causality relationship in all units of the panel data set', while the alternative hypothesis is established as 'at least one of the units of the panel data set has a causality relationship'.

4 Results and Discussions

4.1 Cross-Sectional Dependency and CIPS Panel Unit Root Tests

The cross-sectional dependency between the variables in the study was tested using Lagrange Multiplier (LM) method. The test results are shown in Tab. 1.

When the test results are examined, it is seen that the chi-square test statistics has a probability value of less than 0.05. So, H_0 hypothesis that assumes there is no cross-sectional dependence was rejected and H_1 hypothesis was accepted. In other words, there is a cross-sectional dependency in the data and therefore the second-generation panel unit root tests have to be used.

The results of the CIPS test, which is one of the second-generation panel unit root tests, are shown in Tab. 2.

Here; LGDP, LCO2 and LELCON are the logarithmic values of the variables, while DLGDP, DLCO2 and DLELCON are the first differences of these variables. CV is the critical value (on probability levels of 1 %, 5 % and 10 %) of the test statistics.

Tab. 1: Cross-Sectional Dependency Test Results

	Breusch-Pagan LM Test	
	Chi-square	**Prob.**
Test Statistics	1756.089***	0.0000

*** significant at 1 % significance level.

Tab. 2: Panel Unit Root Test Results

Variables	CIPS Panel Unit Root Test					
	Intercept			*Intercept and Trend*		
	CV (0,01)	CV (0,05)	CV (0,10)	CV (0,01)	CV (0,05)	CV (0,10)
	-2.1	-2.21	-2.4	-2.63	-2.73	-2.92
	Test Statistics			Test Statistics		
LGDP	-1.073			-1.658		
LCO2	-1.987			-2.471		
LELCON	-1.239			-1.509		
DLGDP	-2.383**			-2.733**		
DLCO2	-4.255***			-5.189***		
DLELCON	-3.431***			-4.510***		

*** significant at 1 % significance level. ** significant at 5 % significance level.

When the test results are analyzed, it is seen that the GDP, CO2 and ELCON variables' absolute value of the test statistics that are obtained at the level are lower than the critical values in either intercept or intercept and trend models. Therefore, the hypothesis H_0, which states that the series contains unit roots, i.e., they aren't stationary, cannot be rejected. So, the series is not stationary at the level.

On the other hand, when the test statistics of the first differences of the series are examined, it is seen that the test statistics obtained in both intercept and intercept and trend models are higher than the critical value of 5 % (CV-0.05) with absolute value. In other words, the hypothesis H_0, which states that the first difference of both intercept and intercept and trend models of GDP is not stationary, was rejected and the series was found to be stationary at 5 % significance level. Similarly, the values of test statistics for both intercept and intercept and trend models of CO2 and ELCON variables were found to be higher than the critical values of 1 % (CV-0.01). In other words, for both variables, it is seen that the first differences of both intercept and intercept and trend models are stationary at 1 % significance level.

4.2 Pedroni Panel Cointegration Test

The results of Pedroni cointegration test are shown in Tab. 3.

In the table, it is seen that the test statistics for homogeneous and heterogeneous panels of the Pedroni cointegration test and the probability values of these statistics are given. When the results are examined, it is seen that five of these seven test statistics (Panel v, Panel PP, Panel ADF, Group PP and Group

Tab. 3: Cointegration Test Results

Pedroni Cointegration Test					
Homogeneous			***Heterogeneous***		
	Statistics	**Prob.**		**Statistics**	**Prob.**
Panel v	1.447771*	0.0738	**Group rho**	1.003040	0.8421
Panel rho	-0.119883	0.4523	**Group PP**	-2.228861**	0.0129
Panel PP	-1.822963**	0.0342	**Group ADF**	-4.712019***	0.0000
Panel ADF	-2.579199***	0.0050			

***, **, * are respectively significant at 1 %, 5 % and 10 % significance level.

ADF) were statistically significant at 1 %, 5 % and 10 % significance level. That is, the hypothesis H_0, which assumes that there is no cointegration relationship between the variables, was rejected and H_1 hypothesis was accepted. Therefore, it has been concluded that the chosen variables for the selected European Union countries have a long-run equilibrium relationship, in other words, they act together. Despite the shocks that may occur in the system, these three variables act together in the long-run.

4.3 Dumitrescu-Hurlin Panel Causality Test

The results of the causality test are shown in Tab. 4.

When the test results were examined, it was observed that there were three different results at 1 % significance level. These results showed that one-way causality statistics from economic growth to carbon emission, from electricity consumption to carbon emission and from economic growth to electricity consumption, respectively, are significant.

Tab. 4: Causality Test Results

Causality Direction	**Dumitrescu ve Hurlin Panel Causality Test**	
	Test Statistics	**Prob.**
LGDP $\Longrightarrow$ LCO2	2.4227***	0.0000
LCO2 $\not\Rightarrow$ *LGDP*	0.5079	0.1197
LELCON $\Longrightarrow$ LCO2	7.6987***	0.0000
LCO2 $\not\Rightarrow$ *LELCON*	1.5900	0.0621
LGDP $\Longrightarrow$ LELCON	2.8800***	0.0000
LELCON $\not\Rightarrow$ *LGDP*	0.8075	0.5427

*** significant at 1 % significance level.

5 Conclusions and Recommendations

The importance of energy in sustainable economic growth is not negligible. In addition to the positive results such as the increase in employment due to the need for energy for production, negative results such as carbon dioxide emission are also encountered due to the preferred methods for energy generation.

The energy type that is most needed and which is of vital importance for the sustainability of production is electrical energy. Demand for electricity is increasing at the level of economic growth, which leads to the need to generate more electricity. Primary energy sources (coal, natural gas, oil, nuclear energy, hydroelectric energy, geothermal energy, solar energy, wind energy, tidal and wave energies and biomass energy) are used for electricity generation. In primary energy sources, mostly non-renewable resources are preferred, and electricity production is made more intensively by burning these resources. This causes carbon dioxide emission and increases carbon emission levels.

In this context, considering the energy policies of the European Union, it is observed that there is a sensitivity about sustainable energy and carbon emission. However, this sensitivity does not sufficiently coincide with data containing current energy use. In Bulgaria, Croatia, Cyprus, Czech Republic, Denmark, Estonia, Germany, Greece, Hungary, Ireland, Italy, Latvia, Luxembourg, Malta, the Netherlands, Poland, Portugal, Romania, Spain and the UK, fossil fuel burning methods are still preferred more intensively.

To analyze the causality relationship between GDP, economic growth and the electricity consumption for these selected countries, the natural logarithms of the variables were taken first. Then, with the help of unit root tests, the variables are examined whether they are stationary (i.e., they are resistant to shocks to occur over time). A cross-sectional dependence test was performed before the unit root tests and it was concluded that there was a cross-sectional dependency. This result has necessitated the use of the second-generation panel unit root tests. CIPS test has used for the second-generation panel unit root test. When the results have examined, it has seen that the first differences of GDP, CO2 and ELCON variables were stationary at both intercept and intercept and trend models.

The Pedroni panel cointegration test has been used to determine whether these variables, which analyzed with their first differences, acted together over time. The results have showed that the variables determined for 20 European Union countries were in long-run equilibrium. In other words, these three variables can act together in the long-run against the shocks that may occur in the system.

After the long-run relationship between the variables has been determined, it was aimed to determine the direction of this relationship by using

Dumitrescu-Hurlin panel causality test. When the results of Dumitrescu-Hurlin panel causality were examined a one-way causality was detected for each of the samples, respectively, from economic growth to carbon emissions, from electricity consumption to carbon emissions and from economic growth to electricity consumption.

Looking at these results obtained in the study, it is seen that economic growth increased electricity consumption, electricity consumption increased carbon emissions and thus economic growth increased carbon emissions throughout the European Union. The reason for the increasing carbon emission caused by electricity consumption is that electricity generation following electricity consumption is carried out using primary energy sources (by conventional methods).

Thus, it is understood that the validity of the European Union energy policies has had a limited impact on the period of 1995–2014. This situation has not changed in recent history. According to 2017 data on the official website of the European Commission, when renewable electricity generation with renewable energy sources data are analyzed, it is seen that renewable energy resources have a share of only 26.1 % in electricity generation. In 2017, the European Union has sought to achieve its carbon emission targets more by using nuclear energy for electricity generation. Nuclear energy, which does not cause carbon emission but is a non-renewable energy source, have had a 25.6 % share in electricity generation alone in 2017. In total, the share of conventional methods has declined (48.3 %) slightly due to the intensity of nuclear energy preference (www.ec.europa.eu, 2018).

On the other hand, European Union is the biggest energy importer in the world, because it has a huge foreign dependency on either nuclear energy (uranium) or fossil fuels. EU imports 53 % of its energy demand, which costs 400 billion euros. It imports 42 % of its coal demand, 88 % of its petroleum demand and 66 % of its natural gas demand. Also, it imports nuclear energy (uranium) 29 % from Canada, 15 % from Russia, 15 % from Niger, 15 % from Australia and 14 % from Kazakhstan. (IEA, 2014: 47; www.world-nuclear.org, 26.09.2018).

In summary, on account of using conventional methods in electricity generation more intensely in 20 EU countries, the sharing of renewable energy sources across the European Union is still not at in an effective level. However, due to the persistence of these countries on conventional methods, there are inconsistencies in the implementation of existing policies targeting energy sustainability.

Although the selected member countries have foreign dependency in fossil fuels, they are still using high-cost fossil fuel combustion methods in electricity generation intensely, and they are incapable of keeping their promises on carbon emission. These countries assert that they are preferring the non-renewable energy sources to renewable energy sources in electricity generation because of the relatively higher costs of the renewable sources. However, instead of using imported energy sources, it is possible to terminate their existing foreign dependency with the use of a different type of renewable energy source which can provide the highest efficiency in each location with different characteristics. They will also amortize the high costs they avoid in the long-run. And, as a result, the gains of the current energy policies on carbon emission and sustainable energy will be taken far better.

Policy makers should direct these member states, which use fossil fuels more intensively in electricity generation, to renewable energy sources with more constructive incentives. In the European Union, this step must be taken to eliminate the energy sustainability and carbon emission problem. When the necessary incentives are provided effectively, the European Union will make much faster and faster progress in its fight against carbon emissions than its current situation.

References

Covary, T., (2006). *Renewable Energy: Benefits of Converting Urban Households to Solar Water Heating* (Master Thesis), University of Pretoria, South Africa.

Degunther, R., (2009). *Alternative Energy for Dummies*, Wiley Publishing, Indiana.

Dumitrescu, E.I., Hurlin, C., (2012). Testing for Granger Non-Causality in Heterogeneous Panels, *Economic Modelling*, 29(4), 1450–1460.

Durğun, B., (2013). *Elektrik Tüketimi İle Büyüme Arasında Nedensellik İlişkisi: Türkiye Örneği* (Yüksek Lisans Tezi), Dicle Üniversitesi, Sosyal Bilimler Enstitüsü, Diyarbakır.

Emirmahmutoğlu, F., (2011). *Gelişmekte Olan Ülkelerde Para Krizlerinin Ekonometrik Analizi* (Doktora Tezi), Gazi Üniversitesi, Sosyal Bilimler Enstitüsü, Ankara.

Intergovernmental Panel on Climate Change (IPCC). (2012). *Renewable Energy Sources and Climate Change Mitigation Special Report of the Intergovernmental Panel on Climate Change Summary for Policymakers and Technical Summary*, IPCC, Switzerland.

International Energy Agency (IEA). (2014). Energy Policies of IEA Countries European Union, IEA, France.

Pao, H.T., and Chung-Ming, T., (2011). Multivariate Granger Causality between CO2 Emissions, Energy Consumption, FDI (Foreign Direct İnvestment) and GDP (Gross Domestic Product): Evidence from a Panel of BRIC (Brazil, Russian Federation, India, and China) Countries, *Energy*, 36: 685–693.

Pedroni, P., (1999). Critical Values for Cointegration Tests in Heterogeneous Panels with Multiple Regressors, *Oxford Bulletin of Economics and Statistics*, 61: 653–670.

Peseran, M.H., (2007). A Simple Panel Unit Root Test in the Presence of Cross Section Dependence, *Journal of Applied Econometrics*, 22(2): 265–312.

Polat, M., (2014). *Sürdürülebilir Kalkınmada Elektrik Tüketimi ve Büyüme İlişkisi* (Doktora Tezi), İnönü Üniversitesi, Sosyal Bilimler Enstitüsü, Malatya.

Rufael, Y.W., (2014). Electricity Consumption and Economic Growth in Transition Countries: A Revisit Using Bootstrap Panel Granger Causality Analysis, *Energy Economics*, 44: 325–330.

Ruijven, B.J.V., (2008). *Energy and Development: A Modelling Approach*, Grafisch Bedrijf Ponsen and Looijen BV, Amsterdam.

Saidmurodov, S., (2016). *Orta Asya Ülkelerinde Elektrik Enerji Tüketimi, Ekonomik Büyüme ve Doğrudan Yabancı Yatırım İlişkisi* (Yüksek Lisans Tezi), Kocaeli Üniversitesi, Sosyal Bilimler Enstitüsü, Kocaeli.

Şak, N., (2015). Panel Eşbütünleşme Analizi. Güriş, Selahattin (Der.), *STATA ile Panel Veri Modelleri*, Der Yayınlari, İstanbul.

Salahuddin, Mohammad, Khorshed, A., and İlhan, Ö., (2016). The Effects of Internet Usage and Economic Growth on CO2 Emissions in OECD Countries: A Panel İnvestigation, *Renewable and Sustainable Energy Reviews*, 62: 1226–1235.

Tarı, R., (2008). *Ekonometri*, Avcı Ofset, İstanbul.

Tatoğlu, Yerdelen, F., (2017). *Panel Zaman Serileri Analizi*, Beta Yayıncılık, İstanbul.

Towler, B.F., (2014). *The Future of Energy*, Academic Press, USA.

Usta, C., (2015). *Türkiye'de Enerji Tüketimi Ekonomik Büyüme İlişkisinin Bölgesel ve Sektörel Analizi* (Doktora Tezi), Karadeniz Teknik Üniversitesi, Sosyal Bilimler Enstitüsü, Trabzon.

Electronic References

European Commission; 2018, https://ec.europa.eu/

World Bank World Development Indicators; 2018 https://databank.worldbank.org/data/source/world-development-indicators.

World Nuclear Association; 2018, www.world-nuclear.org

Aysegul Cimen

Foreign Direct Investment and Economic Growth: Evidence from BRICS Countries

1 Introduction

With the increased globalisation and liberalisation among the world, financial markets have become much more integrated. In this borderless world, investments play crucial role for the growth of countries. It is possible to observe the investment inflows and outflows of a country from its balance of payments.

Balance of payments is a statistical record that shows the transactions of a country's residents with rest of the world. With the help of the balance of payments, anyone can have a deeper understanding of a country's overall situation, regardless of the development level of the country.

Emerging markets differ from developed markets in terms of the regulations, size and depth of the markets and the ease of access to meet the funds needed. It is more difficult for emerging markets to find funds due to higher risk and uncertainty compared to developed markets. Besides, investments play a big role as meeting the need for funds especially in the emerging markets. For these reasons, there is a competition among the countries to attract higher volume of FDI inflows. Emerging markets need to provide some advantages to take the attention of foreign investors and to compete with developed countries. Some of the emerging markets are referred to as tax heavens due to the tax advantages they provide to foreign investors. In addition, some of them provide subsidies in order to attract foreign investors.

The American Economist Jim O'Neill (2001) formed the phrase for BRIC in his report for Goldman Sachs for the first time for the country group of Brazil, Russia, India and China. Due to the size, population and land area, these countries are assumed to have potential to be a developed market. On December 24, 2010, South Africa joined the group and formed BRICS.

There is an ongoing debate whether Foreign Direct Investment has an impact on economic growth or vice versa. The aim of this chapter is to analyse the presence and direction of relationship between Foreign Direct Investment and Economic Growth. Data is collected from World Bank database and covers from 1998 to 2017. For the empirical analysis, the emerging market country set known as BRICS (Brazil, Russia, India, China and South Africa) or fragile five is chosen.

This chapter is organized as follows. Section 2 mentions the theoretical framework regarding the relationship between FDI and economic growth whereas

Section 3 describes data and research methodology used for empirical analysis. Section 4 indicates the findings of the study and finally Section 5 provides the conclusion of this chapter.

2 Theoretical Framework

There is an argument among researchers whether foreign direct investment has an impact on economic growth or economic growth has an impact on foreign direct investment. Although this topic has been researched for different country groups, there is not a consensus among the researchers regarding the empirical results.

Mobius (2012: 12) states that emerging markets cover the two third of the world's land mass, which is not possible to neglect. In terms of population, the ratio is almost same. For these reasons, this study has focused on the emerging market country set known as BRICS or fragile five. The other reason is that investment inflow into emerging markets are expected to be greater when compared to the developed markets.

According to the World Trade Report (2018) that is prepared by World Trade Organization, emerging countries' share in global trade could grow from 46 % in 2015 to 57 % by 2030. With such an important potential, economic growth, FDI and its determinants are the attractive topics to be analysed, from the perspective of researchers. Khondoker (2007) states that the emerging markets can attract more FDI with higher growth rate and investment friendly policies compared to the developed countries.

FDI is now considered as one of the most important sources of capital and know-how not only in manufacturing but also in services (Agrawal, 2015). World Trade Report (2018) also emphasises that digital technologies will boost trade especially in services in developing countries.

In order to have a deeper understanding of FDI and its determinants, Ranjan and Agrawal (2011) conduct a study in BRIC countries. The empirical findings imply that market size, trade openness, labor cost, infrastructure, macroeconomic stability and growth prospects are the determinants of FDI inflow.

Although most of the literature focuses on the positive impact of FDI on growth on economy, rising external vulnerability and dependence may be negative consequences of FDI on economic growth (Yalta: 2013).

Empirical results of some studies indicate that there is a unidirectional causality from economic growth to foreign direct investment inflows, which is referred as market size hypothesis. According to market size hypothesis, an accelerated

GDP growth generates new investment opportunities in the host country, which in turn result in higher foreign direct investment inflows (Rodrik, 1999).

Oncu and Celik (2018) has recently studied the relationship between economic growth and foreign direct investment in Brazil, Russia, India, China and Turkey. The findings of the study indicate that there is unidirectional causality from economic growth to foreign direct investment, which supports the market size hypothesis.

On the contrary, some studies contradict with market size hypothesis, which find a unidirectional causality from foreign direct investments to growth in GDP. These findings are explained by FDI-led growth hypothesis. According to FDI-led growth hypothesis, FDI inflows encourage the economic growth of the host country by rising transfer of technology, efficiency and productivity as well as creating new job opportunities.

The growth impact of FDI of the host country depends on the macroeconomic factors and the policies of the host country. Countries with skilled human resources are assumed to benefit from technology transfer, which is a consequence of FDI. (Agrawal:2015). For instance, Wijeweera et al (2010) analyse the relationship between FDI and economic growth over the period of 1997–2004 for 45 countries using a stochastic frontier model. The findings are in line with Agrawal (2015) who claims that FDI inflows result with economic growth given that host country have skilled human capital. Bende-Nabende (2001) investigates whether FDI has caused spillover effects that result in economic growth in ASEAN-5 economies during 1970 and 1996. The empirical findings indicate the significant impact of human factors on FDI inflows and ASEAN Preferential Trade Agreement (APTA).

In addition to unidirectional causalities, studies by Hansen and Rand (2006) find bidirectional causality between the economic growth and FDI. Hansen and Rand (2006) analyse the causal relationship between FDI and GDP in 31 developing countries for a period of 31 years. The findings show that there is bidirectional relation among the variables. Agrawal (2015) also finds bidirectional causality among FDI and economic growth in BRICS economies over the period 1989–2012.

The fourth group of findings point out that there is no statistically significant causal relationship between the variables, which is explained by neutrality hypothesis. For instance, Yalta (2013) investigates the causal relationship between FDI inflow and economic growth in one of the emerging markets- China, for the period 1982 and 2008. Empirical findings imply that there is no statistically significant relationship between variables for the period analysed. These findings are in line with Görg and Greenaway (2004) and Herzer et al. (2008).

3 Data and Methodology

For the empirical analysis, Gross Domestic product (GDP) is chosen as a proxy for economic growth. Both the GDP and FDI data from 1998 to 2017 are collected from World Bank database. For the empirical analysis, the emerging market country set known as BRICS (Brazil, Russia, India, China and South Africa) is chosen. Both of the variables are in natural logarithm and Eviews 9.0 is used for the analysis. Panel causality test is conducted in order to find out the presence and direction of the relationship among variables.

The first step of the empirical analysis is testing for cross- section dependence of residuals. Second step is checking the stationarity of the variables by using Levin, Lin and Chu, Im, Pesaran and Shin W-stat, ADF-Fisher Chi-square and PP-Fisher Chi-square methods. Checking the stationary of the variables is one of the most important preliminary test prior to causality testing.

Third step of the empirical analysis is checking for the causality analysis between economic growth and foreign direct investment inflow to BRICS economies. Dumitrescu and Hurlin (2012) causality test is implemented for the analysis and is chosen due to the fact that it can be used in either situations where N (number of observations) is greater than T (number of periods) or T (number of periods) is greater than N (number of observations).

4 Findings

Tab. 1 shows the test results for cross-section dependence in residuals. Since the probabilities in all Breusch-Pagan LM, Pesaran scaled LM, Bias-corrected scaled LM and Pesaran CD tests are less than 5 percent, the null hypothesis, which states that here is no cross-section dependence in residuals, is rejected.

Tab. 2 indicates the unit root results for both of the variables. Levin, Lin and Chu, Im, Pesaran and Shin W-stat, ADF - Fisher Chi-square and PP - Fisher Chi-square test results are available for both level intercept and level intercept and trend. The null hypothesis states that panel data has unit root or non-stationarity.

Tab. 1: Cross-Section Dependence Test

Test	**Statistic**	**Probability**
Breusch-Pagan LM	2.632.497	0.0033
Pesaran scaled LM	2.532.340	0.0113
Bias-corrected scaled LM	2.400.761	0.0164
Pesaran CD	4.253.709	0.0000

Tab. 2: Unit Root Tests

Gdp	Method	Level	Level		
		Intercept		Intercept and Trend	
		Statistic	Prob.**	Statistic	Prob.**
	Levin, Lin and Chu	-1,839	0,0330	1,81951	0,9656
	Im, Pesaran and Shin W-stat	0,29885	0,6175	1,45408	0,9270
	ADF – Fisher Chi-square	7,19065	0,7073	3,31421	0,9730
	PP – Fisher Chi-square	2,71873	0,9873	2,39210	0,9924
LogGdp	Method	First Difference			
		Intercept		Intercept and Trend	
		Statistic	Prob.**	Statistic	Prob.**
	Levin, Lin and Chu	-2,95	0.0016	-2.39608	0.0019
	Im, Pesaran and Shin W-stat	-2,13	0.0166	-0.97879	0.1638
	ADF – Fisher Chi-square	20,1823	0.0276	13.7154	0.1864
	PP – Fisher Chi-square	31,4620	0.0005	27.9721	0.0018
LogFdi	Method	Level		Level	
		Intercept		Intercept and Trend	
		Statistic	Prob.**	Statistic	Prob.**
	Levin, Lin and Chu	-1,71	0.0435	1.25513	0.8953
	Im, Pesaran and Shin W-stat	-0.35575	0.3610	1.74662	0.9596
	ADF – Fisher Chi-square	9.25858	0.5078	3.43044	0.9694
	PP – Fisher Chi-square	12.9586	0.2260	8.36469	0.5933

(*continued on next page*)

Tab. 2: (continued)

LogFdi	Method	First Difference			
		Intercept		Intercept and Trend	
		Statistic	Prob.**	Statistic	Prob.**
	Levin, Lin and Chu	-2,76	0.0029	-2.28883	0.0110
	Im, Pesaran and Shin W-stat	-3,51	0.0002	-2.85533	0.0021
	ADF – Fisher Chi-square	30.5470	0.0007	25.2106	0.0050
	PP – Fisher Chi-square	91.4151	0.0000	55.1358	0.0000

Tab. 3: Dumitrescu and Hurlin Causality Test

	W-Stat.	**Zbar-Stat.**	**Olasılık**
LOGFDI ⇏ LOGGDP	4.48114	1.66678	0.0956
LOGGDP ⇏ *LOGFDI*	6.25508	3.06312	0.0022

Depending on the method of unit root test, it is not possible to reject the null hypothesis at level for both intercept and intercept and trend, first differences of the variables, the variables are found to be stationary at the first difference level.

Finally, Dumitrescu and Hurlin causality test is conducted in order to find out the direction of the relationship. Tab. 3 shows the findings of Dumitrescu and Hurlin causality test. According to Tab. 3 results, the null hypothesis of LOGGDP ⇏ *LOGFDI* is rejected. It can be said that there is unidirectional causality from economic growth to foreign direct investment.

The findings of the study indicate that there is unidirectional causality from economic growth to foreign direct investment. Unidirectional causality from economic growth to FDI is referred as market size hypothesis. The findings of the study show that this study supports market size hypothesis. Hence, it is important for countries to have higher growth rate in order to become more attractive in terms of foreign direct investment inflows.

5 Conclusion

In this chapter, the causality relationship between Gross Domestic Product (GDP) and foreign direct investment (FDI) is empirically analysed by using panel data analysis. Understanding the relationship between FDI and economic growth is very important for policy makers in order to decide and adapt the most efficient policies.

For the analysis, logarithm of the variables is taken into account to conduct the panel data analysis on Eviews. Emerging market country set known as BRICS or fragile five (Brazil, Russia, India, China and South Africa) for the period 1998–2017 is chosen for the panel data analysis.

The findings of the study indicate that there is unidirectional causality from economic growth to foreign direct investment. Unidirectional causality from economic growth to FDI is known as market size hypothesis in the literature. The findings of the study show that this study supports market size hypothesis.

References

Agrawal, G. (2015). Foreign Direct Investment and Economic Growth in BRICS Economies: A Panel Data Analysis. *Journal of Economics, Business and Management*, 421–424.

Bende-Nabende, A., Ford, J., and Slater, J. (2001). FDI, Regional Economic Integration and Endogenous Growth: Some Evidence from Southeast Asia. *Pacific Economic Review*, 6(3), 383–399.

Dumitrescu, E., and Hurlin, C. (2012), Testing for Granger Non-causality in Heterogeneous Panels. *Economic Modelling*, 29, 1450–1460.

Görg, H., and Greenaway, D. (2004). Much Ado about Nothing? Do Domestic Firms Really Benefit from Foreign Direct Investment? *The World Bank Research Observer*, 19(2), 171–197.

Hansen, H., and Rand, J. (2006). On the Causal Links between FDI and Growth in Developing Countries. *World Economy*, 29(1), 21–41.

Herzer, D., Klasen, S. and Lehmann, F. N. (2008). In Search of FDI-Led Growth in Developing Countries: The Way Forward. *Economic Modelling*, 25(5), 793–810.

Khondoker, A. M. (2007). Determinants of Foreign Direct Investment and Its Impact on Economic Growth in Developing Countries. *MPRA Paper*, Munich Personal RePEc Archive (9457), https://mpra.ub.uni-muenchen.de/9457/1/MPRA_paper_9457.pdf

Mobius, M. (2012). The Little Book of Emerging Markets: How to Make Money in the World's Fastest Growing Markets. John Wiley and Sons.

Oncu, E., and Celik, S. (2018). Foreign Direct Investment and Economic Growth: Panel Causality Analysis in BRICS Countries. *International Journal of Economic and Administrative Studies*, 403–414.

Ranjan, V., and Agrawal, G. (2011). FDI Inflow Determinants in BRIC Countries: A panel Data Analysis. *International Business Research*, 4(4), 255.

Rodrik, D. (1999). *The New Global Economy and Developing Countries: Making Openness Work, Policy Essay No:* 24, Making Openness Work: The New Global Economy and the Developing Countries. Washington, DC: Overseas Development Council

Wijeweera, A., Villano, R., and Dollery, B. (2010). Economic Growth and FDI Inflows: A Stochastic Frontier Analysis. *The Journal of Developing Areas*, 143–158.

World Trade Report (2018), World Trade Organization, https://www.wto.org/english/res_e/publications_e/world_trade_report18_e.pdf

Yalta, A. Y. (2013). Revisiting the FDI-Led Growth Hypothesis: The Case of China. *Economic Modelling*, 31, 335–343.

Özer Özçelik

The Relation between Foreign Direct Investment and Economic Growth in Turkey (2003–2018)

1 Introduction

Countries have several economic targets. Some of them are fair income distribution, stability and economic growth. Achieving and sustaining economic growth is vital. So, factors affecting growth and growth draw more research interest every day. For this reason, the relationship between growth and foreign direct investment has become a subject often investigated by the researchers (Demirtaş and Özgür, 2015: 77).

Globalization trends have influenced the world, removed borders between countries and made it compulsory for the countries to integrate with the world. While developing countries (DC) experience capital problems in economic development processes, the fact that developed countries are in a richer position caused the problem of inefficient resource allocation in the world economy. As the globalization trend increases and with the help of the liberalization of economic and trade policies, the integration between world economies has brought about the free movement of capital among the countries. Thus, the need for foreign direct investment has increased. Foreign direct investment has been the most effective way of eliminating the lack of capital accumulation in developing countries (Ayaydın, 2010: 133).

Foreign Direct Investments can be defined shortly as, "a company's direct foreign capital investments in order to expand its production beyond the borders of its home country by establishing a production facility or purchasing existing production facilities in countries other than the country in which its headquarters is located (Seyidoğlu, 1999: 664).

Investments are of great importance in the development and growth of countries (Yaşar, 2014:202). Development is quite difficult in countries where the level of investment is low and capital accumulation is insufficient. Countries with development difficulty cannot compete with other countries. People's standard of living and welfare begin to decrease. In order to get rid of this unfavourable situation, domestic capital savings are necessary. Countries with the lack of capital can meet this need by foreign direct investment or debt. The difficulty of external debt and domestic savings insufficiency increase the importance of foreign direct investment in developing countries. Foreign Direct Investment plays an important role in economic growth. While Foreign Direct Investments have a positive impact on the economic growth of countries, they have negative effects on the economy (Ayaydın, 2010: 134).

Economic growth can be defined as "the situation that the amount of goods and services produced in a specific region and in a specific time period is more than the previous period." Financial systems play an important role in the economic growth process. The reason is that they undertake the function of supplying funds for the realization of capital accumulation and enable the dissemination of new technologies (Aslan and Küçükaksoy, 2006: 26).

2 Literature on the Relationship between Direct Foreign Investments and Economic Growth

Diverse studies have been carried out on the relationship between foreign direct investment and economic growth for different countries by different methods and most of them have similar findings.

Kahveci and Terzi (2017) examined the causality between foreign direct investment and economic growth, employment, capital accumulation in the 1984–2015 period for Turkey's economy with Sims and DL-VAR causality methods. According to the analysis, there is a positive and unidirectional causality relationship from economic growth and capital accumulation to foreign investments from the East, but there is no causality relationship between foreign direct investments and employment. As a result, economic growth in Turkey positively affects foreign direct investment coming into the country.

Kim et al. (2017) examined the relationship between financial development and economic growth. Fifty five Islamic Cooperation Organization have been examined. In order to get multilateral results, panel data, VAR and Granger causality tests were used. The results obtained from the analyses show that financial development has a positive effect on economic growth.

Meyer and Shera (2017) examined Albania, Bulgaria, Macedonia, Moldova, Romania and Bosnia and Herzegovina during the period of 1999–2013. Panel data set was used. The effect of directly sourced investments on economic growth was investigated. The study is intended to review the practical literature on the impact of cash on economic growth, in order to empirically determine whether these countries have significant relationships between transfer and growth. The results show that revenues have a positive effect on growth and this effect will be higher than GDP.

Sunde (2017) explored the economic growth in Africa as a function of direct foreign investment. The variables are economic growth, foreign direct investment and exports. In the article, autoregressive distributed delay model is applied. The long-term relationship between the variables is investigated with Autoregressive Distributed Lag (ARDL) test approach. Causality direction is investigated by Granger causality test. The article confirmed the cointegration between economic growth, foreign direct investment and exports. Two-way causality from direct foreign investment to economic growth and exports was found.

Alvarado et al. (2017) examined the impact of FDI on economic growth in 19 Latin American countries. Strong empirical evidence is found by using panel data analysis that the impact of FDI on economic growth is not statistically significant in the aggregate. FDI has a positive and significant impact on the product in high-income countries, but in upper middle income countries, the effect is not equal and is not significant. Finally, the impact in low-middle income countries is negative and statistically significant. The findings show that FDI is not an adequate mechanism to accelerate economic growth in Latin America, except in high-income countries.

Acar (2015) tested the relationship between foreign direct investment economic growth and causality analysis in Turkey between 2001 and 2015. According to the analysis, no causality has been found.

Pegkas (2015) investigated the relationship between European countries' foreign direct investment and economic growth between the period 2002 and 2012. Panel data analysis was used. According to the result, foreign direct investment is an important factor that positively affects the economic growth in Eurozone countries.

Amin et al. (2015) investigated Pakistan in their study to examine the relationship between international trade, financial development and economic growth. ADF and PP tests were used to check the integration sequence of variables and the integration of Johansen. The causality direction was tested by Granger causality test. It has been shown that not all variables are stationary and between international trade, financial development and economic growth have been a long-term relationship. According to these results, economic growth in Pakistan has been accelerated.

The study of Abbes et al. (2015) was conducted to improve the level of skill in capital requirements, national savings and economy, and to improve and contribute to market access. The relationship between foreign direct investment and economic growth in 65 countries was measured by joint integration, panel data set and Granger causality tests. The results point to a one-way causality from direct foreign investments to GDP.

Hayaloğlu (2015) investigated the effect of financial development on economic growth in Fragile Five countries (India, Indonesia, Brazil, Turkey and South Africa). Dynamic panel data analysis technique was used in the study covering the period of 1990–2012. The findings of the study, which used different variables as indicators of financial development, show a positive relationship between financial development and economic growth.

Almfraji (2014) investigated how foreign direct investment to Qatar influences its business cycles. Time series analysis was used in the study for the period of 1990–2010. The result shows that the direct investments and economic growth in Qatar have a relatively long-term effect on each other.

Dritsaki and Stiakakis (2014) examine the relationship between foreign direct investment, export and economic growth in Croatia, using annual time series data for the period 1994–2012. Several econometric models are applied, including the bound test (ARDL) approach and the ECM-ARDL model. The results confirm the causal relationship between export and growth in the long term and in the short term.

Omri and Kahouli (2014) estimate an econometric model for the analysis of the relationship between direct foreign investment, domestic capital and economic growth in 13 MENAcountries using a "growth model" framework and concurrent equation models predicted by the common understanding method. The empirical results show that there is a two-way causal relationship between foreign investment and economic growth, local capital and economic growth, and there is a one-way causal relationship between direct foreign investment and local capital throughout the region.

Güneş (2013) used the ratio of money supply (M2Y) to national income (GDP) and the share of employees in total labor force in financial markets as variables in order to represent the level of financial development. VAR and Granger causality tests are used in Turkey's six-month data for the period of 1988–2009. As a result of the analysis, it cannot be concluded that financial development causes economic growth. In the same period, it was found that economic growth increased the share of the employees in the financial markets, but did not affect the M2Y/GNP ratio.

Chang and Lee (2009) examined the relationship between foreign direct investments and financial development and economic growth of 37 countries between 1970 and 2007. Panel data analysise was used in the study. It has been found that the foreign direct investment has an impact on economic growth.

Mah (2009) examines the causality between foreign direct investment and economic growth using foreign direct investments in China. Cointegration test was applied. As a result, foreign direct investment did not cause economic growth.

Karimi and Yusop (2009) examine the causality between economic growth and foreign direct investment for Malaysia using the ARDL bound test, and no significant result was found that there is a relationship between two variables in the long term but only an indirect effect.

Naceur and Ghazouni (2007) analyzed the relationship between financial development and economic growth using unbalanced panel analysis for the 11 MENA countries. The impact of financial development on growth is discussed in terms of both banking and capital markets. According to the result, financial development has a negative or insignificant effect on economic growth. The underdeveloped financial system was defined as the reason for this effect.

Açıkalın et al. (2006) examined the relationship between real wages, growth and foreign direct investment using the 1980–2002 data for Turkey. Because the variables used are not stationary, cointegration analysis is employed. Results indicated that there is a cointegration relationship between real wages, growth and foreign direct investments.

Gui (2004) examines the effect of foreign direct investment on economic growth. The period from 1980 to 2009 of 50 African countries was analyzed. Panel data analysis was used. It was observed that the direct investment in economic growth was negative in the period after 1980, and it was positive from 1995 to 2009.

Beck and Levine (2004) investigated the relationship between financial development and economic growth in a study conducted by analyzing the panel data of 40 countries between 1976 and 1998. They used different variables as indicators of financial development. As a development indicator of stock markets, they used transaction volume and market capitalization and bank loans as financial indicators for the banking sector. As a result of the estimation, they showed the existence of a relationship between financial development and economic growth.

Carkovic and Levine (2002) examined the effect of foreign direct investments on economic growth in 72 developed and developing countries between 1960 and 1995 period with panel data analysis. As a result of the study, no significant effect of foreign direct investments on economic growth has been reached.

3 Modelling the Relationship between Foreign Direct Investment and Economic Growth in Turkey

The data set in the study was created for 2003: Q1-2018: Q1 period. Variable data were obtained from electronic data distribution system of the Central Bank of the Republic of Turkey. For 2003: Q1-2018: Q1 period, a dummy variable was created to include the effects of the global crisis in 2008 on the model. The "Bound Test" approach will be used to determine the effectiveness of foreign direct investments on economic growth.

3.1 Bound Test Approach

The most commonly used cointegration tests in the literature are Johansen (1988) and Johansen and Jesulius (1990) methods based on the system approach with two-stage Engle-Granger (1987) method based on the error term. In order to implement these methods, all variables in the model should not be static at the level [I(0)] and should be static after the first differentials (Pesaran et al., 2001: 289–290). Bound test approach eliminates the problem that the criterion of cointegration method cannot be applied to the series with different cointegration degrees. The equation to be used in the boundary test approach is as follows (Kıran and Güriş, 2011: 72):

$$\Delta eg_t = \alpha + \sum_{i=1}^{m} \beta_i \Delta eg_{t-i} + \sum_{i=1}^{m} \lambda_i \Delta fdi_{t-i} + \emptyset \prime eg_{t-1} + fdi_{t-1} + \epsilon_t$$

3.2 Unit Root Test Results

Augmented Dickey-Fuller (ADF) test and Phillips-Perron (PP) test were used to test whether "eg" and "fdi" variables contain unit roots. The unit root test results are presented in Tab. 2.

Tab. 1: *Unit Root Test Results*

Variable		ADF		PP	
		Intercept-Trend	**Intercept**	**Intercept-Trend**	**Intercept**
eg		-2,6635	-2,6937	-13.6917*	-13.6496*
Δeg		-45.2265*	-45.6850*	-30.7138*	-31.4250*
fdi		-6.2227*	-6.1813*	-5.9257*	-5.8394*
Δfdi		-7.7325*	-7.8769*	-21.4840*	-20.4246*
Critical	**1 %**	-4.1273	-3.5503	-4.1184	-3.5440
Values	**5 %**	-3.4906	-2.9135	-3.4865	-2.9108
	10 %	-3.1739	-2.5945	-3.1715	-2.5930

Note: The sign * indicates that the variable is stationary at the level 1 %. ** indicates the level of 5 %. "Δ" indicates the difference operator, i.e., the first difference values.

Tab. 2: *Optimal Lag Length*

Lag Number	AIC	SC	HQ	LM (1)	LM(4)
1	-1.7276	-1.5879	-1.6729	0.0079	0.0000
2	-2.2272	-2.0159	-2.1447	0.0000	0.0000
3	-3.2618	-2.9776	-3,1511	0,0000	0,0000
4	-3,8105	-3,4521	-3,6712	0,3431	0,1494
5	-3,7551	-3,3211	-3,5869	0,1011	0.1400

According to the results of ADF and PP unit root test in Tab. 1, it is understood that "eg" is I(1) and "fdi" is I(0). Variables were found to be stationary at different levels. The fact that the stationary levels of the variables are different is vital in terms of determining the method to be applied in the analysis. Since the series are stationary at the I(0) and I(1) levels, the Autoregressive Distributed Lag (ARDL) test will be used to demonstrate the relationships between the variables in the study.

3.3 Bound Test Results

In order to implement the bound test, the optimal lag length must be determined first. Akaike Information Criterion, Schwarz Information Criterion and Hannan-Quinn Information Criterion are used to determine the optimal lag length. Depending on the information criteria, the lag length that gives the lowest value is determined as the optimal lag length. However, there should be no autocorrelation problem at the optimal lag length. If there is an autocorrelation problem with the optimal lag length, the lag length that gives the lowest value according to the information criteria is determined as the most appropriate delay length.

When the results of the information criteria are examined, it is determined that the fourth lag length without autocorrelation is the optimal lag length. Following the determination of the optimal lag length, "F statistic" is calculated based on the fourth lag length. After calculating the "F statistic", it is compared with the two critical values, lower and upper, calculated by Pesaran, Shin and Smith (2001). If the "F statistic" is greater than the upper value, there is a long-term relationship between the variables; if it is lower than the lower value, there is no long-term relationship between variables; and if it is between the lower and upper value, no comment can be made (Kıran and Güriş, 2011: 72).

Since the calculated F statistic was less than Peseran's lower critical value at the 5 % significance level, it was concluded that there was no long-term relationship

Tab. 3: *Bound Test Results*

Dependent Variable:	"fdi"	
F Statistics:	2.30	
Critical Values (k=3)		
	Lower Value	***Upper Value***
5 %	2.79	3.67

between "eg" and "fdi" variables. Since no cointegration relationship was determined between the variables, long- and short-term relationships could not be determined.

3.4 Evaluation of Empirical Findings

As a result of the econometric findings obtained from the ARDL model in which the effects of foreign direct investments on economic growth were examined, the long-term relationship between the variables could not be found since the calculated "F statistic (2.30)" was lower than the lower critical value.

The reason for the lack of long-term relationship can be that since direct foreign resources are used in domestic consumption, they do not affect growth. Moreover, foreign direct investments, which stem from the export-oriented growth model, have no effect on growth after the 2008 crisis. As most foreign capital investments to Turkey are portfolio investments, not new investments creating added value, it is another reason for the lack of effect of investment on the economic growth in the long term.

4 Conclusion

Foreign direct investments are investments made by purchasing any company in a country, exporting capital to a new firm, or increasing the capital of a firm. Yet, foreign investments as portfolio investments generally come as bonds and shares. Foreign direct investments have a great importance in terms of enabling countries to achieve economic growth. However, the fact that the future investments are portfolio investments causes capital mobility. These portfolio investments, which are based on high interest rate and high exchange rate, are speculative movements.

As a result of the globalization of capital, especially foreign direct investments increased after the 1990s, foreign direct investments became the most stable and biggest of capital flows. Thus, it became the most important alternative in the development of financial processes. This is because foreign direct investments create employment, introduce new technologies, increase competition, contribute to economic growth by increasing capital accumulation and total factor productivity.

In the study, quarterly data of Turkey for the period of 2003–2018 were used. ARDL Border test was performed due to stagnation as a result of unit root tests, and no relation could be determined between direct foreign investments and economic growth at 5 % significance level. In the literature, Alvarado et al. (2017), Acar (2015), Mah (2009) and Carkovic and Levine (2002) could not find any causal relationship between direct foreign investments and economic growth. The analysis in this study also supports the studies that cannot show the existence of the relationship in the literature.

As a result, it is clear that foreign direct investments can contribute to economic growth and employment if they occur as new investments creating employment, technology and high added value rather than the form of purchases and mergers. In order to attract more foreign direct investments, economic and political stability, as well as the existence and continuation of appropriate conditions, should not be ignored as they are dynamic effects of long-term growth and capital withdrawal.

References

Abbes, M. S, Mostéfa, B, Seghir, M. G and Zakarya, Y. G. (2015). Causal Interactions between FDI, and Economic Growth: Evidence from Dynamic Panel Co-Integration. *Procedia Economics and Finance*. 23, 276–290.

Acar, M. (2015). Doğrudan Yabancı Sermayenin Ekonomik Büyümeye Etkisi: Türkiye Örneği. *Kastamonu Üniversitesi İktisadi ve İktisadi Bilimler Fakültesi Dergisi*, 13, 92–105.

Açıkalın, S., Gül, E. ve Yaşar, E. (2006). Ücretler ve Büyüme ile Doğrudan Yabancı Yatırımlar Arasındaki İlişkinin Ekonometrik Analizi. *Dumlupınar Üniversitesi Sosyal Bilimler Dergisi*, 16, 271–282.

Alvarado, P., Iniguez, M. and Ponce, P., (2017). Foreign Direct Investment and Economic Growth in Latin America. *Economic Analysis and Policy*.

Almfraji, A. M., Almsafir, K. M. and Yao. L. (2014). Economic Growth and Foreign Direct Investment Inflows: The Case of Qatar. *Procedia - Social and Behavioral Sciences* 109, 1040–1045.

Alptekin, V. (2009). Türkiye'de Dış Ticaret – Reel Döviz Kuru İlişkisi: Vektör Otoregresyon (VAR) Analizi Yardımıyla Sınanması, *Niğde Üniversitesi İİBF Dergisi*, 132–149.

Altıntaş, İ., İnançlı, S. ve İnal, V. (2016). Finansal Gelişme ve Ekonomik Büyüme İlişkisi: D-8 Örneği. *Kastamonu Üniversitesi İktisadi ve İdari Bilimler Fakültesi Dergisi.* 14, 36–49.

Amin, Y. M, Gökmenoğlu, K. K. ve Taşpınar, N. (2015). The Relationship among International Trade, Financial Development and Economic Growth. *The Case of Pakistan: 16th Annual Conference on Finance and Accounting,* ACFA, Prague 2015, 29th.

Aslan, Ö. ve Küçükaksoy İ. (2006). Finansal Gelişme ve Ekonomik Büyüme İlişkisi: Türkiye Ekonomisi Üzerine Ekonometrik Bir Uygulama. *Ekonometri ve İstatistik,* 4, 12–28.

Aslan, A. (2008). Türkiye'de Ekonomik Büyüme ve Turizm İlişkisi Üzerine Ekonometrik Analiz, *MPRA Paper No.* 10611.

Ayaydın, H. (2010). Doğrudan Yabancı Yatırımlar İle Ekonomik Büyüme Arasındaki İlişkinin İncelenmesi: Türkiye Örneği. *Dumlupınar Üniversitesi Sosyal Bilimler Dergisi,* 26, 133–145.

Bilgin, O. ve Işık, B. H. (2016). Finansal Gelişme ve Ekonomik Büyüme İlişkisi Türkiye Örneği. *İnsan ve Toplum Bilimleri Araştırma Dergisi,* 5 (7), 1757–1765.

Beck, T., Levine, R. and Loayza, N. (2000). Finance and the Sources of Growth. *Journal of Financial Economics,* 58 (1–2), 261–300.

Carkovic, M. and R. Levine (2002). Does Foreign Direct Investment Accelerate Growth? Financial Globalization: A Blessing or a Curse, *World Bank Conference.*

Chang, C. C. and Lee, P. C. (2009). FDI, Financial Development, and Economic Growth: International Evidence. *Journal of Applied Economics,* XII (2), 249–271.

Demirtaş, C. ve Özgür, I. M. (2015). Finansal Gelişme ve Doğrudan Yabancı Yatırımların Ekonomik Büyüme Üzerindeki Etkileri: Türkiye Örneği. *E-Journal of New World Sciences Academy,* 76–91.

Dickey, D. A. and Fuller, A. W. (1981). Likelihood Ratio Statistics for Autoregressive Time Series with a Unit Root. *Econometrica,* 49 (4), 1057–1072.

Dritsaki, C. and Stiakakis, E. (2014). Foreign Direct Investments, Exports, and Economic Growth in Croatia: A Time Series Analysis. *Procedia Economics and Finance,* 14, 181 - 190.

Gui, L. S. and Diby. (2014). Impact of Foreign Direct Investments on Economic Growth in Africa: Evidence from Three Decades of Panel Data Analyses. *Research in Economics,* 68, 248–256.

Güneş, S. (2013). Finansal Gelişmişlik ve Büyüme Arasındaki Nedensellik Testi: Türkiye Örneği. *Doğuş Üniversitesi Dergisi*, 14 (1), 73–85.

Hayaloğlu, P. (2015). Kırılgan Beşli Ülkelerinde Finansal Gelişme ve Ekonomik Büyüme İlişkisi: Dinamik Panel Veri Analizi. *Ekonomik ve Sosyal Araştırmalar Dergisi*, 11 (1).

Kahveci. Ş. ve Terzi. H. (2017). Türkiye'de Doğrudan Yabancı Yatırımlar Ve Ekonomik Büyüme Arasındaki İlişkilerin Nedensellik Analizleri ile Testi. *Erciyes Üniversitesi İİBF Dergisi*. 49:135–154.

Kahouli, B. and Omri, A., (2014). The Nexus among Foreign Investment, Domestic Capital and Economic Growth: Empirical Evidence from the MENA Region. *Research in Economics*, 68, 257–263.

Karimi, M. S. and Z. Yusop (2009). FDI and Economic Growth in Malaysia. *Munich Personal RePEc Archive* Paper No.14999.

Kıran, B. and Güriş, B. (2011). Türkiye'de Ticari ve Finansal Dışaaçıklığın Büyümeye Etkisi: 1992–2006 Dönemi Üzerine Bir İnceleme. *Anadolu Üniversitesi Sosyal Bilimler Dergisi*, 11 (2), 69–80.

Korgaonkar, C. (2012). Analysis of the Impact of Financial Development on Foreign Direct Investment: A Data Mining Approach. *Journal of Economics and Sustainable Development*, 3 (6).

Mah, J. S. (2009). Foreign Direct Investment Inflows and Economic Growth of China. Division of International Studies, Ewha Womans University, Seodaemun-ku, Seoul, 120–750.

Meyer, D. and Shera, A. (2017). The Impact of Remittances on Economic Growth: An Econometric Model. *Economia*, 18, 147–155.

Naceur, S. B. and Ghazouani, S. (2007). Stock Markets, Banks, and Economic Growth: Empirical Evidence from the MENA Region. *Research in International Business and Finance*, 21 (2), 297–315.

Pegkas. P. (2015). The Impact of FDI on Economic Growth in Eurozone Countries. *The Journal of Economic Asymmetries*, 12, 124–132.

Pesaran, M., Shin, Y. and Smith, R. (2001). Bounds Testing Approaches to the Analysis of Level Relationships. *Journal of Applied Econometrics*, (16), 289–326.

Phillips, P. C. B. and Perron, P. (1988). Testing for a Unit Root in Time Series Regression, *Biometrika*, 75 (2), 335–346.

Seyitoğlu, H. (1999). *Uluslararası İktisat: Teori, Politika ve Uygulama*, Güzem Can Yayınları, 13. Baskı. İstanbul.

Yaşar, E. (2014). *Çokuluslu Şirketler ve Doğrudan Yabancı Yatırımlar*. Hakan Basım Yayın Dağıtım. İkinci Baskı. Ankara.

Resul Yazici and Ayla Yazici

Long-Term Relationship between Economic Growth and External Debt Stock in Turkey

1 Introduction

Developing countries facing foreign currency shortages and saving deficits such as Turkey need to resort to external sources to solve these problems. These countries are dependent on foreign sources because they have to import investment goods due to their shortcomings in terms of technological or raw materials. On the other hand, foreign borrowing is inevitable in order to repay the due debts and to finance the continuous budget deficits, which arise from financing infrastructure investments whose productivity is low in short term. According to Reinhart and Rogoff (2010), negativities such as the increase of budget deficits and loss of the possibility of rolling domestic and foreign debts are increasing. Problems such as non-payment of external and internal debt and inflation are inextricably linked.

According to Ülgen (2005), government revenues should be increased to meet the future debt service in order to succeed in debt management and not to experience these problems. In the case of financial imbalance, the monetary authorities tend to provide new resources at a certain cost. The said cost is the interest rate determined by the demand of the funders. The sustainability of the borrowing process is only possible by the effective use of resources by the authorities. In this way, debt service can be met without resorting to new borrowing. In the same way, economic growth can be achieved by directing the debts to the productive areas. This in return leads to increase in domestic savings and the solution for the foreign exchange shortages. Otherwise, both the currency risk and the high interest rate, and the problem of debt service at the end of the maturity, may slow down the economic growth rate and cause other problems. In particular, the rollover of debts with new debts can reduce credibility of the country and increase interest rates which drag countries into the spiral of "inflation-interest rate-devaluation". Therefore, according to Ulusoy and Cural (2006), unsustainable borrowing disrupts price stability, hinders economic growth potential and makes long-term macroeconomic policies difficult to implement. On the other hand, the increasing debts can cause the government to finance the debt by printing money. In this case, the high amount of debt may be an incentive for the government to reduce the real value of the debt, but this causes inflation and even hyperinflation (Karagöl, 2010). For these reasons, there is a continuous discussion in academic circles on the effects of external borrowing on the economies. In addition to studies that emphasize how this type of borrowing will affect the economy through various channels, some studies focus on the sources and maturity of the external borrowing and utilization areas of the external borrowing.

In this study, the relationship between economic growth and long-term external debt stock in Turkey during the 1974–2017 period is examined. The interaction between foreign borrowing and growth was analyzed in an empirical framework with the help of ARDL analysis. In the study, the literature on foreign borrowing is reviewed and the subject was examined in detailed by the analyses of "Granger Causality", "heteroscedasticity" and "autocorrelation".

2 Related Literature

In this section, cross-country studies on foreign borrowing are initially mentioned and then foreign borrowing studies on Turkey are provided. ElGhouty (2018) pointed out that public debt is a serious problem in recent years in Egypt. Abdelhadi (2013) investigated the relationship between external debt and economic growth in Jordan during the period of 1990–2011 by using econometric techniques. This study indicates that while there is a positive and significant relationship between external borrowing and economic growth in Joordan, there is a negative correlation between the debt service and economic growth. Lau and Kon (2014) studies the link between external borrowing and economic growth in seventeen Asian countries. They found that foreign financial capital positively affected both economic growth and exports. However, due to the uncertainties in the world, they suggest that effective coordination and cooperation in the implementation of debt management to support economic development should be on the agenda of the countries in the region.

Various aspects of the impact of external debt on Turkey's economy are studied. Karluk (2002) has expressed the Turkey's foreign borrowing performance in 1990s in the following way: external debt service (principal and interest) caused a major leak in the economy because of the fact that foreign borrowing fails to create sustainable foreign exchange of revenue which in return adversely affect economic growth. In addition, the political instability, implemented populist policies, incompetence and not-accountability led to a significant internal debt pressure in 1994 in Turkey. The state's constant budget deficits required foreign borrowing even to pay foreign debt. Eventually, for the first time, Turkey had to make domestic borrowing to pay its external debt. The fact that Turkey entered into a spiral of debt made the state unable to perform its basic duties. Similarly, Ulusoy and Küçükkale (1996) concluded that foreign borrowing increased inflation and negatively affected economic growth in the period of 1965–1994. In their study covering the period of 1980–2013, Akan and Kanca (2015) concluded that the external debts lead to increase in inflation by stimulating the total demand. Karagöl (2010) states that in the periods when the external debt stock increased, the growth figures decreased along with the weakening of the economic performance. The analysis of Bilginoğlu and Aysu (2008) covering the years 1968 to 2005 suggests that external debt has negative effect on economic growth in Turkey. Uysal, Özer and Mucuk (2009), in their studies covering the period of 1965–2007, concluded that the external debts adversely affected the national output level in both short and long term. Çevik and Cural (2013) investigated the relationship between domestic and foreign borrowing and economic growth during the period 1989–2012 in Turkey. The study concluded that while external borrowing has a positive effect on economic growth, domestic borrowing has no effect on economic growth. Kamaci (2016) investigated the effects of the external debt on inflation and economic growth for six Central Asian Republics (Azerbaijan, Kazakhstan, Kyrgyzstan, Uzbekistan, Tajikistan and Turkmenistan) and Turkey in the 1995–2014 period. The study concluded that the increase in external debts decreased the economic growth and that the external debts have a negative impact on economic growth and lead countries to the debt spiral as long as they are not transformed into investment. Çiçek, Gözegir and Emre (2010) analyzed the relationship between growth and internal and external debt in Turkey for the 1999–2009 period and concluded that increases in the domestic debt stock has a positive impact on the GDP while increases in external debt stock has a negative impact on GDP. Study of Tülümce and Yavuz (2017) suggest that there is a relationship between growth and debt in Turkey and concluded that this relationship occurs in the negative direction.

Similar analysis methods are used in growth studies in the literature. For instance, Koyuncu the Sarıtaş (2017) examined the relationship between globalization and growth with ARDL boundary approach and found no significant relationship in the short term while they found a significant relationship in the long run. In addition, there are other studies examining the relationship between growth variable and macro-economic variables. The study of Koyuncu and Özen (2017) examine the relationship between economic growth and the terrorist attacks in Turkey by the ARDL analysis. They found no short- and long-term causality relationship between the growth and terrorist events.

The above summarizes the previous studies on growth and external debts stock. Next section provides data and methodology used in the study.

3 Data and Methodology

In this study, the long-term relationship between economic growth and external debt stock in Turkey is tested with cointegration test. The sample of the study covers the years between 1974 and 2017 and employs GDP growth (x521) and external debt stocks (x454) as variables. The data is taken from World Development Indicators (WDI).

To test the existence of a cointegration relationship between two series with ARDL boundary test approach, the following model is estimated:

$$\Delta x454_t = \beta_0 + \sum_{i=1}^{p} \beta_i \Delta x454_{t-i} + \sum_{i=0}^{q} \alpha_i \Delta x521_{t-i} + \theta_0 x454_{t-1} + \theta_1 x521_{t-1} + \varepsilon_t \quad (1)$$

Where x454 series shows the value of external debt stock of Turkey between 1974 and 2017.While $\theta_0, \theta_1$the coefficients on the right side of the equation shows the long-term relationship between the series,β_i, α_i coefficients provide a short-term relationship between the series. As can be predicted, Δ is the first-order difference operator, $\beta_0$is the constant term of the model and $\varepsilon_t$is the white-noise error term of the model.

ARDL boundary test approach tests the null hypothesis of $H_0 : \theta_0 = \theta_1 = 0$ (i.e., there is no cointegrating association among series) against to the alternative hypothesis of $H_1 : \theta_0 \neq \theta_1 \neq 0$(i.e., there exists cointegrating association among series). If the F-statistic value gathered from ARDL boundary test is beyond the upper limit at a particular significance level then H_1hypothesis is accepted. On the other hand if the F-statistic value is smaller than lower limit at a particular significance level then H_0 hypothesis is accepted. Finally, any F-statistic value falling into the area between the lower and upper limits indicates indecisive zone.

In addition to ARDL boundary test, given the existence of cointegration association among series, the following model is estimated to get short-run and long-run coefficients:

$$x454_t = \beta_0 + \sum_{i=1}^{p} \beta_i \Delta x454_{t-i} + \sum_{i=0}^{q} \alpha_i \Delta x521_{t-i} + \varphi ECM_{t-1} + \varepsilon_t \quad (2)$$

In equations above, β_i and α_i display the dynamic coefficients bringing the model to the balance in the long run; $ECM$is error correction term; φ stands for the speed of adjustment at which the model reverts to long run balance after a shock occurred in short run. The speed of adjustment term is expected to be negative and statistically significant.

4 Estimation Results

The stationarity analysis of the series was performed by using the Philips-Perron (PP) unit root test. PP unit root test results for the level values of the series are reported in Tab. 1 and the PP unit root test results for the first differences of the series are reported in Tab. 2.

As seen in the PP unit root test results, it is seen that x454 series is stationary in I (1) i.e., first difference. x521 series is I (0), meaning that stable at the level. Since none of the existing series are integrated into two or more degrees, we can test whether there is co-integration by applying the ARDL boundary test approach to these series.

The ARDL (1,3) model, which has the lowest criterion value (BIC = 10,250499) among the 20 different models estimated in the light of the evaluations made under the Schwarz Information Criteria (BIC), has been found to be the model with the most appropriate delay. The results of the ARDL boundary test to investigate the existence of co-integration between the X454 series and the x521 series are shown in Tab. 3. Accordingly, since the F-statistic = 3.909329 value is greater than the upper-limit values determined for the 10 % significance level, it indicates that there is a cointegration relationship between the series and therefore the null hypothesis must be rejected. These results, therefore, show that

Tab. 1: PP Unit Root Test Results (Levels)

X454	
	Constant with Trend
t-statistics	-3.041164
Prob. Value	0.1334
X521	
	Constant with Trend
t-statistics	-6.631982
Prob. Value	0.0000

Tab. 2: ADF Unit Root Test Results (First Difference)

X454	
	Constant with Trend
t-statistics	-5.329404
Prob. Value	0.0004

Tab. 3: Boundary Test Results for Co-Integration

***F Statistics:* 3.909329**	Critical Values	
Significance Levels	***Lower-bound****I*(0)	***Upper-bound****I*(1)
10 %	2.44	3.28
5 %	3.15	4.11
2.5 %	3.88	4.92
1 %	4.81	6.02

Tab. 4: Long-Term Coefficients Belonging to ARDL (1,3) Model

Dependent Variable: x454			
Variable	***Coefficient***	***t-Statistic***	***Prob.***
X521	52.235108	4.056646	0.0002

Tab. 5: Error Correction Model Estimation Results of ARDL (1,3) Model

	***Dependent Variable:* x454**		
	Coefficient	***t-Statistic***	***Prob.***
ΔLOG(X521)	-1.428408	-0.851226	0.4000
ΔLOG(X521(-1))	-6.485795	-2.826523	0.0075
ΔLOG(X521(-2))	-2.864626	-1.605206	0.1167
ECM$_{t-1}$	-0.131959	-2.832739	0.0073
ECM=x454-(52.2351* (x521))			

there is co-integration (a long-term relationship) between economic growth and external debt stock in Turkey during the period under study.

As can be seen from Tabs. 4 and 5 of ARDL Model Error Correction Model (ECM) estimation results, the long-term coefficient of X521 variable, 52.235108, is statistically significant, which is in parallel with the result of the cointegration test obtained above. In other words, there is a long-term relationship between GDP growth (x521) and external debt stocks (x454). The coefficient of the error correction term (indicating the speed of the model returning to the long-term equilibrium) takes the expected negative sign and is statistically significant. There is a statistically significant relationship between GDP growth and external debt stocks both in the short term and in the long term. In the short term, the coefficients are statistically significant and negative in only one of the three

Tab. 6: Autocorrelation Test

Breusch-Godfrey Serial Correlation LM Test:			
F-statistic	0.277864	Prob. F(2,36)	0.7590
Obs*R-squared	0.653695	Prob. Chi-Square(2)	0.7212

Tab. 7: Heteroskedasticity Test

Heteroskedasticity Test: ARCH:			
F-statistic	0.083808	Prob. F(1,40)	0.7737
Obs*R-squared	0.087814	Prob. Chi-Square(1)	0.7670

delays. On the other hand, GDP growth and external debt stocks interact in the same direction in the long run and this relationship is significant at 1 %.

Breusch-Godfrey serial correlation test was performed to determine whether the predicted model had an autocorrelation problem and the results were reported in Tab. 6. According to the test results, H0 cannot be rejected because the test statistic of 0.653695 is not statistically significant. So there is no autocorrelation problem in the predicted model.

In the above mentioned Tab. 7 about the ARCH Heteroskedasticity test was used to test whether the predicted model had heteroskedastic variance. According to the test results, H0 cannot be rejected because the test statistic of 0.087814 is not statistically significant. In other words, there is no problem of heteroskedastic variance in the predicted model.

Finally, CUSUM parameter stability test was applied for the parameters of the predicted model. As can be seen from the Graph-1, since the cumulative sum of the recursive residuals does not go outside of the lines drawn for %5 significance level, the parameters of estimated model are stable.

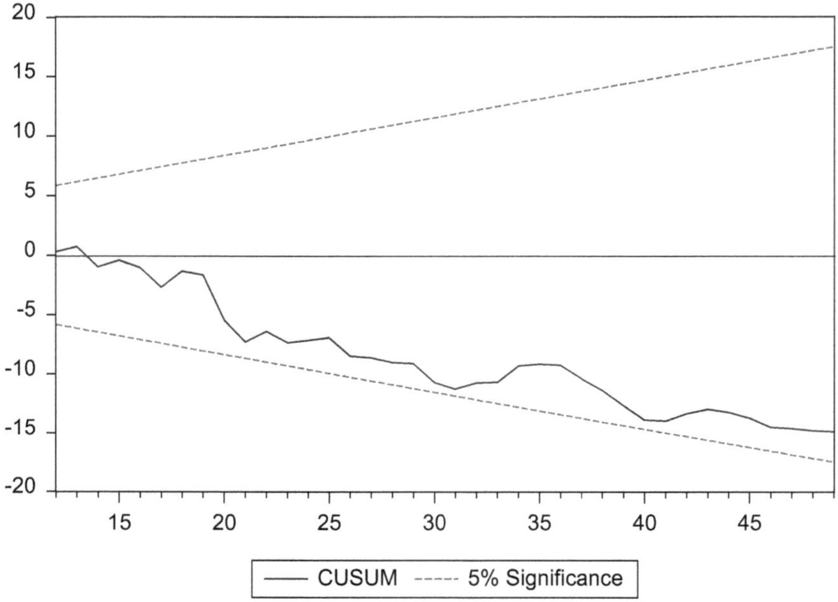

Graph 1: CUSUM Graph

4 Conclusion

The expansionary fiscal policy measures implemented by countries to reduce risks in the real economy and the financial system and to avoid economic stagnation disrupt the budget balance of the public sector. The sustainability and the management of external debts are becoming increasingly difficult due to competition among countries and other instabilities in the global financial system. Therefore, it is necessary to bring the debt stock to a certain level and to reduce the dependence after reaching the leverage effect of the borrowing. Otherwise, negative effects will be unavoidable for the country's economy. Therefore, necessary measures should be taken to facilitate debt management and to reduce borrowing costs. In this context, firstly, the structure of the resources provided by borrowing, where and how they are spent should be questioned. The use of these resources for future investments will be the most important policy change that will pave the way for the country. Simultaneously, structural reforms should be implemented in order to reduce foreign dependency. Their main objective should be to finance the growth from national resources through increasing domestic savings, and to ensure that the production capacity is directed at increasing imports-substitution and increasing exports.

This study questions the long-term relationship between economic growth (x521) and the external debt stock (x454) in Turkey by ARDL bounds testing. According to the findings, it was found that there is a relationship between x454 and x521 both in the long term and in the short term. While there is a negative relationship in the short term, it is seen that the relationship is positive in the long term. It was also tested that whether the model had autocorrelation and heteroskedastic variance problem. Results indicate that both problems were not in the model.

References

Abdelhadi, S.A. (2013). "External Debt and Economic Growth: Case of Jordan (1990–2011)". *Journal of Economics and Sustainable Development*, 4(18), 26–33. 01.03.2019 tarihinde https://iiste.org/Journals/index.php/JEDS/article/view/8834 adresinden alınmıştır.

Akan, Y. and Kanca, O.C. (2015). Türkiye'de Dış Borçlanma, Büyüme ve Enflasyon İlişkisi: Var Yaklaşımı (1980–2013). *Hacettepe University Journal of Economics and Administrative Sciences*, 33(3), 1–22.

Bilginoğlu, M.A. and Aysu, A. (2008). Dış Borçların Ekonomik Büyüme Üzerindeki Etkisi: Türkiye Örneği. Erciyes Üniversitesi İktisadi ve İdari Bilimler Fakültesi Dergisi, Sayı: 31, Temmuz-Aralık, 1–23.

Çevik, N.K. and M. Cural (2013). İç Borçlanma, Dış Borçlanma ve Ekonomik Büyüme Arasında Nedensellik İlişkisi: 1989–2012 Dönemi Türkiye Örneği. *Maliye Dergisi*, 165, 115–139.

Çiçek, H., Gözegir, S. and Emre, Ç. (2010). Bir Maliye Politikası Aracı Olarak Borçlanma ve Ekonomik Büyüme İlişkisi: Türkiye Örneği (1990–2009). C.Ü. *İktisadi ve İdari Bilimler Dergisi*, 11(1), 141–156.

ElGhouty, A.S. (2018). "Public Debt and Economic Growth in Egypt". *Business and Economic Research*, ISSN 2162-48602018, 8 (3). 01.03.2019 tarihinde https://www.researchgate.net/publication/327440536_Public_Debt_and_Economic_Growth_in_Egypt adresinden alınmıştır.

Ülgen, G. (2005). Türkiye'de Dış Borcun Sürdürülebilirliği. *Marmara Üniversitesi İ.İ.B.F Dergisi*, 20(1), 19–34.

Karagöl, E.T. (2010). Geçmişten Günümüze Türkiye'de Dış Borçlar. *Siyaset, Ekonomi ve Toplumsal Araştırmalar Vakfı*, Ağustos, 1–32.

Karluk, R.S. (2002). Türkiye Ekonomisi, No:1295, Beta Yayınları, İstanbul.

Kamacı, A. (2016). Dış Borçların Ekonomik Büyüme ve Enflasyon Üzerine Etkileri: Panel Eşbütünleşme ve Panel Nedensellik Analizi. *International Journal of Cultural and Social Studies (IntJCSS)* August 2(1), 165–175.

Koyuncu, C. and Sarıtaş, T. (2017). "Analysis of Globalization and Economic Growth for Turkey with ARDL Model." *Anadolu Üniversitesi Sosyal Bilimler Dergisi*, 17(2), 51–66.

Koyuncu, C. and Özen, E. (2017). Terörizmin Büyüme Üzerindeki Etkileri: Türkiye Örneği. Dimitrov, D. K., Nikoloski, D., and Yılmaz, R. (Ed.), *III. International Balkan and Near Eastern Social Sciences Congress Series*, Proceeding Book, Edirne, Turkey, 212–217.

Lau, E. and Kon, Thian-Ling (2014). "External Debt, Export and Growth in Asian Countries: 1988–2006." *Journal of Applied Sciences*, 14: 2170–2176. 01.03.2019 tarihinde https://scialert.net/fulltext/?doi=jas.2014.2170.2176 adresinden alınmıştır.

Reinhart, C.M. and Rogoff, K.S. (2010). Bu Defa Farklı Finansal Çılgınlığın 800 Yıllık Tarihi. (Çev.: Konyar, Levent), NTV Yayınları, İstanbul.

Tülümce, S.Y. and Yavuz, E. (2017). Türkiye'de Borçlanma ve Ekonomik Büyüme Arasındaki İlişki. International Journal of Management Economics and Business, ICMEB, 17(Special Issue), 1034–1048.

Ulusoy, A. and M. Cural (2006), Türkiye'de 1980 Sonrası Dönemde İç Borçların Sürdürülebilirliği, *ZKÜ Sosyal Bilimler Dergisi*, 2(4), 1–21.

Ulusoy, A. and Y. Küçükkale (1996). Türkiye'de Dış Borçların İktisadi Büyüme ve Enflasyon Üzerine Etkisi: Granger Nedensellik Testi. *Ekonomik Yaklaşım Dergisi*, 7(21), 13–25.

Uysal, D., Özer, H. and Mucuk M. (2009). Dış Borçlanma ve Ekonomik Büyüme İlişkisi: Türkiye Örneği (1965–2007). *Atatürk Üniversitesi İktisadi ve İdari Bilimler Dergisi*, 23(4), 161–178.

Eda Ozen

Do Loans Contribute to the Macro Economy? The Case of Turkey

1 Introduction

Financial globalization and the increasing financial depth it has brought have pushed the financial sector into new searches in the last century. While the existing financial system is insufficient to respond to the needs of all the nations in the world, problems may arise in transferring the existing capital accumulation to macroeconomics due to the constraints in the banking system. This situation is in search of transferring the actors of financial system to macroeconomics effectively. As globalization becomes widespread, other macroeconomic variables, particularly exports, are affected by the financial system. At the same time, the effects of macroeconomic variables on globalization should not be ignored. For example, the empirical study of Okşak (2018) on Turkey emphasizes that globalization and exports move in the same direction.

The financial sector is gaining more and more importance in developing economies due to the lack of capital accumulation depending on economic growth and the increase in debt stock. The banking sector, which is one of the financial actors of these countries in terms of sustaining financial activities, is of great importance. This is because when the financial system is mentioned in these economies, the deposit banks come to mind at the first place. How macroeconomic variables are kept under control and the sustainability of macroeconomic variables, especially the growth, is the main research question for Turkey as an emerging economy.

In this study, the effects of credit on macroeconomic indicators in Turkey are investigated and it is attempted to reveal the extent to which the financial system is effective.

2 Related Literature

Studies examining the impact of credits on macroeconomic indicators are also present throughout the literature. In this context, some of the empirical researches on the effect of credits on macroeconomic variables that have been used in this study are as follows:

Beck et al. (2010) compare the data of 100 conventional and Islamic banks in the pre-crisis period between 1995 and 2007 with the panel data analysis method. In the study, data obtained from Bankscope were used to create and compare the indicators of business orientation, effectiveness, asset quality and stability of conventional and Islamic banks. As a result of this comparison, it is concluded that that Islamic banks have higher asset quality and better capital adequacy than conventional banks while the use of loans and funding is less efficient in Islamic banks. When the macroeconomic indicators in the economic crisis have been taken into consideration, it is seen that the credit losses during the crisis have been lower in the Islamic banking system. Arslan and Yapraklı (2008) employed total bank loans and inflation (PPI) to determine the relationship between inflation and bank lending in the period between the years 1983 and 2007 in Turkey. As a result of the analysis using Johansen co-integration analysis and error correction model, it is estimated that bank loans in the long run positively affect inflation. On the other hand, inflation has a negative effect on bank loans. Granger causality tests show that there is a causal relationship between variables.

Castro (2013) has analyzed the link between macroeconomic developments and banking credit risk for GIPSI countries (Greece, Ireland, Portugal, Spain and Italy) sample. Using quarterly data from 1997 to 2011 and applying dynamic panel data approaches, the researcher observed that credit risk increased significantly as a result of GDP growth and decreasing stock and housing price indices. In addition, it has been concluded that credit risk increases in relation to variables such as unemployment and interest rate increase and credit growth.

Araç and Özcan (2014) analyzed the relationship between financial developments and economic growth in Turkey using quarterly data between the years 1987 and 2012. Using eight time series, Johansen cointegration test, Pesaran boundary test and Granger causality test methods were used for the analysis of financial development. According to the results of tests, there is a long-term relationship between economic growth and financial development indicators. The study supports the supply-side hypothesis and the demand following hypothesis.

Mashamba et al. (2014) investigated the relationship between deposit interest rates and savings deposits of banks in Zimbabwe in the period between 1980 and 2006. In addition, macroeconomic variables (GDP, per capita income and inflation) affecting bank deposits were analyzed. According to the results of the study that used ordinary least squares (OLS) method, there is a significant correlation between macroeconomic variables, deposit interest rates and bank deposits.

Some of the empirical studies on conventional and participation banks and macroeconomic indicators are summarized above. Some examples from different studies in the literature on banks and the banking system are summarized in the following paragraphs. When the negative effects of banking on economy were mentioned, banking crises were the first problem that came to mind. In this context, in the empirical study of foreign banks and banking crisis, Yalçınkaya Koyuncu and Yılmaz (2015) pointed out that foreign banks contributed more to credit stability in times of crisis and that foreign ownership in the Turkish banking sector decreased the probability of bank failures. Yazıcı (2017) has done theoretical investigations on the functioning of the financial system and the operations of participation banking on the financial system. In another study (Yalcinkaya Koyuncu, 2011) on the existence of banks and foreign banks, an empirical analysis examining how the banking market is affected in the periods when foreign banks are widespread. In another study, Yazıcı and Yazıcı (2017) examine the causes and consequences of the non-development of capital markets due to the weighted structure of the money markets in the Turkish financial system. The study also emphasizes the importance of financial literacy in the development of the financial system.

Having literature review, this study empirically examines how the credit provided by conventional banks affects the macroeconomy.

3 Data and Methodology

In this part of the study, the effect of conventional banks' loans on the macro economy is analyzed by using quarterly data between2010: Q1 and 2017: Q1 with panel data analysis. In this study, bivariate and multivariate fixed effect model (FEM) are used. Export, investment, employment, household consumption and national income are other macroeconomic indicators included in the study. The definitions and sources of the variables used in the analysis are summarized in Tab. 1 below.

Tab. 1: Definition and Sources of Variables

kkredi	Amount of credit granted by the participation bank	Participation Banks Association
int2	Discount Rate	IMF
indp	Industrial Production/Index	IMF
goods1	Goods, Value of Exports, FOB, US Dollars (million$)	IMF
expgs1	Exports of goods and services/Current prices, million euro	Eurostat
gfcf	Gross Fixed Capital Formation/Domestic Currency/Millions	IMF
gdp1	Gayrisafi Yurtiçi Hasıla (Alıcı fiyatlarıyla)/Gelir Yöntemiyle	Central Bank
goods2	Goods, Value of Imports, CIF, US Dollars (million$)	IMF
emp	Employment	IMF
hce	HouseholdConsumptionExpenditure, Nominal/ DomesticCurrency/Millions	IMF

The bivariate and multivariate FEM used in the analysis are described below. National Income Models:

$$LOGGDP1_{it} = \beta_{1i} + \beta_2 LOGKKREDI_{it} + u_{it} \text{ (1A)}$$

$$LOGGDP1_{it} = \beta_{1i} + \beta_2 LOGKKREDI_{it} + \beta_3 LOGINT2_{it} + \beta_4 LOGINDP_{it} + \beta_5 LOGEXPGS1_{it} + u_{it} \text{ (1B)}$$

Export Models:

$$LOGEXPGS1_{it} = \beta_{1i} + \beta_2 LOGKKREDI_{it} + u_{it} \text{ (2A)}$$

$$LOGEXPGS1_{it} = \beta_{1i} + \beta_2 LOGKKREDI_{it} + \beta_3 LOGINT2_{it} + \beta_4 LOGINDP_{it} + \beta_5 LOGGOODGS2_{it} + u_{it} \text{ (2B)}$$

Invesment Models:

$$LOGGFCF_{it} = \beta_{1i} + \beta_2 LOGKKREDI_{it} + u_{it} \text{ (3A)}$$

$$LOGGFCF_{it} = \beta_{1i} + \beta_2 LOGKKREDI_{it} + \beta_3 LOGINT2_{it} + \beta_4 LOGINDP_{it} + \beta_5 LOGEXPGS1_{it} + u_{it} \text{ (3B)}$$

Employment Models:

$$LOGEMP_{it} = \beta_{1i} + \beta_2 LOGKKREDI_{it} + u_{it} \quad (4A)$$

$$LOGEMP_{it} = \beta_{1i} + \beta_2 LOGKKREDI_{it} + \beta_3 LOGINT2_{it} + \beta_4 LOGINDP_{it} + \beta_5 LOGEXPGS1_{it} - u_{it} \quad (4B)$$

Household Consumption Models:

$$LOGHCE_{it} = \beta_{1i} + \beta_2 LOGKKREDI_{it} + u_{it} \quad (5A)$$

$$LOGHCE_{it} = \beta_{1i} + \beta_2 LOGKKREDI_{it} + \beta_3 LOGINT2_{it} + \beta_4 LOGINDP_{it} + \beta_5 LOGGDP1_{it} + u_{it} \quad (5B)$$

Where *it* sub-index is the value of the observation of the *ith* bank in the year *t* in relation to the related variable; β_{1i}model indicates that the constant term is different for each bank; u_{it}represents the error term of the regression model.

4 Estimation Results

The estimation results are reported in separate tables for each macroeconomic variable included in the analyses. The Model A in each table represents the bivariate FEM while the Model B represents the multivariate FEM. All of the variables (dependent and independent) included in the models are logarithmic variables. In this context, each parameter value obtained in the analysis refers to the percentage effect on the dependent variable.

In the above-mentioned Tab. 2 about national income model, Model 1A displays the bivariate FEM results. Results in Model 1A indicate that 1 % change in the LOGKKED variable leads to a 0.65 % increase in national income. When we look at the results in Model 1B, it can be seen that 1 % increase in LOGKKEDI variable cause 0.22 % increase in national income while 1 % increase in LOGINDP variable cause 0.81 % increase in national income. Finally, it is observed that 1 % increase in LOGEXPGS1 provides an increase of 0.49 % on national income. Moreover, it is seen that 1 % increase in LOGINT2 variable caused a decrease of 0.24 % in national income.

In the above-mentioned Tab. 3 about export model. The Model 2A presents bivariate FEM results in the export model above. It is seen that 1 % change in LOGKKREDI in model 2A provides a 0.32 % increase on export. When we look at multivariate multi-fixed effect model results at the model 2B, it is seen that 1 % increase in LOGKKREDI variable leads to 0.17 % increase in export, 1 % increase in LOGINDP variable results in %0.89 surge in export, 1 % increase in LOGINT2 variable cause %0.04 increase in export,a 1 % increase in LOGGOODS2 variable provides a %0.17 increase in export.

Tab. 2: National Income Models

	Model 1A	*Model 1B*
C	19,89863	18,97782
P-value	*0,0000*	*0,0000*
LOGKKREDI	0,656849	0,224238
P-value	*0,0000*	*0,0000*
LOGINT2		-0,244238
P-value		*0,0000*
LOGINDP		0,811067
P-value		*0,0000*
LOGEXPGS1		0,498346
P-value		*0,0000*
Num. of Obs.	*405*	*405*
Num. of Banks	*14*	*14*
Periods of Quarterly	*29*	*29*
R-square	*0,887666*	*0,956462*
F stat.	*220,1283*	*500,1058*
Prob(F stat.)	*0,0000*	*0,0000*

Tab. 3: Export Models

	Model 2A	*Model 2B*
C	4,871683	1,187249
P-value	*0,0000*	*0,0073*
LOGKKREDI	0,323959	0,178000
P-value	*0,0000*	*0,0000*
LOGGOODS2		0,173590
P-value		*0,0000*
LOGINT2		0,044475
P-value		*0,1410*
LOGINDP		0,893269
P-value		*0,0000*
Num. of Obs.	*405*	*405*
Num. of Banks	*14*	*14*
Periods of Quarterly	*29*	*29*
R-square	*0,688531*	*0,798068*
F stat.	*61,58089*	*89,96999*
Prob(F stat.)	*0,0000*	*0,0000*

In the above-mentioned Tab. 4 about investment model, Model 3A shows bivariate FEM results. One percent change in the LOGKKED variable in model 3A results in an increase of 0.79 % on investment. When the results of the Model 3B multivariate fixed effect model are examined, it can be observed that 1 % increase in LOGKKEDI variable leads to 0.22 % increase in investment, 1 % increase in LOGINDP variable causes 1.85 % surge ininvestment, finally 1 % increase in LOGEXPGS1 variable cause an increase of 0.38 % on investment. Furthermore, it is seen that 1 % increase in LOGINT2 variable in the model causes a decrease of 0.20 % on investment.

In the above-mentioned Tab. 5 about employment model above, Model 4A shows the results of the bivariate FEM results. It is seen that 1 % change in LOGKKED in model 4A provided an increase by 0.15 % on employment.

When we look at the results of the model 4B multivariate fixed effect model results, it can be observed that 1 %increase in LOGKKEDI variable leads to 0.04 % increase in employment, 1 % increase in LOGINDP results in 0.13 % surge in employment and finally 1 % increase in LOGEXPGS1 variable cause %0.19 increase in employment. It is seen that 1 % increase in LOGINT2 variable in the model caused a decrease in employment by 0.03 %.

Tab. 4: Invesment Models

	Model 3A	*Model 3B*
C	-2,270895	-4,576728
P-value	*0,0000*	*0,0000*
LOGKKREDI	0,797952	0,226901
P-value	*0,0000*	*0,0000*
LOGINT2		-0,203725
P-value		*0,0000*
LOGINDP		1,854534
P-value		*0,0000*
LOGEXPGS1		*0,380651*
P-value		*0,0000*
Num. of Obs.	*378*	*378*
Num. of Banks	*14*	*14*
Periods of Quarterly	*27*	*27*
R-square	*0,882612*	*0,973358*
F stat.	*194,9513*	*773,6729*
Prob(F stat.)	*0,0000*	*0,0000*

Tab. 5: Employment Models

	Model 4A	*Model 4B*
C	14,373380	13,633C5
P-value	*0,0000*	*0,0000*
LOGKKREDI	0,150776	0,043281
P-value	*0,0000*	*0,0000*
LOGINT2		-0,033114
P-value		*0,0001*
LOGINDP		0,136606
P-value		*0,0000*
LOGEXPGS1		*0,194958*
P-value		*0,0000*
Num. of Obs.	*392*	*392*
Num. of Banks	*14*	*14*
Periods of Quarterly	*29*	*29*
R-square	*0,811617*	*0,90994*
F stat.	*116,0176*	*222,2813*
Prob(F stat.)	*0,0000*	*0,0000*

Tab. 6: Household Consumption Models

	Model 5A	*Model 5B*
C	2,138633	-12,419420
P-value	*0,0000*	*0,0000*
LOGKKREDI	0,591465	0,076846
P-value	*0,0000*	*0,0000*
LOGINT2		-0,013133
P-value		*0,0241*
LOGINDP		0,184126
P-value		*0,0000*
LOGGDP1		*0,724021*
P-value		*0,0000*
Num. of Obs.	*378*	*378*
Num. of Banks	*14*	*14*
Periods of Quarterly	*27*	*27*
R-square	*0,916626*	*0,996033*
F stat.	*465,2922*	*5316,6000*
Prob(F stat.)	*0,0000*	*0,0000*

In the above-mentioned Tab. 6 about household consumption model, Model 5A shows the bivariate FEM results. One percent change in the LOGKKED variable model 5A has 0.59 % increase in household consumption. When the model 5B multivariate FEM results are examined, an increase of 1 % in LOGKKEDI variable leads to 0.07 % increase in household consumption, 1 % increase in LOGINDP variable cause % 0.18 increase in household consumption, finally 1 % increase in LOGGDP1 variable leads to an increase of 0.72 % on household consumption. Moreover, it is seen that 1 % increase in LOGINT2 variable in the model causes a decrease of 0.01 % in household consumption.

5 Conclusion

As a result of the analysis conducted in this study, it is seen that the loans extended by the conventional banks have a positive effect on all the macroeconomic variables included in the study. Among the macroeconomic variables used in the analyses, national income, investment and household consumption are highly affected by credits.

As can be seen from the results of the analysis, it is possible to say that the credits have a significant effect on the economy dynamics. Thus, our hypothesis "credits contribute to macroeconomics" is confirmed. With this result, it may be possible to expand the credit volume and increase the impact on macroeconomics.

References

Araç, A., and Özcan, S. K., (2014). The Causality between Financial Development and Economic Growth: The Case of Turkey. *Journal of Economic Cooperation and Development*, 35(3), 171–198.

Arslan, İ., and Yapraklı, S., (2008). Banka Kredileri ve Enflasyon Arasındaki İlişki: Türkiye Üzerine Ekonometrik Bir Analiz (1983–2007). *İstanbul Üniversitesi İktisat Fakültesi Ekonometri ve İstatistik Dergisi*, 7, 88–103.

Beck, T., Demirgüç Kunt, A., and Merrouche, Q., (2010). Islamic vs. Conventional Banking: Business Model Efficiency and Stability, Policy Research Working Paper, The World Bank, 5446.

Castro, V., (2013). Macroeconomic Determinants of the Credit Risk in the Banking System: The Case of GIPSI. *Economic Modelling*, 31, 672–683.

Mashamba, T., Magweva, R., and Gumbo, L. C., (2014). Analysing the Relationship between Bank's Deposit Interest Rate and Deposit Mobilisation: Empirical Evidence from Zimbabwean Commercial Banks (1980–2006). *IOSR Journal of Business and Management*, 16(1), 64–75.

Okşak, Y., (2018). Cointegration and Causality Analysis of Globalization and Exports for Turkey. *Journal of Economics Bibliography*, 5(2), 122–128.

Yalcinkaya Koyuncu, J., (2011). Foreign Bank Presence and Bank Spreads: Evidence from Turkey. *The AUCO Czech Economic Review*, 5(1), 64–75.

Yalcinkaya Koyuncu, J., and Yilmaz, R., (2015). The Impact of Privatization on Export in Transition Economies: A Panel Study. *Anadolu Üniversitesi Sosyal Bilimler Dergisi*, 15(2), 57–62.

Yazıcı, A., and Yazıcı, R., (2017). Institutional Changes in Businesses and the Importance of Quality Management Systems for Economic Development: The Case of Turkey. *Journal of Current Researches on Business and Economics*, 7(2), 17–26.

Yazıcı. R., (2017). *Finansal Sistemde Faiz Sorunsalı Ve Katılım Bankacılığı.* İstanbul: Kriter yayınevi.

Levent Korap and Ali Konak

An Empirical Note on Uncovered Interest Parity Condition with Turkish Evidence

1 Introduction

Understanding the behavior of economic agents in financial markets requires the knowledge of what motives drive the contruction of expectations. In this line, one of the main recent issues of interest in policy design process is to reveal the fundamental building blocks of exchange rates and interest rates in international macroeconomics, and in turn such a policy debate based on theoretical underpinnings of exchange rate determination of economic agents would be of special concern for the effectiveness of interventions in exchange markets, revealing also some main motives that rule the exchange rate movements. As Isard (2006) emphasizes, the uncovered interest parity (UIP) condition would constitute a central focal point in contemporaneous exchange rate determination models and to the extent that the UIP is valid at short time horizons, official intervention cannot succeed in changing the spot exchange rate relative to the expected future spot rate unless the authorities choose to allow interest rates to change.

Following briefly Huisman et al. (1998), the UIP condition would hold if the return on a domestic currency deposit equals the expected return from converting the domestic currency into the foreign currency, investing it in a foreign deposit and then converting the proceeds back into the domestic currency at the future expected exchange rate. Thus the UIP assumes the existence of arbitrage in international markets linking the interest and exchange rates. If the *ex-post* uncovered interest differential reflects the degree of capital mobility, then it implies that the sum of the risk premium and rational expectation error may diminish over time since the interdependence of world financial markets has increased (Sul, 1999). Or, in other words, if capital is perfectly mobile, then investors around the world will be indifferent between holding their portfolios in domestic or foreign securities, which are also perfectly comparable denominated in different currencies because they obtain the same return from these assets (Bhatti and Moosa, 1995). Consequently, through the joint assumptions of rational expectations, risk neutrality, free capital mobility and the absence of taxes on capital transfers, expected excess returns in the foreign exchange markets then must equal zero on average (Baillie and Bollerslev, 2000).

There exists a large literature of theoretical and empirical papers examining the interest parity condition, of which most papers also fail to give evidence in favour of the UIP hypothesis. Likewise, Flood and Rose (2002) touch on this issue in the sense that although the UIP theorem predicts that countries with high interest rates should, on average, have depreciating currencies, much empirical papers indicate that such currencies in general have tended to appreciate. These findings, in general, are attributed to that the forward rate is a biased predictor of the future spot rate. For this failure of the predictive power of the UIP hypothesis in empirical papers, Chinn and Meredith (2004) consider that much of the published studies examining the UIP phenomenon have been using financial instruments with relatively short maturities of 12 months or less, for which they assume some potential reasons such as constraints on sample size and difficulty of obtaining long-term fixed maturity interest rate data, while they report good performance of the UIP hypothesis using bonds with maturity ranging from 5 to 10 years. Also, Christensen (2000) attributes the rejection of the UIP theory to both the lack of assuming rational expectations and the existence of time-varying risk premia. As emphasized by Sachsida et al. (2001), the so-called peso problem can be considered one of the main reasons of empirical lack of the UIP theorem since most countries do not work with a pure floating exchange rate regime. In a fixed rate regime, due to a small probability of large alteration in the exchange rate within the period covered by the analysis, one can be misled to the conclusion that agents are showing systematic errors in their short run predictions, i.e., they are not rational, and this can lead to biased estimates of slope parameters of the UIP equations in samples that are too short to accurately reflect the small probability of large events (Chinn and Meredith, 2004). Since the rational expectations assumption is one of the fundamental building blocks of the UIP theorem, the failure of the empirical tests applied can be a result of apparent lack of rationality in the exchange rate expectation. Beyaert et al. (2007) also express that regime shifts stemming from institutional, political and economic changes subject to modern world economies is responsible for the UIP puzzle estimated by researchers. Regimes switch 'infrequently' at dates that are unknown and so economic agents make rational forecast errors that are correlated with the forward premium or the interest rate spreads.

At this point, some papers have emerged on why the slope coefficient in the regression of the change in the logarithm of the spot exchange rate on the forward premium is less than unity or even negative. This would imply that investors in the foreign exchange market do not behave rationally since they would not take the profit of predictable excess returns. See also, among many others, Froot and Thaler (1990), Lewis (1995) and Engel (1996) on this issue. However, some others are able to give evidence in favour of the UIP theorem. See, for instance, Han (2004). Chinn and Meredith (2004) explain the contradiction between short- and long-term estimation results rejecting the validity of UIP theorem in the short run but supporting it in long horizon estimates in the sense that the long horizon results differ sharply from the short horizon results because the model's 'fundamentals' play a more important role in trying down exchange rate movements over longer horizons.

Our aim in this note is to test the UIP condition based on theoretical fundamentals in line with economic theory. The next section gives such a theoretical framework, while the third section tries to conduct an empirical model using data from the Turkish economy. Finally, the last section concludes.

2 Theoretical Bases

We now try to construct analytically the relationships between the unbiasedness hypothesis on which the UIP theorem is based and covered (CIV) plus uncovered interest parity (UIP) relationships. For this purpose, we will follow McCallum (1994) and Chinn and Meredith (2004).

Let s_t be the price of foreign currency in units of domestic currency at time t, and let f_t denote the one period forward value of s, i.e., the home currency price in period t of a unit of foreign exchange to be paid for and delivered in period $t+1$. Then f_t might be said to be an unbiased predictor of s_{t+1} if $\alpha = 0.0$ and $\beta = 1.0$ in the relation:

$$\alpha + \beta f_t = E_t s_{t+1} \tag{1}$$

where $E_t s_{t+1} \equiv E\left(s_{t+1}/\Omega_t\right)$ is is the conditional expectation of s_{t+1} formed on the basis of the information set Ω_t available at time t. With rational expectations, expectational error $\varepsilon_{t+1} = s_{t+1} - E_t s_{t+1}$ will be uncorrelated in the population with all elements of Ω_t so that we can rewrite Equation 1 as:

$$s_{t+1} = \alpha + \beta f_t + \varepsilon_{t+1} \tag{2}$$

Equation 2 can be estimated by means of ordinary least squares (OLS) if ε_t is white noise. Rearranging this yields Equation 3:

$$s_{t+1} - s_t = \alpha + \beta\left(f_t - s_t\right) + \varepsilon_{T+1} \tag{3}$$

Equation 3 is a more generalized form in conducting unbiasedness tests under the test hypothesis $\beta = 1.0$.

Let us now define covered and uncovered interest parity relationships based on the assumption of arbitrage between spot and forward foreign exchange markets. If the conditions for risk-free arbitrage exist, the ratio of the forward to the spot exchange rate will equal the interest differential between assets with otherwise similar characteristics measured in local currencies. As for CIP relationship and following the notation in Chinn and Meredith (2004), if we define s_t as considered above, $f_{t,t+k}$ forward value of s for a contract expiring k periods in the future, $i_{t,k}$ one plus the k-period yield on the domestic instrument, and $i^*_{t,k}$ the corresponding yield on the foreign instrument, all in natural logarithms, risk-free arbitrage condition regardless of investor preferences can be written in Equation 4 below:

$$f_{t,t+k} - s_t = \left(i_{t,k} - i^*_{t,k}\right) \tag{4}$$

Following Taylor (1995), in other words, assuming the nonexistence of any barrier to arbitrage across international financial markets should lead us to hypothesize that the interest differential on similar assets, adjusted for covering in the forward foreign exchange market the movement of currencies at the maturity of the underlying assets, converge continuously to be equal to zero. To the extent that investors are risk averse, however, the forward rate can differ from the expected future spot rate by a premium that compensates for the perceived riskiness of holding domestic versus foreign assets as shown in Equation 5 below:

$$f_{t,t+k} = s^e_{t,t+k} - rp_{t,t+k} \tag{5}$$

Expected change in exchange rate can be expressed by substituting Equation 5 into Equation 4, from period t to period $t+k$ to be expressed as a function of the interest differential and the risk premium:

$$\Delta s^e_{t,t+k} = \left(i_{t,k} - i^*_{t,k}\right) - rp_{t,t+k} \tag{6}$$

UIP requires that the risk-premium in Equation 6 is zero through the assumption of risk-neutral investors. Making use of rational expectations in exchange rates for the purpose of direct testing, future realizations of s_{t+k} will equal the value expected at time t plus a white-noise error term that is uncorrelated with all information known at t, including the interest differential and the spot exchange rate:

$$s_{t+k} = s^{re}_{t,t+k} + \xi_{t,t+k} \tag{7}$$

where $s^{re}_{t,t+k}$ is the rational expectation of the exchange rate at time $t+k$ formed in time t. Substituting Equation 7 into Equation 6 gives the following relationship:

$$\Delta s_{t,t+k} = \left(i_{t,k} + i^*_{t,k}\right) - rp_{t,t+k} + \xi_{t,t+k} \tag{8}$$

where the left-hand side of Equation 8 is the realized change in the exchange rate from t to $t + k$. As emphasized by Sachsida et al. (2001), a constant can be added to the above equation, which is aimed to capture any risk premium demanded by economic agents. Such a constant may also capture asymmetric information or other economic considerations that can justify the existence of a differential in yields of bonds measured in local currency.

3 GMM Estimation

The theoretical UIP model constructed in the former section is tried to be estimated in a somewhat similar way to Sarantis (2006) and Aslan and Korap (2010), considering the Turkish lira/US dollar bilateral currency exchange rate that presents daily average of spot rates quoted for the US dollar on national market expressed as national currency per US dollar. The exchange rate data are represented by one-period ahead expected exchange rate return in natural logarithms using the formula $\ln(s_{t+1}/s_t)$ where ln is the natural logarithm operator. Data for interest rates are of the form short-term, i.e., the monthly treasury average compound domestic borrowing rate for Turkey and 3-month Treasury bond interest rate for the United States. We use in the model estimation process below the share prices as instrument. All quoted interest rates are in percentages. Hence, following Sarantis (2006), the rates used in the estimation are measured by $r = \ln(1 + i/100)$. Besides, stock returns are measured by $\ln(p_t/p_{t-1})$, where p is the 2010: 100 based stock price index for the Turkish and US economy. The model includes also three variables as instruments in order to capture the potential interdependence of financial markets.

We use monthly frequency data over the period 2002M01–2017M12 with 192 observations which represent the implementation of flexible exchange rate system for the Turkish economy after the economic crisis year 2001. The exchange rate and the interest rate for Turkey are obtained from the electronic data delivery system of the Central Bank of the Republic of Turkey (https://evds2.tcmb.gov.tr/) and the electronic data delivery system of the Ministry of Development (https://www.sbb.gov.tr/), while all the other data are taken from the electronic data delivery system of the OECD Main Economic Indicators (https://stats.oecd.org/). Since exchange rates and interest rates are jointly determined, we consider both exchange rates and interest rate differentials as endogeneous variables. We estimate the model with the generalized method of moments (GMM) estimator of Hansen (1982). The GMM estimator selects parameter estimates so that the correlations between the instruments and disturbances are as close to zero as possible, as defined by a criterion function. For estimation purposes, we need some instruments when applying to the GMM procedure, and we choose the 12-month lagged values, the exchange rate differential, interest rate differential plus stock return differential ($return_{stock}$) as instruments. The GMM estimates reported below use the Newey and West (1987) weighting matrix, which ensures that the GMM estimates and their standard errors are robust to heteroskedasticity and autocorrelation of unknown form.

We now estimate whether the UIP relationship can be verified for the future exchange rate return employing short-term interest rate data from the Turkish versus the US economy. The exchange rate data are represented by one-period ahead expected exchange rate return in natural logarithms using the formula $\ln(s_{t+1}/s_t)$ where ln is the natural logarithm operator.

In Tab. 1, we report the GMM estimation results of the standard UIP relationship with serial correlation robust t-statistics in parentheses employing the future spot exchange rate (s_{t+1}) and short-term interest differential. Since we use more instruments than parameters to estimate, the validity of overidentifying restrictions is tested by the Hansen's (1982) J-statistic. Under the null hypothesis that the overidentifying restrictions are satisfied, the J-statistic times the number of regression observations is asymptotically χ^2 with degrees of freedom equal to the number of overidentifying restrictions.

Tab. 1: GMM Estimates of the UIP Relationship $\left(\boldsymbol{\Delta s_{t+1}} = \boldsymbol{\alpha} + \boldsymbol{\beta}\left(\boldsymbol{i_t} - \boldsymbol{i_t^*}\right) + \boldsymbol{u_t}\right)$

α	β	$Adj.R^2$	$J-statistic$	$\alpha=0$	$\beta=1$
0.0160	-0.0977	0.0411	5.1881	9.5486	-31.427
(t-stat 3.09)	(t-stat -2.80)		(prob. 0.08)	(prob. 0.00)	(prob. 987.7)

Instruments used: C $s_{t-12}(i_{t-12} - i^*_{t-12}) return_{stock,t-12}$

Endogeneity test

Null hypothesis: $(i_t - i_t^*)$ is exogenous

	Value	df	Probability
Difference in $J-stats$	0.0477	1	0.83

Instrument Orthogonality C test

		Value	df	Probability
Null hypothesis:	s_{t-12} is exogenous	3.8148	1	0.06
	$(i_{t-12} - i^*_{t-12})$ is exogenous	2.3331	1	0.13
	$return_{stock,t-12}$	2.3343	1	0.13

Numbers within parentheses next to regression coefficients are the heteroskedastcity and autocorrelation consistent t-values. $Adj.R^2$ is the adjusted coefficient of determination statistic, and $J - statistic$ is the Hansen's (1982) $J - statistic$ for overidentification restrictions. For the restrictions $\alpha = 0$ and $\beta = 1$, the Wald statistics are distributed as a χ^2 (1) under the null.

In Tab. 1, we find anomalous estimation result as for theoretical model construction above with estimates of α being close to zero and with estimated slope coefficient β which is negative, although both have significance in acceptable statistical levels. Thus, our findings confirm the failure of the UIP hypotheses in the sense that over short horizons we give support to the common perception in the economics literature that the exchange rates move inversely with interest differentials (Chinn and Meredith, 2004). We must note that the smaller lagged values was also tried to be employed to the data. Although estimating similar results, the $J - statistic$ to test the validity of overidentifying restrictions under the null hypothesis was rejected for small lagged values of the variables. But using 12-lags fitted to the statistical prerequisites.

Further, the determination coefficient is very low and close to zero; thus, these results reveal that interest rate differentials alone cannot possibly explain short horizon exchange rate movements. Wald tests restrictions that $\alpha = 0$ or $\beta = 1$ under χ^2 (1) give supportive estimation results to those estimated in the unrestricted GMM system equation as well. Endogeneity test indicates that we are unable to reject the exogenous characterictic of interest differential variable. Also, the null hypothesis of exogeneity for instruments used cannot be rejected by the orthogonality test.

Following Chinn and Meredith (2004) and Aslan and Korap (2010), we can attribute these perverse relationships between interest rates and exchange rates to using short horizon data. However, when considered longer horizon data for the G-7 countries Chinn and Meredith (2004) somewhat support the UIP hypothesis, with slope parameters that are positive and closer to the hypothesized value of unity than to zero. Thus some robustness checks of our findings with longer horizon data such as five- or ten-year homogenous interest rate data and exchange rate return should be applied to verify our main findings in this note. Such a task is thought to be implemeted in future complementary papers.

4 Concluding Remarks

In contemporaneous macroeconomics, one of the main recent issues of interest is to examine the fundamental building blocks of exchange rates and interest rates based on theoretical underpinnings of exchange rate determination.

Inferences from these controversies reveal the knowledge of what motives drive the construction of expectations and in turn highlight whether they can help policy makers for the choice of appropriate stabilization policies. In this empirical note, we investigate one of the central focal points in exchange rate determination models upon the Turkish economy. For this purpose, we construct a theoretical model based on uncovered interest parity (UIP) relationship relating expected exchange rate return to the interest rate differentials, and then estimate it by applying to GMM methodology. Our estimation results reveal that we verify the failure of the UIP theorem using short horizon interest differential and future spot exchange rate data as was found in much empirical papers in the economics literature. But, we finally note that these findings contradict Aslan and Korap (2010) that give support to the validity of the UIP hypothesis in the long run for the Turkish economy by employing contemporaneous multivariate cointegration methodologies. Thus, future chapters must also further search this discrepancy so as to see whether the empirical findings verify the estimation results found in this chapter.

References

Aslan, Ö. and Korap. H.L. (2010). Does the Uncovered Interest Parity Hold in Short Horizons? *Applied Economics Letters*, 17, 361–365.

Baillie, R.T. and Bollerslev, T. (2000). The Forward Premium Anomaly Is Not as Bad as You Think. *Journal of International Money and Finance*, 19, 471–488.

Beyaert, A., García-Solanes, J., and Pérez-Castejón, J.J. (2007). Uncovered Interest Parity with Switching Regimes. *Economic Modelling*, 24, 189–202.

Bhatti, R.H. and Moosa, I.A. (1995). An Alternative Approach to Testing Uncovered Interest Parity. *Applied Economics Letters*, 2, 478–481.

Chinn, M.D. and Meredith, G. (2004). Monetary Policy and Long-Horizon Uncovered Interest Parity. *IMF Staff Papers*, 51(3), 409–430.

Christensen, M. (2000). Uncovered Interest Parity and Policy Behavior: New Evidence. *Economics Letters*, 69, 81–87.

Engel, C. (1996). The Forward Discount Anomaly and the Risk Premium: A Survey of Recent Evidence. *Journal of Empirical Finance*, 3, 123–192.

Flood, R.P. and Rose, A.K. (2002). Uncovered Interest Parity in Crisis. *IMF Staff Papers*, 49(2), 252–266.

Froot, K.A. and Thaler, R.H. (1990). Foreign Exchange. *Journal of Economic Perspectives*, (4), 179–192.

Han, B. (2004). Is the Forward Premium Puzzle Universal? *Applied Economics Letters*, 11, 131–134.

https://evds2.tcmb.gov.tr/

https://stats.oecd.org/

https://www.sbb.gov.tr/

Hansen, L.P. (1982). Large Sample Properties of Generalized Method of Moments Estimators. *Econometrica*, 50, 1029–1054.

Huisman, R., Koedijk, K., Kool, C., and Nissen, F. (1998). Extreme Support for Uncovered Interest Parity. *Journal of International Money and Finance*, 17, 211–228.

Isard, P. (2006). Uncovered Interest Parity. IMF Working Paper, WP/06/96.

Lewis, K.K. (1995). Puzzles in International Financial Markets. In G. Grossmand and K. Rogoff (Eds.), *Handbook of International Economics*, 3. Amsterdam: Elsevier Science, 1913–1971.

McCallum, B.T. (1994). A Reconsideration of the Uncovered Interest Parity Relationship. *Journal of Monetary Economics*, 33, 105–132.

Newey, W. and West, K. (1987). A Simple Positive Semi-Definite, Heteroskedasticity and Autocorrelation Consistent Covariance Matrix. *Econometrica*, 55, 703–708.

Sachsida, A., Ellery Jr., R. and Teixeira, J.R. (2001). Uncovered Interest Parity and the Peso Problem: The Brazilian Case. *Applied Economics Letters*, 8, 79–181.

Sarantis, N. (2006). Testing the Uncovered Interest Parity Using Traded Volatility, A Time-Varying Risk Premium and Heterogeneous Expectations. *Journal of International Money and Finance*, 25, 1168–1186.

Sul, D. (1999). Does Ex-Post Uncovered Interest Differential Reflect the Degrees of Capital Mobility? *Applied Economics Letters*, 6, 97–102.

Taylor, M.P. (1995). The Economics of Exchange Rates. *Journal of Economic Literature*, 33, 13–47.

İbrahim Al

The Stability of the Demand for Money in Turkey

1 Introduction

Demand for money is one of the most popular topics in macroeconomics. Money demand theories have sought the answer to the following question. What motivates economic agents to hold money? Neo-Classic theory, except for Pigou, accepts only the transactions motive. However, Keynesian and Monetarist theories accept three motives, which are the transaction, the precautionary and the speculative motives. Speculation motivation have been included by Keynes to the money demand theory. This contribution led to the inclusion of interest rate in the money demand function. In this context, it is assumed that the demand for money is basically a function of income and interest rate.

Macroeconomic theories have different results about stability of demand for money. According to Neo-Classical and Monetarist theories, the demand for money is stable. However, it is not stable according to Keynesian theory. Neo-Classic theory accepts the velocity of circulation is fixed. Besides, Friedman (1956) believes that the velocity of circulation of money is predictable. This means that the money demand function is stable and insensitive to interest rate. However, in Keynesian theory the velocity of circulation is changeable and money demand function is unstable and unpredictable and very sensitive to interest rates. If so, the changing of money supply has little impact on production in an economy (Lee and Chien, 2008: 3185). In this situation, fiscal policy should be more preferable than monetary policy in Keynesian theory. If not so, money supply has a potential impact on both economic activity and inflation (Albilescu and Pepin, 2018).

The stable money demand means that there is a predictable and reliable relationship between the monetary aggregates and the variables which are income and the alternative cost of holding money, in the money demand function. Hence, the amount of money demand can be accurately estimated by the money demand function (Hacker and Hatemi-J, 2005: 1731). However, financial innovations, technological developments, economic crises, expectations, etc. disrupt the stability of demand for money. The use of information and communication technologies in monetary sector has emerged the new payment instruments. These instruments have changed the demand for central bank's reserve money multiplier and the functioning of monetary transmission mechanism. Hence, base money, money multiplier and money supply may become unstable (Akyazı and Artan, 2006: 9–12).

Whether the demand for money is stable or not affects the strategies of monetary policy. For example, stable demand for money implies a stable money multiplier. If it is stable, then it is easier to predict the effect of a given money supply on the aggregate money income. Hence, a central bank can achieve to the price stability task by controlling money supply (Pradhan and Subramanian, 2003: 336). So, in an economy where the demand for money is stable, the central bank may choose the money supply as the intermediate target. In this situation, money supply is the most suitable monetary policy instrument. But it can choose an interest target when the demand for money is unstable. Hence, interest rate is the most appropriate instrument for the conduct of monetary policy (Kumar et al., 2013: 979).

Monetary targeting and exchange rate targeting strategies have been implemented to achieve price stability task in Turkey before 2001. But these strategies have failed. Inflation targeting has been implemented in Turkey since 2002. Implicit inflation targeting had been implemented in the 2002–2005 period and explicit inflation targeting has been implementing since 2006. The main policy tool of inflation targeting strategy is policy rate. The purpose of this study is to empirically re-investigate the parameter stability of long-run money demand function in Turkey for the 2006Q1–2018Q3 period. Thus, it can be evaluated whether the strategy of the implemented monetary policy is appropriate in this term. The rest of the chapter is as follows: In Section 2, the empirical literature of the stability of money demand in foreign countries and Turkey is given. In Sections 3 and 4, econometric method, data and findings are explained. The last section concludes and presents the policy implications.

2 Literature

Owing to its importance, the money demand function, including traditional determinants (income and interest rate) and sometime others (exchange rate, inflation rate, stock market index, etc.), has been intensively investigated in empirical research for a number of countries. For example, Hoffman et al. (1995), for U.S., Japan, Canada, U.K. and West Germany; Bahmani-Oskooee and Shabsigh (1996), for Japan; Bahmani-Oskooee and Bohl (2000), for Germany; Pradhan and Subramanian (2003) for India; Hecker and Hatemi-J (2005) for Sweden; Bahmani (2008) for fourteen countries in Middle East; Kumar et al. (2013), for Nigeria; Hamdi et al. (2015), for six Gulf Cooperation Council Countries; Lee and Chien (2008), for China; Manap (2009), for Malasia and Atgür and Altay (2015), for Turkey and Indonesia.

Some studies have investigated the stability of Turkey money demand function. The empirical evidence on the stability of demand for money in Turkey is mixed. For example, Balaylar and Duygulu (2004), Yılancı (2012), Dritsaki and Dritsaki (2012), Özcan and Arı (2013), Tüzün et al. (2017) found that demand for money is unstable in Turkey. However, Akıncı (2003), Halıcıoğlu and Uğur (2005), Gencer and Arısoy (2013) found that demand for money is stable.

Dritsaki and Dritsaki (2012) searched the stability of money demand function for the period 1989M5–2010M5 in Turkey. The result showed that there is a long-run relationship but the money demand function is instable. Yılancı (2012) investigated the stability of the money demand function in Turkey from 1989Q1 to 2011:Q2 by employing bounds test and rolling bounds test approaches. The result showed that the money demand function is instable in the analysis period. Özcan and Arı (2013) investigated the stability of M2 using monthly data for the period 2005M12–2012M10. They examined the presence of long run equilibrium relationship among M2 monetary aggregate, real income, interest rate, exchange rate through Johansen Cointegration test and analyzed the stability of money demand using Cusum and Cusum Square tests. According to cointegration test, there are long-run relationship among the variables. However, the stability of money demand function is rejected. Atgür and Altay (2015) investigated the relationship between the money demand and its determinants during the inflation targeting period in Turkey by using Autoregressive Distributed Lag (ARDL) Model and Cusum Test. The results have shown that there is no relationship between income level, interest rate, inflation and money demand function in both short-run and long-run.

Akıncı (2003) investigates the relationship between real money balances, real income and the opportunity cost variables in Turkey for the period 1987Q1–2003Q3. The estimated results indicate that there is a long-run relationship between real currency, private consumption expenditure as a scale variable, interest rates on government securities and the exchange rate. Halıcıoğlu and Uğur (2005) analyze the stability of the M1 in Turkey for the period 1950–2002. They estimate and test the stability of the demand for money by ARDL bound test and Cusum and Cusum Square stability tests. They show that money demand function is stable in Turkey. Gencer and Arısoy (2013) investigated the long-run money demand for Turkey's economy. They tested empirical relationship among real money, real income, interest rate, inflation and exchange rate for the period 1989Q1–2010Q4. ARDL bound test indicates that there is a long-run relationship between real money and other variables. The results show that real income and exchange rate have positive effect, whereas inflation and interest rate have negative effect on real money demand.

Many studies have used the cointegration technique to search the long-run stability of the money demand function. If there is a cointegration among variables, then money demand function is stable. However, cointegration relationship may be damaged due to structural instability. Therefore, formal instability tests as Cusum and Cusum Square should be applied on cointegrating relationship to determine the stability of estimated parameters (Bahmani, 2008: 81). Although there are cointegration in many studies, which investigate the stability of demand for money, it has been found to be unstable according to the Cusum and Cusum Square stability tests in the literature.

3 Method

Granger and Yoon (2002) introduce a hidden cointegration test. "They investigate the presence of a cointegrating relationship not between the aggregate series but between their components, which they call hidden cointegration. That is, they allow for the possibility that, even if no linear cointegration exists, there may be along-run relation between the positive and negative non-stationary components of some series" (Hatemi-J and Irandoust, 2012: 372). Granger and Yoon (2002) introduced hidden cointegration test mainly based on Engle and Granger (1987). Hatemi-J and Irandoust (2012) test the possible asymmetric links between variables by applying hidden cointegration analysis within a multivariate maximum likelihood framework. It is based on Johansen cointegration technique. This method can be explained as follows (Hatemi-J and Irandoust, 2012: 373):

Suppose X_t and Y_t are two random walk time series:

$$X_t = X_{t-1} + \varepsilon_t = X_0 + \sum_{i=1}^{t} \varepsilon_i$$

$$Y_t = Y_{t-1} + \eta_t = Y_0 + \sum_{i=1}^{t} \eta_i$$

where t = 1,2,...T and X_0, Y_0 are initial values and ε_i and η_i denote mean zero white noise disturbance terms. A standard cointegration exists if $\{X_t\ ; Y_t\}$ are cointegrated by one cointegrating vector. When movements of X_t and Y_t are asymmetric, it is possible to detect hidden cointegrations between them. Granger and Yoon (2002) define positive and negative shocks as follows:

$$\varepsilon_i^+ = \max(\varepsilon_i, 0), \quad \varepsilon_i^- = \min(\varepsilon_i, 0)$$
$$\eta_i^+ = \max(\eta_i, 0), \quad \eta_i^- = \min(\eta_i, 0)$$
$$\varepsilon_i = \varepsilon_i^+ + \varepsilon_i^- \; and \; \eta_i = \eta_i^+ + \eta_i^-$$

Thus:

$$X_t = X_{t-1} + \varepsilon_t = X_0 + \sum_{i=1}^{t} \varepsilon_i^+ + \sum_{i=1}^{t} \varepsilon_i^-$$

$$Y_t = Y_{t-1} + \eta_t = Y_0 + \sum_{i=1}^{t} \eta_i^+ + \sum_{i=1}^{t} \eta_i^-$$

Then the notations can be simplified with:

$$X_t^+ = \sum_{i=1}^{t} \varepsilon_i^+, \; X_t^- = \sum_{i=1}^{t} \varepsilon_i^-, \; Y_t^+ = \sum_{i=1}^{t} \eta_i^+, \; and \; Y_t^- = \sum_{i=1}^{t} \eta_i^-$$

So:

$$X = X_0 + X_t^+ + X_t^-, \; and \; Y = Y_0 + Y_t^+ + Y_t^-$$

Consequently:

$$\Delta X_t^+ = \varepsilon_t^+, \quad \Delta X_t^- = \varepsilon_t^-, \quad \Delta Y_t^+ = \eta_t^+, \quad and \quad \Delta Y_t^- = \eta_t^-.$$

Hatemi-J and Irandoust (2012) calculate the first difference ($\Delta X = X_t - X_{t-1}$) for both of the time series and sort observations to positive and negative movements ($\Delta X_t^+ \; and \; \Delta X_t^-$). They also calculate the cumulative sum of positive (negative) changes, at a given time, for all variables ($X_t^+ = \sum \Delta X_t^- and \; X_t^- = \sum \Delta X_t^-$) via equations that are presented above. Similar calculations are implemented for Y. The variables X and Y are said to have hidden cointegration if their components are cointegrated. The process is estimated by implementing the Johansen multivariate maximum likelihood approach.

4 Data and Empirical Findings

In general, the demand for money is assumed to depend on a scale variable and the opportunity cost of holding money. Following the literature, we assume that income and interest rate are the main determinants of the demand for money.

$$\frac{M}{P} = f(Y, R)$$

where M denotes nominal money supply, P price index, Y a scale variable representing the transaction volume in economy and R denotes opportunity cost of holding money. Thus, the following formulation in log linear form is adopted.

$$lnm_t = \beta_0 + \beta_1 lnY_t + \beta_2 lnR_t + \varepsilon_t$$

With $m_t = \frac{M_t}{P_t}$, where m_t is money supply, Y_t is real gross domestic product (real GDP) and R_t is nominal interest rate. β_0 is positive constant, β_1 is output elasticity and expected positive andβ_2 is interest rate elasticity and expected negative.

The data used in this study are obtained from electronic data dissemination system of the Central Bank of the Republic of Turkey. In our analysis, we use M2 monetary aggregate, GDP in real terms and 3-month interest rates (weighted average interest rates for deposits in Turkish Lira).

All data are quarterly observations of the variables, and the study covers the period from 2006Q1 to 2018Q3. In this study, M2 monetary aggregate was deflated by consumer price index. Real M2 and real GDP seasonal adjusted by Census X-13 technique. In order to reduce the variability of the data, the logarithmic form of them was used. All variables are in natural logarithms. Later, we separated all variables to the positive and negative components.

Firstly, we test the stationary characteristics of the related variables by using Phillips-Perron unit root test. Because, Phillips-Perron test rebuts autocorrelation and heteroskedasticity (Hatemi-J and Irandoust, 2015, 220). Unit root test results of the positive and the negative cumulative shocks of the variables are given in Tab. 1.

As can be seen in Tab. 1, these positive and negative components of M2, Y and R are non-stationary. The test results show that positive and negative components of the variables are integrated at the first level.

Secondly, we test for cointegration in order to avoid spurious results. For this reason, we select VAR lag order. The optimal lag order was selected by Schwarz Information Criteria and Hannan-Quinn Information Criteria. Optimal lag order is 1 for equations with both positive and negative components. Also, there is no autocorrelation problem.

Hatemi-J–Irandoust hidden cointegration test results are given in Tab. 2. As can be seen in Tab. 2, there is no cointegration among negative components of variables. Besides, trace test indicates one cointegration among positive components of variables at the 0.05 level. But maximum eigenvalues test indicates no cointegration at the 0.05 level. For this reason, we say that there is no cointegration among the positive components.

Tab. 1: The Phillips-Perron Unit Root Test Results

	With a Constant				With Both a Constant and a Trend			
	Level		First Difference		Level		First Difference	
M2+	-1.6862	(15)	-12.0060	(12)	-4.5262	(3)	-11.6578	(12)
	[0.4319]		[0.0000]*		[0.0036]*		[0.0000]*	
M2-	-0.1062	(6)	-6.3165	(7)	-2.4967	(3)	-6.2519	(7)
	[0.9429]		[0.0000]*		[0.3284]		[0.0000]*	
Y+	-0.3678	(3)	-7.8669	(0)	-2.3847	(0)	-7.9597	(1)
	[0.9796]		[0.0000]*		[0.3828]		[0.0000]*	
Y-	-0.3618	(0)	- 5.9975	(2)	-1.8904	(1)	-5.9374	(2)
	[0.9075]		[0.0000]*		[0.6446]		[0.0000]*	
R+	1.7888	(4)	-4.9538	(1)	-0.6248	(3)	-5.1208	(3)
	[0.9997]		[0.0002]*		[0.9730]		[0.0006]*	
R-	-1.3170	(3)	-4.4198	(2)	-1.0514	(3)	-4.5314	(1)
	[0.6147]		[0.0009]*		[0.9269]		[0.0036]*	

Note: The number in parentheses is the chosen order lags for the Phillips Perron test. The asterisk indicates the unit root hypothesis is rejected at the 1 % significance level based on the models selected by the criteria. The number in brackets is p-value.

Tab. 2: Hatemi-J-Irandoust Hidden Cointegration Test Results

Positive and Negative Components	Null Hypothesis	Alternative Hypothesis	Trace Statistic	Max-Eig. Statistic	p-value
$(M2^+, Y^+, R^+)$	r=0	r≥1	40.89780		0.0105
	r=1	r=2	17.17987		0.0734
	r=0	r≥1		23.7193	0.0537
(M2, Y, R)	r=0	r≥1	22.69552		0.5238
	r=0	r≥1		14.56509	0.5363

Note: r denotes the number of cointegrated vectors. The optimal lag order was selected by Scwarz Information Criteria and Hannan-Quinn Information Criteria. Null and alternative hypotheses are arranged according to the results.

5 Conclusion

Economic crises, technological developments and financial innovations disrupt the stability of demand for money. However, the stability is important for the monetary policy strategy. If the demand for money is unstable, the monetary targeting strategy should not be implemented. Instead, a strategy that targets the interest rate should be preferred. In this study, the stability of demand for money have been investigated by Hatem-J and Irandoust hidden cointegration test in Turkey's economy for the 2006Q1–2018Q3 period. According to the results, there is no cointegration among the positive components of variables or negative components of variables. Hence, it is said that, demand for money is unstable in Turkey. For this reason, the Central Bank of the Republic of Turkey should not apply monetary targeting strategy as before 2001. It is known that explicit inflation targeting strategy is applied in Turkey since 2006. The main policy instrument of this strategy is short-term interest rates. So, this monetary policy strategy or interest rate targeting is consistent with results.

References

Akıncı, Ö. (2003). Modeling the Demand for Currency Issued in Turkey. *Central Bank Review*, 3(1), 1–26.

Akyazı, H. & Artan, S. (2006). The Reflections of the New Economy on the Monetary Policy and Central Banking. Münich Personal RePEc Archive. MPRA Paper No. 603. http://mpra.ub.uni-muenchen.de/603/

Albulescu, C. T. & Pepin, D. (2018). Money Demand stability, Monetary Overhang and Inflastion Forecast in the CEE Countries. http://hal.archieves-ouvertes.fr/hal-01720319/document.

Atgür, M. & Altay O. N. (2015). "Enflasyon Hedeflemesi Sürecinde Para Talebi İstikrarının ARDL Modeli Yaklaşımı İle Analizi: Türkiye ve Endonezya Örneği" Eskişehir Osmangazi Üniversitesi İİBF Dergisi, 10(1), 79–97.

Bahmani, S. (2008). Stability of the Demand for Money in the Middle East. Emerging Markets Finance & Trade. 44(1), 62–83.

Bahmani-Oskooee, M. & Bohl, M. T. (2000). German Monetary Unification and The Stability of the German M3 Money Demand Function. Economic Letters, 66, 203–208.

Bahmani-Oskooee, M. and Shabsigh, G. (1996). The Demand for Money in Japan: Evidence from Cointegration Analysis. Japan and the World Economy, 8, 1–10.

Balaylar, N. A. and Duygulu, A. A. (2004). "Türkiye'de Para İkamesi Olgusu ve Para Talebinin İstikrarı", Dokuz Eylül Üniversitesi İktisadi ve İdari Bilimler Fakültesi Dergisi, 19(2): 33–54.

Dritsaki, M. and Dritsaki, C. (2012). The Stability of Money Demand : Evidence from Turkey. The IUP Journal of Bank Management, 11(4), 1–22.

Friedman, M. (1956). The Quantity Theory of Money A Restatement. In M. Friedman, ed., Studies in the Quantity Theorry of Money. University of Chicago Press, Chicago.

Gencer, S. and Arısoy, İ. (2013). The estimation of Long Run Broad Money Demand (M2Y) in Turkey: Evidence from Time Varying Parameters Approach. Ege Academic Review, 13(4), 515–526.

Granger, C. W. and Yoon, G. (2002). Hidden Cointegration. University of California, Department of Economics Working Paper, San Diego.

Hacker, R. S. and Hatemi-J, A. (2005). The Effect of Regime Shifts on the Long-Run Relationships for Swedish Money Demand. Applied Economics, 37, 1731–1736.

Halicioglu, F. and Uğur, M. (2005). On Stability of the Demand for Money in a Developing OECD Country: The Case of Turkey". Global Business and Economics Review, 7(2/3), 203–213.

Hamdi, H., Said, A. and Sbia, R. (2015). Empirical Evidence on the Long-Run Money Demand Function in the Gulf Cooperation Council Countries. International Journal of Economics and Financial Issues, 5(2), 603–612.

Hatemi-J, A. and Irandoust, M., (2012). Asymmetric Interaction between Government Spending and Terms of Trade Volatility New Evidence from Hidden Cointegration Technique. Journal of Economic Studies, 39(3), 368–378.

Hoffman, D. L., Rasche, R. H. and Tieslau, M. A. (1995). The stability of Lung-Run Money Demand in Five Industrial Countries. Journal of Monetary Economics, 35, 317–339.

Kumar, S., Webber, D. J. and Fargher, S. (2013). Money demand stability: A Case study of Nigeria. Journal of Policy Modeling, 35(6), 978–991.

Lee, C. C. and Chien, M. S. (2008). Stability of Money Demand Function Revisited in China. Applied Economics, 40, 3185–3197.

Manap, T. A. A. (2009). Stability of Lung-Run Money demand Function: Evidence From Malaysia. IIUM Journal of Economics and Management, 17(2), 261–285.

Özcan, B. and Arı, A. (2013). An Analysis on Determinants and Stability of Money Demand: The Case of Turkey. Yönetim ve Ekonomi, 20(2), 105–120.

Pradhan, B. K. and Subramanian, A. (2003). On the Stability of Demand for Money in a Developing Economy Some Empirical Issues. Journal of Development Economics, 72(1), 335–351.

Tüzün, O., Ceylan, F. and Ekinci, R. (2017). Türkiye'de Para Talebinin İstikrarı: Zamana Göre Değişen Eşbütünleşme Testi. Social Sciences Studies Journal, 3(12), 2252–2260.

Yılancı, V. (2012). Testing the Stability of Money Demand in Turkey: Evidence from Rolling Bounds Test. Dumlupınar Üniversitesi Sosyal Bilimler Dergisi, 33, 67–74.

Esra N. Kilci

A Review of the Role of Fixed Exchange Rate Regime, Excessive Credit Growth and Deposit Insurance in Financial Crises: Examples from Emerging Market Economies

1 Introduction

The emerging market economies including Mexico, Argentina, East Asian Countries and Turkey experienced financial crises, which had quietly devastating effects in terms of their economies in the 1990s and in the beginning of the 2000s. The common result of these financial crises is that these crises mainly resulted from increase in excessive risk taking and thereby moral hazard problems combined with the macroeonomic imbalances. The concept of moral hazard problem, which is commonly used to explain financial deterioration in economies focuses on issues such as fixed exchange rate regime, deposit insurance and excessive credit growth. Accordingly, excessive credit growth as a result of mismanaged financial liberalization processes and high external borrowing, fixed exchange rate regimes supported by IMF and implicit and/or explicit deposit insurance mechanisms implemented by governments led to increase in moral hazard problems in the countries' financial markets and aggravated financial and macro-economic deterioration in these countries and a resulting liquidity or currency crisis quickly turned into a large-scale financial crisis.

In these countries such as East Asia countries and Turkey, there had been remarkable macroeconomic imbalances. On the other hand, it has been widely emphasized by the researchers that these crises were not only the consequence of macroeconomic deterioration but also the consequence of specific institutional inadequacies and incorrect practices, which created moral hazard in financial systems, bringing with excessive risk-taking behavior and inefficient investments. Firstly, implementing incorrect monetary and fiscal policies was an important factor that weakens the economic and financial systems of developing countries. In these countries, in order to control the high and variable inflation, which is one of the main problems of these economies, fixed exchange rate regimes were often used. Generally, programs implemented with IMF support and monitored based on the fixed exchange rate regimes played a triggering role in the formation of crises by creating moral hazard problems in the financial system. Financial actors increased their open positions and were exposed to high exchange rate risk, based on the fixed exchange rate commitment of the authorities responsible for monetary and fiscal policies. When the problems grew, the realization of speculative attacks against the national currency led these agents to the brink of bankruptcy due to negative shocks.

In addition, excessive credit growth was one of the early indicators of financial crises experienced in emerging market economies. Especially following the comprehensive study by Krugman (1998), the concept of moral hazard has been used prevalently to clear up excessive risk taking behavior of borrowers and creditors prior to the breakout of the Asian 1997–1998 currency and banking crises. Moral hazard problem was commonly used to explain financial crises, connecting them to the incautious behavior of banks, borrowers, corporations, creditors, depositors and investors and became part of the argument explaining the formation of large financial bubbles in emerging markets, specifically in East Asia. When a credit bubble has occurred, it seems impossible to avoid a burst, whatever the type of exchange rate regime, a credit bubble is likely to produce increasing fragility in the financial sector. Corsetti et al (1999a) defined one properties of moral hazard problem at a financial level as excessive borrowing by domestic financial intermediaries to support excessively high investment rates (Silva and Yoshitomu, 2001: 1–6).

The last factor which is reviewed in this study and which is considered to lead to increase in moral hazard problems is deposit insurance mechanism. Demirguc-Kunt and Detragiache (1998) found that in cases which interest rates were liberalized, institutional environment was weak, insurance coverage to depositors was high and the funding was financed by government instead of the private sector, explicit deposit insurance system tended to increase the likelihood of banking crises in a study based on 61 countries for the period of 1980–2017. Similarly, Demirguc-Kunt and Kane (2002), in another study, found that it was not possible to develop financial stability by using deposit insurance system in the lack of effective regulation and supervision mechanisms and transparency. They emphasized that if supervisory regulations had not the ability to limit the excessive risk-taking motives effectively, deposit insurance mechanism could be highly detrimental.

Prior to the financial crises experienced in emerging market economies such as East Asia economies and Turkey, it has been seen that the countries pegged their exchange rates to the U.S. dollar and had current account deficits. Sustainable current account deficits put downward pressure on these economies' currencies. As a result of high capital inflows arising from the fixed exchange rate regime implemented, the banking sector in these countries was heavily borrowing from foreign banks mostly in dollars. In the meantime, domestic banks were lending to domestic companies in local currencies. As a result, large currency mismatches accumulated in the balance sheets. While the assets of the banking sector were denominated in domestic currency on a large scale, their liabilities were mainly denominated in dollars. Moreover, implicit and explicit insurances that were provided by the government in these countries triggered the moral hazard problem.

In this study, the role of factors as fixed exchange rate regime, excessive leverage and credit growth and deposit insurance system, which have been considered to trigger moral hazard problems in emerging market economies in the academic literature, is reviewed briefly by giving examples from several emerging market economies including Turkey. Finally, the necessity and the importance of the effective regulatory and supervisory mechanisms and the existence of a sound financial system to prevent crises are emphasized in Section 5.

2 Fixed Exchange Rate Regime

Based on the past experiences of the countries, it is indicated that, countries implementing the exchange-rate-based stabilization programs have achieved success in the fight against inflation and improved fiscal discipline and achieved faster improvement than those countries that adopted stabilization programs based on monetary aggregates by some researchers. Nonetheless, the use of foreign currency as a nominal anchor in combating inflation brings with a dangerous process ending with the collapse of the fixed exchange rate regime, depending on the specific characteristics of the countries. The main factors leading to the collapse of the implemented exchange-rate-based stabilization programs can be summarized as implementation of inconsistent fiscal policies, the existence of a weak and fragile banking system, unfavorable terms of trade shocks and the absence of a previously announced release date or strategy (Serdengecti, 2002: 1).

Emerging market economies such as Argentina, Mexico, Russia and Turkey implemented exchange-rate-based stabilization programs in order to control inflation in the past. These programs, on the other hand, brought the economies in a very dangerous position and lead to increasing risks in both financial markets and real economies. As a result of the increase in dollarization of liabilities, the decrease in interest rates and the excessive appreciation of the real exchange rate, some indicators as current account deficit became unsustainable. In addition, capital inflows had accelerated following the implementation of the exchange-rate-based program. While the proportion of the direct investments was limited in capital inflows, the ratio of portfolio investments and borrowing from abroad by banks and private sector was very high. This situation supported the moral hazard problems, suggesting that the implementation of fixed exchange rate regime provided an implicit guarantee to economic agents. Capital inflows accelerated as the government offered a guarantee to the private sector that the exchange rate would not change; in this way, the vulnerability of the economies to external shocks increased significantly.

In these economies implementing fixed exchange rate regimes, as capital inflows increase liquidity, domestic nominal interest rates decline and, as a result, domestic expenditures increase. The upward trend in imports lead to trade deficit while capital inflows continue. Due to capital inflows, undesirable revaluations in foreign exchange rates create an asymmetry between the expectations of real and financial sectors in the economy. Complications in exchange rate management are reflected in the expectations related to inflation as a result of the indexation in the goods and services markets. At this point, it is necessary to take into account the inelastic price structure in these markets. Because the backward decision-making behavior resulting from the indexing and the process of taking the decisions considering future expectations in the financial markets create assymmetry in the expectations and behaviors of economic agents. This asymmetry between the financial markets and goods and services markets increase the cost of stability resulting from the overvaluation in the foreign exchange rates (Ozturk, 2003: 179).

Since fixed exchange rate regimes provide guarantee to the economic agents that the exchange rate will remain the same, it encourages excessive risk taking through increasing open positions. As emerging market economies have limited funding facilities in terms of their national currency, the foreign exchange rate risk increases in parallel with the increase in foreign exchange denominated liabilities. In fact, fixed exchange rate regimes might increase the foreign exchange rate risk in two ways. Firstly, implicit guarantees might lead to an increase in total external borrowing or bring with shortening the maturity of external liabilities by encouraging interest arbitrage (investing in domestic financial instruments that generate higher returns by borrowing at low cost in foreign currency). Fixed exchange rate regimes can also encourage domestic investors to keep their assets and liabilities in foreign currency by providing implicit exchange rate guarantee, thus encouraging the tendency to dollarization (Ghosh, 2006: 17).

One of the important examples that fixed exchange rate regimes triggered financial crises is the case of Thailand (1997-East Asia crisis). In the case of East Asia, several economies had maintained fixed exchange rates against the U.S. dollar until the crisis. Thailand and other countries had their national currencies pegged to a basket of currencies, with the U.S. dollar having a prevailing weight. This was extensively perceived by economic agents as an official guarantee to minimize foreign exchange rate risk and to encourage trade, foreign direct investments and other capital inflows. The appreciation of U.S. dollar since 1995, against currencies of other major developed countries, might have contributed to a perception of unsustainable exchange rates in East Asia (Kawai et al, 2005: 190). Thailand, having fixed the value of its national currency against the dollar, gave a competitive advantage to Thai export at the beginning. Unfortunately, there had been inconsistency between the monetary policy and the defacto pegged exchange rate arrangement in the pre-crisis period. As a result of increase in moral hazard problems combined with unsustainable current account deficit, the speculative attack started. The government defended its national currency by using foreign exchange reserves and tried to prevent the depletion of foreign exchange reserves by resorting to the forward market to support its currency, even though its real net positions were damaged. Thailand had to leave the fixed exchange rate regime at the point where the negative forward market position equated the country's net reserves. The devaluation of the Thai baht in July 1997 triggered a huge panic among investors that led to presumably one of the most massive outflows of capital (Kawai et al, 2005: 186).

As a result of the devaluation, the depreciation of value of the national currency and doubling the value of the dollar denominated debt meant bankruptcy of many companies that used high leverage in dollar terms but were dependent on dollar denominated earnings. Naturally, banks which were lending to these companies and had the expectation of continuation of the fixed exchange rate regime could not pay back their debt. With the increases of bankruptcies, there had been a major contraction in economic activity and Thailand experienced destructive consequences in terms of its economy due to debt deflation (Feldstein, 2002: 5–8). The devaluation in Thailand led to speculative pressure against neighbouring countries which had their currencies pegged to the U.S dollar, especially Indonesia, Malaysia and the Philippines. Even Hong Kong and Singapore came under pressure in spite of their strong current account and fiscal positions. The situation which is commonly referred to contagion effect led to financial turbulence in the other countries (Miller and Luangaram, 1998: 29).

Turkey and Mexico cases are the other examples. In these emerging market economies, speculative attacks to national currencies combined with the other vulnerabilities triggered currency and financial crises. In the case of Mexico, the attacks took place after the increase in political risk in 1994 and although the Central Bank of Mexico intervened in the foreign exchange market and increased interest rates to high levels, the attack could not have been stopped. The Central Bank, in the end, had to devalue the peso. Similarly in Turkey in 2001, the increasing political uncertainty between the political authorities caused the pressure to increase in financial markets and after the speculative attack, the fixed exchange rate regime was abandoned. In Turkey, it had been actually planned to strengthen public financing, to lower interest rates by reducing the budget deficit, to reduce the inflation to single digit values and to ensure a stable growth rate with the disinflation program based on fixed exchange rate regime and launched in 1999. The disinflation program seemed to have eliminated the foreign exchange rate risk due to the 18-month-period foreign exchange band, which was announced in the beginning. The risk of default was reduced through fiscal policy measures and structural reforms implemented within the program. In this way, as the expected return of foreign investors exceeded the risk-free return and default risk premium, the capital flows were accelerated by creating an arbitrage opportunity on market interest rates (Alper, 2001: 6). However, it was seen that most of the capital flowing into the country had been in the form of portfolio investments and in the form of loans taken by the banking sector. Unfortunately, the high liquidity and mobility of portfolio investments led to rapid capital outflows and increased the depth of financial crisis by exacerbating the perceived risk as a result of increasing problems and volatility in the financial markets.

The stabilization program based on a fixed exchange rate regime has been tried to be implemented in an economy in which there was a weak banking sector that had significant interest rate risk and foreign exchange rate risk in balance sheets and that had insufficient capital adequacy ratios (Colak, 2001: 20). The fact that the large-scale capital inflows to the country were not sterilized by the monetary authorities in the first year of the program had brought a severe increase in money supply and a significant expansion in domestic credit volume. The deterioration in the quality of loans as a result of excessive risk taking was an important factor contributing to the emergence of the crisis with the losses experienced in the reserves to be able to maintain the fixed exchange rate regime. The excessive credit growth also had an indirect negative impact on the disinflation program, leading to an increase in domestic consumption spendings and a deterioration in trade balance (Ari and Dagtekin, 2008: 17). A similar process was experienced in Argentina. After the growing foreign trade deficit caused a serious pressure on the national currency, real interest rates rose considerably. These high interest rates led to the extreme weakening of the economy and resulted in rising public deficit to a great extent. The economic slowdown caused the rise in interest rates of domestic debt and decrease in tax revenues. Argentina's fixed exchange rate system became even more unstable when the full convertibility of the capital account was provided. With the increasing concerns regarding the sustainability of fixed exchange regime and devaluation expectations of 'peso', the capital outflows led to an economic and financial collapse.

3 Excessive Leverage and Credit Growth

When the financial crises in emerging market economies are analyzed, it is seen that one of the common developments encountered in almost all countries during the pre-crisis period is the excessive growth in leverage and credits. Excessive leverage of enterprises heightens the adverse effects of a sharp devaluation on foreign-currency denominated debt as well as the resulting rise in the interest rates of both domestic and foreign debt. It supports moral hazard on the part of the borrowers and magnifies the domino effect of insolvency and bankruptcy on the whole financial system. It also enables the hedge funds to engage in greedy speculation on a large scale (Lau, 2001: 14). The loans used by the private sector and the public sector, which are borrowed from abroad, means an increase in the amount of loans lended in the country and become an important cause of the financial crises, especially in cases where creditors do not renew their loans and the debtors fall into default. Rapid credit growth indicates that credit risk increases and, in a sense, bring with an increase in non-performing loan ratio. The financing of the credits through foreign borrowing in emerging market economies including Turkey and Korea had been a major factor that led to illiquidity and financial volatility in the past.

The problem with the increase in loans is in fact, rather than the growth of the loans, these credits grew very rapidly, caused excessive risk-taking and this situation led to a large increase in non-performing loans and resulted in large losses in loans in the following period. For example, in a study carried out by Corsetti et al (1999b), it was emphasized that the ratio of non-performing loans significantly before the financial crisis. One of the reasons for excessive risk-taking was that banks and other financial institutions did not have qualified loan officers, risk management systems and management experience in order to be able to evaluate risks and react timely and effectively. This problem was further aggravated when credit expansion was experienced (Mishkin, 2001: 9). In the case of East Asia crisis, one of the major characteristics and early fundamental causes of the financial crisis was the increasing trend in leverage ratio especially in Korea, Malaysia and Thailand as a result of increases in short-term borrowing and excessive credit growth. High short-term external debt and high leveraging led to increase in financial sector fragility. High debt to equity ratios of financial institutions and other corporations magnified the problems. Between 1990 and 1996, it has been seen that the ratio of banking sector credits to GDP grew by more than % 50 in Philippines and Thailand, % 27 in Malaysia and around %15 in Hong Kong, Indonesia, Singapore and Korea (Corsetti et al, 1999b). Implicit government guarantees made easier to take credit from abroad with a low cost and in large amounts. As a result of international lending boom and availability of cheap capital which was transformed to domestic loans in the presence of weak supervision, banks financed riskier projects instead of low-risk projects, and corporations increased their debt significantly leading to deterioration in their highly leveraged balance sheets.

The experience in East Asia revealed that the highly leveraged and vulnerable corporate sectors were major determinants of the depth of the crisis. Due to the high economic growth, the adverse effects of inefficient resource allocation were camouflaged while insider financial flows without due diligence did not create problems. However as the economies got into the crisis, the problems related to poor corporate governance were exposed. Currency devaluation suddenly boosted the size of external debt, which was measured in terms of the national currency and debt service obligations. High interest rates also sharply increased domestic debt service obligations of the corporations, causing the domestic corporations go into financial distress. These vulnerabilities affected the banks because of their exposure to the corporations. This created a liquidity crisis and deepened the recessionary pressures, which caused further damage to the corporate sector. The crisis revealed that the existence of a disciplined corporate sector with sustainable debt-to-equity ratios was, therefore, important to prevent exchange rate and interest rate shocks (Kawai et al, 2005: 192). Moreover, prior to the Asian financial crisis, it has been seen that early warning systems concentrated on government external finances and neglected increase of private debt and high leverage ratios. On the other hand, this debt had the potential to become public liabilities because of implicit guarantees.

In Korea, for instance, for the corporate sector, the ratio of debt to capital rose to cover %400 for 'chaebols'[1] while it was %50 before the crisis. The banks financed this debt by borrowing from abroad significantly. Excessive borrowing from abroad by commercial banks inevitably led to the solvency problems and played a great role in Korean financial crisis (Mishkin; 2001, 11). In fact, the increase in liquidity resulting from capital inflows contributed to the increase in loans to households and companies and financed the asset prices bubble and the increase in consumption and investment spendings in emerging market economies. On the other hand, the large increase in the external borrowing, mainly

---

1 Monopolist or oligopolistic holdings which are in the form of 'family company'.

in the short-term, brought about a severe maturity mismatch between the assets and liabilities of the banking sector in these countries (Özkan, 2005: 566). Many Korean banks that borrowed excessively from abroad in foreign currency had aggresively lended to domestic 'chaebols' in local currency 'won'. When the 'won' depreciated sharply against the U.S dollar, Korea experienced a severe banking crisis.

In the pre-crisis period of Turkey, since banks, which operated in a financial system, in which there were not enough monitoring, evaluation and selection mechanisms, increased their loans, there was seen a severe growth in risky loans. Especially the increase in consumer loans was noteworthy. According to the CBRT data, the consumer credit volume which was 1.004,3 billion Turkish Lira as of the end of 1999, increased by %300 in real terms and reached 4.504,5 billion Turkish Lira as of the end of October, 2000 (Uygur, 2001: 13). Moreover, the contribution of the exchange- rate-based program was great in the rapid increase in loans in Turkey. The increase in the capital inflows parallel with the stabilization program led to the increase in the amount of loanable funds in terms of banks. However, the increase in loans resulted in an increase in default risk, leading to a decline in asset quality and a deterioration in the balance sheets of the banking sector. The failure to manage the credit risk effectively and the lack of regulation and supervision mechanisms were among the main factors in the deterioration experienced in the balance sheets.

4 Unlimited Deposit Insurance

Deposit insurance schemes were implemented by several countries to prevent bank runs and to provide liquidity to banks against insolvency problems and bankruptcies. On the other hand, many studies regarding financial crises signals to the role of the deposit insurance and government guarantees in explaining how moral risk problems trigger financial crises. Deposit insurance is an important source of risk. While the authorities intend to ensure depositor confidence and to prevent bank runs with deposit insurance schemes, it comes with an undesirable consequence of encouraging banks to take on excessive risk. That is, deposit insurance leads to the reduction in the incentive of depositors to monitor banks that lead to excessive risk-taking (Anginer et al, 2014). The fact that the liabilities of the domestic banks are under the guarantee of the government leads to an increase in excessive risk taking behavior and thereby an increase in moral hazard problems for both depositors and banks because they know that their deposits will be saved by the government if there is a panic in the banking sector.

Demirguc-Kunt and Detragiache (2002) studied the relationship between deposit insurance and the occurrence of banking crises and examined the question of whether deposit insurance increased or decreased banking stability empirically by using data belonged to 61 countries in the period of 1980–1997. They found that the probability of a banking crisis was greater when the government offered explicit deposit insurance, and they emphasized that the existence of deposit insurance had a great role in explaining the occurrence of banking crises by causing moral hazard problems. They produced empirical evidence that explicit deposit insurance increased banking system vulnerability in countries with weak institutional environments and where the interest rates were deregulated. The results of their analysis, therefore, signaled that explicit deposit insurance tended to be detrimental to bank stability.

In another study carried out by Demirguc-Kunt and Huizinga (2004), it was found that implementing an explicit deposit insurance scheme brought with it a tradeoff between increased depositor safety and reduced market discipline by bank creditors. In a study conducted by Krugman (1998), it was illustrated how financial intermediaries that were provided implicit guarantees would choose investments that were too risky. Implicit guarantees also provide adverse incentives to international lenders to lend without following adequate supervisory, control and risk management systems in place. One of the implications of such mechanisms is overinvestment caused by excessive lending as several projects with negative net present value are financed and undertaken. The second implication is that prices of domestic assets increase beyond their real economic value leading to overvaluation of asset prices. In fact, these overinvestment and overvaluation might have led to the outstanding economic growth in many economies in East Asia in pre-crisis period (Chowdhry, 2000: 145).

The negative impact of the deposit insurance scheme on bank stability tends to be stronger when the coverage offered to depositors is more extensive and when it is financed and managed by the government rather than the private sector. The characteristics of a country's private and public contracting environments have been shown to be important in adoption and design of deposit-insurance mechanism (Demirgüç-Kunt and Kane, 2002). In most countries with explicit deposit insurance, the schemes insure deposits only up to a certain limit, providing a limited-coverage deposit insurance. In some countries, such as Turkey, the schemes provide blanket guarantee and ensure full coverage. The advantage of the deposit insurance system, which provides a blanket guarantee, is that it completely eliminates bank runs. On the other hand, it leads to a significant increase in moral hazard problems.

It is obvious that particularly in emerging market economies, the guarantees provided by the government in different ways and degrees lead to moral hazard problems in financial markets. With the lack of effective regulatory and supervisory mechanisms and the neglect of the principle of transparency, the banking sector and the corporate sector have the tendency to use excessive debt and there becomes deterioration in balance sheets. With the provision of deposit insurance, the depositors, without making the necessary analysis with the belief that the government will rescue them, direct their funds to the risky banks by taking into account the high interest returns. In the same way, the banks use the funds in very risky activities. The deposit insurance creates a perception that they will be rescued from the viewpoint of depositors and banks, resulting in excessive risk taking. That is, if the good scenario occurs, they will have high returns, on the other hand, in the event of the bad scenario, they tend to be discautious and there is over-lending as they know that they will be rescued. In the event that the regulatory and supervisory mechanisms do not function effectively, the deposit insurance and similar government guarantees result in the failure of banks in taking into account the minimum limits on liquidity and capital adequacy.

Deposit insurance, explicit or implicit, encourages moral hazard problems and increases systemic risk for both the depositors and the lenders who are owners of financial institutions. Deposit insurance mechanism effectively enables an insured financial institution to attract deposits with government guarantee, regardless of its own financial conditions and without the need for prudential supervision and regulation. Nevertheless, the regulatory agencies in most countries lack the ability to identify and correct problem before it is too late. The inadequacy of qualified personnel and the incentive for the financial institution to fraud also triggers moral hazard problem (Lau, 2001: 66). In addition, government-directed credit and implicit guarantees of financial institutions and businesses which are called 'too big to fail' promote moral hazard on the parts of financial institutions (lenders) and businesses (borrowers); for instance, financial institutions tend to over-lend to businesses that are called 'too big to fail'; businesses which consider themselves 'too big to fail' tend to overborrow as in the case of Hyundai of South Korea (Lau, 2001: 62). In East Asia crisis, implicit guarantees which were provided to banks and businesses deemed 'too big to fail' by governments encourage moral hazard on the part of both borrowers and lenders (Lau, 2001: 13).

In East Asia countries, it was seen that the banking sector developed large asset-liability mismatches and unhedged foreign exchange borrowings, which were invested in non-tradable sectors and short-term funds, which were transferred into property with much longer maturities in the run-up to the crisis.

All this left the banks vulnerable to currency fluctuations and to interest rate volatility. As domestic financial systems were not well-regulated when capital account liberalization was accelerated in the 1990s and regulatory and supervisory mechanisms weakened in risk-capital management in the following period, moral hazard problem increased in the financial markets and explicit or implicit government guarantees, which were provided to individual financial institutions, supported the excessive risk-taking and moral hazard incentives severely (Kawai et al, 2005: 191).

Laeven (2002) evaluated the relationship between risk-taking behavior and governance structure of many banks in 14 economies including Korea, Indonesia, Malaysia and Thailand by using the cost of deposit insurance. The results showed that the cost was high particularly for banks with concentrated private ownership, which were predominantly owned by a single company or another financial institution, indicating that these banks tended to take the big risks. On the other hand, banks with dispersed ownership engaged in a relatively low level of risk-taking. Finally, he found that the cost of deposit insurance, as a proxy for bank risk, did have some power in predicting bank failures. The findings supported the view that existing government deposit insurance programs encouraged moral hazard for banks. He also indicated that banks which were characterized by concentrated private ownership and operated in an environment with weak institutions tended to take great risks (Laeven, 2002: 135).

In the case of East Asia, banks behaved in a risky manner due to the presence of implicit deposit guarantees and fixed-exchange rate regimes. Credit risk of the banking sector rose significantly by increasing moral hazard problem due to the lack of efficient regulatory and supervisory mechanisms and no penalty for banks managers. Deposit insurance and other implicit guarantees are mostly defined as the main source of moral hazard problems for banking sector in the Asian economies. According to this reasoning, bank deposits are at least implicitly guaranteed by all governments due to the importance of the bank liabilities in the domestic payments system, and such guarantees create and encourage moral hazard on the side of the banks, which then lend to speculative projects. Especially in Korea, banks had taken excessive risks since they knew that the governments would not allow them go bankrupt because of the logic of 'too big to fail' (Chang, 2000: 781).

The deposit insurance leads to higher interest rates of deposits and shorter maturities. Without analyzing the banks' risk profile, the depositors only take into consideration the interest returns. With the loss of market discipline in the banking sector, it is inevitable that moral hazard problems occur and increase. This structure, in Turkey, as in the other emerging market economies, invited the depositors and banks to take excessive risks in order to earn higher returns. Given the fact that BRSA (Banking Regulation and Supervision Agency) became operational only at the end of 2000, the absence of autonomous institution acting independently from the political authorities hampered effective control over the banks (Ari and Dagtekin, 2008: 7).

Unlimited deposit insurance, which was implemented after the financial crisis of 1994 in Turkey and that contributed quite positively in overcoming the crisis by having significant impacts on reducing panic in the financial markets, had played a negative role in the crisis of 2000–2001 (Serdengecti, 2002: 8). This instrument had damaged instead of making contribution because of the presence of a banking sector in which regulation and control mechanisms were weak and it encouraged moral hazard problem causing behaviors in the banking sector. Therefore, the fiscal obligations of the government had increased due to acquisitions and recovery process of the problematic banks (Celasun, 2002: 13). Securing all deposits encouraged the banking sector to offer high interest rates to deposits. Here, the risk was undertaken by SDIF (Savings Deposit Insurance Fund) and the moral hazard problem increased in the whole economy as a result of the transfer of some deposits by banks to the group companies (Çolak, 2001: 24).

5 Conclusion

The rising frequency of the financial crises and the resulted losses of these in emerging market economies since 1980s have led to the development of many theories that tried to explain the causes and the formation processes of these financial crises. One of the results of these theories that researchers focused that the country's vulnerability to financial crises increased in the lack of sound financial system and effective regulatory and supervisory mechanisms. Accordingly, factors such as the fixed exchange rate regime, deposit insurance and excessive credit growth in addition to the accumulated macroeconomic imbalances in the pre-crisis period encouraged excessive risk taking and led to an increase in moral hazard problems in financial markets of these emerging market economies in case of the inadequate regulatory and supervisory mechanisms. The crises experienced in these countries clearly showed that the implementation of fixed exchange rate regimes could have very dangerous consequences in economies which financial liberalization processes was not managed correctly and gradually and when there were not efficient regulatory and supervisory mechanisms. In order to prevent future crises and to achieve financial stability, the existence of a strong financial system and a healthy banking system as well as sound financial balances are of great importance. For countries with a fragile financial system, the use of exchange-rate-based regimes is highly risky although it does have some successes such as reducing inflation or attracting capital. In case of the collapse of the exchange rate, the currency crisis might turn into a large-scale financial crisis.

In most of these emerging market economies, the macroeconomic policies implemented such as fixed exchange rate regimes did not control aggregate demand, supported excessive credit growth in the domestic economy and enhanced the excessive external dependence on foreign borrowing. If the more consistent policies had been maintained, excessive economic growth could have been slowed down, appreciation of real effective rate and current account deficit could have been reduced and leverage ratio (debt to equity ratio) could have been controlled efficiently. In the cases of East-Asia Countries and Turkey, with the implementation of the fixed exchange rate regime, capital inflows in the form of portfolio investments and short-term external borrowing led to a rapid increase in bank lending and the excessive risk-taking behavior of economic agents made the countries very fragile against speculative attacks. The weaknesses of the banking sector gradually increased due to high external borrowing and exchange rate and maturity mismatches accumulated on the balance sheets. The exchange rate regime provided investors with a guarantee that the exchange rate would remain fixed or pegged, and this led to an increase in moral hazard problems. In particular, the deterioration in bank balance sheets made it difficult to distinguish high-risk banks from low-risk banks. The explicit and implicit deposit insurances was another important factor in these countries contributing to the moral hazard problem in financial markets, leading to the neglect of the risks of the banking sector.

Although there are several studies indicating that bank insolvency might increase due to contagion effect and even sound and healthy banks could go bankrupt in the absence of deposit insurance in the academic literature, unlimited deposit insurance practices encourage excessive risk-taking behavior in countries where the risk in the banking sector is not managed effectively and regulatory-supervisory mechanisms do not work well. The banks offer high interest rates because they know that they will be rescued by the government, while the depositors act solely on the basis of interest yields and make their funds available to the risky banks without analyzing the banks' risk profile. Therefore, deposit insurance practice does not always seem the right option for emerging market economies and should be considered carefully. Strengthening of the banking system should be one of the primary objectives of the policymakers in reducing the moral hazard problem caused by the deposit insurance practice.

The financial crises experienced in Turkey and other emerging market economies have clearly demonstrated that improving auditing standards, increasing transparency and objectivity in the practices and implementing corporate governance principles are highly essential to improve the soundness of a country against financial crises.

In this regard, the existence of strong banking regulation and supervision mechanisms is essential in order to reduce the moral hazard problem, which results from excessive risk-taking behavior and to prevent financial crises. To optimize financial leverage ratio by balancing credit growth, to allocate sufficient capital and liquidity reserves, to ensure transparency with the aim of eliminating information asymmetries, to implement financial auditing and corporate governance processes and to take corrective measures timely have great priority for financial stability. The fact that depositors can monitor the activities of banks and they can have accurate and complete information about the areas in which their funds are invested is only possible through the establishment of strong regulatory and supervisory mechanisms as well as effective monitoring of the banking sector activities. In this way, moral hazard problems in financial markets could be minimized. Accordingly, to minimize the likelihood of a systemic failure of a country's economy and financial system, the measures which tries to reduce excessive leverage of both banking sector and companies, the practices such as unlimited deposit insurance practices and the improper and inappropriate policies such as fixed exchange rate regimes should be implemented by policy makers and moral hazard incidences should be reduced. In addition, having a sound, solvent and well-reformed financial sector is key to prevent crises in emerging market economies. This will increase the flexibility of these countries to cope with external negative shocks and to take corrective measures in both pre-crisis and crisis periods. Moreover, it is emphasized that low leverage ratios make possible to raise interest rates to fight against speculative currency attacks.

References

Alper, C. E. (2001). The Turkish Liquidity Crisis of 2000: What Went Wrong? *Russian and East European Finance and Trade*, 37(6), 51–71.

Anginer, D., Demirguc-Kunt, A. and Zhu, M. (2014). How Does Deposit Insurance Affect Bank Risk? Evidence from the Recent Crisis, *Journal of Banking and Finance*, 48, 312–321.

Ari, A. and Dagtekin, R. (2008). Early Warning Signals of the 2000/2001 Turkish Financial Crisis, *International Journal of Emerging and Transition Economies*, 1(8), 191–218.

Celasun, M. (2002). *2001 Krizi, Öncesi ve Sonrası: Makroekonomik Bir Değerlendirme*, University of Utah, 1–56.

Chang, H. J. (2000). The Hazard of Moral Hazard: Untangling the Asian Crisis, *World Development*, 28(4), 775–788.

Chowdhry, B. and Goyal, A. (2000). Understanding the Financial Crisis in Asia, *Pacific-Basin Finance Journal*, 8(2), 135–152.

Colak, O. F. (2001). Finansal Kriz ve Bankacılık Sektöründe Yeniden Yapılandırma Programı Üzerine Bir Eleştiri, *Gazi Üniversitesi İ.İ.B.F Dergisi*, 15–30.

Corsetti, G., Pesenti, P., Roubini, N., & Portes, R. (1999a). The Asian crisis: An overview of the empirical evidence and policy debate. In P. Agénor, M. Miller, D. Vines, & A. Weber (Eds.), *The Asian Financial Crisis: Causes, Contagion and Consequences* (Global Economic Institutions, pp. 127–163). Cambridge: Cambridge University Press.

Corsetti, G., Pesenti, P. and Roubini, N. (1999b). What Caused the Asian Currency and Financial Crisis? *Japan and the World Economy*, 11(3), 305–373.

Demirguc-Kunt, A. and Detragiache, E. (1998). The Determinants of Banking Crises: Evidence from Developing and Developed Contries, *IMF Staff Papers*, 45(1), 81–110.

Demirguc-Kunt, A. and Kane, E. J. (2002). Deposit Insurance around the Globe: Where Does It Work? *Journal of Economic Perspectives*, 16(2), 175–195.

Demirguc-Kunt, A. and Detragiache, E. (2002). Does Deposit Insurance Increase Banking System Stability? An Empirical Investigation. *Journal of Monetary Economics*, 49(7), 1373–1406.

Demirguc-Kunt, A. and Huizinga, H. (2004). Market Discipline and Deposit Insurance. *Journal of Monetary Economics*, 51(2), 375–399.

Feldstein, M. (2002). Economic and Financial Crises in Emerging Market Economies: Overview of Prevention and Management, *NBER Working Paper* 8837, 1–37.

Ghosh, A. (2006). Capital Account Crises: Lessons for Crisis Prevention, IMF, Prepared for the High Level Seminar on Crisis Prevention, Singapore, 1–24.

Kawai, M., Newfarmer, R. and Schmukler, S. L (2005). Financial Crises: Nine Lessons from East Asia, *Eastern Economic Journal*, 31(2), 185–207.

Krugman P. (1998). What Happened to Asia? Mimeo. Available at: http://www.bresserpereira.org.br/Terceiros/Cursos/Krugman-WhatHappenToAsia.pdf

Laeven, L. (2002). Bank Risk and Deposit Insurance. The World Bank Economic Review, 16, No: 1. 109–137. Available at: http://documents.worldbank.org/curated/en/750461468326138447/Bank-risk-and-deposit-insurance

Lau, L. J. (2001). Lessons from the East Asian Currency Crisis, Presentations, Department of Economics, Stanford University. Available at: http://www.cuhk.edu.hk/vc/doc/Presentations/011020.pdf

Miller, M. and Luangaram, P. (1998). Financial Crisis in East Asia: Bank Runs, Asset Bubbles and Antidotes, *National Institute Economic Review* 165(1), 66–82.

Mishkin, F. (2001). Financial Policies and the Prevention of Financial Crises in Emerging Market Countries, NBER Working Paper 8087, 1–42.

Ozkan, F. Gulcin (2005). Currency and Financial Crises in Turkey 2000–2001: Bad Fundamentals or Bad Luck? *The World Economy*, 28(4), 541–572.

Ozturk, S. (2003). Sabit Döviz Kuru Politikasının Krizlere Olan Etkisi: 1997 Güneydoğu Asya ve 2000 Kasım-2001 Şubat Türkiye Krizleri, *Yönetim ve Ekonomi: Celal Bayar Üniversitesi İktisadi ve İdari Bilimler Fakültesi Dergisi*, 10(1), 171–185.

Serdengeçti, Süreyya (2002). Şubat 2001 Krizi Üzerine Düşünceler, Merkez Bankası Bakış Açısından Çıkarılacak Dersler, ODTÜ VI. Uluslararası Ekonomi Konferansı Açılış Konuşması, Ankara, 1–9.

Silva, L. A. P and M. Yoshitomi (2001). Can "Moral Hazard" Explain the Asian Crises? *ADB Institute Research Paper Series*, 29, 1–72.

Uygur, Ercan (2001). Krizden Krize Türkiye: 2000 Kasım ve 2001 Şubat Krizleri, *Türkiye Ekonomi Kurumu Tartışma Metni*, 7 Nisan 2001, 1–40.

Gizem Akbulut Yildiz and Bengu Tosun

The Effect of Globalization on Foreign Trade: The Case of BRICS Countries

1 Introduction

International trade theories that started with Adam Smith were developed for explaining how countries carried out more profitable trading along with globalization. Although globalization is not a new concept, there is also no common definition of the term either. While some writers express that globalization is the driving power of a country as a whole, some writers state that it only has influence on certain fields of a country. More clearly, on the contrary to the views stating that globalization will increase trading, technology transfer and employment of a country, there are also some writers suggesting that it is a movement that may widen the gap between the countries. Nevertheless, there is also no consensus with regards to when globalization implicitly emerged either. Because globalization movement does not only affect a country economically but also affects in various manners such as culturally, socially and demographically.

Twenty first century did not only increase the pace of globalization among world economies but it also presented the increasing level of competition between developed and developing countries on the other hand. Alongside the developing globalization and increasing level of competition, both developed and also developing economies are closely associated with each other economically, socially, politically and culturally. More specifically, developing countries want to increase their economic activities, raise their physical and human capital and sustain their comparative advantages (Shahbaz et al., 2016: 2). International movement of goods and services, financial capital, information and society fall within the more explicit indicators of globalization (Figge and Martens, 2014: 876).

Economic globalization includes cross border flow of goods and services, international capital flows, decrease in tariffs and trade barriers, migration, expansion of technology and cross border information. Globalization is the source of many discussions and conflicts just like any other big source of power. Wide effects of globalization on different aspects of life attracted great attention in the last three decades. Counties, particularly the developing countries, accelerate to close their gaps with regards to globalization and increase their influences on economic growth, poverty, inequality, environment and cultural dominance (Samimi and Jenatabadi, 2014: 1).

Definitions with regard to the types of globalization are presented in Table 1. As it may be seen in Tab. 1, globalization is of particular interest to many fields such as culture, ecology and legal infrastructure, economy being in the first place.

Developing countries are concentrated on the regions that have the greatest population in the world. At the beginning of the century, the prospect of these countries underwent a radical change by means of the most dynamic growth performance in the world and decrease of population growth rate, which caused increase in GNP per capita close to developed countries. This situation was made possible through increasing economic integration levels of developing countries in global economy carried out in trading and finance industries (Radulescu, Panait and Voica, 2014: 606). BRICS countries are also among developing countries. BRICS statement is the abbreviation of the initials of Brazil, Russia, India, China and South Africa. One of the significant features of the countries within BRICS countries that differs them from other developing countries is that they

Tab. 1: Types of Globalization Source: Sliburyte and Ostaseviciute (2009: 947–948).

Competition	Field companies are adopting new strategies practically in every field of their business in order to survive in the big new global market. They have to quit from many competitive markets and search for new businesses.
Cultural	Development of intercultural expanded by multiculturalism and rising of a new case called "world culture".
Ecologic	The main problems of ecologic globalization are global warming and pollution.
Economic	A greater global connection of economic activities by means of international trade, capital flow and migration.
English	English is the most popular language in the world. Using a common language increases both communication and also globalization.
Financial	Generation of global financial markets and decreasing the barriers against external financing.
Industrial	Development of world-wide production markets, decreasing the borders (time, distance and others) between producers and consumers. Acceleration of free movement of goods, materials and labor.
Informational	Use and precocity of satellites, telephones, internet and other communication and data transfer connect geographically distant places.
Ethical/Legal	Establishment of international criminal courts, Lahey Court and other international juridical organizations.

both have crowded population and, therefore, they also have a higher share in the world economy. Another factor is that they have high ratio of natural resources and mine reserves. Therefore, their having a say in the world trade along with globalization movements increases the relative importance of these countries.

The KOF Globalization Index was developed by Dreher (2006) in the study conducted on the purpose of presenting the globalization performance of countries. KOF Globalization Index published by Swiss Economic Institute is calculated by weighting of three criteria as economic, political and social globalization. Annual index values that were published since 1970 have been valued between 1 and 100. In accordance with these values, Brazil is in the 96th place with 59.64, Russia is in the 56th place with 69.06, India is in the 101st place with 56.77, China is in the 87th place with 61.23 and South Africa is in the 58th place with 68.63. When it is generally evaluated, Russia is in the best position among approximately 185 countries and India is the country that has the weakest performance.

In recent years, the increase in the number of studies examining the effects of globalization attracts attention. However, its relationship with economic growth is examined in majority of these studies and the number of studies that examine the effects of globalization on foreign trade is quite few. From this point of view, the objective of the study is to examine the effect of globalization on foreign trade. The study, which is conducted on BRICS countries, comprises the period of years 1990–2015. In the second part of the study, the studies in the literature with regards to the subject will be summarized. Then, information with respect to the analysis will be discussed and findings obtained will be explained.

2 Literature Summary

Chen and De Lombaerde (2014) researched the effect of globalization and regionalization on foreign trade in the study they conducted on BRICS countries. In this study, which comprises the period of years 1990–2009, fixed effects model was performed. In accordance with the analysis results, globalization has a positive and statistically significant effect on both export and also import.

The objective of the study carried out by Savrul and İncekara (2015) is to measure the effect of globalization on international trade. The study, which was conducted on 12 Black Sea Economic Cooperation Organization, comprised the period of years 1992–2014. In accordance with the analysis, which was performed with least squares method, globalization has a positive and statistically positive effect on trade.

With reference to Surugiu and Surugiu (2015), international trade has an important share on countries' GDP. Various companies coming from different countries seek new growth opportunities beyond national boundaries. Important sectors of economy such as information and communication technologies (ICT) and transportation are supported by international trade. Therefore, it is emphasized in their study that international trade is a significant result of globalization.

Borchert and Yotov (2017) researched how globalization affects trade in their study. The study, which comprises the period of years 1986–2006, includes 69 countries. In accordance with the results of the gravity model, it was determined that the effect of distance on international trade diminishes in progress of time and it is probably the effect of new technologies associated with 'globalization' or of separation of production.

In the study carried out by Hussain (2017) on Pakistan, gravity model was estimated by using the data with regards to 15 countries that Pakistan do business with. In the study, which comprises the period of years 2003–2013, analysis was performed by using Pseudo Poisson Maximum Likelihood estimation model. In accordance with the analysis result, globalization has a positive and statistically significant effect on export.

In the study carried out by Metin and Akcan (2017), the effect of foreign trade on economic globalization was examined. The study, which was conducted on Turkey, comprises the period of years 1970–2016. In accordance with the findings obtained as a result of Granger causality analysis, while economic and political globalization are the causes of foreign trade, no causality relationship was determined between social globalization and foreign trade.

Maiga et.al (2018) researched the relationship between globalization, Foreign Direct Investment (FDI) and export in the study they carried out in West African ECOWAS region. In the study, which comprises the period of years 1980–2014, Panel VAR and Granger causality analyses were performed. In accordance with the analysis results, alongside causality between non-export GDP and short term export, there is also a statistically significant and positive relationship.

3 Data Set, Method and Findings

In the study, the effect of globalization on foreign trade for BRICS member countries was examined. Panel data analysis was used to examine the relationship between variables in the study that was carried out with the data within the scope of the period of years 1990–2015. In the study, the sum of export and import values obtained from World Bank database was used in representation of foreign trade volume, and KOF Globalization Index published by KOF Swiss Economic Institute was used in representation of globalization.

The equation used in the study performed to examine the relationship between variables is stated below:

$$\ln trade_{it} = \alpha_{it} + \beta_1 gi_{it} + \varepsilon_{it} \quad (1)$$

In the equation, i represents the country, t represents the period and $trade_{it}$ represents foreign trading volume and gi_{it} represents Globalization Index. Foreign trading volume variable was included in the model by taking natural logarithm.

It is primarily necessary to search stationarity of the series in panel data analysis. When nonstationary series are used, analyses may give biased results. Therefore, at first the stationarity of the series was researched and in consequence of tests it was observed that level value of the series is stationary. After the determination of stationarity, which model out of Classical, Fixed Effects or Random Effects models will be chosen was determined in consequence of some specification tests. In this study, F, Lagrange multiplier (LM) and Hausman tests were used to determine the suitable model. Test results are prepared in Tab. 2.

In accordance with F and LM test results, it may be observed that classical model is not suitable. The result obtained from Hausman test displays that fixed effects model is inconsistent and random effects model is effective. Thereupon, heteroscedasticity, autocorrelation and cross sectional dependency tests were applied on random effects model to determine the deviations from basic assumptions. Test results are presented in Tab. 3.

In consequence of basic assumption tests, it was observed that the model has heteroscedasticity and autocorrelation problems. However, in consequence of cross sectional dependency test of Frees, there is no cross sectional dependency within the model since test statistics is smaller than critical values. In order to eliminate deviations from basic assumption, random effects model was re-estimated by means of clustered standard errors estimator. The results of the estimation are presented in Tab. 4.

Tab. 2: Results of Specification Tests

Tests	Stat.	Prob.
F Test	87.95***	0.000
LM Test	737.39***	0.000
Hausman Test	2.05	0.1519

Note: *** displays %1 significance level.

Tab. 3: Basic Assumption Tests

Heteroscedastic	
W0 = 3.8956610	df(4, 125) Pr > F = 0.00513206
W50 = 2.2451802	df(4, 125) Pr > F = 0.06789632
W10 = 3.7715060	df(4, 125) Pr > F = 0.00624337
Autocorrelation	
Bhargava et.al. Durbin Watson	0.24025408
Baltagi-Wu Local Uniformly Optimum Constant Test	0.34918919
Cross Sectional Dependency	
Frees' Test	1.290 Frees Q Distribution: 0.05: 0.1297 0.01:0.1870

Tab. 4: Clustered Standard Errors Estimator Results

lntrade	**Coefficient**	**St. Error**	**z**	**P>t**
gi	0.0985816***	0.0055403	17.79	0.000
constant	20.86753***	0.4867034	42.88	0.000

Note: ***, displays %1 significance level.

In accordance with the findings obtained, there is a positive and statistically significant relationship between foreign trade and globalization. Hereunder, a one unit increase in Globalization Index increases foreign trading volume approximately by 0.1 % unit.

4 Conclusion

BRICS countries are among the countries that grab attention in World markets in terms of both their geopolitical positions and also their economic potentials. While countries, which are developed in terms of trading volume, were considered at the forefront from past to present, developing countries attract more attention at the present time. BRICS countries' gaining high level of acceleration particularly in recent years is associated with globalization movements to a considerable extent. In this regard, the effect of BRICS countries' globalization performances on foreign trade is researched in the study. In accordance with the finding obtained as a result of analysis in the study, which comprises the period of years 1990–2015, globalization has a positive and statistically significant effect on trading volume. Consequently, the effort of these countries to be integrated to the international markets contribute to their foreign trade development. Further to that, it indicates that globalization processes of BRICS countries will decrease the weight of many developed countries in the markets with regards to foreign trade.

References

Borchert, I., and Yotov, Y. V. (2017). Distance, Globalization, and International Trade. *Economics letters*, 153, 32–38.

Chen, L., and De Lombaerde, P. (2014). Testing the Relationships between Globalization, Regionalization and the Regional Hubness of the BRICS. *Journal of Policy Modeling*, 36, S111–S131.

Dreher, A., (2006). Does Globalization Affect Growth? Evidence from a New Index of Globalization. *Applied Economics* 38, 1091–1110.

Figge, L., and Martens, P. (2014). Globalisation Continues: The Maastricht Globalisation Index Revisited and Updated. *Globalizations*, 11(6), 875–893.

Hussain, M. (2017). Globalization and Gravity Model of Trade of Pakistan: A PPML-Estimator Analysis. *Management and Administrative Science Review*, 6(1), 15–27.

KOF (2019), *KOF Globalization Index*, Swiss Economic Institute, Zurich.

Maiga, O. A., Hu, X., Mekongcho, T. M., and Coulibaly, S. K. (2018). Effects of Economic Globalization, Foreign Capital Influx on Export in ECOWAS. *Global Economy Journal*, 18(4).

Metin, İ., and Akcan, A. T. (2017). The Effect of Globalization on Foreign Trade: Turkey Case. *Journal of Current Researches on Business and Economics*, 2, 257–268.

Radulescu, I. G., Panait, M., and Voica, C. (2014). BRICS Countries Challenge to the World Economy New Trends. *Procedia Economics and Finance*, 8, 605–613.

Samimi, P., and Jenatabadi, H. S. (2014). Globalization and Economic Growth: Empirical Evidence on the Role of Complementarities. *PloS one*, 9(4), e87824.

Savrul, M., and Insecara, A. (2015). The Effect of Globalization on International Trade: The Black Sea Economic Cooperation Case. In International Conference on Eurasian, 88–94.

Shahbaz, M., Mahalik, M. K., Shah, S. H., and Sato, J. R. (2016). Time-Varying Analysis of CO2 Emissions, Energy Consumption, and Economic Growth Nexus: Statistical Experience in Next 11 Countries. *Energy Policy*, 98, 33–48.

Sliburyte, L., and Ostaseviciute, R. (2009). Theoretical Aspects of Economic Globalization Impacts on Emerging Economies. *Economics and Management*, (14), 947–953.

Surugiu, M. R., and Surugiu, C. (2015). International Trade, Globalization and Economic Interdependence between European Countries: Implications for Businesses and Marketing Framework. *Procedia Economics and Finance*, 32, 131–138.

World Bank (2019), World Development Indicators.

Derya Mercan and Serif Canbay

Theoretical Framework of Asset Prices Channel

1 Introduction

Only a few areas of monetary economics have extensively been studied as much as the monetary transmission mechanism. The literature on the monetary transmission mechanism has improved considerably in line with the changing characteristics of the financial system (Borio and Zhu, 2008:1). The monetary transmission mechanism focuses on the effects of changes in monetary policy on inflation and economic activities. The periodic emergence of economic shocks forces policy makers to choose between high inflation volatility and output balance (Hofmann and Peersman, 2017: 2).

Mishkin (1996, 2001), Kuttner and Mosser (2002), Goodhart (2001), Bernanke and Gertler (1999, 2001), Filardo (2001), Goodhart and Hofmann (2001), Cecchetti et al. (2000) have made recommendations on the effects of asset prices on the economy and whether policy makers should react against asset price movements. Mishkin (1996, 2001) and Kuttner (2002) described the transmission mechanism of monetary policy and explained each monetary transmission channel in general. Goodhart (2001), Bernanke and Gertler (1999, 2001), Filardo (2001), Cechetti et al. (2000), Goodhart and Hofmann (2001) addressed the asset price channel and investigated the effects of asset price movements on the economy. Considering the literature on the effects of the monetary policy on the economy through the asset price channel generally it is observed that monetary policy shocks have a significant effect on the economy through asset prices.

The transmission channels of monetary policy are examined under four headings. These are the interest channel, the credit channel, the asset price channel and the expectation channel. The interest rate channel operates via the short-term real interest rates, the credit channel operates via the credit supply volume, and the expectation channel operates via the expectations of economic agents regarding the future periods. Lastly, the asset prices channel mechanism, which constitutes the theoretical basic framework of this study, operates via the stock prices, housing prices and exchange rates. In the next chapters, the definition and the process of asset prices channel are discussed.

2 Definition and Types of Asset Prices Channel

The asset prices channel, which is one of the monetary policy transmission channels, can be defined as the process of affecting the aggregate output and price levels by the monetary policy operations of the central bank through affecting the asset prices. The risks of financial instability reduce economic activity below the desired levels. Central banks, which are trying to stabilize the economy in the long term, may need to react to existing asset price movements in order to prevent these drawbacks. In order to slow down the increase in asset prices, central banks may choose the way of monetary tightening to prevent financial instability and negative macroeconomic consequences in a booming economy. This policy assumes that central banks are able to determine whether real-time asset prices movements too fast or coincide with key indicators (Assenmacher-Wesche and Gerlach, 2010: 2).

Due to the provision of large amounts of consumer goods in emerging markets, the goods prices may react very slowly to the changing global monetary conditions. On the other hand, asset prices, such as housing and commodity prices react faster since the real estate and commodity supplies are inelastic and cannot be expanded easily. Therefore, the imbalances in these markets are balanced by fairly rapid price adjustments (Belke, Orth and Setzer, 2010: 2). In the literature, the asset price channel in the monetary transmission channels of monetary policy has three categories, affecting the economy other than debt instruments (Mishkin, 2001: 1):

1. Stock Prices Channel
2. Housing Prices Channel
3. Exchange Rates Channel

The stock prices channel operates through the Tobin's Q effect, company balance sheet effect and household liquidity and wealth effect. However, the effect of capital cost in the real estate price channel, the expected valuation effect on housing prices, the effect of interest rate on housing supply and the effects of consumer and firm wealth on consumption are effective on the operation of real estate prices channel. In the exchange rate channel, net exports and effects on the balance sheet are effective. Figure 1 shows the asset prices transmission channels and the factors affecting these channels.

The general operation of the asset price channel is as follows: When the central bank decides to decrease the policy interest rate, corrections in the short-term money market interest rates will occur. Economic agents reallocate their savings toward interest-free assets such as real estate, foreign exchange and stocks. The increase in demand for these assets leads to an increase in asset prices. High stock

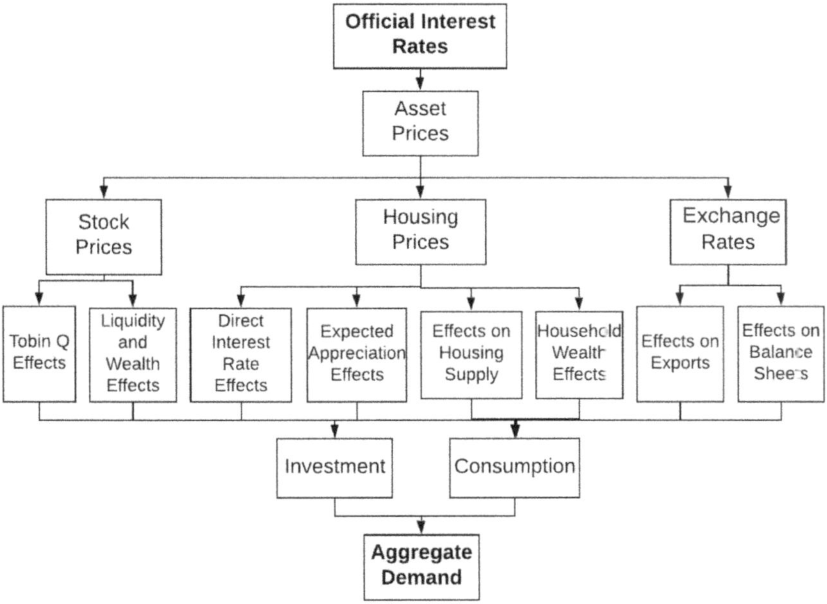

Fig. 1: Asset Prices Channel Mechanism

prices encourage companies to invest more by increasing their market values. In addition, household wealth increases and a higher consumption level is reached. Finally, the expansion in domestic demand leads further economic growth. This process will be examined and detailed in Section 2, under the headings of stock prices channel, real estate prices channel and exchange rates channel.

3 Operation of Asset Price Channel

In this section, the process of the asset price channel, which is one of the monetary transmission channels, will be examined under the headings of stock prices channel, real estate prices channel and exchange rates channel and the sub-headings of these channels in detail.

3.1 Stock Prices Channel

The stock prices channel can be defined as the process of affecting the aggregate output and price level with a change in the monetary policy decisions by affecting the stock prices and thus the investments. Tobin's q theory and Modigliani's life cycle consumption model are effective in the operation of the stock prices channel. In this monetary transmission mechanism, changes in monetary policy affect the economy through stock prices. According to the transmission mechanism, when the central bank changes the money supply or the interest rates, the relative prices of financial assets change. In this case, stock prices are affected, stimulating the investments and expenditures of companies and households. And, changes in investments and expenditures affect the total amount of output.

The effects of the monetary transmission mechanism of the monetary policy on the economy through the stock market can be examined under two headings:

1. Effects of stock prices on investment
2. Household liquidity and wealth channel

3.1.1 Effects of Stock Prices on Investment

The effect of the monetary transmission mechanism on the investment through stock prices operates through the Tobin's q ratio. The asset prices play an important role on the investment and consumption decisions of economic agents. Tobin's q theory is the best method to show that asset prices can be used for determining the market value of a firm's fixed capital stock. Tobin's q theory establishes a natural connection between asset prices and corporations' investments (Claessens and Köse, 2017: 8).

Nobel laureate economist James Tobin (1969) explained a money-capital model and used the q ratio in this model. Tobin's q ratio is expressed as the ratio of the firm's market value to the capital replacement cost. The higher the q value means the higher the market value of the firm compared to the capital renewal cost. Then, the companies will be able to buy more investment goods by exporting less shares. In this case, investment expenditures will increase. Tobin (1978) explains the effects of rising stock prices on capital cost with q theory. The central bank's influence on capital cost and q ratio is indirect, but strong.

When an expansionary monetary policy is implemented, the amount of money in the households increases and they want to spend the excess. The stock market is one of these investments. In this case, demand for stocks increases and stock prices increase. Increase in the stock prices will increase the q ratio and make the investment attractive for companies. Therefore, total demand and investments increase (Mishkin, 2004: 620). This transmission mechanism can be shown as follows:

Money supply ↑ => Stocks Prices ↑ => Tobin's q ↑ => Investments ↑ => Aggregate Demand ↑

3.1.2 Household Liquidity and Wealth Effects

The liquidity and wealth channel built on the life cycle model of consumption, where household wealth is an important determinant of consumption expenditure, developed by Modigliani and Brumberg (1954) and Ando and Modigliani (1963). In this model, consumption is a function of not only permanent income but also wealth. According to this, the amount of wealth of the household affects consumption not only through the income flow it generates, but also through the market value that provides a direct source of purchasing power by eliminating the effects of temporary changes in income during the life cycle (Ando and Modigliani, 1963: 76).

Modigliani models consumption as a function of income and wealth. Accordingly, the real increase in the wealth of households increases consumption expenditures. Normally, the downward trend in policy interest rates has a positive effect on housing, stock and bond prices. This mechanism directly increases the real wealth and consumption of households. This mechanism also works through the credit channel. Total wealth increase means higher collateral value for more credits. This wealth and collateral effect increases total demand by stimulating total consumption and investments (Başçı, Özel and Sarıkaya, 2008: 484).

The present value of an asset or a durable good is negatively proportional to the long-term real interest rate and is positively proportional to the return of the asset. Thus, for example, stock prices can be expressed as the discounted present value of the future expected return on the investment. Therefore, it is observed that the causality between asset prices and macroeconomic performance continues in both directions. The positive and strong expectation of growth increases expectations for future earnings and potential stock prices. This two-way causality makes it difficult to distinguish the real effect of asset prices on aggregate demand (Mohanty and Turner, 2008: 13).

When an expansionary monetary policy is implemented, interest rates decrease and bonds become less attractive than stocks. The demand for stocks increases and consequently the stock prices stimulate. This stimulation of the stock prices causes an increase in the wealth of individuals. Investments and aggregate demand increase due to increased total wealth. The mechanism of this channel can be shown as follows:

Money Supply ↑ => Stock Prices ↑ => Total Wealth ↑ => Investments ↑ => Aggregate Demand ↑

3.2 Housing Prices Channel

The housing (or real estate) price channel can be defined as the process of affecting the aggregate demand and price level by the changes in the monetary policy decisions through housing, land, etc. real estate prices and thus the investments and expenditures of households. Modigliani life cycle consumption model is effective through the operation of this channel. In this transmission mechanism, investments or expenditures of firms or households are affected by the direct effects such as the effects of capital utilization cost, interest rates and income effects and the indirect effects such as housing and rent wealth and collateral effects. Consequently, changes in investments and expenditures affect the total amount of output (Milcheva and Sebastian, 2010: 3).

Financial innovation is another factor that is believed to play a role in increasing the impact of interest rates on housing activity. In advanced mortgage markets, consumers have easier access to credit loans and tend to leverage more. In the presence of financial frictions, if leverage is high, then the impact of changes in interest rates on consumer wealth and housing market will be stronger. In addition to this effect, there may also be growth through securitization (Sá, Towbin and Wieladek, 2011: 2). However, housing tends to have a significant share of household wealth and individuals can borrow money in exchange for this wealth. The increase in house prices may cause an increase in consumption through this leverage effect (Claessens and Köse, 2017: 11).

Changes in short-term interest rates affect the housing market and thus the volume of economic activity directly or indirectly. Some of these channels are as follows (Mishkin, 2007: 5):

1. Direct effects of interest rates
2. Interest rate effects on expected appreciation of house prices
3. Interest rate effects on housing supply
4. Household wealth and collateral effects

3.2.1 Direct Effects of Interest Rates

Short-term interest rates are related with housing prices and mortgage loans. Due to the maturity structure, long-term rates react to short-term rates, so mortgage prices are affected. In response to the expansionary monetary conditions, the mortgage prices decline and hence mortgage loans are increased. Rising housing prices increase the collateral value of mortgage loans and increase the asset position and lending capability of banks (Jordà, Schularick and Taylor, 2015: 37).

When an expansionary monetary policy is implemented, short- and long-term interest rates decrease and reduce the user cost of capital. As a result, investments and aggregate demand increase. This transmission mechanism is presented as follows:

Short-Term Interest Rates ↓ => Long-Term Interest Rates ↓ => User Cost of Capital ↓=> Investments↑ => Aggregate Demand ↑

3.2.2 Interest Rates Effects on Expected Appreciation of Housing Prices

It is generally accepted that monetary policy shocks have a significant impact on real economic activities. However, there are disagreements on the transmission mechanism in which the impact occurs. While the traditional monetary view argues that the monetary policy affects the real economy by changing the user capital cost which determines the fixed investment and durable consumer goods expenditures, the new credit view claims that it affects real economy by improving the general credit conditions and increasing the credit supply for bank-dependent borrowers by strengthening the borrowers' balance sheet through monetary expansion. Despite the different views on the transmission mechanism of money and credit, there is a common idea that asset prices play an important role in the spread of monetary shocks to the real economy since housing constitutes the majority of the household's wealth in particular (HKMA, 2008: 221).

From a monetary policy perspective, it is necessary to establish a link between asset prices and commodity prices in order to determine whether different price dynamics in asset and commodity prices change the relationship between money and inflation. The basic idea is that different supply price elasticities lead to differences in the dynamic characteristics of price adjustment against a global liquidity shock. While commodity prices adapt very slowly to changing global monetary conditions due to excess supply of consumer goods in emerging markets, asset prices such as housing and commodities react more quickly since real estate and commodity supply are not easily expandable. Therefore, imbalances in these markets are usually offset by price adjustments (Belke, Orth and Setzer, 2010: 1).

When an expansionary monetary policy is implemented, interest rates decrease and house prices increase. The expectation that an expansionary monetary policy will be implemented in the future increases the expected real appreciation rate of housing prices. It decreases the user cost of capital and increases the demand for housing and construction. As a result, investments and aggregate demand increase. The expected appreciation of housing prices and the interest rate effects can be schematized as follows:

Money Supply ↑ => Interest Rates ↓ => Expected Real Appreciation Rate of Housing Prices ↑ => Investments ↑ => Aggregate Demand ↑

3.2.3 Interest Rate Effects on Housing Supply

Housing prices have an impact on housing supply through investment with the effects of Tobin's q. As the supply is constant since time is needed to build new housing units, an increase in demand is reflected as an increase in housing prices (Goodhart, 2008: 8). The increase in housing prices due to high demand affects economic activity. First, based on the Tobin's q theory, housing investment can be further encouraged. In particular, when the ratio between housing prices and construction costs is more than one, it is profitable for individuals or construction companies to build new housing. New housing supply depends on interest rates and other demand shocks as well as the sensitivity to housing price movements, competition in the construction sector, building regulations, land planning, presence of expert labor and new housing financial applications (Giuliodori, 2004: 5).

An expansionary monetary policy reduces cost of housing finance by lowering interest rates. The decrease in costs increases the demand for housing and thus housing prices rise. The fact that real estate prices are higher than the construction costs lead construction companies to produce more housing for more profit. Thus, both the housing supply and the total output increase. This transmission mechanism can be schematized as follows (Mishkin, 2001: 5):

Money Supply ↑ => Interest Rates ↓ => Housing Prices ↑ => Housing Supply ↑ => Aggregate Demand ↑

3.2.4 Household Wealth and Collateral Effects

The housing market plays an important role in transferring monetary policy shocks to consumption. Unlike other investment assets, housing is distributed more evenly in the population. Housing constitutes more than half of the total net value of households. As a result, changes in the real estate values affect the consumption decisions. In addition, the use of properties as collateral in the credit market increases the effect of the housing market on the monetary policy transmission mechanism by changing the value of the balance sheet position of the borrowers. The wealth effect is based on the life cycle hypothesis of Modigliani. An expansionary monetary policy stimulates consumption by increasing housing wealth. The increase in consumption increases the total demand (Milcheva and Sebastian, 2016: 78). The wealth effects of housing prices on consumption can be schematized as follows:

Money Supply↑ => Interest Rates ↓ =>Housing Prices ↑ => Consumption ↑ =>Aggregate Demand↑

3.3 Exchange Rate Channel

The exchange rate channel is defined as the process of changing the aggregate demand and price level by affecting the value of national currency and thus net exports through a change in monetary policy decisions. The exchange rate channel is theoretically based on the Mundell-Fleming theorem. The Mundell-Fleming model, which is used for analyzing exchange rate movements, is an open-country adapted version of the traditional IS-LM model, which actually examines a closed economy system. The model shows that a fixed exchange rate, free capital movement and an independent monetary policy cannot be implemented in an economy simultaneously. In this model, the real and nominal variables that play a role in determining the exchange rate are shown in a simple way (Claessens and Köse, 2017: 22).

Changes in the monetary policy have effects on prices, trade volume and investments by changing the exchange rate. Short-term interest rates affect the exchange rate in the first stage of the transmission mechanism. In the second stage, changes in exchange rates are transferred to import and domestic good prices, followed by changes in real values such as exports, imports and investments. In addition to the changes in short-term interest rates, monetary authorities may intervene directly in the foreign exchange markets and affect short-term exchange rate movements. Although the exchange rate is affected by unsterilized intervention by changing the money supply, there are different empirical findings on unsterilized interventions. Interventions made in order to affect the exchange rate are successful especially if it is announced to the public and compatible with monetary and fiscal policies (Egert and Macdonald, 2009: 36).

The effects of the monetary transmission mechanism of the monetary policy on the economy through the exchange rate channel can be examined under two headings (Mishkin, 2001:7):

1. Effect of Exchange Rates on Export
2. Effect of Exchange Rates on the Balance Sheet

3.3.1 *Effect of Exchange Rates on Export*

The exchange rate channel has become an important transmission channel by influencing the market through the exchange rates of monetary policy especially in small and open economies. There are two important conditions to discuss about the presence of the exchange rate channel. First, monetary shocks should be effective on the exchange rate. Second, changes in exchange rates should have an impact on aggregate demand and prices. The power of the exchange rate channel depends on how much the exchange rates are affected by monetary shocks, the level of openness of economies and the sensitivity of net exports to changes in exchange rates (Boughrara and Erriadh, 2003: 5).

When the expansionary monetary policy is implemented, the real interest rate decreases. Accordingly, domestic currency demand decreases and foreign currency demand increases. As a result, the value of the national currency in foreign currency decreases and the exchange rate appreciates. The prices of domestic goods become cheaper relative to foreign goods and as a result of this, net exports increase. Net exports increase leads to an increase in total output. The effect of monetary policy on the economy through exchange rate is shown schematically as follows (Mishkin, 1996: 5):

Money Supply => Interest Rates ↓ => Exchange Rates ↑ => Net Export ↑ => Aggregate Demand↑

3.3.2 *Effect of Exchange Rates on the Balance Sheet*

When countries have foreign currency denominated debt, the exchange rate appreciates with the decreasing value of the local currency against foreign currency if the expansionary monetary policy is implemented. As a result, the amount of foreign currency required to paying the debt of economic agents and the burden of financial debts increases. However, debt-financed assets are usually shown in the national currency and, therefore, their value does not increase with expansionary policy, and even their relative net worth becomes reduced by foreign currency. This increases moral hazard and adverse selection problems and, therefore, decreases the amount of funds obtained through debt. As a result, total investment and total consumption decrease. This transmission channel can be schematized as follows (Mishkin, 2001: 7):

Money Supply ↑ => Interest Rates ↓ => Exchange Rates ↑=> Net Wealth ↓ => Investments ↓ => Aggregate Demand ↓

The effects of the exchange rate channel on the economy through net exports and balance sheet works in the opposite direction. This leads to the uncertainty of some of the links between real exchange rates and macroeconomic results. For example, an appreciation of the exchange rate may lead to an increase in investment by increasing the marginal profit of capital with increasing exports by making the domestic goods relatively cheaper. However, the higher price of imported goods and inputs may reduce profits and, therefore, investments. The general effect of the changes in the exchange rate on the investment varies depending on which of these effects is dominant (Claessens and Köse, 2017: 23).

4 Conclusion

Asset price channel of monetary policy has three main components. The first is the stock price channel, the second is the housing price channel and the third is the exchange rate channel. The operation of the asset price channel is extremely important to see the effects of changes in monetary policy decisions. Accordingly, it is important to find out the direction in which a change in monetary policy affects aggregate demand through its reflections on asset prices, when the monetary authority implements a change in monetary policy by taking into account the economic conditions. When the monetary authority changes its monetary policy decisions by taking into account the current economic conditions, it is important to determine the impact of the change in asset prices on the aggregate demand level in terms of the effectiveness of the policy implementations. The effects of the change in the decisions of the monetary authority on the macroeconomic indicators emerge through the reflections of the stock prices on investment and the liquidity and wealth effects of the households.

There is also a relationship between the changes in monetary policy decisions and the exchange rates. Exchange rate movements can affect numerous macroeconomic variables as well as affecting expectations directly. The exchange rate depends on a large number of internal and external variables. At this point, the effects of monetary policy decisions should not be ignored. The monetary policy strategies that the central bank will implement in order to stabilize the exchange rate movements have a significant effect. Therefore, it is of vital importance that the monetary authority addresses the exchange rates in such a way that they do not have negative effects on macroeconomic variables.

While the relationship between monetary policy and housing prices is discussed in the literature, the reflections of monetary policy channels on the housing sector are taken into consideration. Especially in economies that the housing has a significant place in the economic activity volume, accurate identification of the relationship between monetary policy and housing prices is one of the basic conditions for shaping the policy implementations correctly.

References

Ando, A., and Modigliani, F. (1963). The "Life Cycle" Hypothesis of Saving: Aggregate Implications and Tests. *The American Economic Review*, 53(1), 55–84.

Assenmacher-Wesche, K., and Gerlach. S. (2010). *Financial Structure and the Impact of Monetary Policy on Property Prices*. Mimeo, University of Frankfurt.

Başçı, E., Özel, Ö., and Sarıkaya, Ç. (2008). The Monetary Transmission Mechanism in Turkey: New Developments. *BIS papers*, 35, 475–499.

Belke, A., Orth, W., and Setzer, R. (2010). Liquidity and the Dynamic Pattern of Asset Price Adjustment: A Global View. *Journal of Banking and Finance*, 34(8), 1933–1945.

Bernanke, B., and Gertler, M. (1999). Monetary Policy and Asset Price Volatility (No. w7559). Federal Reserve Bank of Kansas City, *Economic Review*, 84(4), pp. 17–52.

Bernanke, B. S., and Gertler, M. (2001). Should Central Banks Respond to Movements in Asset Prices? *American Economic Review*, 91(2), 253–257.

Borio, C., and Zhu, H. (2008). Capital Regulation, Risk-Taking and Monetary Policy: A Missing Link in the Transmission Mechanism? *Bank for International Settlement*, 268. Basel, Switzerland.

Boughrara, A., and Erriadh, C. (2003). What Do We Know about Monetary Policy and Transmission Mechanism in Morocco and Tunisia?. In 10th Annual Conference of Economic Research Forum (ERF), Marrakech, Morocco.

Cecchetti, S. G., Genberg, H., Lipsky, J., and Wadhwani, S. (2000). Asset Prices and Central Bank Policy. *Geneva Report on the World Economy 2*

Claessens, S., and Köse, M. A. (2017). Asset Prices and Macroeconomic Outcomes: A Survey. *BIS Working Papers*, 676. Basel, Switzerland.

Egert, B., and MacDonald, R. (2009). Monetary Transmission Mechanism in Central and Eastern Europe: Surveying the Surveyable. *Journal of Economic Surveys*, 23(2), 277–327.

Filardo, A. (2001). Should Monetary Policy Respond to Asset Price Bubbles? Some Experimental Results. (No. RWP 01–04). *Federal Reserve Bank of Kansas City Working Paper No: 01-04.*Goodhart, C. (2001). What Weight Should Be Given to Asset Prices in the Measurement of Inflation? *The Economic Journal*, 111(472), 335–356.

Goodhart, C., and Hofmann, B. (2001). Asset Prices, Financial Conditions, and the Transmission of Monetary Policy. In Conference on Asset Prices, Exchange Rates, and Monetary Policy, Stanford University (pp. 2–3).

Goodhart, C., and Hofmann, B. (2008). House Prices, Money, Credit, and the Macroeconomy. *Oxford Review of Economic Policy*, 24(1), 180–205.

Giuliodori, M. (2004). Monetary Policy Shocks and the Role of House Prices across European Countries (No. 015). Netherlands Central Bank, Research Department. Working Paper No:15.

HKMA (Hong Kong Monetary Authority). (2008). The Housing Market Channel of the Monetary Transmission Mechanism in Hong Kong. *BIS Papers*, 35, 221–234.

Hofmann, B., and Peersman, G. (2017). Monetary Policy Transmission and Trade-Offs in the United States: Old and New, BIS Working Papers 649, June. Basel, Switzerland.

Jordà, Ò., Schularick, M., and Taylor, A. M. (2015). Betting the House. *Journal of International Economics*, 96, S2–S18.

Kuttner, K. N., and Mosser, P. C. (2002). The Monetary Transmission Mechanism: Some Answers and Further Questions. *Federal Reserve Bank of New York Economic Policy Review*, 8(1), 15–26.

Milcheva, S., and Sebastian, S. (2010). Housing Channels of Monetary Policy Transmission in European Industrial and Transition Countries. *Eres2010, No: 159, European Real Estate Society, 1-67.*

Milcheva, S. and Sebastian, S. (2016). The Housing Market Channel of Monetary Policy Transmission in the Euro Area. *Journal of European Real Estate Research*, 9(1), 76–97.

Mishkin, F. S. (1996). The Channels of Monetary Transmission: Lessons for Monetary Policy. NBER Working Paper 5464, Cambridge, National Bureau of Economic Research.

Mishkin, F. S. (2001). The Transmission Mechanism and the Role of Asset Prices in Monetary Policy. NBER Working Paper 8617, Cambridge, National Bureau of Economic Research.

Mishkin, F. S. (2004). *The Economics of Money, Banking and Financial Markets.* 7. Ed., Pearson Education, USA.

Mishkin, F. S. (2007). Housing and the Monetary Transmission Mechanism. NBER Working Paper 13518, Cambridge, National Bureau of Economic Research.

Modigliani, F., and Brumberg, R. (1954). Utility Analysis and the Consumption Function: An Interpretation of Cross-Section Data. *Franco Modigliani*, 1, 388–436.

Mohanty, M. S., and Turner, P. (2008). Monetary Policy Transmission in Emerging Market Economies: What Is New?. *BIS Papers*, 35, 1–59.

Sá, Filipa, Pascal Towbin, and Tomasz Wieladek. (2011). Low Interest Rates and Housing Booms: The Role of Capital Inflows, Monetary Policy, and Financial Innovation. *Globalization and Monetary Policy Institute Working Paper* 79, FRB Dallas.

Tobin, J. (1969). A General Equilibrium Approach to Monetary Theory. *Journal of Money, Credit and Banking*, 1(1), 15–29.

Tobin, J. (1978). Monetary Policies and the Economy: The Transmission Mechanism. *Southern Economic Journal*, 44, 421–431.

Yuksel Oksak

Does Value Added Created in Industrial Sector in Turkey Trigger Export? ARDL Analysis

1 Introduction

The difficulties in measuring the added value of the countries in exports led to new value-added measurements. These new values provide the basis for more accurate measurements. Exportation of local products through trade is at the head of these values, because now the world becomes even smaller in terms of trade. Products produced at any point can be sent to another point of the world without losing their commercial value. The important part here is that countries can now exchange goods and services more easily. Another name for this system is the global value chain. Global value chains have become a channel for countries and companies to gain access to the world markets; thus, new opportunities for revenue and profits are discovered (Vrh: 2017). Value chains evolve rapidly in the last decade. The process of considering the value-added exports was first developed by Hummels, Ishii and Kei-Mu (2001) and later by Koopman, Wang and Wei (2008). Pioneer empirical analyses of value-added trade offer some explanatory facts. The increasing use of imported components and the fact that part of the production process is done outside the country in order to reduce the wages appear in the final exports. The industrial sector, which is in close relation with many other sectors, especially the trade sector, plays an important role in economic growth in the economy. Koyuncu and Yılmaz (2015: 58) state that the efficiency level is another factor affecting the export decision of firms. The industrial sector has supply and demand from almost all other sectors in the market. Therefore, the industrial sector is critical for the increase in exports. Exports stimulate the industrial sector by selling industry-created products to other countries to make a profit. In this way, both the country develops, and new fields of employment have emerged. The main issue in industrialization is to increase the share of industrial sector in the Gross National Product to higher levels.

Quoting Syrquin and Chennery, Pamukçu and Boer (1999: 5) gave three basic explanations on the share of the industrial sector in GNP. The same explanation can be found in the discussion paper by Arısoy (2008: 2):

i. Demand-based explanation (Engel effect leading to change in the composition of final demand in favor of non-food sectors).

ii. Foreign trade-based explanation (changes in the comparative advantage of the country in parallel with capital and human capital accumulation).
iii. Technology-based explanation (increased share of industrial products as input per unit output).

As a result of Turkey's liberalization of the economy in 1980 with the Decision on January 24, 1980, the import substitution industrialization strategy, which applied until 1980, was abandoned and was replaced with export-led growth strategy whereby export sector was promoted. However, during this process, the fact that the industrial production is dependent on the importation of capital and intermediate goods has proved that the exports are highly dependent on imports. Therefore, it is necessary to examine the relations between industrial production, export and import with time series methods which take into account the interrelationships between these macroeconomic variables. In this study, the long-term relationship between exports and value added in the industrial sector in Turkey during the period 1969–2017 is questioned with the ARDL bounds test.

2 Related Literature

When a literature survey on the industry sector, export and value-added triangle has been carried out, it is observed that most of the studies are in the axis of economic growth. A notable part of these studies mention that the industrial sector is the driving force in the economy, and in doing so gives particular place to Kaldor's Law. In the empirical literature of McCombie (1983: 279–294), Millin and Nichola (2005: 47–62), Thirlwall (1983: 346–348), Mamgain (1999: 295–309), Necmi (1999: 653–654) Arısoy (2008: 7) and Ateşoğlu's (1993: 67–68), Kaldor's Law is presented in three different models as given in Tab. 1:

Tab. 1: Different Models of Kaldor's Law. Source: Arısoy, İ., "Kaldor Yasası Çerçevesinde Türkiye'de Sanayi Sektörü ve İktisadi Büyüme İlişkisinin Sınanması", Eskişehir Osmangazi Üniversitesi İİBF Dergisi, 2013.

MODEL 1	$RGSMH = \alpha_1 + \beta_2 IND + \varepsilon_t$	$B_1>0$
MODEL 2	$IEMP = \alpha_2 + \beta_2 IND + \varepsilon_t$	$B_2>0$
MODEL 3	$RGSMH = \alpha_3 + \beta_3 IEMP + \Phi ES + \varepsilon_t$	$B_3>0, 0<\Phi$

RGSMH, IND, IEMP and ES indicate real gross national product, real industrial production value, industrial sector employment volume and employment volume in sectors other than industrial sector, respectively.

In Arisoy (2013)'s study, Model 1 presents the first law of Kaldor stating that industry sector is the most important driving force of the growth in the detailed manner. According to Kaldor, the growth of the industrial sector is also to ensure the growth of other sectors with the wide employment opportunity. There is a positive correlation between industrial sector growth and economic growth. When similar academic research are examined in this context, we observe that regression analyses suggest the validity of Kaldor's Law. Model 2 presents Kaldor-Verdoorn Law.

It emphasizes that the increase in the industrial sector will lead to an increase in the productivity of the industrial sector at a faster rate. The validity of the Kaldor-Verdoorn Law is provided by the $\beta 2 > 0$ restriction.

In his study on Kaldor's Law, Arısoy (2013) adopted the approach of Mamgain (1999) and used real industrial value-added per labor force (LRPRD) instead of the IEMP industrial sector employment volume used as an indicator of the labor productivity in Model 2.

With Model 3, Kaldor assumes that there is a negative relationship between labor productivity and production amount in the industrial sector due to the static and dynamic increasing returns to scale; however, there is a negative relationship between labor productivity and production volume and employment in other sectors other than industry sector (such as agriculture and services) due to the law of diminishing returns. Kaldor suggested that the marginal product of the labor (as per the law of diminishing returns) will be transferred to the industrial sector from agriculture and similar sectors where the average product is low, and the labor productivity will increase in the industrial sector and hence production will increase as a whole (Kaldor, 1968).

Countries should have competitive ability in the export sector to grow their industry. Large differences between gross export and domestic market value are very important in this regard. Because this transformation will increase the added value of the country. Exports means an increase in global value added (Ceglowski: 2017). China has the largest share in this export. China's exports have increased tremendously over the past three decades. Because the intense growth in Chinese technology and the integration of this growth into the industry is one of the reasons increasing the exports. However, researchers such as Branstetter and Lardy (2006), Fung (2013), Lall (2000), Srholec (2007), Tang, Zhang, and Findlay (2013) point out that China is producing at low-added value level. They justify this by arguing that China preferred to sell technology instead of products (Wen: 2018). Another study on international trade is conducted by Koyuncu and Yalçınkaya Koyuncu (2017: 655). In this, an empirical study was conducted on the relevant data of 79 countries for the period of 1989–2015 and a statistically significant relationship was found between information communication technologies and international trade.

In their working paper, Koopman, Wang and Wei (2008) point out that the export-oriented policy preferences often lead to a significant difference in the intensity of imported intermediate inputs in the processing export production and in other demand sources (for domestic final sales and normal exports). At the same time, they emphasize that processing exports consists of more than 50 % of China's exports every year since at least 1996 and hence HIY formula will lead to an important estimate of the contribution of value added in China's exports. Yilmaz and Koyuncu (2010: 86) examined the effect of imports from China on the poverty levels of importing countries. In this study, important evidence is presented between a country's imports from China and poverty. In another study on China, Koyuncu and Yılmaz (2010: 161) demonstrate a positive and statistically significant relationship between labor productivity and imports from China.

It can be said that a steady increase in Turkey's exports is a driving force on economic growth.

Therefore, if we aim at economic growth, economic policies should be developed to increase value added exports. Most of the import items in the industrial sector consist of intermediate and capital goods. Therefore, although the increase in the imports of the industrial sector seems to be triggering growth in the short term, academic studies conducted suggest that these imports have a negative effect on growth in the long run. In this context, it is necessary to implement stable and sustainable economic policies that will minimize our foreign trade deficit.

In the countries, the contribution of industries for value-added production are undeniable. The added value of the country will increase through the products produced by the producers. The more value added in the country, the more common is the new products. This is due to fact that new value-added products lead to new products that lead to new employment areas which lead to new competitive environments.

3 Data and Methodology

In this study, the existence of long-term relationship between the industrial sector value added (x673) and exports (x673) in Turkey during the period 1969–2017 is questioned by empirical analysis. Data was collected from the World Bank (WDI). The following model is estimated to apply the ARDL boundary test:

$$\Delta x442_t = \beta_0 + \sum_{i=1}^{p} \delta_i \Delta x442_{t-i} + \sum_{i=0}^{q} f_i \Delta LOGx673_{t-i} + \gamma_0 x442_{t-1} + \gamma_1 LOGx673_{t-1} + \varepsilon_t \quad (1)$$

Here x442 series the share of national income of Turkey's exports, shows the added value of x673 industry.In equation 1 above, γ_0 and γ_1 terms stand for long-term coefficients; δ_i and ϕ_i terms represent short-term coefficients; Δ is first degree difference operator; β_0 is constant term of the model and ε_t is white noise error term of the model.

For the cointegration test, ARDL boundary test approach tests the null hypothesis of $H_0 : \gamma_0 = \gamma_1 = 0$(i.e., there is no cointegrating association among series) against the alternative hypothesis of $H_1 : \gamma_0 \neq \gamma_1 \neq 0$(i.e., there exists cointegrating association among series). If the F-statistic value gathered from ARDL boundary test is beyond the upper limit at a particular significance level then H_1 hypothesis is accepted. On the other hand if the F-statistic value is smaller than lower limit at a particular significance level then H_0 hypothesis is accepted. Finally, any F-statistic value falling into the area between the lower and upper limits indicates indecisive zone.

$$x442_t = \beta_0 + \sum_{i=1}^{p} \beta_i \Delta x442_{t-i} + \varphi ECM_{t-1} + \varepsilon_t \quad (2)$$

Also the following error correction model is estimated in order to get both short- and long-run coefficients:

$$x442_t = \beta_0 + \sum_{i=1}^{p} d_i \Delta x442_{t-i} + \sum_{i=0}^{q} f_i \Delta LOGx673_{t-i} + \eta ECM_{t-1} + \varepsilon_t \quad (2)$$

In equation 2 above, δ_i and ϕ_i display the dynamic coefficients bringing the model to the balance in the long run; *ECM* is error correction term; η stands for the speed of adjustment at which the model reverts to long run balance after a shock occurred in short run. The speed of adjustment term is expected to be negative and statistically significant.

Meantime a causality test by utilizing Granger Causality/Block Exogeneity Wald Tests is implemented to see if there is a causality relationship between the two variables.

4 Estimation Results

Stationary analysis of the series was investigated using Augmented Dickey Fuller (ADF) unit root test. The ADF unit root test results for the level values of the series are reported in Tab. 2 while the ADF unit root test results for the first differences of the series are reported in Tab. 3.

As seen in the ADF unit root test results, LOGx673 and x442 series were found to be I (1), i.e., they were stationary in the first differences. Since none of the existing series are integrated into two or more degrees, we can test whether there is co-integration by applying the ARDL boundary test approach to these series.

By permitting a maximum of 6 delays for all series, the most optimal delay number was determined according to Schwarz (BIC) criteria. According to the BIC criterion, the most suitable model is ARDL (1,4). This ARDL (1,4) model has been selected from 30 different models according to BIC criteria. Fig. 1 below shows the number of lags for the first 20 models providing the lowest BIC value.

The results of the ARDL boundary test to investigate the existence of co-integration between the LOGx673 series and the x442 series are shown in

Tab. 2: ADF Unit Root Test Results (Levels)

LOGx673	
	Constant-With Trend
t-statistic	-2.560790
Prob. Value	0.2993
X442	
	Constant-With Trend
t-statistic	-2.68366
Prob. Value	0.2477

Tab. 3: ADF Unit Root Test Results (First Difference)

LOGx673	
	Constant-With Trend
t-statistic	-5.793399
Prob. Value	0.0001
X442	
	Constant-With Trend
t-statistic	-6.239788
Prob. Value	0.0000

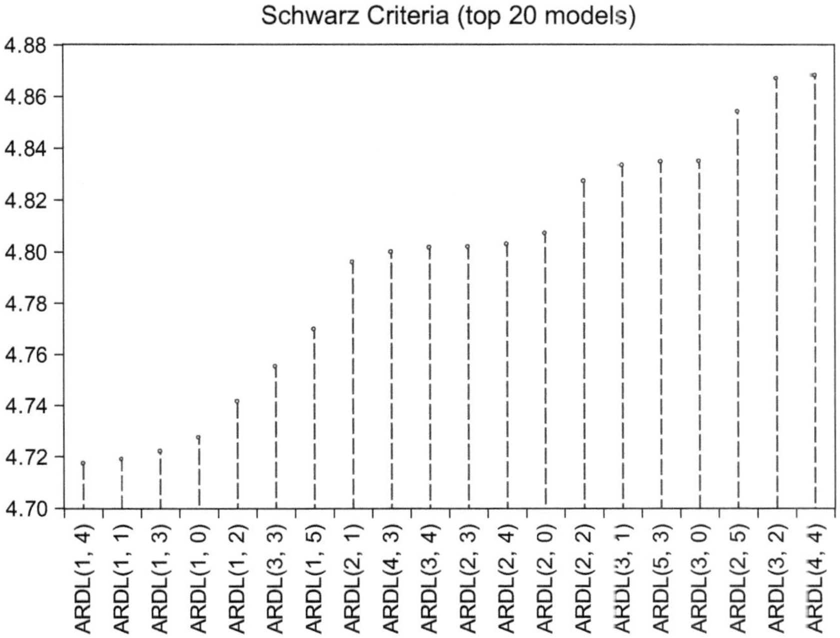

Fig. 1: The Best 20 Models According to the BIC Criterion

Tab. 4: The Results of the ARDL Boundary Test for Cointegration

F-Statistics: 4.764123	*Critical Values*	
Significance Level	***Lower-Bound*** $I(0)$	***Upper-Bound*** $I(1)$
10 %	2.44	3.28
5 %	3.15	4.11
2.5 %	3.88	4.92
1 %	4.81	6.02

Tab. 4. Accordingly, since F-statistic = 4.764123 value is greater than the upper-limit values determined for the 5 % significance level, it indicates that there is a cointegration relationship between the series and therefore the null hypothesis should be rejected. These results indicate that there is a co-integration (a long-term relationship) between value added in the industrial sector and exports in Turkey in the examined period.

Tab. 5: The Long Term Coefficients Belonging to ARDL (1,4) Model

Dependent Variable: ***x442***			
Variable	***Coefficient***	***t-Statistic***	***Prob.***
LOG(X673)	*1.891175*	*1.685988*	*0.0998*

Tab. 6: Error Correction (ECM) Estimation Results of ARDL (1,4) Model

	Dependent Variable: x442		
	Coefficient	***t-Statistic***	***Prob.***
ΔLOG(X673)	-15.929869	-3.042452	0.0042
ΔLOG(X673(-1))	10.896977	2.017037	0.0506
ΔLOG(X673(-2))	-10.426953	-1.957914	0.0574
ΔLOG(X673(-3))	-10.636048	-1.980819	0.0547
ECM_{t-1}	-0.058616	-3.126109	0.0033
ECM=x442-(1.8912*LOG(x673))			

As can be seen from Tab. 5 and Tab. 6 of ARDL Model Error Correction (ECM), the long-term coefficient of LOGX673 is 1.891175 and is statistically at 10 %, which does not confirm the result we obtained in the ARDL boundary test.. In other words, there is a long-term relationship between industrial sector value added and exports. The coefficient of the error correction term (indicating the speed of the model returning to the long-term equilibrium) takes the expected negative sign and is statistically significant. There is a statistically significant relationship between industrial sector value added and exports in both short and long term. In the short term, the coefficients receive a negative sign in three different lags while they receive a positive sign in one lag. On the other hand, in the long run, industrial sector value added and export co-integrate in the same direction and this relationship is significant at 10 %.

In order to determine the causality relationship between the series, Granger causality test was applied with Toda Yamamoto approach on Tab. 7.. While 1.848707 is obtained as the Schwarz information criteria (SIC) value for unconstrained VAR model with 1 lag, 2.131518 is obtained as the Schwarz information criteria (SIC) value for unconstrained VAR model with 2 lags.

Therefore, the most appropriate lag for the respective VAR model was 1 (i.e., p = 1). The highest degree of co-integration between LOGX673 and X442 series was found to be 1 (i.e., dmax = 1). Therefore, the unrestricted VAR (2) model is estimated since total of the most appropriate lag number and the highest degree

Tab. 7: Granger Causality Test

Dependent variable: LOGX673			
Excluded	**Chi-sq**	**df**	**Prob.**
X442	3.143687	2	0.2077
All	3.143687	2	0.2077
Dependent variable: X442			
Excluded	Chi-sq	df	Prob.
LOGX673	5.444448	2	0.0657
All	5.444448	2	0.0657

of integration is 2 lags, and causality testing has been conducted and the results are reported below. According to the causality results, there is a unidirectional causality from industrial value added to exports.

5 Conclusion

In this study, the long run relationship between value added in the industrial sector (x673) and exports (x442) in Turkey in the period 1969–2017 are investigated by using ARDL bounds test. According to the findings, it was found that there is a relationship between x673 and x442 both in the long term and in the short term. Long-term co-integration between the two series was found to be in the same direction. In addition, it was observed that there was a unidirectional causality from industrial value added to exports as a result of the test conducted with Toda Yamaoto approach.

References

Arısoy, İ. (2008), "Türkiye'de Sanayi Sektörü - İktisadi Büyüme İlişkisinin Kaldor Hipotezi Çerçevesinde Test Edilmesi", *Türkiye Elektrik Kurumu Tartışma Metni*, s.2. http://www.tek. org.tr

Arısoy, İ. (2013), "Kaldor Yasası Çerçevesinde Türkiye'de Sanayi Sektörü ve İktisadi Büyüme İlişkisinin Sınanması", *Eskişehir Osmangazi Üniversitesi İİBF Dergisi*, 8(1), 143–162.

Ateşoğlu, H. S. (1993), "Manufacturing and Economic Growth in the United States", *Applied Economics*, 25, 67–69.

Branstetter, L. and Lardy, N. (2006), *China's Emergence of Globalization (NBER Working Paper No. 12373)*. Washington, D.C: National Bureau of Economic Research.

Ceglowski J. (2017), "Assessing Export Competitiveness through the Lens of Value Added", *The World Economy*. doi: 10.1111/twec.12362.

Fung, H. G. (2013), "The Integration of China's Economy with the World", *Chinese Economy*, 46(4), 3–5. doi:10.2753/ces1097-1475460400.

Hummels, D., Ishii, J. and Kei-Mu. Y., (2001), "The Nature and Growth of Vertical Specialisation in World Trade", *Journal of International Economics*, 54:75–96. doi:10.1016/S0022-1996(00)00093-3.

Kaldor, N. (1968), "Productivity and Growth in Manufacturing Industry: a reply", *Economica*, 35, 385–391.

Koopman, R., Wang, Z. and Wei, S. (2008), *How Much of Chinese Exports Is Really Made in China? Assessing Domestic Value-Added When Processing Trade Is Pervasive*. NBER Working Paper Series, no. 14109: 1–49, National Bureau of Economic Research, Cambridge, MA. doi:10.3386/w14109.

Koyuncu, C. and Yilmaz, R. (2010). "Chinese Exports and Productivity Gains: Panel Evidence", *Asian Pacific Economic Literature Journal*, 24(2), 161–170.

Koyuncu, J. Y., and Koyuncu, C. (2017). "The Association between ICT and Export and Import: Panel Analysis", *Cataloging-In-Publication Data*, 655–660.

Koyuncu J., Y., Yılmaz, R. (2015), "The Impact of Privatization on Export in Transition Economies: A Panel Study", *Anadolu Üniversitesi Sosyal Bilimler Dergisi*, 15(2), 57–61.

Lall, S. (2000), "The Technological Structure and Performance of Developing Country Manufactured Exports", *Oxford Development Study*, 28(3), 337–369. doi:10.1080/713688318

Mamgain, V. (1999), "Are the Kaldor–Verdoorn Laws Applicable in the Newly Industrializing Countries", *Review of Development Economics*, 3(3).

Mccombie, J. S. L. (1983), "Kaldor's Laws in Retrospect", *Journal of Post Keynesian Economics*, 5, 414–429.

Millin, M. and Nichola, T., (2005), "Explaining Economic Growth in South Africa: A Kaldorian Approach", *International Journal of Technology Management and Sustainable Development*, 4(1), 47–62.

Necmi, S., (1999), "Kaldor's Growth Analysis Revisited", *Applied Economics*, 31(5), 653–660.

Pamukçu, T. ve Boer, P. (1999), "Technological Change and Industrialization: An Application of Structural Decomposition Analysis to the Turkish Economy," *Ekonomik Yaklaşım*, Cilt 10, Sayı 32, s.5–30.

Srholec, M. (2007), "High-Tech Exports from Developing Countries: A Symptom of Technology Spurts or Statistical Illusion?" *Review of World Economics*, 143(2), 227–255. doi:10.1007/s10290-007-0106-z

Tang, Y., Zhang, Y., and Findlay, C. (2013). "What Explains China's Rising Trade in Services?" *Chinese Economy*, 46(6), 7–31. doi:10.2753/ces1097-1475460601

Thirlwall, A.P. (1983), "A Plain Man's Guide to Kaldor's Growth Laws", *Journal of Post Keynesian Economics*,5, 345–358.

Vrh N. (2017), "The Convergence in Domestic Value-Added of Exports in the EU", *Post-Communist Economies*,29 (3), s.405–430.

Wen, D. (2018), "Domestic Value Added in China's Exports to the World and Its Partners", *The Chinese Economy*, 51: 45–68.

Selahattin Bozkurt

Sadrettin Tosbi's Overview of the Turkish Economy and Suggestions for Solution (Parliamentary Minutes 1961-1965)

1 Biography

Born in 1913 (1329) in İstanbul, Sadrettin Tosbi completed his elementary, secondary and high school education at Galatasaray High School. He graduated from İstanbul University, Academy of Economics and Commercial Sciences in 1935. He continued his education at Heidelberg University in Germany between 1935 and 1938 and achieved his PhD here at Faculty of Economics and State Sciences.[1]

Having completed his army service, he was appointed as Associate Director of Domestic Markets in the Ministry of Commerce in Ankara and then he was promoted as the Director of Companies in the Ministry of Commerce in 1941.[2]

He started his academic life in 1946 by being granted professorship in Cooperation Department at Economy and Business School of Istanbul and worked there until 1961. Apart from his lecture notes, he also had seven published works. Tosbi was elected as Kütahya MP (Member of Parliament) from Republican Peasant Nation Party (CKMP) in 1961.[3]

Having completed his one-term deputyship (four years), Tosbi returned back to his academic life. In 1968, he started to work as Director of the School of Economics and Commerce of Aksaray and retired in 1978. He was married with no children. He died on June 26th, 2004.

Tosbi, with his colourful and dedicated personality, was a well-beloved teacher who contributed to the education of many young people in academic life. In the field of politics, he was a valuable, outspoken parliamentarian who

---

1 Sadrettin Tosbi'nin Hal Tercümesi, TBMM Arşivi, Sicil No:1. Dönem 306, Selahattin Bozkurt, Kütahya Milletvekilleri ve Millet Meclisi'ndeki Faaliyetleri (1961-1980), Yayınlanmamış Doktora Tezi, Dumlupınar Üniversitesi Sosyal Bilimler Enstitüsü, Kütahya 2017, s. 80

2 Tosbi, Hal Tercümesi, Bozkurt, a.g.t., s. 80, Mustafa Kalemli, Kütahya'nın Yasama Organı Üyeleri, 1920-2001, Ankara 2001, s. 17–18, TBMM Albümü 1920-2010, C. II, s.811, II. Baskı, Ankara 2010

3 Tosbi'nin Hal Tercümesi, Bozkurt, a.g.t., Kalemli, a.g.e., s.17-18

always expressed his ideas boldly and freely in The National Assembly. He served as Party Group President (Floor Leader) and Member of Council of Europe. Tosbi didn't write his memoirs. However, Aziz Nesin mentioned some of Tosbi's adventures in his book titled "Benim Delilerim".

2 A New Era Begins

The State of the Republic of Turkey was officially established in 1923 with the proclamation of the Republic. The newly established state tried to pass to the multiparty system twice but it did not succeed. Therefore, in the period until 1950, the country was governed by one-party rule in a rather undemocratic way.

The developments occurred after World War II forced Turkey to switch to a multiparty democratic system. As a result, in 1946 a multi-party system was introduced. For the first time power changed hands in the state as a result of the elections held in 1950. The Democratic Party, which had liberal discourses especially in the economy, came to power. Between 1950 and 1960, ruling the country uninterrupted, the Democratic Party followed an economic policy based on imports. In agriculture, mechanization was brought to the fore and production was increased. New industrial facilities were established. A freer environment than the previous one-party period was created in relation to the democratic demands and the rights and freedoms of the people. Despite these positive developments, the economic system based on imports was impaired after 1957 and difficulties arose in foreign borrowing. Under the pressure of non-constructive criticism of the opposition, the Democratic Party government began to follow strict economic policies. The tight policies adopted by the government in the economy and the devaluation pressure on the Turkish currency caused the public to be displeased. Upon these developments, the government's negative pressure on the opposition and dissatisfaction among the people led to a number of incidents in the country.

Upon the above-mentioned negative developments in Turkey, on May 27th, 1960, the army seized power. The military administration tried to create a more democratic environment after the coup. A new constitution was made. However, these efforts wouldn't be successful because the new arrangements left the past ruling Democratic Party members out of politics and brought the opposition of the past, the Republican People's Party, to the fore more. Besides, in the post-1960 period, the army rose to prominence and often intervened in politics.

Although Turkey switched to a democratic system again with the elections held on October 15th 1961, the presence of two military coup attempts in 1962 and 1963 made the process more troublesome. The 1961 elections also revealed another fact: no political party could reach the majority to form the government alone, which introduced Turkey with period of coalitions for the first time. The lack of stability in the parliament brought about problems in democratic life and economy. Lack of stability in the parliament brought about problems in democratic life and economy.

Having been elected MP from CKMP in Kütahya in 1961, Tosbi served his term with 40 speeches, seven law proposals and four parliamentary questions and became the most active of the deputies of Kütahya ns the parliament. The reason for this is his academic personality, his education and his interest in country issues. Although his speeches encompassed many different fields, he was mostly interested in the creation of economic and economic institutions.[4]

3 His Thoughts on Agricultural Policy

According to the Tosbi, the most important reason for underdevelopment of agriculture in Turkey and low production in some key agricultural products was mispricing policies of governments on agricultural products.

> *"…if the price policy continues this way, then it is inevitable that wheat production will decline in Turkey in the coming years."*[5]

He argued that together with this pricing policy, importing wheat imported from overseas would finish agriculture in Turkey and as a result, each farmer would only be able to produce enough for his family, which would lead to a complete external dependence for the needs of the non-agricultural segments. In order to avoid such a problem, he urged the government to support the farmers by buying especially the basic agricultural products at above the cost prices.

He added"*Whatever the cost of the goods produced by the Turkish peasants, it is obligatory to provide income to the villagers and to feed our people by buying their products at a price above the cost.*" Moreover, since a significant portion of the Turkish people are engaged in agriculture, they have to be supported by the state for their subsistence.[6]

Since sugar beet cultivation in Turkey is not sufficient for the country's sugar needs, enough benefit cannot be obtained from this product in terms of animal feed either. As such, grain products are used as animal feed. In this case, the

4 Veriler; TBMM Zabıt Cerideleri I. (XII) Dönem Tutanaklarından Derlenmiştir. Bozkurt, a.g.t., s. 103–104
5 Millet Meclisi Tutanak Dergisi, C.I, B.31, (10.1.1962), s.634
6 Millet Meclisi Tutanak Dergisi, C.I, B.31, (10.1.1962), s.634-635

country comes up against a grain deficit. Therefore, production of sugar beet should be increased through meticulous planning and planting of crops which can be animal feed should be supported.[7]

He argued that it was necessary to increase the capacity of sugar factories in Turkey and construct new ones. This would not only contribute significantly to the economic situation of the farmers and the peasants but also bring the currency to the country as it would develop the sugar industry.[8]

Tosbi, wanted the country to move to a planned system for economic progress and development of agriculture. He stated that labour and capital being adequate in Turkey, all we had to do for the country's development was to make conscious use of the land and to increase the production by directing the labour force to agricultural production. He added that soil analysis wasn't done in Turkey and so, it was not known what production the land of the country was suitable for. By doing soil analysis urgently and evaluating the climatic conditions, he urged the agricultural production to be directed accordingly. By guaranteeing the landowners to buy the product they produced, he saw switching to industrialization in agriculture as economic salvation of the country.[9] Thus, supply-demand balance would be provided, as well as realizing the foreign exchange needs of the country by exporting abroad.

4 Population-Industry-Economy

Tosbi, saying that the most important problem in Turkey was capital, stated that it could be solved by the labour factor. For this purpose, he emphasized that the existing factories, especially those in the private sector, should be employed at full capacity. He revealed that the factories operated by the private sector did not work at full capacity and this was a big capital loss. According to Tosbi, the goal of our industrial policy should be that all existing factories should be on full capacity operation.[10]

Tosbi, believed that it wasn't true to say that the cost of the products some factories produced was more expensive than the same product imported from abroad, because the imported products were subsidized by their governments. Also in Turkey, the government must subsidize factories manufacturing these kinds of products.

---

7 Millet Meclisi Tutanak Dergisi, C.I, B.31, (10.1.1962), s.635
8 Millet Meclisi Tutanak Dergisi, C.XVII, B.92, (27.6.1963), s.626
9 Millet Meclisi Tutanak Dergisi, C.XXVII, B.57, (20.2.1964), s.238
10 Millet Meclisi Tutanak Dergisi, C.III, B.56, (25.2.1962), s.527-528

According to Tosbi, Turkey should export cotton, one of its most important export product, as an industrial product rather than raw. For this purpose, Tosbi emphasized that cotton should be processed in textiles. He explained that such a move would both improve the industry and employ labour in the country, as well as bringing a large amount of foreign currency to the country.[11]

Tosbi, also focused on the population factor for the country's development. He was opposed to the members of the government who asserted that population growth would slow the pace of development and so strongly criticized their suggestion of contraception to prevent population growth.

Tosbi said "*In my opinion, this is a highly erroneous idea in many ways… The more the active population of a country is, that is, the number of citizens who have the power to work is more than the number of those who do not work, handicapped etc., the more prosperity and blessings there is in that country. The salvation of Turkey and becoming a great country will be through the increase of the population… Turkey of 50 million will certainly be a more prosperous, much stronger, much more reputable Turkey than today's Turkey of 30 million… We are taking measures to reduce the Turkish generation and prevent Turkish children from adding their power to the Turkish potential. This can't happen ..*"[12]

Today, the biggest problem in the developed Western countries is the population. These countries, whose population does not increase, seek to obtain qualified labor from underdeveloped countries, which leads to other problems in those countries. However, with its population exceeding 80 million today, Turkey has become potential player in the world. Therefore, it is understood how these evaluations of Tosbi in 1962 were correct.

Tosbi's opinions on the development of domestic industry are as follows. He wanted the domestic industry to be protected and supported without making any concessions on quality production or making domestic producers monopoly. In addition, he also pointed out that while supporting the domestic industrialists, an unjustly rich class should not be created.

5 Planned Economy and Economic System

In the 1960s, there was no significant economic system implemented in Turkey or planning in the economy. Although the mixed economic model from the past seemed to be implemented, unemployment rate and decapitalization were overwhelming due to the economic strategies of DP government and

---

11 a.g.y.

12 Millet Meclisi Tutanak Dergisi, C.IX, B.6, (16.11.1962), s.195-196

resulting depression between 1950 and 1960. Therefore, the capital shortage of governments for new investments was reflected in parliamentary debates.

Tosbi, insistently argued that there wasn't an economic system in Turkey and therefore transition to planned economy was out of the question. Therefore, he added, Turkey should rapidly switch to a planned economy by determining its own economic system.

> *"... a plan is not feasible unless the system is certain. Each system has a plan that fits. The system is the basis of the plan, as a plan is only feasible within a system."*[13]

Tosbi explained the economic model of the current coalition government as follows: *"the current government is twenty-five per cent statists, thirty per cent liberals, twenty per cent socialists and finally fifteen per cent neo-liberals"*[14] and compared this situation to mixed ice cream.

He emphasized that in case of the establishment of a planned economic system in Turkey, a strong government intervention was required on it. Otherwise, he explained, a planned economy would not be successful without state intervention.

"Since rapid development is a necessity, a systematic, a planned intervention is needed in social life. Only the state, the highest authority, can make such an intervention. The state will intervene in social and economic life. The best way to be held by the state is the planned intervention. However, if the state does not anticipate on what field of the society, on which elements of the economy and to what extent the intervention will be, negative consequences may arise." He pointed out that the success of the economic plan depended on the degree of state intervention: the more radical the state intervention, the more successful the economic plan. He stated that any reduction in intervention would mean failure of the plan. However, he emphasized the need to establish an institution that would be able to follow the data in the planned economy and to process the data correctly.[15]

He also criticized the lack of an institution that could give direction to the national economy of Turkey. He stated that the Planning Department of the Prime Ministry should be transformed into an organ to organize the economy rather than being a research institution. This institution needed to be authorized at a high level in the determination of economic policies. In doing so, he asked scientists to develop policies. The direction of the Turkish economy should be

---

13 Millet Meclisi Tutanak Dergisi, C.V, B.90, (22.5.1962), s.331.
14 Millet Meclisi Tutanak Dergisi, C.II, B.48, (17.2.1962), s.447
15 Millet Meclisi Tutanak Dergisi, C.XXVII, B.57, (20.2.1964), s.236

the task of this department. "*The duty to lead Turkey's national economy should be taken under the guarantee of the Planning Department.*"[16]

He stated that the Planning Office should be connected directly to the Parliament, not to the Prime Ministry, in order to avoid any pressure from the government or political influence. He also said that it would be correct for the State Institute of Statistics to process and announce the data accurately and without any political pressure.[17]

Tosbi's view of the Turkish economy during the period when he was an MP between 1960 -1964 was transition to a correct production policy through a rapid analysis of Turkish lands and, at the same time, gearing to industrial agricultural products. Population growth should not be stopped and manpower should be directed to production. Turkey's biggest capital is its fertile land and population. By using the full capacity of industry, it is necessary to prevent capital from being kept idle. A certain economic system should be established in Turkey and Turkey should definitely switch to the planned economy. Prodigality should be avoided.

References

Kalemli M., (2001), *Kütahya'nın Yasama Organı Üyeleri*, 1920-2001, Ankara.

Sadrettin Tosbi'nin Hal Tercümesi, *TBMM Arşivi*, Sicil No: I. Dönem 306.

Bozkurt S.(2017), Kütahya Milletvekilleri ve Millet Meclisi'ndeki Faaliyetleri (1961-1980), Yayınlanmamış Doktora Tezi, Dumlupınar Üniversitesi Sosyal Bilimler Enstitüsü, Kütahya

TBMM Albümü 1920-2010, C. II, II. Baskı, Ankara 2010.

Veriler; TBMM Zabıt Cerieleri I. (XII) Dönem Tutanaklarından Derlenmiştir.

Millet Meclisi Tutanak Dergisi, C.I, B.31, (10.1.1962)

Millet Meclisi Tutanak Dergisi, C.II, B.48, (17.2.1962)

Millet Meclisi Tutanak Dergisi, C.III, B.56, (25.2.1962)

Millet Meclisi Tutanak Dergisi, C.V, B.90, (22.5.1962)

Millet Meclisi Tutanak Dergisi, C.IX, B.6, (16.11.1962)

Millet Meclisi Tutanak Dergisi, C.XII, B.49, (14.2.1963)

Millet Meclisi Tutanak Dergisi, C.XVII, B.92, (27.6.1963)

Millet Meclisi Tutanak Dergisi, C.XXVII, B.57, (20.2.1964)

Millet Meclisi Tutanak Dergisi, C.XXVII, B.57, (20.2.1964)

16 Millet Meclisi Tutanak Dergisi, C.XXVII, B.57, (20.2.1964), s.237

17 Millet Meclisi Tutanak Dergisi, C.XII, B.49, (14.2.1963), s.554-555

Ahmet Uyaniker and Ali Apali

1295 R. (1879 M.) Year August Investigation of Records of Salary Payments in the Ottoman Government Ceyb-i Humayun

1 Introduction

The treasure means to keep something and save it. The name of the Arabic "hazn" root, which is name-space, has been translated into Turkish as a treasure. Government cash, valuables and related documents are stored and protected (Orhonlu, 1998: 130). State income expenditures were collected and government costs were collected therefrom. Ottoman state XVIII. He was using only one treasure system to the hundredth. The treasury was divided into two parts, internal and external treasury. XVIII. The century has begun a very delightful period. Over time, the treasure of Amire began to decline. In 1835, the mint was merged with the Hazine-i Amire in order for the state to regain its qualification as the main treasure. Darphane-i Amire has been established. However, this activity is insufficient. In 1838 it was separated from the mint and the Hazine-i Amire. Hazine-i Amire and Mensure Treasury were merged to establish financial supervision. After the declaration of the Imperial Edict in Gülhane in 1839, the period of treasure in the Ottoman finance was ending. A single treacherous turn has been passed. Treasury units in the Ottoman Empire were classified in different forms such as outer treasure, inner treasure, treasury of ceyb-i hümayun.

The external treasury, which is also called as "Rural Treasury", "Treasure-i Amire", "Financial Treasury" or "Imperial Council Treasury", was the main treasury of the state where income was collected and used by laws (Terzi, 2000: 1). The administration of the Treasure-i Amire was undertaken by the chief treasurer, who was the most competent person in charge of the grand vizier and financial affairs appointed by the Sultan himself as the chief of state affairs. The Ottoman state treasure is also called the Treasure-i Amire or the Treasure of the One for being on the outside of the palace. It is in middle courtyard at Topkapı Palace. Ruznamek registered by the pen. Books are books that contain all kinds of daily allowances and records. The administration is the grand vizier and the ledger. The room where the calculation of all the income and expenses of the state is made is a rented room. The items and coins that were to enter the warehouse were taken over by ruznamçeciler, exhibitionist, exhibitionist and tent mehterbashi (Terzi, 2000: 1). Every night, the amount of money that went into and out of the treasure was made up. The defendants, whose records of income and expenditures are kept, are called by name. The books containing only the figures of currency figures are called eccas-i nukud and the book of the fathers. Outside, that is, when there is a shortage in the treasury, borrowing money from this treasury and collecting the revenues from the treasury would be returned.

Another treasure unit in the Ottoman Empire is the inner chamber. The expenses of the inner treasure were held by the Sultan. The name of this treasure is given the names of the treasury of the Enderun or Treasure-i Hassa. This treasure was not only made of gold and silver coins, but also in the gift items of the monarch's own personal possessions. The official at the head of the inner treasure is the treasure. In the 17th century this treasure house was introduced. The inner treasure also has its own divisions. Precious goods and jewels were kept in treasures of inner treasures. These treasures, which are referred to by the name of the chamber treasure, the basement treasure and the family names, are the functions of the inner treasure. The treasure room, the treasury Pavilion, which was built by Sultan Mehmed the Great during the building of the palace in 1451–1481, has been used as palace treasury since its inception. In the basement there are gold, silver and sticks. There are precious harnesses in the Raht treasure. In the treasure hill, the sultan dressed on the sultan, It is the treasure where the goods are. The part that does not work is the basement treasure where old and scrapped hiding is stored. Especially during the expedition, when the money was stolen, the money was cut from the silver mallets in the basement treasure and unused. There were precious goods presented at the birth of the silk, Sultan or princes. The upper treasure is the treasure treasure. This treasure is being used in urgent need times. The inner treasury, palace treasury, worked like a credit bank for the outer treasury. The main sources of income of the domestic treasury are the has, mukataa and foundation incomes, corn mint mint income, various gifts and confiscation income (Tabakoğlu, 1985: 59–67).

Ceyb-i hümayun is part of the inner treasure. The Ceyb-i Hümâyûn is a peculiar term used for personal treasure, which means the private slaughter, which governs the sultan's special income and expenses.

The meaning of this term, which comes from the union of the words of ceyb (ceb) with the word of hümâyûn, which informs that something belongs to the sultanate, is the word of the sultan (Pakalın, 1983: 265).

Ceyb-i Humayun is a special treasure where the income determined for the sultan's special expenditures is collected together and the expenditures are recorded one by one. In the Ottoman Empire, from the Classical Period to the Tanzimat, the accounting of the private income and expense items belonging to the Sultan was held by this treasure. Although Tanzimat has been carrying out some new applications within the framework of seeking to connect the Treasury of Ceyb-i Hümâyûn to a certain system, this treasure continued to exist until the collapse of the Ottoman State (Sahillioğlu, 1993: 465). Sometimes these incomes, which can be used in the form of hidden appropriations, can sometimes be given to save the treasury, the ruler and the grand vizier. In the latter case they had to return the allocated amounts. As a result, domestic treasury funds have become a kind of treasury loan. Apart from these, there were incomes called "ceyb-i hümâyun coin" to cover the personal expenses of the sultan. The expenses of the palace kitchen expenses, the pensions of the palace, the private productions connected to the sultan, which are in the form of a personal expenses, are covered from the general budget and recorded in the "delivery" chapters of the cost budgets. Jobs related to Ceyb-i Humayun were seen in the treasure of harem-i hümâyun and later in the treasure of ceyb-i hümâyun. The master is a high-ranking officer with the name "secret guru" (Terzi, 2000: 2). The necessary amount of money sent by the treasury every month, this apartment circulated in line with the request of the ruler. Ceyb-i Hümâyun continued until the abolition of the Sultanate.

2 Multiple Treasury System in Ottoman Empire

XVII. Until the last quarter of the century, Hazine-i Amire was the only treasure in the Ottoman finance organization. The state revenues that reached the center were collected in this treasure and the necessary needs were met from this treasure. XVIII. In the late 19th century, the mint gained importance in Ottoman finance. In 1792, as an extension of the reforms that were to be made in the military territory in the end of the Ottoman-Russian war, during the reign of Selim, the Irâd-ı Cedid Treasure was established as an independent institution. Thus, the only treasure system was abandoned and the period of multiple treasures was passed (Cezar, 1986: 100).

İrad-ı Cedid Treasury

It is also known as Nizam-ı Cedid Hazinesi. III. It was the budget established in 1793 to meet the expenses of the Nizam-ı Cedid army on the order of Selim. As a result of the meeting chaired by the Sultan, a budget was set apart from the usual budget revenues and a decision was made to divide the revenue sources from the budget and the general budget. The new treasure created by this decision was also called İrad-ı Cedid (Yardımcı and Ayvaz, 2017: 255). According to the Irad-i Jedid laws, the daily income and expenditure papers given to the head of Irad-i

Cedid and the head ledger are examined at the end of the month and three copies of the monthly book are prepared. Babıali, Chief Accountant, and Ruznamçe Kalemesi were given the balance sheet at the end of the year.

The surplus money was transferred to the special Irad-i Cedid treasure in the Darphane-i Amire. As a result of the Kabakçı Mustafa Pasha rebellion, Sultan III. This treasure was abolished when Selim was lowered from the throne, and the accumulated money was transferred to the treasure of the Darphane-i Amire.

Zahire Treasury

It was established to meet Istanbul's food and beverage needs. III. It was founded during the Selim period. This treasure is not funded by the income of certain income sources but rather by the funds that are brought to the capital, that is, by the revolving fund, and it is separated from other treasures.

Tersane Treasury

After the establishment of Iraad-ı Cedidin, some attempts were made for the shipyard costs from the end of 1804 and the shipyard treasury was established in February 1805 and the salaries, rationing, shipbuilding and equipment costs of the shipyard personnel started to be met here (Terzi, 2000: 893). Over time, silk official proceeds and house price hikes were among the major income items of the Tersane Treasury. The main expenses of the meeting are salary payments and settlement expenses, expenses for the necessary materials for the shipyard. In addition, the prices of medicines and medical devices given to hospitals and ships were paid by the Tersane Treasury (Gencer, 1985: 116).

Mukataat/Mansûre Treasury

In order to meet the expenses of the Asakir-i Mansure-i Muhammedi army established after the removal of the Janissaries, the sources of income were needed. The revenues transferred to governors or mutasariffs by the administration of fifteen of the Anatolian sancağas from 1820, without being governor or mutasarrif, were transferred to the new treasure called Muqataat Treasury, which was initially allocated to cover Asakir-i Mansur-i Muhammediyye expenses and collected some mukataa incomes (Cezar, 1986: 256). After the interest of the Timar system and the Janissary Quarter, in 1834 the name of the Mukataat Treasure was turned into the Mansour Treasury.

Redif Treasury

To fulfill the expenses of the Redif units, a branch of Asâkir-i Mansûre, the Redif organization was established on July 8, 1834. For this reason, some examples were sent to the places where the organization was established, and according to this example, a dress that was dyed, a local kadi or a nobody approved cost was sent to Istanbul together with the accounting for the cost of a battalion. After the incoming accounts had been appropriately received starting from Seraskerlik and containing the Order of Payment, the indicated amount was paid in Redefine (Shaw, 1983: 73).

3 31/5 Number and Y.PRK.HH. Fund Coded Book Transcription

The book begins with the accounting records of the salary amounts of the Hazine-i Humayun Kethüdası and the civil servants. Belgede was also an institution where the Treasury-Kethuda and his officers served. Yavuz Sultan Selim Khan was established during the time of the treasure kethüarlardan, was kept responsible for the storage and storage of the entry and exit into the saddle. The memorial at the head of this institution was called the treasure khetüdası. They kept the treasury coffers of the treasury-owned relic's books and the rulers of those sold or destroyed, and handed them over to successors in their infidels (Pakalin, 1983: 791). The persons and their salaries recorded with these duties are shown in Tab. 1.

Tab. 1: With the Treasure-i Humayun Kethüdası and the salaries of the importers and officers

	Guruş	Nefer	Hesab	İcmal
Hazine-i Hümayun Kethüdası Hacı Hasan Bey Bendeleri	10.000	1	000	
Hazine-i Hümayun Başkâtibi Hasan Bey Bendeleri	2250	1	000	
Hazine-i Hümayun İkinci kâtibi Ethem Bey Bendeleri	1400	1	000	
Hazine-i Hümayun Kaftancısı Şevket Bey Bendeleri	1400	1	000	
Hazine-i Hümayun Üçüncü Kâtibi Bekir Bey Bendeleri	1000	1	000	
Hazine-i Hümayun Sergulamı Rıza Bey Bendeleri	800	1	000	
Hazine-i Hümayun Dördüncü Kâtibi Ahmet Bey Bendeleri	600	1	000	
Hazine-i Hümayun Gulam-ı Sanisi Kamil Efsa Bendeleri	500	1	000	
Hazine-i Hümayun Kapucu Fedayi Nuri Bey Bendeleri	500	1	000	
Yekün	**18400**	**9**	**000**	**18.450**

According to Tab. 1, nine people were working as salaried employees in the Hazine-i Humayun Kethüdalığı. Among them, the highest salary is the Hazine-i Humayun Kethüdas registered with the name of Hacı Hasan Bey with 10.000 gurush, while the lowest salary is with Gulam-ı Sanisi Kamil Bey and the Coverer Fedayi Nuri Bey with 500 gurush. While the sum of the salaries of all these employees was 18400 gurush, this amount was recorded as 18450 gurush in icmal and, therefore, a deviation of 500 gurush was in question. This deviation was due to a collection error of 500 gurush when the total was taken. In the ongoing part of the document, the amounts of the salaries of the Cardinals were recorded.

Tab. 2 shows the salaries of staff members who are staff members for forty-two persons. According to this, salaries of 22,750 gurush are shaped according to different positions. First-class relatives receive the highest salary, while fourth-class relatives are those who receive the lowest salary.

According to Tab. 3, the total salary paid for Hazine-i Hümayun, which is 126 employees, is 24,400 gurush. Among these employees, the highest salary is the salaries of 1300 gurush belonging to 2 persons registered as head jail. The lieutenant has been taken under this section as a grand total. Accordingly, the total salary payment for people up to this amount is 65,600 gurush.

The salary amounts of Babessaade Hademeleri are recorded on the following page. Babu's-Saade is the place where the throne of the Sultans came out on the throne, on the couches and in the feast ceremonies. The most important gate of the palace is Babu's-Saade because of its symbolic characteristic is the place where the divan square and the rerun school and the sultan's apartments are located. This door which passes through courtyard is the first place in the palace because it is the knot point of the one with Enderun and the sultan is sitting in front of this door in ceremonies such as culms and festivals. The sarcophagus has the earthen Darü's-Saade ages and Akağalar and Enderun civil servants.

Tab. 2: Hırka-ı saadet Congierge Servants Average Salaries

	Guruş	**Nefer**	**Hesab**	**İcmal**
Has oda Kethüdası Necip Bey Bendeleri	2250	1	000	
Hırka-i Şerif Ser Hademesi Mucip Bey Bendeleri	1500	1	000	
Hırka-i Şerif Birinci Sınıf Hademeleri Bendeleri	5500	10	550	
Hırka-i Şerif İkinci Sınıf Hademeleri Bendeleri	5000	10	500	
Hırka-i Şerif Üçüncü Sınıf Hademeleri Bendeleri	4500	10	450	
Hırka-i Şerif Dördüncü Sınıf Hademeleri Bendeleri	4000	10	400	
Yekün	**22.750**	**42**	**000**	**22.750**

Tab. 3: Hazine-i Hümayun Congierge Servants Average Salaries

	Guruş	**Nefer**	**Hesab**	**İcmal**
Hazine-i Hümayun Ser Hademeleri Bendeleri	2600	2	1300	
Hazine-i Hümayun Ser Hademe Muavinleri Bendeleri	800	2	400	
Hazine-i Hümayun Birinci Sınıf Hademeleri Bendeleri	2400	8	300	
Hazine-i Hümayun Ser Hademeleri İkinci Sınıf Hademeleri Bendeleri	2500	10	250	
Hazine-i Hümayun Üçüncü Sınıf Hademeleri Bendeleri	2000	10	200	
Hazine-i Hümayun Dördüncü Sınıf Hademeleri Bendeleri	14100	94	150	
Yekün	**24.400**	**126**	**000**	**24.400**
				65.600

Tab. 4: Babüssade Congierge Servants Average Salaries

	Guruş	**Nefer**	**Hesab**	**İcmal**
Babüssaade Ağası Ümit Efendi Bendeleri	2250	1	00	
Cüce Osman Ağa Bendeleri	208	1	00	
Babüssade Ser Hademesi Hüseyin Ağa Bendeleri	200	1	00	
Babüssaade Hademeleri Bendeleri	1800	12	150	
Yekün	**4458**	**15**	**000**	**4458**

Tab. 4 shows that the total number of Babessaade residents is 15 people and the total salary paid to these employees is 4458 gurush. The highest salary is the Babüssaade Ağa while the lowest salary is the relatives.

Tab. 5 reveals that the sum of the salaries of the Tidaran-i Hassa Hademas is 6200 gurush, and the highest salary of 32 people is paid to Hüseyin Efendi, the Tirderan Kethüdası.

Tab. 6 shows salary payments for a total of 5042 gurush for 16 employees. The salary of the employee registered with the name "Arabi Muallimi Evveli Efendi Servants" which has the highest salary from these salary payments is the salary of the employee who is registered as "Kuran-ı Kerim Muavini Efendi Servants" while the salary of the employee is the salary of 81 gurush.

Tab. 7 contains records of the salaries of the relatives and capers. Accordingly, the highest wage in salary payments of 2500 gurus his head concierge registered

Tab. 5: Tidaran-i Hassa Congierge Servants Average Salaries

	Guruş	**Nefer**	**Hesab**	**İcmal**
Ser Tirdaran Hassa Ahmed Aga Bendeleri	1300	1	00	
Tirderan Kethudası Hüseyin Efendi Bendeleri	2500	1	00	
Tirderan Eskileri Bendeleri	800	4	200	
Tirderan ...Efendi Bendeleri	200	1	000	
Tirderan hademeleri Bendeleri	2750	25	150	
Yekün	**6200**	**32**	**00**	**6200**

Tab. 6: Mektep-i Hanifi of Hazine-i Hümayun Concierge Hodja and Magisters Servants Average Salaries

	Guruş	**Nefer**	**Hesab**	**İcmal**
Kuran-ı Kerim Hocası Efendi Bendeleri	125	1	00	
Kuran-ı Kerim Muavini Efendi Bendeleri	81	1	00	
Arabi Muallimi Evveli Efendi Bendeleri	1250	1	00	
Muallimi Sani Efendi Bendeleri	250	1	00	
Muallimi Salisi Efendi Bendeleri	83	1	00	
Muallimi Rabei Efendi Bendeleri	85	1	00	
Farisi Muallimi Efendi Bendeleri	208	1	00	
Riyaziye Muallimi Efendi Bendeleri	625	1	00	
Sülüs ve Resim Hacaları Efendileri Bendeleri	666	2	333	
Rika Hocası Efendi Bendeleri	700	1	000	
İmla Hocası Efendi Bendeleri	167	1	000	
Mektep Müdürü İle Hanende Muallimi Efendiler Bendeleri	500	2	250	
Neyzen Muallimi İle Keman Ustası Efendiler Bendeleri	300	2	150	
Yekün	**5042**	**16**	**000**	**5042**
				81.300

as "Erzak Serhademesi Aga Servants". The lowest salary is the salary of those registered as "Suffe Concierge Servants".

According to Tab. 8, the salary of 17 employees is 2762, the highest salary is 1000 gurush, while the lowest salary paid is 42 salaries.

Tab. 9 shows the wages of the municipal police and servants in the Treasury of Humayun. However, in this section an account fault was identified. Accordingly,

Tab. 7: Erzak-ı Concierge Suffe Third Doorman Servants Average Salaries

	Guruş	Nefer	Hesab	İcmal
Erzak Serhademesi Aga bendeleri	300	1	00	
Serhademe Muavini Bendeleri	250	1	00	
Erzak hademeleri Bendeleri	600	3	200	
Erzak hademesi Bendeleri	150	1	00	
Suffe Hademesi Bendeleri	150	1	00	
Suffe Hademesi Bendeleri	700	7	100	
Üçüncü Kapıcıları Bendeleri	400	2	200	
Yekün	**2500**	**16**	**00**	

Tab. 8: Eshab-ı Sala Servants Served as Retail

	Guruş	Nefer	Hesab	İcmal
Ziyafet-i şeb Takımı Memuru Efendi Bendeleri	1000	1	00	
Bekçiler Agası Efendi Bendeleri	083	1	00	
Hırka-ı Şerif ser Müezzini Efendi Bendeleri	500	1	00	
Daire Kahvecisi Aga Bendeleri	104	1	00	
Daire Kilercisi Aga Bendeleri	083	1	00	
Dolap Uşagı Bendeleri	042	1	00	
Hırkka-ı Şerid Sakaları Bendeleri	150	3	50	
Mezbele Keşan Neferatı bendeleri	500	5	100	
Birinci ila İkinci..... Mekteb Sakaları Bendeleri	300	3	100	
Yekün	**2762**	**17**		

Tab. 9: Etfal-i Muhacirin and Zabıtan and Hizmetçiyan-ı Servants that are in Daire-i Hazine-i Humayun Average Salaries

	Guruş	Nefer	Hesab	İcmal
Etfal-i Muhacirin Zabitanı Bendeleri	1650 (**1400**)	7	200	
Etfal muhacirin Teblekeşan ve Hizmetçiyanı Bendeleri	2000	00	00	
Muhacirin Etfal Bendeleri	2250 (**1500**)	75	20	
Yekün	**4900**	**82**		

a total of 1,600 gurush should be 1400, and a total of 1,550 gurushes are required. However, there is no error in the documents and the totals are taken correctly.

Tab. 10 shows the salaries of health workers working in the pharmacy at the Treasury of Humayun. According to the records, 2500 gurush for employees and

Tab. 10: Residents' Survival and Surgeon Servants Amount Salaries at the Treasure-i Hümayun Pharmacy

	Guruş	Nefer	Hesab	İcmal
Sertabib nuri Bey Bendeleri	2500	1	00	
Eczacı Mustafa Efendi Bendeleri	666	1	00	
Eczacı Muhammed Efendi bendeleri	250	1	00	
Eczacı Çevamnaki Bendeleri	250	1	00	
Yekün	**2.666**	**4**		**2.666**
				95.178

Tab. 11: Topkapı Saray-ı Humayunu Matbahı Treasures of the Treasures in the Maturity of the Constitution Aşçıyan and Teblekeşan and the Officer Servants Average Salaries

	Guruş	Nefer	Hesab	İcmal
Harem-i hümayun Matbah-ı ve Kilerciyle Katip ve Muavini Bendeleri	1200	3	400	
Aşçıbaşı Bendeleri	800	1	000	
Aşçıyan Bendeleri	8000	27	000	
Teblekeşan Bendeleri	5000	25	200	
Helvahane Hademeleri Bendeleri	1500	04	000	
Kantarcı ve Kilerci Defer Bilici Bandeleri	750	3	250	
Sebze ve Hitab Memurları Bendeleri	400	02	200	
Matbah Kapıcısı Bendeleri	200	1	000	
Matbah Çöpçüsü bendeleri	150	1	000	
Helvacı Camii İmamı ve Kayyumu ve Şeyh Efendiler Daileri	300	3	100	
Hazine Hademeleriyle ve Katibi bendeleri	800	2	400	
Hazine Hademeleri Teblekeşanı Bendeleri	2250	19 **(17)**	150	
	21650	91	000	
				116.828

250 gurush paid for salaried workers. Also in this part of the document there is a record of 95.178 showing the total salaries of the employees registered up to this point.

In the last part of the document related to salary payments, the total salaries of 91 employees are 21650 gurush. According to this, the lowest salary is "Imam of Helvacı Mosque and Kayyumu and Shaykh Efendiler Daileri", while the highest salary is the employees registered as "Chef Servants".

4 Conclusion

The document shows the accounting records of the monthly salaries paid to the employees in the Hazine-i Hümayun office. Rumi, 116.828 gurush, the total amount of the document dated August 18, 1295 (August 30, 1879), both appeared at the end of the accounting records and in the explanatory section at the end of the document. The transcription of the disclosure at the end of the verse is as follows:

> *"Daireyi Hazineyi Humayun Mevcud Bendegân Kullarına evatıf-ı İlliyeyi Cenab-ı Mülükaneden İhsan-ı Şahane Buyrulan birer maaş bedeli olan balada muharrer yalnız 116.828 guruş Ceyb-i Humayun-u Şahaneden makbuz olduğuna müşir iş bu defter bi tanzim mabeyn-i hümayunu mülükane Cenab-ı Aliyesine Takdim kılındı. 18 Agustos 1295"*

According to the document dated August 30, 1879, the highest salary is the Hazine-i Hümayun Kethüdası Hacı Hasan Bey Bendeleri "and is the salary of the manager of the position near the sarcophagus. The lowest salary registered to the lieutenant is 42 salaried salaries of the employee who are registered as "Cabinet Lieutenants". This shows that salary difference is about 238 times among those working in treasury. Besides, it is the place where the treasury chapters are located where the most employees are located. It is here that 126 employees are working and accordingly the salary of 24.400 gurush is paid in total salary payments. The minimum number of employees is the pharmacy in which four people working in the health field are located.

References

Afyoncu E., (2002). *Sorularla Osmanlı İmparatorluğu II*, İstanbul.

Akyıldız A., (1993). *Tanzimat Dönemi Osmanlı Merkez Teşkilatında Reform*, İstanbul.

Başbakanlık Osmanlı Arşivleri, Sıra No: 5/31, Fon Kodu: Y.PRK.HH.

Cezar Y., (1986). *Osmanlı Maliyesinde Bunalım ve Değişim Dönemi*, İstanbul 1986.

Eren A., (1999). Osmanlı Ekonomisinde Kurumsal Gelişmeler, *Osmanlı Ansiklopedisi* III, Ankara.

Gencer A. İ., (1985). *Bahriye'de Yapılan Islahat Hareketleri ve Bahriye Nezareti'nin Kuruluşu* (1789–1867), İstanbul.

Genç M., (2009). *Osmanlı İmparatorluğunda Devlet ve Ekonomi*, İstanbul.

Halaçoğlu Y.,(1998). *Osmanlılarda Devlet Teşkilâtı ve Sosyal Yapı*, Ankara.

Orhonlu C. (1998). Hazine, TDVİA XVII, İstanbul.

Pakalın M. Z., (1983). *Osmanlı Tarih Deyimleri ve Terimleri Sözlüğü I*, İstanbul.

Sahillioğlu H., (1993). Ceyb-i Hümâyun, *TDVİA* VII, İstanbul.

Shaw S. J., (1983). *Osmanlı İmparatorluğu ve Modern Türkiye II, nşr. (M.Harmancı)*, İstanbul.

Tabakoğlu A., (1999). Osmanlı Malî Yapısının Ana Hatları, *Osmanlı Ansiklopedisi* III, Ankara.

Tabakoğlu A., (1985). *Gerileme Dönemine Girerken Osmanlı Maliyesi*, İstanbul.

Terzi A. T., (2000). *Hazine-i Hâssa Nezareti*, Ankara.

Uzunçarşılı İ. H., (2017). *Osmanlı Devletinin Saray Teşkilatı*, Ankara.

Yardımcı M. E., E. Ayvaz. (2017). Osmanlı Mali Sisteminde İrâd-ı Cedid Hazinesi ve Muhasebe Kayıtları (1799–1800), *Bingöl Üniversitesi Sosyal Bilimler Enstitüsü Dergisi* 7.

Baris Yildiz

A Conceptual View to Corruption and Broken Windows Theory Approach"

1 Introduction

Although corruption is not a new problem, it is considered as a social disease and can be seen in most of the developing countries (Chowdhury, Desai and Audretsch, 2018a: 40). Corruption refers to behaviors such as embezzlement, nepotism, bribery, exorbitant pricing, influence peddling and committing fraudulent acts, besides the abuse of public service for private gains (Chetwynd, Chetwynd and Spector, 2003: 6). In other words, corruption is an abuse of public service or institutions for private gains (Hira, 2016). Corruption may occur when a public official in the public sector grants privilege to a civilian citizen. This situation will reveal the phenomenon called bribery which can be considered as the rewarding of the public official granting the privilege (Delavallade, 2006: 223).

Some economists, such as Tanzi (1999), advocate the positive aspects of corruption in a moderate manner. According to them, the most efficient investors will pay the highest bribe. Thus, the resources will be transferred to the most efficient areas as a result of the corruption committed. On the other hand, they also argue that corruption can ensure that businesses are carried out faster, and that the level of wages received by employees in the public sector can be kept low through bribery. In brief, they consider that corruption is useful grease lubricating the engine of economic growth, and an economic agent (Aliyu and Elijah, 2008: 1). However, this moderate perspective on corruption has been replaced by more realistic and negative views in recent years.

2 Main Reasons for the Emergence of Corruption

Corruption is a social problem that emerges with the emergence of the state institution, and it also continues its existence at the present time. Although the state seems to be the main phenomenon in the emergence of corruption, there are many economic, social political, cultural and psychological reasons on the basis of it (Eren and Künü, 2018: 1471).

State intervention is the best option used to deal with the market failure. However, state interventions in the economy may increase corruption in some cases since they disrupt the effective distribution of resources and cause the degeneration of state employees (Acemoğlu and Verdier, 2000). The environment required for the increase in corruption is established when severe economic arrangements of the state and unfair and unequal practices come together along with the weakening of the rule of law (Chowdhury, Desai and Audretsch, 2018b: 53). The increase in the rate of education, improvement of investment environment for foreign investments to come, and the improvements made for integration into the international economy may decrease the rates of corruption (Abdelbaki, 2017). The mutual relationship between informality and corruption is usually analyzed using the corruption index. The extent of corruption and informality appears to be complementary in low-income countries, and it is stated that there is no strong relationship between these two in high-income countries (Dreher and Schneider, 2010: 230).

One of the factors that may lead to corruption is the fiscal decentralization. Decentralization is to grant power to the local authority to generate and spend local income. In this case, bureaucrats/authorities at the local level can easily get access to opportunities for corruption since they are responsible for the implementation of laws. Here, geographical location is another factor affecting the relationship between decentralization and corruption. People in rural areas may tend to further pay bribes since they further rely on public services (Chowdhury, Desai and Audretsch, 2018a: 45).

There are also many economic and social reasons, such as trade restrictions, state subsidies, price controls, multiple currency practices, exchange allocation plans, lower wages in the public service, natural resource equipment such as oil and gold, and some sociological factors, for the emergence of corruption (Mauro, 1997: 4–6).

3 Some Damage Caused by Corruption

Corruption may affect the purchases of public goods and services depending on the offer of the person who gives the best bribe rather than the one who offers the best price-quality combination (Blackburn, Bose and Haque, 2011: 407). This situation causes corruption caused by public officials to affect the extent and distribution of state expenditures (Liu and Mikesell, 2014). For instance, corruption may negatively affect the incentive structure by excluding labor-intensive projects in which bribery is not so significant or other income generating opportunities. Furthermore, corruption may change the in cash and kind distributions of social transfer expenditures. This change is observed in the form of an increased share of in-kind transfers within social transfers if corruption has occurred in a democratic country (Gupta, Davoodi and Alonso-Terme, 2002: 40). While the change in the distribution of public expenditures is at the expense of the reduction of social expenditures such as education, health, recreation, religion spending and culture, it may occur in favor of defense, fuel, energy and general public services (Delavallede, 2006; Jajkowicz and Drobiszová, 2015).

Increasing public expenditures in low-income countries may reduce economic growth by causing budget deficits. This may lead to higher social costs, which can be accompanied by the inefficiency of expenditures and increasing corruption (Dzhumashev, 2014). Public finance aims to reduce poverty by increasing economic growth especially in low-income countries (Hillman, 2004:1067). Although the direction of corruption on economic growth is often unclear, it may show the effects of the hypotheses called wheel lubrication and wheel sandblasting (Dwiputri, Arsyad and Pradiptyo, 2018). The corruption, which slows down the economic growth rate, increases the gap between the rich and the poor (Timofeyev, 2011: 39) and may negatively affect the traditional basic functions of the government, such as the redistribution of income, along with the stabilization of the economy (Hessami and Uebelmesser, 2016: 94).

The long-term effect of corruption on economic growth may also appear in the form of a delay in economic growth by directly reducing efficiency and indirectly restricting investments (Anoruo and Braha, 2005: 50). Furthermore, corruption has nonignorable indirect effects on state investment expenditures, human capital development, total employment (Aliyu and Elijah, 2008) and military expenditures. It can be interpreted that the interactions between corruption and investments and corruption and military expenditures have strong negative effects on economic growth (d'Agostina, Dunne and Pieroni, 2016).

The countries with high levels of corruption can achieve faster economic growth when they implement a comprehensive economic liberalization. However, this growth cannot ensure the distributive justice due to degenerated structures of the countries, on the contrary, it may increase the poverty (Choi and Woo, 2011:192). The funds allocated to struggle against poverty can be exploited by the people with good connections in the public and private sectors along with the effect caused by corruption and may affect the targeting of social programs to those who really need them (Timofeyev, 2011: 39).

Corruption may affect income inequality and poverty through various ways such as asset ownership, human capital formation, education inequality, factor accumulation uncertainty, growth, biased tax systems and poor targeting of social programs (Gupta, Davoodi and Alonso-Terme, 2002: 25).

As it is seen, indirect effects of corruption through some economic and management factors may lead to the emergence of poverty. The increasing corruption depending on economic factors decreases economic investments, destroys the market structure, prevents competition, increases business costs and increases income inequality. The increasing corruption depending on management factors may led to the orientation of state investments to unnecessary projects in which bribe is taken, deterioration of compliance in safety and health regulations and thus the erosion of institutional capacity of public services (Chetwynd, Chetwynd and Spector, 2003: 6–7).

When the relationship between corruption and education is examined, it is indicated that high and increasing corruption may significantly decrease access to school. In his empirical study, Dridi (2014) stated that there was a strong connection between corruption and secondary school enrollment rates. Moreover, he also determined that a one-unit increase in corruption reduces enrollment rates by almost 10 %.

Corruption and accountability play an important role in determining the level of tax efforts of developed and developing countries, affect tax revenues and may weaken the tax policies. Corruption has a negative effect on the taxpayer's confidence in the state and willingness to collaborate (Hillman, 2004:1067; Bird, Martinez-Vazquez and Torgler, 2008: 61). Another factor that causes tax revenues to decrease is the extent of informal economy. Corruption may increase the extent of informal economy. Therefore, increasing corruption moves this cycle further up and completes it by causing decrease in tax revenues and increase in the amount of public debt (Cooray, Dzhumashev and Schneider, 2017).

The negative and significant effect of corruption on capital investments is also important. This is much more apparent especially for Small and Medium-scaled Businesses. However, bribery has no effect on the efficiency of investment for large companies including state, semi-state and foreign capital companies (O'Toole and Tarp, 2014:589).

Corruption Perception Index (CPI) is calculated by Transparency International for perceived public sector corruption levels according to international experts and businessmen. According to the index, failure to control corruption is considered as one of the most important arguments that cause the crisis of democracy in the world (CPI, 2018).

4 Measures to Be Taken in the Fight against Corruption

The biggest source of corruption is malicious public officials. Therefore, when it is attempted to ensure financial constraint in a country, it is first necessary to limit the corruption of public employees and the expenditures caused by it. Increases in the state's level of expenditures do not constitute a problem alone. The problem is the use of increases in expenditures by policy makers for private gains and inadequacy of more efficient and fair allocations (Liu and Mikesell,

2014: 355). This supports the idea that corruption may be further observed in countries with a large public sector (Hopkin, 2002: 580) and therefore brings the reduction of size of the state in fighting against corruption to the agenda (Brown and Cloke, 2004:276). However, when the data of the corruption perception index in 2018 are examined, it is noteworthy that many countries with high public sector size within top 20 are the least degenerated countries. Therefore, to express that the fight against corruption can be done only by downsizing of the state will be a very simple way for the solution. Accordingly, it can be said that the fact that the public sector acts in an order and to serve as a model to the rest of the economy is more important than its size (Hopkin, 2002: 581).

It is important to establish a good management system in the fight against corruption. In this case, it is stated that the institution that should come to the forefront is the health system (Lewis, 2006: 44). Good management decreases the negative effects on economic activities by promoting transparency and accountability in fiscal, monetary and financial policies and supports the efforts to directly reduce corruption (Baldacci et al., 2008: 1336; Arvate et al., 2010). Some opinions suggesting that the prevention of all corruption is extremely costly, and therefore it is the best option to intervene only in some of the corruption are remarkable (Acemoğlu and Verdier, 2000: 207). According to them, for instance, more targeted and different policy approaches adapted according to specific types of firms (such as small- and medium-sized enterprises–SMEs and large firms) for a policy aimed at eliminating the negative effect of corruption on capital investments will be potentially more effective (O'Toole and Tarp, 2014: 589).

When fighting against the problems caused by corruption is generally evaluated, the factors such as i) sound management of natural resources, ii) Broad-based, labor-intensive growth, iii) Effective expenditures for education and health, iv) Effective targeting of social programs, v) Ensuring a low level of inequality in access to education (Gupta, Davoodi and Alonso-Terme, 2002: 40) vi) Legislation on freedom of information on issues such as national budgets, vii) Justice reform, viii) Establishment or strengthening of public institutions responsible for the fiscal control of the government, such as the National Ombudsman, Anti-Corruption Agency and the Inspector General, ix) Public service reform and professionalization, x) Reform of public procurement systems, xi) Election reform, and xii) Inclusion of non-governmental organizations in the fight (Brown and Cloke, 2004: 276) seem to be important.

5 Broken Windows Theory Approach to Corruption

The Broken Windows Theory refers that the smallest problem or a bad behavior that may exist in a place may lead to cause some other crimes and then the crime may spread (Yazıcı, 2018: 848). According to the theory which was first expressed by Wilson and Kelling (1982:30), no crime should be left unpunished, no matter how minor it is. Each factor that causes disruptions should be considered important and eliminated due to the fact that it is likely to cause more serious crimes in the future. According to the theory, broken windows or problems (corruption) are perceived more quickly by criminals (bribers). If minor crimes such as breaking the window with stones are disregarded and the broken glass is not repaired, events that may cause more damage to the entire building may occur later in the process. Failure to fight minor crimes may give a signal that the system is careless or that sufficient attention is not paid to minor issues. According to this situation adapted to corruption, anti-corruption plans targeting minor disorders are important and it is necessary to focus on them.

Fight against corruption gives a strong indication of the state's determination to ensuring the general welfare. To approach international corruption through Broken Windows Theory indicates that a society is determined to fight against corruption. Although the legal environment of the fight against international corruption has improved dramatically in recent years especially with the studies of institutions such as Organisation for Economic Co-operation and Development (OECD) and International Monetary Fund (IMF), developing countries still fall behind the developed countries. To approach corruption through Broken Windows Theory changes the legal framework of anti-bribery laws in three different ways. Firstly, broken windows approach will help to define corruption again and from a different perspective as insecurity and irregularity. Secondly, the Broken Windows Theory will strengthen fighting against corruption by focusing more on minor bribery. Thirdly, the Broken Windows Theory will further emphasize the partnership between public and private sector in the fight against corruption (Alford, 2012: 1261–1277).

6 Conclusion

Although the fight against corruption ensures many public interests, developing countries still fall behind the developed countries with respect to fighting. Therefore, one of the most important determinants of corruption is the level of development of countries. Furthermore, it appears that severe and damaged economic arrangements of the state are another important factor that feeds corruption. However, many economic and social reasons, such as the accompanying weak legal system, practices causing inequality in society, management approach moving away from international integration, bad investment environment, low level of education and high level of informal economy, deepen the corruption and its consequences.

One of the most important consequences of corruption is the waste of public resources, as it is revealed in the literature. The most important reason for this is the inadequate decisions related to projects of the people working in the implementing units of the public due to bribery and even the fact that the projects that are important for the country are given to insufficient firms. Thus, the value of the economic transaction decreases due to corruption, which prevents competition because it creates an opportunity by forming a contract which is not normally preferred (Delavallade, 2006: 223). Furthermore, bad investment environment causes corruption and consequently difficulties in attracting foreign direct investments by reducing confidence in the country, and reduction in the amount of capital investment in the country, and therefore, it negatively affects the economic growth. While the negative effect of corruption on economic growth basically emerges by its effects on human capital and political instability (Dridi, 2013: 121), it also causes social unrest by giving rise to income inequality and poverty.

Corruption also contributes to the increased role of the informal economy in macroeconomics. Increased informal economy, on the other hand, leads to the reduction of tax revenues and consequently serious budget deteriorations. Furthermore, corruption changes the composition of public expenditures against the required new equipment expenditure activities, health and education. Thus, public investments and the efficiency of the country's infrastructure are decrease (Aliyu and Elijah, 2008: 2).

These reasons indicate that it is important for governments to fight against corruption. The use of a single method in the fight against corruption does not seem sufficient. One of the most important ways of fighting is the good management practices to prevent corruption of public employees. Good management practices emerge with the policies that promote transparency and accountability in the public sector. Furthermore, serious fight against informality will ensure that the state policies to prevent corruption can be welcomed by the society. The increase in the quantity and quality of education and health expenditures in the country will contribute to the reduction of income inequalities by contributing to the development of human capital in the long term. The fact that the reduction in income inequalities is supported by the faith in the rule of law will contribute to the emergence of a spontaneous resistance to corruption in society.

The adoption of the Broken Windows Theory approach will contribute to further increasing the resistance to fight against corruption. Despite very few opinions indicating that fighting against all corruptions is extremely costly and therefore intervention in the elected ones seems to be the best option, the approach of Broken Windows Theory seems important in terms of the society's belief and support to the fight.

References

Abdelbaki, H. H. (2017). Investigation of Economic Determinants of Corruption in Egypt under Mubarak Regime. *International Research Journal of Finance and Economics*, 160, 14–25.

Acemoğlu, D., and Verdier, T. (2000). The Choice between Market Failures and Corruption. *American Economic Review*, 90 (1), 194–211.

Alford, R. P. (2012). A Broken Windows Theory of International Corruption. *Ohio St. LJ*, 73 (5), 1253–1283.

Aliyu, S. U. R., and Elijah, A. O. (2008). Corruption and Economic Growth in Nigeria: 1986–2007. MPRA Paper, 1–20. https://mpra.ub.uni-muenchen.de/12504/ (Erişim Tarihi: 18.12.2018).

Anoruo, E., and Braha, H. (2005). Corruption and Economic Growth: The African Experience. *Journal of Sustainable Development in Africa*, 7 (1), 43–55.

Arvate, P. R., Curi, A. Z., Rocha, F., and Miessi Sanches, F. A. (2010). Corruption and the Size of Government: Causality Tests for OECD and Latin American Countries. *Applied Economics Letters*, 17 (10), 1013–1017.

Baldacci, E., Clements, B., Gupta, S., and Cui, Q. (2008). Social Spending, Human Capital, and Growth in Developing Countries. *World Development*, 36 (8), 1317–1341.

Blackburn, K., Bose, N., and Haque, M. E. (2011). Public Expenditures, Bureaucratic Corruption and Economic Development. The Manchester School, 79(3), 405–428.

Bird, R. M., Martinez-Vazquez, J., and Torgler, B. (2008). Tax Effort in Developing Countries and High Income Countries: The Impact of Corruption, Voice and Accountability. *Economic Analysis and Policy*, 38 (1), 55–71.

Brown, E., and Cloke, J. (2004). Neoliberal Reform, Governance and Corruption in the South: Assessing the International Anti-Corruption Crusade. *Antipode*, 36 (2), 272–294.

Chetwynd, E., Chetwynd, F., and Spector, B. (2003). Corruption and Poverty: A Review of Recent Literature. *Management Systems International*, 600, Water Street, SW Washington, DC 20024 USA, https://pdf.usaid.gov/pdf_docs/PNACW645.pdf (Date of Access: 01.03.2019)

Choi, E., and Woo, J. (2011). Liberal Reform, Political Corruption, and Socio-Economic Impacts in Asia and Eastern Europe. *International Journal of Comparative Sociology*, 52 (3), 181–196.

Chowdhury, F., Desai, S., and Audretsch, D. B. (2018a). Corruption, Entrepreneurship, and Social Welfare A Global Perspective. *Corruption: An Unsolved Puzzle* (pp. 39–51). Springer, Cham.

Chowdhury, F., Desai, S., and Audretsch, D. B. (2018b). Corruption, Entrepreneurship, and Social Welfare: A Global Perspective. *Corruption, Regulatory Regime, and Entrepreneurship* (pp. 53–65). Springer, Cham.

Cooray, A., Dzhumashev, R., and Schneider, F. (2017). How Does Corruption Affect Public Debt? An Empirical Analysis. *World Development, 90*, 115–127.

CPI (2018). Corruption Perceptions Index 2018, https://www.transparency.org/news/feature/cpi_2018_global_analysis (Date of Access: 12.01.2019)

d'Agostino, G., Dunne, J. P., and Pieroni, L. (2016). Government Spending, Corruption and Economic Growth. *World Development*, 84, 190–205.

Delavallade, C. (2006). Corruption and Distribution of Public Spending in Developing Countries. *Journal of Economics and Finance*, *30*(2), 222–239.

Dreher, A., and Schneider, F. (2010). Corruption and the Shadow Economy: An Empirical Analysis. *Public Choice*, 144 (1–2), 215–238.

Dridi, M. (2013). *Corruption and Economic Growth: The Transmission Channels*. Published in: *Journal of Business Studies Quarterly*, 4 121–152

Dridi, M. (2014). Corruption and Education: Empirical Evidence. *International Journal of Economics and Financial Issues*, *4*(3), 476–493.

Dzhumashev, R. (2014). The Two-Way Relationship between Government Spending and Corruption and Its Effects on Economic Growth. *Contemporary Economic Policy*, *32*(2), 403–419.

Dwiputri, I. N., Arsyad, L., and Pradiptyo, R. (2018). *The Corruption-Income Inequality Trap: A Study of Asian Countries* (No. 2018–81). Economics Discussion Papers.

Eren, M., Künü, S. (2018). Yolsuzluk Ve Ekonomik Büyüme İlişkisi: E7 Ülkeleri İçin Bir Uygulama. I. International Iğdir Congress on Multidisciplinary Studies November 6–8 Iğdır-Turkey. Congress Book of Full Texts. İksad Publishing House, 1470–1476.

Gupta, S., Davoodi, H., and Alonso-Terme, R. (2002). Does Corruption Affect Income Inequality and Poverty? *Economics of Governance*, 3(1), 23–45.

Hessami, Z., and Uebelmesser, S. (2016). A Political-Economy Perspective on Social Expenditures: Corruption and In-Kind versus Cash Transfers. *Economics of Governance*, 17 (1), 71–100.

Hillman, A. L. (2004). Corruption and Public Finance: An IMF Perspective. *European Journal of Political Economy*, 20 (4), 1067–1077.

Hira, A. (2016). Broken Windows: Why Culture Matters in Corruption Reform. *Journal of Developing Societies*, *32*(1), 1–16.

Hopkin, J. (2002). States, Markets and Corruption: A Review of Some Recent Literature, *Review of International Political Economy*, 9(3), 574–590.

Jajkowicz, O., and Drobiszová, A. (2015). The Effect of Corruption on Government Expenditure Allocation in OECD Countries. *Acta Universitatis Agriculturae et Silviculturae Mendelianae Brunensis*, 63(4), 1251–1259.

Lewis, M. (2006). Governance and Corruption in Public Health Care Systems. The Center for Global Development. Working Paper Number 78.

Liu, C., and Mikesell, J. L. (2014). The Impact of Public Officials' Corruption on the Size and Allocation of US State Spending. *Public Administration Review*, *74*(3), 346–359.

Mauro, P. (1997). Why Worry About Corruption? Economic Issues (6), International Monetary Fund, USA.

O'Toole, C. M., and Tarp, F. (2014). Corruption and the Efficiency of Capital Investment in Developing Countries. *Journal of International Development*, *26*(5), 567–597.

Tanzi, V. (1999). *Governance, Corruption, and Public Finance: An Overview. Governance, Corruption, and Public Financial Management*. Manila, Philippines: Asian Development Bank, 1–20.

Timofeyev, Y. (2011). How Corruption Affects Social Expenditures: Evidence from Russia. *Global Journal of Business Research*, 5(4), 39–51.

Yazıcı, N. (2018). Hile Üçgeni: Fırsatların Önlenmesinde Kırık Camlar Teorisi. *Üçüncü Sektör Sosyal Ekonomi*, 53(3), 843–851.

Wilson, J. Q. and Kelling, G. L. (1982), Broken Windows, *The Atlantic Monthly*, 249 (3), 29–38.

Bahar Arabaci, M. Engin Sanal and Adil Oguzhan

Working Women's Perceptions of GenderBased Discrimination

1 Introduction

Throughout history, men and women have been compared in many respects, and the resulting differences have been effective in determining the roles to be assumed by women and man in social life. While these roles have been the determinants of the roles, attitudes and behaviors of men and women in social life by the reproduction of these roles in the socialization process and the influence of social conditioning, they have also led to the emergence of the expectation that men and women behave in accordance with traditional gender roles in working life and consequently gender-based discrimination in working life.

In this context, in our study aiming to determine gender-based discrimination practices against working women and women's perceptions in this respect, the literature review on the subject was performed and the case was discussed theoretically, and the study was supported by a quantitative research the sample of which consisted of women working in Bursa Province, in the textile sector in which women are intensely employed in Turkey. According to research results, it was revealed that working women had low perceptions of gender-based discrimination.

1.1 The Concepts of Gender Discrimination and Perception of Gender Discrimination

Although the concept of discrimination was mostly used in the meaning of racism until the 1970s, it is a process of social inequality far beyond it, and in the most basic sense, it refers to the fact that characteristics of some groups become dominant and constitute the basis of discriminatory behaviors (Reskin, 1993: 241). Gender-based discrimination in working life is the unequal distribution of opportunities, resources and rewards because of being a woman or man regardless of employee's competencies or job performance (Kırel, Kocabaş and Özdemir, 2010: 5; Onay, 2009: 1102). Although women's share in employment increased and they were involved in male-dominated jobs, men have been in a more advantageous position than women in labor relations, especially in earnings (Tienda, Smith and Ortiz, 1986: 1). Although labor market in OECD countries made a significant progress in gender equality as a result of the increase in female labor force from the 1960s (Olfert, Moebis, 2006: 45), according to a study covering 15 countries in Europe, discrimination depending especially on atypical employment on business, professional and sectoral basis is still going on although the differences in wages and salaries tend to contract (Petrongolo, 2004: 1-3).

Despite a threefold increase in female labor force and a decrease in discrimination in the labor market from the second half of the twentieth century in the USA, gender-based wage discrimination continues despite decreasing. The two main reasons for this are women's behavioral characteristics such as the influence on their business continuity due to their maternity functions and their preference for part-time jobs, and discrimination (England, 2005: 280). One third of gender-based wage differences at the international level result from gender-based occupational discrimination. The employment of women in low-paid jobs, even if they are qualified, increases women's poverty (Río and Alonso-Villar, 2010: 338). Another dimension of the issue is the instability of the employment of working women. There are two important reasons for this. The first one is that women and men are separated to a certain extent on the issues such as wage and job security; therefore, women are further exposed to occupational discrimination. Secondly, women further go out of labor market, become unemployed and show less mobility among jobs (Frederiksen, 2008:931–932). In this context, discrimination in labor markets has negative consequences such as low wages and low income of women compared to men, failure to benefit from female labor force even if they are qualified, decrease in their ability to adapt to changing conditions of the market, and the fact that gender-based occupational discrimination negatively affects the preferences and education of girls and boys on working areas and decreases efficiency and competitiveness within the global economy (Río and Alonso-Villar, 2010: 338).

Gender discrimination in the workplace occurs both horizontally and vertically. Horizontal discrimination, which is also referred to as glass walls in the literature, occurs in the distribution of jobs between men and women. Vertical discrimination, which is defined as a glass ceiling, refers to the distribution of the hierarchical status between women and men in the work, such as the fact that women are assistants and men are executives (Rotolo and Wilson, 2007: 560). Intentional gender discrimination in the workplace is often associated with the desire to protect privilege, which is also supported by the current literature (Snizek and Neil, 1992: 404). In a study investigating the reasons of gender-based wage differences in the public and private sectors in Australia, gender-based wage differences among low-wage workers can be explained by features related to gender-based productivity independently of sectors, while wage differences faced by more than 50-60 percent of women among high-wage workers cannot be explained. This is related to the presence of glass ceilings (Barón and Cobb-Clark, 2010: 240).

On the other hand, gender-based discrimination in working life can be either direct or indirect. Direct (open) discrimination is explained by the negative conditions and treatment of the employee due to her/his gender (Arısoy, Demir, 2007: 712). Direct discrimination is considered as the privileged treatment of the person of different gender, although the employees have similar characteristics (Demir, 2011: 766). Although there is no exact definition of indirect (implicit) discrimination, it is defined by lawyers as the negative influence on a gender group due to the resulting situation although there is no suspicious incident which would suggest discrimination when it is considered objectively (Arısoy, Demir, 2007: 713).

Different or similar behavior of the working individual due to his/her gender is defined as the perceived gender discrimination (Onay, 2009: 1102). The perceived gender discrimination, which is an individual perception of discriminatory and different treatment of the person, originates from female or male group membership (Foley, Ngo, Loi and Zheng, 2015: 652). It is important for women or men to perceive the discrimination applied against their own gender in order to ensure the quality of working life and organizational peace. Because perceptions may lead to polarization by affecting the behaviors of women or men to the other group (Demir, 2011: 766). In a study investigating the relationship between perceived gender discrimination, individual career success and career anchors among 300 female employees in a large French company, it was determined that there was a negative relationship between perceived gender discrimination and individual career success, however, the relationship between two variables was controlled by career anchors. While anchors such as managerial, technical and life style increase the effect of perceived gender discrimination, anchors such as security and autonomy mitigate this effect (Herrbach and Mignonac, 2012: 25).

There is a significant relationship between perceived gender discrimination and perceived gender bias. When this relationship is considered, individuals' prejudices about gender affect their perception of gender discrimination. Men and women's perceptions of gender discrimination differ in this regard. While men perceive discrimination personally, women consider that they are exposed to discrimination due to social roles attributed to their gender and them (Onay, 2009: 1102–1103). In a study on police officers carried out in Canada, it was determined that there was a difference in perceptions of gender-based discrimination among male and female police officers and that the level of stress in female officials was higher compared to males (Dowler and Arai, 2008: 133). The perception of gender discrimination for women is related to certain outcomes. They stand out as low power, prestige status, high levels of work conflict, increasing depression, low self-confidence and anxiety. The most important difference between gender groups is that women perceive discrimination against their fellow humans, and this prejudice results from the situations faced by sexes in individual decisions and working conditions (Onay, 2009: 1102-1103). In a study carried out among 234 female audit employees working in the public sector in the USA, it was determined that gender-based discrimination was reported at a low level by female employees when female stakeholders are more in number, ethical climate is strong, alternative forms of work are further supported and the welfare of employees is supported by the top management at the highest level. Moreover, it was determined that gender-based discrimination had a low correlation with organizational citizenship behaviors and a high correlation with the desire to win (Dalton, Cohen, Harp and McMillan, 2014: 1).

2 Material and Method

In the study, which was carried out to determine women's perceptions of gender-based discrimination in working life, the sample consisted of women working in the textile industry in Bursa province. The information of the companies operating in Bursa province and the number of employees were obtained through the individual application from Bursa Social Security Institution. In line with the information obtained, it was determined that there were a total of 26,658 employees consisting of 17,597 men and 9,061 women in 488 textile mills that employ ten and more workers. In the study, many workplaces were contacted, 500 questionnaires were distributed, but a total of 220 questionnaires were returned from only 13 workplaces. The data were collected through convenience sampling method with 95 % confidence and 6.5 % error (Çakıcı, Oğuzhan and Özdil; 2015:168).

Z: Confidence interval P: Probability of success q: probability of failure d: Error rate

$$n = \frac{NZ^2pq}{d^2(N-1)+Z^2pq} \quad n = \frac{(8065)1,96^2(0,50)(0,50)}{(0,065)^2(8065-1)+1,96^2(0,50)(0,50)} = 221$$

In the study, a questionnaire form consisting of 34 questions was prepared. 13 out of 34 questions were aimed at determining socio-demographic variables since it was assumed that socio-demographic variables could affect women's perceptions of gender discrimination, and the other 21 questions are related to recruitment, dismissal, charging, promotion/advancement, working conditions and relations with colleagues and managers and the phenomenon of discrimination was applied to women employees due to gender and aimed at determining employees' perceptions of discrimination. In the study, Likert scale was used in questions for measuring the perception of female employees on gender based discrimination in working life. The correlation values between the items in the Likert scale were analyzed, the internal consistency test, *Cronbach's Alpha* (α) was applied, and it was determined that the alpha coefficient obtained as a result of the test was α=0.908 (Altunışık et al., 2005: 115). This also shows that the Likert Scale, which we applied to determine female employees' perceptions of gender discrimination, has a high reliability.

3 Results

3.1 Distribution of Socio-Demographic Characteristics of the Participants

When the age distribution of the participants was analyzed, it was determined that, 38.6 % were between 18 and 28 years old, 37.3 % were between 29 and38 years old, 21.8 % were between 39 and 48 years old and 2.3 % were at the age of 49 and above. While 33.2 % of 220 subjects were primary school graduates, 36.8 % were high school graduates, 15 % had associate's degree and 15.0 % had bachelor's degree and above. While 60 % of the participants were workers, 0.9 % were group heads, 7.7 % were chiefs and 31.4 % were civil servants. Of the participants involved in the questionnaire, it was determined that 65.5 % had 1–19 years working experience, 27.3 % had 11–20 years working experience, 6.4 % had 21–30 years working experience and 0.9 % had 31–40 years working experience. In terms of their distribution according to marital status, it was determined that 65 % were married, 33.2 % were single and 1.8 % were divorced/widowed. Furthermore, it is seen that 74.3 % of the participants involved in the questionnaire had a family income below 2250 TL. It was determined that 77 % of the subjects were in province, district and metropolitan during the upbringing period. When mothers and fathers' educational status was examined, it was determined that 74.6 % of fathers and 81.4 % of mothers of the participants received primary and secondary education or were illiterates.

3.2 Descriptive Statistics of Working Women's Views on Discrimination Scale

The frequency values of the responses of the working women to the Likert scale items on the discrimination scale are presented in Tab. 1.

When descriptive statistics of working women on discrimination scale are examined in Tab. 1, it is seen that the item regarding the fact that gender is an effective factor in the distribution of jobs in the workplace has the highest importance among the items related to discrimination scale. The item regarding the fact that they, as women, cannot receive a recompense for their works in the workplace is on the second rank. The item regarding the fact that men are provided with more wage increases compared to women in the workplace is on the third rank. They were followed by the items regarding the fact that women do not receive the same salary as the male employees who are in the same position and have equal efficiency in the workplace and women do not have equal rights with men in terms of promotion/advancement, and it was revealed that they were among the top five options.

3.3 The Independence of Gender-Based Discrimination Scale from Socio-Demographic Structures of Employees

As a result of the Chi-Square independence test, which was performed to reveal the independence of the gender-based discrimination scale from socio-demographic structures of employees, it was found out that the item regarding the fact that men are primarily preferred in the recruitment of workers in the workplace was not independent of the working women's educational status, place where they lived during the upbringing period and the department worked. The fact that male labor force is preferred to female labor force due to the nature of the work in the department worked is not interpreted as the fact that they are completely discriminated.

It was concluded that the item regarding the fact that when it is required to dismiss workers during economic crisis periods, female employees are primarily dismissed was not independent of the employee's age, working year, number of children and the employment status of her husband. In this case, it is seen that the age and seniority of the working women are important during the periods of economic crisis and that women with children and unemployed husbands are further affected in cases of dismissal.

It was determined that the item regarding the fact that female employees are exposed to negative attitudes and behaviors of male employers in the workplace because they are women was not independent of the working women's seniority,

Tab. 1: Descriptive Statistics of Working Women's on Discrimination Scale

		Strongly agree	Agree	No idea	Disagree	Strongly disagree	Mean	Standard deviation
		(5)	(4)	(3)	(2)	(1)		
	STATEMENTS	f_i						
		% f_i						
X1	In my workplace, men are primarily preferred in the recruitment of workers.	4	21	40	108	47	2.21	0.948
		1.8	9.5	18.2	49.1	21.4		
X2	In my workplace, in the department where I work, men are primarily preferred in the recruitment of workers	2	10	26	120	62	1.95	0.815
		0.9	4.5	11.8	54.5	28.2		
X3	In my workplace, when it is required to dismiss workers for economic crisis or similar reasons, female employees are primarily preferred.	1	17	33	106	63	2.03	0.888
		0.5	7.7	15.0	48.2	28.6		
X4	In my workplace, I am exposed to negative attitudes and behaviors of male employers because I am a woman.	-	6	4	99	111	1.57	0.669
		-	2.7	1.8	450	50.5		
X5	To be a woman leads to the negative attitudes and behaviors of male managers in my workplace.	-	3	9	103	105	1.59	0.638
		-	1.4	4.1	46.8	47.7		
X6	In my workplace, I am exposed to negative attitudes and behaviors of my male colleagues because I am a woman.	-	6	6	99	109	1.59	0.680
		-	2.7	2.7	45.0	49.5		
X7	In my workplace, male employees do not want to communicate with female employees	-	11	21	11	77	1.85	0.790
			5.0	9.5	50.5	35.0		
X8	In my workplace, the working conditions of male employees are easier compared to female employees.	1	10	27	119	63	1.94	0.794
		0.5	4.5	12.3	54.1	28.6		
X9	In my workplace, I have to work more than my male colleagues.	1	4	16	128	71	1.80	0.686
		0.5	1.8	7.3	58.2	32.3		
X10	In my workplace, there is discrimination in determining the working conditions between male and female employees with similar characteristics	5	12	34	106	63	2.05	0.930
		2.3	5.5	15.5	48.2	28.6		

(continued on next page)

Tab. 1: (continued)

		Strongly agree	Agree	No idea	Disagree	Strongly disagree	Mean	Standard deviation
		(5)	(4)	(3)	(2)	(1)		
X11	In my workplace, gender is an effective factor in the distribution of jobs.	7	50	39	72	52	2.49	1.172
		3.2	22.7	17.7	32.7	23.6		
X12	In my workplace, women do not receive the same salary as the male employees who are in the same position and have equal efficiency.	5	22	73	72	48	2.38	1.007
		2.3	10.0	33.2	32.7	21.8		
X13	In my workplace, men are provided with more wage increases compared to women.	8	22	66	81	43	2.41	1.028
		3.6	10.0	30.0	36.8	19.5		
X14	In my workplace, as a woman, I cannot receive a recompense for my works.	17	39	17	99	48	2.45	1.228
		7.7	17.7	7.7	45.0	21.8		
X15	In my workplace, women do not have equal rights with men in terms of promotion/advancement.	6	27	35	108	44	2.29	1.009
		2.7	12.3	15.9	49.1	20.0		
X16	In my workplace, women have to work harder than men to come to a higher position.	4	24	29	109	54	2.16	0.978
		1.8	10.9	13.2	49.5	24.5		
X17	In my workplace, male employees get promoted faster than female employees.	5	23	43	104	45	2.27	0.977
		2.3	10.5	19.5	47.3	20.5		
X18	In my workplace, maternity function prevents promotion/advancement.	3	23	40	107	47	2.22	0.945
		1.4	10.5	18.2	48.6	21.4		
X19	I'm humiliated in my workplace due to my gender.	-	3	2	83	132	1.44	0.590
		-	1.4	0.9	37.7	60.0		
X20	I suffer oppression in my workplace due to my gender.	-	3	3	81	133	1.44	0.597
		-	1.4	1.4	36.8	60.5		
X21	I suffer verbal abuse in my workplace due to my gender.	1	2	1	75	141	1.40	0.599
		0.5	0.9	0.5	34.1	64.1		

employment status of their husband and the place where they lived during the upbringing period. Accordingly, it is seen that working women's perceptions that they are exposed to discrimination in their relations with their employers are significantly affected by the place where they lived during the upbringing period and their seniority. Similarly, it was determined that the fact that working women are exposed to negative attitudes and behaviors of their employers because of gender and their current duty, the number of children they have and the place where they lived during the upbringing period were dependent. There is also dependence between working women's exposure to negative attitudes and behaviors in their relations with their colleagues and the number of children they have and the place where they lived during the upbringing period. Nevertheless, it was revealed that the item regarding the fact that male employees do not want to communicate with female employees was dependent on educational status, number of children and the place where they lived during the upbringing period.

Furthermore, it is seen that there is dependence between women's idea that their conditions are more difficult than men's working conditions and the total working year. It was determined that the perception that working women had to work more than their male colleagues was not independent of the working woman' age, number of children and the department worked. Furthermore, it was observed that the item regarding the fact that there is discrimination between men and women with similar characteristics in the workplace was not independent of the working year, the number of children and the employment status of the working woman's husband. It was determined that there was dependence between the item regarding the fact that gender is an effective factor in the distribution of jobs, one of the items of the gender discrimination scale in working life, and the department worked and total monthly family income.

It was revealed that the women thinking they cannot receive the same salary as the men who are equal with them in the workplace had dependence on working year, number of children and the department worked. Furthermore, it was determined that the item regarding the fact that men are provided with more wage increases in the workplace was not independent of the current duty, working year, number of children and the department worked. Moreover, it is seen that there is dependence between the item regarding the fact that working women cannot receive a recompense for their works and the duty and working year of the working woman.

It is observed that there is dependence between the item regarding the fact that women do not have equal rights with men in terms of promotion in the workplace and the number of children and department worked. There is also dependence between the item regarding the fact that women have to work harder than men to come to a higher position and the working year and total family income. It was found out that the item regarding the fact that male employees get promoted faster than female employees was not independent of the total family income, the number of children and the employment status of the husband. Furthermore, it was revealed that the item regarding the fact that maternity function prevents promotion was dependent on educational status and the number of children.

It is understood that those thinking that they are humiliated in the workplace because of their gender are not independent of the number of children they have and the employment status of their husbands. It was also revealed that there was dependence between those suffering oppression in the workplace due to gender and their current duty, total working year, the number of children, the employment status of their husbands and total monthly family income. Furthermore, it was found out that the item regarding the fact that women suffer verbal abuse in the workplace due to their gender was not independent of the number of children and the employment status of their husbands.

4 Discussion, Conclusion and Recommendations

In the historical process, women and men have been the subject of many comparisons in terms of biological, physiological, genetic and social aspects. The differences obtained as a result of these comparisons led to the emergence of the concept of "social gender" by the shaping of attitudes and behaviors expected of men and women and the reflection of these expectations on various institutions and organizations.

The social gender roles acquired through socialization are the determinants of the attitudes and behaviors of the gender in social life and also effective in working life, along with the influence of social conditioning. In this context, organizational life has been shaped by male-specific roles and attitudes since organizations are usually established and managed by men (Bacacı-Varoğlu, 2001: 323). Accordingly, women are less preferred than men in organizations, and when they are preferred, they have become eligible to work at lower levels than men and in jobs and professions that are appropriate to their gender. This is explained by the concept of discrimination based on gender in working life.

The most important reflection of gender-based discrimination is the separation of jobs as women's jobs/men's jobs. Gender discrimination, which starts with occupational orientation, recruitment and distribution of jobs, is a phenomenon encountered in different periods of working life, such as woman's working as a man's subordinate, imposing glass ceilings in the promotion stage, lower wages than men, women's exposure to psychological and sexual harassment of women by their colleagues and employers who regard women's work as contrary to gender roles, and the fact that women are primarily dismissed due to the widespread opinion that they bring additional income to the family during the periods of economic crisis.

The fact that the employee is evaluated according to his/her gender and subjected to different treatment due to his/her gender regardless of his/her competencies and job performance is an important problem for the organization in terms of ensuring both employee and working welfare.

In this context, in our study aiming to determine gender-based discrimination practices against working women and women's perceptions in this respect, the literature review on the subject was performed and the data obtained related to the subject were tested with an empirical analysis. In line with data obtained, as it is seen in Table 1, it was determined that the women working in Bursa province, who constituted the sample of our study, had low perceptions of gender-based discrimination.

As a result of the studies on the relationship between gender discrimination and the perception of gender discrimination, it is seen that there is a negative relationship between them, supporting the results obtained in our study. For instance, according to the results of a study carried out by Hallock, Hendricks and Broadbent, no strong relationship was found between the perception of gender discrimination and the statistical measures on wage discrimination against women although women perceive gender discrimination quite a lot. In fact, there is a low negative relationship between these two. These results are also supported by the studies of Kuhn (1987) and Hampton and Heywood (1993) (Hallock, Hendricks and Broadbent, 1998: 262). Similarly, the fact that discrimination is usually more perceived if it is applied by men rather than women is also supported by of Krumm and Corning (2008: 1120). These research results show that there is a negative relationship and differences between gender discrimination and perception of gender discrimination. The working women in Turkey are exposed to many discriminatory practices in working life but they have a low level of perception of discrimination. For instance, Rich and Palaz (2008:186) the presence of significant and persistent gender-based wage discrimination since the 1980s was seen in Turkey.. However, in a similar study carried out in Ankara University, it was concluded that the perception of discrimination of employees was low (Ciner, 2003: 160).

Whether this is because especially individuals with low education could not perceive discrimination or even considered it usual as a result of the internalization of traditional gender roles imposed on individuals by social institutions in the process of socialization or because the businesses operating in the textile industry, which is an important branch of textile sector where women are employed intensively due to their natural abilities, improved the working conditions of women due to legislations and organizational policies to ensure operational efficiency is a separate subject of study.

References

Altunisik, R., Coskun, R., Bayraktaroğlu, S., and Yıldırım, E. (2005). *Sosyal Bilimlerde Araştırma Yöntemleri SPSS Uygulamalı*. Sakarya Kitabevi. Sakarya.

Arisoy, İ. A. and Demir, N. (2007). Avrupa Birliği Sosyal Hukukunda Ayrımcılıkla Mücadele Kapsamında Kadın Erkek Eşitliği. *Ege Akademik Bakış Dergisi*, 7(2), 707–725.

Bacaci Varoglu, D. (2001). Örgütsel Yaşamda Toplumsal Cinsiyet Rolleri. Yönetim ve Organizasyon. *Nobel Yayın Dağıtım*. 323–339.

Barón, J. D. and Cobb-Clark, D. A. (2010). Occupational Segregation and the Gender Wage Gap in Private- and Public-Sector Employment: *A Distributional Analysis the Economic Record*, 86(273), 227–246.

Cakıcı, M., Oguzhan, A. and Ozdil, T. (2015). İstatistik. Ekin Yayınları

Ciner, O. (2003). *Halkla İlişkiler Sektöründe Cinsiyete Dayalı Ayrımcılık*. (Ankara Üniversitesi Sosyal Bilimler Enstitüsü Halkla İlişkiler Ve Tanıtım Anabilim Dalı, Yayınlanmamış Yüksek Lisans Tezi)

Dalton, D. W., Cohen, J. R., Harp, N. L. and McMillan J. J. (2014). Antecedents and Consequences of Perceived Gender Discrimination in the Audit Profession. *Auditing: A Journal of Practice and Theory*, 33(3), 1–32.

Demir, M. (2011). İş Yaşamında Ayrımcılık: Turizm Sektörü Örneği. *Uluslararası İnsan Bilimleri Dergisi*, 8(1), 760–784.

Dowler, K. and Arai, B. (2008). Stress, Gender and Policing: The Impact of Perceived Gender Discrimination on Symptoms of Stress. *International Journal of Police Science and Management*, 12(2), 123–135.

England, P. (2005). Gender Inequality in Labor Markets: The Role of Motherhood and Segregation. *Social Politics*, 12(2), 264–288.

Foley, S., Ngo, H., Loi, R. and Zheng X. (2015). Gender, Gender Identification and Perceived Gender Discrimination. *Equality, Diversity and Inclusion: An International Journal*, 34(8), 650–665.

Frederiksen, A. (2008). Gender Differences in Job Seperation Rates and Employment Stability: New Evidence from Employer-Employee Data. *Labour Economics*, 15(5), 915–937.

Hallock, K. F., Hendricks, W. and Broadbent, E. (1998). Discrimination by Gender and Disability Status: Do Worker Perceptions Match Statistical Measures. *Southern Economic Journal*, 65(2), 245–263.

Herrbach, O. and Mignonac, K. (2012). Perceived Gender Discrimination and Women's Subjective Career Success: The Moderating Role of Career Anchors. *Industrial Relations*, 67(1), 25–50.

Kirel, C., Kocabas, F. and Ozdemir, A. A. (2010). İşletmelerde Algılanan Cinsiyet Temelli Ayrımcılık: Eskişehir'de Özel Sektörde Bir Alan Araştırması. *Çimento İşveren Dergisi, Çimento Endüstri İşverenleri Sendikası*, 24(3), 4–15.

Krumm, A. J. and Corning, A. F. (2008). Perceived Control as a Moderator of the Prototype Effect in the Perception of Discrimination. *Journal of Applied Social Psychology*, 38(5), 1109–1126.

Olfert, M. R. and Mobis, D. M. (2006). The Spatial of Gender-Based Occupational Segregation. *The Review of Regional Studies*, 36(1), 44–62.

Onay, M. (2009). Algılanan Cinsiyet Ayrımcılığının Sonuçları ve Konuyla İlgili Ampirik Bir Çalışma. *Ege Akademik Bakış Dergisi*, 9(4), 1101–1125.

Petrongolo, B. (2004). Gender Segregation in Employment Contracts. *Journal of the European Economic Association*, 2(2–3), 331–345.

Reskin, B. (1993). Sex Segregation in the Workplace. *Annual Reviews of Sociology*, 19(1), 241–270.

Rich, J. and Palaz, S. (2008). Why Has Occupational Sex Segregation in Turkey Increased since 1975? *Labour*, 22(1), 185–218.

Río, C. D. and Alonso-Villar, O. (2010). Gender Segregation in the Spanish Labor Market: An Alternative Approach. *Social Indicators Research*, 98(2), 337–362.

Rotolo, T. and Wilson, J. (2007). Sex Segregation in Volunteer Work. *The Sociological Quartely*, 48, 559–585.

Snizek, W. E. and Neil, C. C. (1992). Job Characteristic, Gender Stereotypes and Perceived Gender Discrimination in the Workplace. *Organization Studies*, 13(3), 403–427.

Tienda, M., Smith, S. A. and Ortiz, V. (1986). Industrial Restructuring, Gender Segregation and Sex Differences in Earnings. *CDE Working Paper*, 86–23.

Ugur Saylan

Sister Cities and Tourism: The Case of Turkey

1 Introduction

Tourism is a bridge between countries, regions and cities. This bridge, which has been established by tourism, will be transformed into a stronger structure with the sister city relations of the municipalities. It will also be possible to develop cooperation in the fields of culture and tourism between countries with sister city relations. The aim of this study is to reveal the effects of municipalities on sister city relations and tourism. In the study, firstly, the concept of sister city was explained and information about the relationship between the sister city and tourism was given. Emphasizing the importance of these relations in terms of tourism, the responsibilities of the municipalities were investigated. In addition, the study investigated sister cities of municipalities in Turkey are given information about their current status.

2 Sister City Concept

Sister Cities International states that a sister city, county or state relationship is a broad-based, long-term partnership between two communities in two countries. Sister city organizations can include representatives from nonprofits, municipal governments, the private sector and other civic organizations. Each sister city organization is independent and pursues the activities and thematic areas that are important to them and their community including municipal, business, trade, educational and cultural exchanges and projects with their sister city (Sister Cities International, 2019). Sister City Relations (SCR) is an official partnership established by two cities from different countries. The sister city relationship is conceptualized with various synonyms in the literature and is often referred to by different names such as “town twinning”, “city-to-city partnership” and “friendship cities”. After the Second World War, the concept of sister city was introduced for the first time during the US Eisenhower administration to facilitate mutual understanding and international peace. Nowadays, it is more widely adopted by inland settlements around the world for various purposes such as promoting economic cooperation and local tourism, providing humanitarian assistance and developing political relations. The development of sister city relations is not only a movement driven by globalization, but also an important indicator of urban entrepreneurship. In this process, the city governments not only promote the internationalization of urban governments and policies, but also try to create multi-choice mutual channels for the local community. Prior to the 1980s, those reciprocal channels in sister city relations were mostly built with cultural, social and political purposes. This is particular the case in sister city relations between Europe and Africa involving educational/medical help, and also sister city relations within Anglophone or European countries having similar political settings for policy learning. At the same time, sister city relations now have been more economic-oriented, and local economic development has become a priority, and even an expected result, for sister city relations. Since the 1990s, local governments have become the main initiators of sister city relations and have shown a proactive and spontaneous stance in the development of sister city relations. Sister city programs are used as a strategy to create urban image, establish socio-economic links, attract foreign direct investments and improve international trade. Sister city relations are mostly focused on cities in developed countries, where political systems and cultural roots are similar and whose twinning objectives are different (Liu and Hu, 2018).

In the beginning, sister city relations, based on cultural understanding and peace with citizen diplomacy, are further developed in today's society. Politicians increasingly demand to establish real relations in which local governments are actively involved. A meaningful sister city relationship is an asset for any community and its nation. Economic development is the main motivation tool for establishing a sister city relationship. In order to be successful in sister city relations, an effective public relations campaign is required, which informs communities about a strong policy development, professionalism and opportunities for international connections (Cross, 2010). Although the history of sister city relations does not date back to old times, an increase has been witnessed in their number in recent years. Sister cities provide opportunities to share local government experience, enhance local services, improve economic cooperation, develop tourism and increase intercultural relations and activities. In addition to these opportunities and developments, a process that includes benefits such as the enhancement of local administrative mechanisms and participation of citizen are also targeted (Akman, 2016).

The proposal to become a sister city is usually done through diplomatic channels. It is forwarded to the municipalities through the Ministry of Foreign Affairs or mutual contacts between municipalities are established. In order to be a sister city with any city from abroad, the Municipal Assembly Decision and the Ministry of Interior require approval. The most important issue that is considered in the decision of the Municipal Assembly and the permission of the Ministry of Interior is the equivalence between the cities. It is ideal for cities to be close or equivalent in terms of their importance within the country, their population, economic and commercial status, cultural structure and geographical characteristics (İBB, 2019). It is a project that can be more meaningful after the sister city relationship is established. Some of the programs that can be implemented in this context are as follows (TDBB, 2019):

- Youth and Education,
- Business/Commerce,
- Disaster Management,
- Conflict Resolution,
- Competition,
- Information and Experience Sharing,
- Culture Exchange and Tourism.

3 Sister City and Tourism Relationship

Among the local administrations, municipal administrations have the strongest relations with tourism. All kinds of duties and responsibilities of municipal administrations are closely related to tourism. Considering that tourism provides regional development, tourism policies to be implemented in the region will have positive results such as economic development and job creation. In this context, the sister city relations established with the policies implemented by the municipalities can contribute to the development of regional tourism with a good marketing activity. The studies on the relationship between the sister city and tourism in the literature are examined.

In a study by Liu and Hu (2018), they examined by using the correlation analysis whether Chinese cities are positively related to the number of foreign visitors and the number of international flights in their relations with their sister cities. According to the results of this study, it is determined that China cities, which have more number of sister cities, have an increase and a higher relationship with international direct foreign investment networks, number of international flights and foreign tourists. In addition, it was found in the study that economically developed cities, especially big cities by the sea, tend to develop more sister city relations.

According to Cross (2010), New Zealand's portfolio of sister cities reflects its location on the Pacific Rim and its political/economic positioning as part of Asia. Increasing interest in China as a business place is the same as the need to increase sister city activities. Firm-level engagement with Japan through sister city links is to focus at the consumer level on education and tourism, with some efforts in niche export sectors such as food and beverage.

Carruthers (2006) investigated the sister cities of the People's Republic of China and New Zealand and their effects on tourism. China, which has been isolated from the world stage for a long time, especially after the reforms in the early 1980s, the development of sister cities is seen as the best way to understand different cultures. The results of the study indicate that both New Zealand and Chinese cities believe that sister city relationships can play important roles in fostering tourism growth and are initiators of economic development. Chinese place importance on developing long-term relationships, thus tourism, cultural and educational exchanges are essential in building up a successful relationship that can lead to economic development. In order to achieve the most effective sister city relationship, inter-city cooperation should be provided including tourism marketing, projects and funding.The evaluation of the tourism-related activities of the municipalities within the framework of the sister city can both make them more successful through mutual cooperation and have some gains such as the development of regional tourism from the mutual tourist arrivals and the increase of the revenues of the touristic enterprises due to their relations with the sister cities. In addition, it is possible for the local people to visit the destination of the other sister municipality for tourism purposes and the sister city relationship can serve this purpose.

4 Sister Cities of Municipalities in Turkey

According to the studies on sister cities in Turkey, it is seen that they do not have a very long history. In this context, there is not enough work on what is the concept of sister city and how it should be perceived. It is seen that the studies are handled only with certain aspects of the subject (Geziciand Kocaoğlu, 2018).

Sister cities are seen as a significant means to provide international cooperation among local administrations. In Turkey, it is observed that sister city relationship that began in 1960s has increased considerably after the 2000s. While there were 160 sister city in Turkey until the 2000s, 1.547 sister city relationship were established in 2016 and the number was increased almost ninefold. It is not true to describe these relations only as a numerical increase. In addition to the numerical increase, it is seen that the quality of sister city relationship has changed (Akman, 2016). The following table gives the number of sister cities of cities in Turkey in 2016.

According to Tab. 1 the total number of sister cities of municipalities in Turkey in 2016 is 1547. The majority of international municipal sister city cooperation

Tab. 1: The Number of Sister Cities of Municipalities in Turkey in 2016. Source: Gezici, H. S. and Kocaoğlu, M. (2018). Dünya'da ve Türkiye'de Kardeş Şehir Uygulamaları. Çağdaş Yerel Yönetimler Dergisi, 27 (2), 129–130.

Adana	22	Konya	48
Adiyaman	3	Kutahya	14
Afyonkarahisar	16	Malatya	5
Agri	2	Manisa	21
Amasya	5	Kahramanmaras	5
Ankara	126	Mardin	8
Antalya	82	Mugla	37
Artvin	-	Mus	-
Aydin	21	Nevsehir	13
Balikesir	26	Nigde	6
Bilecik	9	Ordu	4
Bingol	-	Rize	4
Bitlis	1	Sakarya	15
Bolu	8	Samsun	24
Burdur	3	Siirt	-
Bursa	113	Sinop	6
Canakkale	28	Sivas	8
Cankiri	-	Tekirdag	32
Corum	3	Tokat	7
Denizli	16	Trabzon	17
Diyarbakir	2	Tunceli	-
Edirne	26	Sanliurfa	6
Elazig	2	Usak	5
Erzincan	1	Van	2
Erzurum	7	Yozgat	4
Eskisehir	35	Zonguldak	22
Gaziantep	36	Aksaray	-
Giresun	7	Bayburt	-
Gumushane	1	Karaman	1
Hakkari	-	Kirikkale	4
Hatay	6	Batman	-
Isparta	7	Sirnak	1
Mersin	34	Bartin	3
Istanbul	281	Ardahan	1
Izmir	142	Igdir	2

(*continued on next page*)

Tab. 1: (continued)

Kars	4	Yalova	35
Kastamonu	1	Karabuk	5
Kayseri	14	Kilis	2
Kırklareli	25	Osmaniye	4
Kirsehir	11	Duzce	6
Kocaeli	44		
TOTAL		1547	

is concentrated in the metropolitan municipality and their districts. Istanbul ranks first with 281 cooperation. Istanbul Metropolitan Municipality have 53, and the district municipalities of Istanbul have 228 cooperations. After Istanbul, the second city with the most cooperation is Izmir (142). The third city with the most cooperation is Ankara (126). And then Bursa (113) and Antalya (82) have the most cooperation. As of 2016, there are 1397 municipalities in Turkey. Three hundred and ninety two of these municipalities have sister city relations with the municipality of 127 countries. Number of municipalities that established a sister city relationship in 2009 was 317. Despite the double increase in the total number of sister cities, there is no increase in the number of municipalities establishing these relations. It is understood that municipalities, which had established sister city relations before, continued to expand their relationship networks. It is seen that the cooperation activities are mainly made by large scale municipalities which are more developed in terms of capacity and possibility. It is understood that small-scale districts and towns municipalities with limited capacity and facilities are not able to benefit sufficiently from the cooperation activities. Regarding the regional distribution of international municipal cooperation, regional disparities are noteworthy. While Marmara Region is the most collaborative region, it is observed that there are fewer cooperations in the Aegean and Mediterranean regions where tourism activities are intense. The minimum number of cooperation was established by the municipalities in the Eastern and Southeastern Anatolia Regions. As of 2016, Aksaray, Artvin, Batman, Bayburt, Bingol, Cankiri, Hakkari, Mus, Siirt and Tunceli have no sister city relations with any municipality.

International sister city relationship of municipalities in Turkey has spread throughout the world. Twenty seven percent of the sister city relations were with the municipalities of the EU member states. When added, the cities of Balkan countries are 26 percent (formerly Yugoslavia-forming countries, Bulgaria and

Romania) and the cities of other European countries such as Ukraine, Belarus, Norway and Switzerland are 4 percent, more than half of the sister cities of the municipalities in Turkey (%57) are European cities. Sister city relationship established with the Asian continent and established relationships with the Turkic States make up with one quarter of all the sister city relationship in Turkey. The relations with the cities in the Middle East and North Africa are 8 percent (TBB, 2019).

Developing relations between cities in a cultural context will be able to mediate different cultures to each other, to strengthen commercial ties, to contribute to the promotion of tourism and to carry out efficient studies in the exchange of information. As it is not established in the framework of a tangible goal of sister city relationship in Turkey, these relations generally shake hands and stay on the paper after giving the city pennants and some gifts. In the face of changing mayors and lack of leadership, sister city relations are forgotten over time between the municipality's routine workload. When the reasons for the success of the municipalities who are successful in the sister city relationship in Turkey is examined, it is seen that they have the unit responsible from the maintenance of the international relations or have personnel assigned to this subject. These municipalities have staff who speak foreign languages. They also care about archival work (Özcan, 2006).

5 Conclusion

The changes in the demands and needs of the citizens and the responsibilities of the local authorities make the processes of the local city administration difficult. Establishment of sister city relationship and development of tourism will be beneficial in solving these problems in cities. Municipalities have failed to solve some problems in the face of increasing and various responsibilities. At this point, sister cities can play an active role in solving various problems by sharing their experiences. They can also collaborate to solve common problems. They can make some progress not only in solving problems but also in improving the quality of local services, promotion of a place and socio-cultural cooperation. For this reason, it is seen that establishing cooperation between municipalities is important. In addition, one of the most important advantages of the sister city relationship is that it provides municipalities with the opportunity to benefit from the European Union and World Bank funds.

The total number of sister cities of municipalities in Turkey in 2016 was 1547. The majority of the international municipal sister city cooperation is concentrated in the metropolitan municipality and their districts. Regarding the regional distribution of international municipal cooperation, regional disparities are noteworthy. While Marmara Region is the most collaborative region, it is observed that especially the number of cooperations in the Aegean and Mediterranean Regions, where tourism activities are intense, is less.

The benefit expected from the establishment of sister city relations is generally to ensure that different cultures recognize each other, to develop tourism relations, to establish and strengthen commercial relations, to provide information and technology transfer. The establishment and successful implementation of the sister city relations, together with the protection and development of cultural assets and economic development, bring about sectoral development especially in the field of tourism. Moreover, it can be seen that the transformation of tourism movements between cities into income generating activities is directly proportional to the increase in the number of overnights. To increase the number of overnights and tourism revenues, partnerships between municipalities should be established and a common promotional and business division should be made to encourage overnights. In order to increase tourism revenues, joint investments will be possible with a healthy partnership platform between cities.

References

Akman, Ç. (2016). Evaluating the Current Situation via Town Twinning Practices in Turkey. *Journal of Suleyman Demirel University Institute of Social Sciences, CIEP Special Edition*, 1055–1071.

Carruthers, D. (2006). *New Zealand and Chinese Sister Cities and Their Implications for Tourism. Master of Tourism*, University of Otago, New Zealand.

Cross, B. (2010). Sister Cities and Economic Development: A New Zealand Perspective. *Transylvanian Review of Administrative Sciences*, 30, 104–117.

Gezici, H. S. and Kocaoğlu, M. (2018). Dünya'da ve Türkiye'de Kardeş Şehir Uygulamaları. Çağdaş Yerel Yönetimler Dergisi, 27 (2), 113–139.

İBB. (2019, March 13). Istanbul Metropolitan Municipality. https://www.ibb.istanbul/SitePage/Index/151

Liu, H. and Hu, X. (2018). Are 'Sister Cities' from 'Sister Provinces'? An Exploratory Study of Sister City Relations (SCRs) in China. Networks and Spatial Economics, *In Press*, 1–19.

Özcan, Ü. (2006). Yerel Yönetimler Arasında Ortaklıklar ve Kardeş Şehir İlişkileri El Kitabı.

Sister Cities International. (2019, March 13). https://sistercities.org/about-us/what-is-a-sister-city-3/

TBB. (2019, March 13). Union of Municipalities of Turkey. http://www.yereldiplomasi.gov.tr/kardes-sehirler-istatistiki-veriler/

TDBB. (2019, March 13). Union of Turkish World Municipalities. Kardeş Şehir El Kitabı: http://www.tdbb.org.tr/tdbb/wp-content/uploads/2016/01/kardessehirelkitabi.pdf

Figen Taskin

Sustainable Tourism Policy of World Tourism Organization

1 Introduction

The World Tourism Organization (UNWTO) plays a key role in the worldwide dissemination and promotion of sustainable development and sustainable tourism objectives. The UNWTO sets out the problems and objectives of the tourism sector, which is the most important sector of sustainable development in the international system. Sustainable tourism is critical for the future of the world. According to the UNWTO World Tourism Barometer, international tourist arrivals increased by 7 percent to 1.3 billion in 2017 (Dünya Gazetesi, 2017) and are expected to increase by 60 percent by 2020 (the World Counts). Tourism exerts great pressure on natural resources due to excessive consumption, especially in regions where resources are scarce. The tourism industry contributes immensely to environmental pollution and global warming due to greenhouse gas emissions of means of transportation of tourists and goods and energy used for their accommodation (Ştefănică 2017: 87).

Environmental problems and global warming are making their presence feel strongly these days. Therefore, the negative impacts of the tourism sector on the environment should be eliminated or minimized. The UNWTO should continue its efforts to achieve sustainable tourism objectives. This study briefly reviews the sustainable tourism practices that the UNWTO has undertaken since its establishment and highlights the significance of the 2030 Agenda for Sustainable Development and the Berlin Declaration on Transforming Tourism.

The UNWTO is an agency of the United Nations and responsible for the promotion of responsible, sustainable and universally accessible tourism. The aim of the study is to point out the efforts of the UNWTO for the achievement of sustainable tourism objectives. The WTO, a leading international organization in the field of tourism, promotes tourism as the driving force of economic growth, inclusive development and environmental sustainability and promotes the development and dissemination of global knowledge and tourism policies. The study focuses on the efforts of the UNWTO to ensure that sustainable tourism pioneers the management of all resources in such a way that economic, social and aesthetic needs are met while cultural integrity, basic ecological processes, biological diversity and life support systems are preserved, as noted by Lu and Nepal (Göktepe, 2009)..

2 United Nations World Tourism Organization (UNWTO)

The United Nations (UN) was established in the aftermath of the Second World War to establish peace in 1945. According to its Charter, the UN aims to preserve international peace and security, to develop friendly relations among nations based on respect for the principle of equal rights and self-determination of peoples, to cooperate for the solution of international economic, social, cultural and humanitarian problems and to promote respect for fundamental human rights and freedoms and to be a center of harmony among nations to achieve these common objectives. In order to achieve these objectives and solve the problems of humanity, the UN also cooperates with specialized agencies, which are autonomous organizations. All specialized agencies enter into relations with the UN through negotiation agreements. Some of them had already been established before World War I. Some were associated with the League of Nations. Others were established at the same time as the UN. Others were created by the UN to meet arising needs (The United Nations, 2019).

The UN, which aims to solve international problems of economic, social, cultural and humanitarian character, has established an organization for the development of tourism, a sector with economic, social and cultural aspects. The International Union of Official Tourist Publicity Organizations (IUOTPO) had been established in 1934 before the UN. The first International Congress of National Congress of Tourism held in London in 1946 arrived at a decision that a new international non-governmental organization should be established to replace the IUOTPO. The First Constitutive Assembly of the International Union of Official Travel Organizations (IUOTO) was held in 1947 in the Hague and a temporary center was established in London.

The European Travel Commission (ETC), which is the first regional commission within the IUOTO, was established in 1948. Afterwards, regional commissions were established in Africa (1949), Middle East (1951), Central Asia (1956) and the Americas (1957). The IUOTO gained official United Nations advisory status in 1948. After an IUOTO initiative, the UN declared 1967 as the International Tourism Year with the slogan "Tourism, Passport to Peace. " The Intergovernmental Conference held in 1969 in Sofia and the UN General Assembly put pressure for the creation of an intergovernmental organization for independent tourism. The Charter of the WTO was adopted at the

IUOTO Special General Assembly held in Mexico City on September 27, 1970, which has been celebrated as "the World Tourism Day" since then.

The Secretary General of the WTO was established in Madrid on June 1, 1976. An agreement was signed to transform the WTO to an executive body of the United Nations Development Programme (UNDP) that can establish technical cooperation with governments.

The Manila Declaration on World Tourism was adopted at the World Tourism Conference held in Manila in 1980. At the conference, all aspects of tourism were addressed from its dynamic role in the changing world to the responsibilities of states for its development and from environmental protection to making sure that low-income countries benefit economically and socially from it (Esenkal, Cozeli vd., 2016). The very same year, the World Conservation Strategy (WCS) was published. It is a very important document for the historical development of the concept of sustainable development prepared by such organizations as International Union for Natural Resources and Nature Conservation (IUCN) and World Wildlife Fund (WWF) (Bozlağan (2010: 1017).

The Acapulco Document was adopted by the WTO at the World Tourism Conference held on 21 and August 27, 1982, in Acapulco, Mexico, with the participation of seventy-nine state representatives and fifty-seven observers (The World Tourism Organization, 1982). The World Tourism Conference was held to implement the goals set out in the Manila Declaration. It was an important step in the implementation of the concepts, principles and criteria in the Manila Declaration, which has proven useful for states, tourism experts and all other related bodies to realize the importance of changes in administrative and operational approaches to tourism. The conference was primarily focused on how far the goals in Manila were reached. The conference manifesto assessed the current situation of the world and stated that tourism could be a vital force to get rid of chaos. The adaptive power of tourism breaks international intolerance, prejudices and misconceptions and creates an atmosphere of understanding. Therefore, tourism is more vital than ever to improve the quality of life of all people and contribute to the preservation of peace, regardless of religious, socio-economic and political differences. Tourism eliminates the economic gap between developed and developing countries and contributes to the establishment of a new international economic order.. However, the current world order and increasing armed conflicts prevent the development of world tourism. Therefore, state representatives and observers have great responsibilities to establish relationships between countries.

3 Sustainable Development Policy of World Tourism Organization

Sustainable development and environment were discussed for the first time at the UN Stockholm Conference held in 1972 (Ekiztepe, 2016: 34). The concept of sustainable development was discussed and defined in *Our Common Future*, also known as the Brundtland Report.

The Brundtland Report was adopted by the UN General Assembly in 1987. It originates from the Decision of the General Assembly (No: 38/161, Date: December 19, 1983) stipulation that a special commission should be established, including the proposed strategies for sustainable development, to prepare a report on environmental and global issues until 2000 and beyond. The commission then adopted the name of the World Commission on Environment and Development. The decision of the General Assembly also stipulated that the Assembly should use the report of the Special Commission as a basis for the preparation of the *Environmental Perspective to the Year 2000 and Beyond* (The United Nations, 1987).

Article 27 of the Brundtland Report defines the concept of sustainable development as "Humanity has the ability to make development sustainable to ensure that it meets the needs of the present without compromising the ability of future generations to meet their own needs. The concept of sustainable development does imply limits – not absolute limits but limitations imposed by the present state of technology and social organization on environmental resources and by the ability of the biosphere to absorb the effects of human activities. But technology and social organization can be both managed and improved to make way for a new era of economic growth. The Commission believes that widespread poverty is no longer inevitable. Poverty is not only an evil in itself, but sustainable development requires meeting the basic needs of all and extending to all the opportunity to fulfil their aspirations for a better life. A world in which poverty is endemic will always be prone to ecological and other catastrophes."

The Brundtland Report does not address tourism directly. It is, however, recognized that tourism should also be sustainable for sustainable development. Article 24 of Section 3 titled Some Causes of Extinction, in which the word "tourism" is mentioned, states that although Kenya allocated 6 percent of its territory as parks and reserves for tourism, the protected land is subject to pressure from farmers. Article 65 states that such National Conservation Strategies as more promotion of wildlife-based tourism can be an important tool for coordinating conservation and development programs.

The Hague Declaration on Tourism was adopted by the WTO in the Inter-Parliamentary Conference on Tourism, jointly organized by the WTO and the Inter- Parliamentary Union in 1989. The Declaration stated that a pristine nature and a non-degenerated cultural and social environment are essential conditions for the development of tourism. In addition, historical and natural areas, which are the common heritage of humanity, should be protected, and the economic well-being of local populations should be taken into account and their participation in tourism should be encouraged (Esenkal: 575). The Declaration also stated the intrinsic connection between tourism and environment should be considered and effective measures should be taken accordingly. These measures are as follows:

- Domestic and international tourists should be educated to make sure that they preserve and respect the natural, cultural and human environment in places where they visit.
- The integrated planning of tourism development should be promoted based on the concept of "sustainable development" proposed in the Report of the World Commission on Environment and Development (Brundtland Report) and in the report "The Environmental Perspective to the Year 2000 and Beyond" of the United Nations Environment Programme (UNEP) adopted by the UN General Assembly.
- Access to such sites at certain periods should be restricted to respect the carrying capacity levels of sites visited by tourists.
- An inventory of historical, archaeological, artistic, cultural, religious, scientific, social, technical and recreational sites and natural tourists should be compiled.
- Public zoning plans should pay attention to rational use and protection.
- Alternative types of tourism should be developed.
- Tourists should be provided with products and facilities without posing a threat to the social and cultural identity of local populations.
- Public and private sectors should cooperate at national and international level to achieve these objective.

The Declaration refers to the alternative forms of tourism based on resistance to cultural and historical change and respect for and integration with the environment.

The WTO participated in the UN Conference on Environment and Development held in Rio de Janeiro (Brazil) in 1992, where "Agenda 21" was developed. The UN action plan for Agenda consisted of 40 topics and 115 programs. However, the action plan made only a few references to eco-tourism, which focuses on encouraging sustainable development and integrating all social groups to the process. Despite this, tourism was the first sector to pursue the suggestions of Agenda 21 and all commercial sectors had to develop the industrial version of Agenda 21 at the international level. A separate Agenda 21 was published for tourism in 1996. The plan was developed jointly with the WTO, the World Travel and Tourism Council (WTTC) and the World Council (EC) composed of international NGOs established to monitor the recommendations of the Rio Conference.

Agenda 21 plan had 3 general objectives: (1) to establish a system and procedures that implement sustainable development at the international level, (2) to identify measures to ensure sustainability in tourism and (3) to discuss that self-regulation is the most effective strategy for implementing sustainable development in tourism (Aall, 2014: 2569).

2002 was declared the International Year of Ecotourism. The World Ecotourism Summit was held in Quebec, Canada, and the Quebec Declaration on Ecotourism was adopted. Ecotourism was defined at the World Ecotourism Summit as a conservation approach that guarantees the sustainability of natural resources and protects the socio-cultural integrity of local populations while supporting their economic development (Erdoğan, 2014).

The WTO participated in the World Summit on Sustainable Development where the programme Sustainable Tourism – Eliminating Poverty (ST-EP) was held. The final declaration of the Summit made a direct reference to the sustainable development of tourism. The transformation of the WTO into a specialized body of the UN was endorsed by the Assembly (Resolution No: 453 XV) and recognized by the UN General Assembly (Resolution No: A/RES/58/232).

The Sustainable Development Goals were set at the UN Conference on Sustainable Development held in 2012 in Rio de Janeiro. The aim of the Conference was to create a set of universal objectives addressing urgent environmental, political and economic issues. The United Nations adopted the 2030 Agenda for Sustainable Development at a special summit held on September 25, 2015 (Avrupa Birligi Türkiye Delegasyonu, 2019). The Agenda stated "We recognize that social and economic development depends on the sustainable management of our planet's natural resources. We are, therefore, determined to conserve and sustainably use oceans and seas, freshwater resources, as well as forests, mountains and drylands and to protect biodiversity, ecosystems and wildlife. We are also determined to promote sustainable tourism, tackle water scarcity and water pollution, to strengthen cooperation on desertification, dust storms, land degradation and drought and to promote resilience and disaster risk reduction. In this regard, we look forward to COP13 of the Convention on

Biological Diversity to be held in Mexico in 2016." Everybody should be provided with full and productive employment and work to achieve sustainable and inclusive economic growth. Sustainable tourism policies that create jobs and promote local cultures and products should be designed and implemented (The United Nations Sustainable Development Goals Knowledge Platform, 2019). The impact of sustainable tourism on sustainable development should be addressed to encourage local cultures to achieve sustainable consumption and production patterns by 2030.

The UNWTO recognizes that it is responsible for implementing the Sustainable Development Goals to support tourism as a tool for the promotion of global sustainable development and poverty reduction (The United Nations World Tourism Organization, 2019)

More than 30 representative of NGOs, civil society groups and academia from 19 African, Asian, European and Latin American countries launched the Berlin Declaration on Transforming Tourism to improve the vision of the 2030 Agenda for Sustainable Development between March 3 and 6, 2017. They also expressed their concern about the current tourism model failing to meet the standards set forth by 2030 Agenda for a fair, inclusive and egalitarian world transformation.

A special session was held on October 3 at the 2018 WTO Public Forum to shed more light on developments in the tourism sector. The innovation and digital transformation for sustainable and inclusive tourism session held by the WTTC, UNWTO, International Trade Center (ITC) and World Trade Organization (WTO) had a high-level panel of speakers who addressed how degeneration could be prevented and how the global tourism industry could be maintained. They highlighted the significance of global cooperation for trade and tourism and encouraged the greater participation of the tourism sector in trade policy.

Tourism is the third largest sector in international trade, constituting 10.4 % of global gross domestic product (GDP) and providing employment to 313 million people worldwide, and therefore, plays a critical role in achieving the Sustainable Development Goals (The United Nations World Tourism Organization 2018). As the World Trade Organization People Forum was held in 2018, this common communication aims to highlight the significance of tourism and the critical role that the WTO plays in ensuring the seamless and foreseeable functioning of trade, including the tourism sector.

According to the WTTC, the G20 countries invested in biometrics and new airport infrastructure to make existing terminal facilities and processes more efficient, safe and free of problems, and created 7 to 19 million new jobs. Moreover, travel and tourism grew by 4.6 % in 2017, which is one and a half times the growth rate of the world economy, and it is predicted that it will continue to exceed the growth rate of the world economy.

According to the main theme of Trade 2030, the 2018 subthemes of the WTO Public Forum are sustainable trade, technology-efficient trade and a more comprehensive trading system. According to the UNWTO Tourism Towards 2030 long-term outlook, international tourist arrivals worldwide will increase by 3.3 % by 2030 and that this increase will contribute to emerging economies. The market share of emerging economies, which increased from 30 % in 1980 to 45 % in 2016, is expected to reach 57 % in 2030, equivalent to more than 1 billion international tourists.

4 Conclusion

On September 27, 1970, the World Tourism Organization adopted the notion of organizing tourism and using it as a means to integrate people all over the world. An agreement was signed for WTO to become an executive body of the United Nations Development Programme (UNDP) and to cooperate with governments. Following this development, it was decided that the WTO was to conduct research to contribute to the establishment of a new international economic order that will eliminate the economic gap between developed and developing countries through tourism.

The Brundtland Report, drawn after the UN Stockholm Conference held in 1972 and adopted by the UN General Assembly in 1987, discussed and defined the concept of sustainable development. Nevertheless, there was no recognition of and regulation on the fact that tourism should be sustainable for sustainable development.

In the United Nations Conference on Environment and Development held in Rio de Janeiro (Brazil), where "Agenda 21" was developed , eco-tourism was addressed only a few times to encourage all groups in society to participate in thematic breadth and sustainable development. Despite lack of attention, tourism was the first sector to follow the recommendations of Agenda 21, and all commercial sectors had to develop the industrial version of Agenda 21 at the international level. A separate Agenda 21 for tourism was published in 1996.

The WTO participated in the World Summit on Sustainable Development where the programme Sustainable Tourism – Eliminating Poverty (ST-EP) was held. The Sustainable Development Goals were set at the UN Conference on Sustainable Development held in 2012 in Rio de Janeiro. The United Nations adopted the 2030 Agenda for Sustainable Development at a special summit held on September 25, 2015. The Agenda stated, "We are determined to promote sustainable tourism, tackle water scarcity and water pollution, to strengthen cooperation on desertification, dust storms, land degradation and drought and to promote resilience and disaster risk reduction." Sustainable tourism policies will be designed and implemented to achieve sustainable consumption and production patterns by 2030 in order to promote local cultures and products for sustainable development of tourism and to provide everybody with full and productive employment.

A special session was held at the WTO's 2018 Public Forum on October 3 to shed more light on developments in the tourism sector. A special session was held on October 3 at the 2018 WTO Public Forum to shed more light on developments in the tourism sector. "The innovation and digital transformation for sustainable and inclusive tourism" session held by the WTTC, UNWTO, International Trade Center (ITC) and World Trade Organization (WTO) had a high-level panel of speakers. As a result of all these efforts, tourism, which is the third largest sector in international trade, constituting 10.4 % of global gross domestic product (GDP) and providing employment to 313 million people worldwide, has made significant contributions to the realization of the Sustainable Development Goals.

References

Aall, Carlo. (2014). Sustainable Tourism in Practice: Promoting or Perverting the Quest for a Sustainable Development? *Sustainability*. 6, 2562–2583. Retrieved online March, 5, 2019.

Avrupa Birliği Türkiye Delegasyonu (2015). AB, 2030 Sürdürülebilir Kalkınma Gündeminin BM tarafından kabulünü memnuniyetle karşılıyor. Retrieved online March, 5, 2019.

Bozlağan, Recep (2010). Sürdürülebilir Gelişme Düşüncesinin Tarihsel Arka Planı. *Sosyal Siyaset Konferansları Dergisi*, (50), 1011–1028

Development and International Economic Co-operation (1987). Environment, Report of the World Commission on Environment and Development. Retrieved online March, 2, 2019.

Dünya Gazetesi (2017). Küresel turist sayısı 2017'de 1,3 milyar kişiye ulaştı. Retrieved online March, 3, 2019.

Ekiztepe, Burçak Akıncı (2016). Sürdürülebilir Kalkınma ve Gelişim Süreci. Hüseyin Çeken, Sürdürülebilir Turizm (Temel Kavramlar ve İlkeler) (27–54). Ankara: Detay Yayıncılık.

Erdoğan, Nazmiye (2014). Turizm, Çevre ve Sürdürülebilirlik. Reyhan Hakan vd., Sosyal Çevre Bilimleri (143–185). Edition: 1, Ankara: Siyasal Kitabevi.

Esenkal Çözeli, Füsun, Bal, Kürşat, Tümen, Nazlı, Yaşar, İrfan, Aydemir, Burhan (2016). Uluslararası Turizm Anlaşmalarının Dayandığı Uluslararası Temel Belgeler (Sözleşmeler). Murat Doğdubay, 15. Geleneksel Turizm Sempozyumu Bildiriler Kitabı (563–581), Ankara: Detay Yayıncılık.

Göktepe, Sevgi (2009). Alternatif Turizm Kavramı. Retrieved online March, 5, 2019.

Ştefănică, M. (2017). Environmental Impact of Transportation in the Tourism Industry – Dimensions and Actions. Studies and Scientific Researches. Economics Edition, 25, 84–89.

The United Nations (1987). Environmental Perspective to the Year 2000 and Beyond. Retrieved online February, 23, 2019.

The United Nations (2019). Funds, Programmes, Specialized Agencies and Others. Retrieved online February, 23, 2019.

The United Nations Sustainable Development Goals Knowledge Platform (2019). Transforming our world: the 2030 Agenda for Sustainable Development. Retrieved online February, 23, 2019.

The United Nations World Tourism Organization (2018). Tourism and the Sustainable Development Goals – Journey to 2030. Retrieved online February, 23, 2019.

The United Nations World Tourism Organization (2019). Who we are? Retrieved online February, 23, 2019.

The World Counts (2019). The Negative Environmental Impacts of Tourism. Retrieved online March, 19, 2019.

The World Tourism Organization (1982). Acapulco Document. Retrieved online February, 23, 2019.

Selim Tuzunturk

The Probabilistic View of the Impact of Past Experience on Intention to Purchase in White Goods

1 Literature

Longman English Dictionary (1987) defines *experience* as (i) the gaining of knowledge or skill which comes from practice in an activity or doing something for a long time. It is the fact or state of having been affected by or gained knowledge through direct observation or participation (Merriam-Webster, 2019). People's expectations are set in part by their previous experiences (Schwager and Meyer, 2007). *Product experiences* occur when consumers interact with products (Brakus et al., 2009: 52). The *customer experience* originates from a set of interactions between a customer and a product, a company, or part of its organization, which provoke a reaction (Gentile et al., 2007: 397). Every company provides a customer experience which may be good, bad or indifferent (Richardson, 2010). This customer experience is the internal and subjective responses of customers which come out of any direct or indirect contacts[1] of customers with companies (Schwager and Meyer, 2007). Brand-related stimuli, such as brand design and identity (e.g., name and logo), packaging, and marketing communications (e.g., advertisements and brochures), and environments (e.g., stores) constitute the major source of subjective, internal consumer responses, which is referred to as brand experience (Brakus et al., 2009: 53).

Customer experience encompasses every aspect of a company's offering the quality of customer care, of course, but also advertising, packaging, product and service features, ease of use and reliability (Schwager and Meyer, 2007). The *experience factor* plays an important role in determining the *success of a company* such that business must focus on the customer experience (Yang and He, 2011: 6738). A successful brand shapes customers' experiences by embedding the fundamental value proposition in the offerings' every feature (Schwager and Meyer, 2007). Successful products involve customers' senses, emotions,

1 Direct contacts such as purchasing and using a product and also contacting with the service facilities of the product. Indirect contacts such as word-of-mouth recommendations or criticisms of people around us, advertising activities of the products, and new reports or reviews about the products.

thoughts, acts, values and relations in different ways (Gentile et al., 2007: 404). Richardson (2010) states that to be a really successful company on a long-term basis customer experience needs to be seen. Ultimately, *customer experience management*, which is the collection of processes that a company needs to be tracked and organized. Every interaction between a customer and the company through the customer lifecycle needs to be taken into consideration. The following table (Schwager and Meyer, 2007) represents the customer experience management in the context of subject matter, timing, monitoring, audience and purpose:

Tab. 1: Customer Experience Management (CEM). **Source:** Schwager and Meyer (2007).

What	When	How Monitored	Who Uses the Information	Relevance to Future Performance
Captures and distributes what a customer thinks about company.	At points of customer interaction: "touch points".	Surveys, targeted studies, observational studies, "voice of customer" research.	Business or functional leaders, in order to create fulfillable expectations and better experiences with products and services.	Leading: Locates places to add offerings in the gaps between expectations and experience.

Purchase intention refers to a plan to purchase an exacting good or service in the future (Rizwan et al., 2014: 58). It has an aspect that the consumer will purchase a product after evaluation (Younus et al., 2015: 2). In simplest of terms, purchase intention is the likelihood of a customer buying the same product again based on their purchase history, or it can also be the need of a product which is driving the customer toward a purchase (Bhasin, 2018). The greater the purchase intention is, the greater a consumer's desire is to buy a product (Nasermoadeli et al., 2013: 128). Bhasin (2018) stresses the significance of purchase intention with the following sentences below:

> *"Purchase intention is one favorable factor that can ensure the long life of any business. As long as the customers want to buy your products, irrespective of the availability of similar products in the market, you can stay alive with steady growth."*

Customer purchase intention serves as an early indication of the sales of the final products (Pandey and Srivastava, 2016: 55). The purchase intention is an effective tool to predict the buying process (Mirabi, et al. 2015: 268). For a seller or a business, purchase intention is something that will affect their sales very much (Bhasin, 2018). Marketing managers use purchase intentions (i) as a leading indicator of future demand[2] for their products, (ii) to assess how their marketing actions will impact those future sales and (iii) in some cases, to measure consumer demand for new products using concept and product tests (Morwitz, 2012: 181).

Obviously, the customer will have their own ideas or their own previous experience on what they want to purchase (Bhasin, 2018). Customer experience plays a fundamental role in determining the customers' preferences, which then influence their *purchase decisions* (Yang and He, 2011: 6740). Customer experience has been used as a base to predict the customer purchase intention (Nasermoadeli et al., 2013: 128). Some recent studies that investigate the proposed relation are as follows: Yang and He (2011) investigated the relationship between the dimensions of the customer experience and purchase intention in a retail context. Researchers found that two of the dimensions have a positive direct effect on purchase intentions and one dimension has an indirect impact on purchase intentions. Kim and Chung (2011) found that past experiences have a positive impact on purchase intention with organic products. Lee et al. (2013) found that consumer intentions to purchase athletic team merchandise are significantly associated with personal values, team identification, brand/product attitude, product attributes, expectancy, previous purchase and satisfaction. Mohmed et al. (2013) investigated three factors (trust, past experience and social presence) that may have relationships with the intention to purchase in e-commerce. Researchers found that all three factors have strong and positive correlation with buyers' intentions and purchasing behaviors. Nasermoadeli et al. (2013) investigated the relationship between the dimensions of the customer experience in the process of going to the cinema, watching the movie at the cinema, the purchase intention and found a positive relationship between them. Rizwan et al. (2014) investigated the effect of image, low price, past experience, brand attachment and product awareness on customer purchase intention in Levi's jeans buyers. The regression analysis of this research showed that past experience had a significant positive relationship with purchase intention. Rasheed et al. (2014) found a significant relationship between past experience and purchase intention in counterfeit mobile phones. Ghouri et al. (2017) found that purchase orientation, prior online purchase experience and online trust

---

2 Purchase intentions are one of the primary inputs that marketing managers use to forecast future sales (Morwitz, 2012: 181).

have positive effect on the customer purchase intention in online shopping. Song et al. (2017) determined that the past experience exerted a strong influence on consumers' purchase intention toward traceable beef.

In the context of the above literature that indicates the positive relationship between the past experience and purchase intention, one of the purposes of this chapter is to find out the stated relationship in white goods market. The other purpose of this chapter is to discover the customer experience and purchase intention relation in a probabilistic manner. By doing so, it is aimed to look at customer experience and purchase intention relation from a different stand point.

2 Research Design and Methodology

The target population of this study is the *Generation X population* born between 1965 and 1980 in Bursa, Turkey, and who bought white goods from the brand VESTEL, which was established in 1997. The VESTEL brand is a domestic product of Turkey. The common characteristics of Generation X are as follows (Kane, 2018): (i) being individualistic (independent, resourceful and self-sufficient), (ii) being flexible (adopt well to change), (iii) having balanced values of work and life (appreciate fun in the workplace and espouse a work hard/play hard mentality) and (iv) technologically adept (comfortable with PDAs, smartphones, email, laptops, tablets and other technology employed in the legal workplace).

Convenience sampling method was used, which is a nonprobability sampling method and useful in small-scale, exploratory studies where one wishes simply to gain greater familiarity with the population (Weiers, 2002: 146). A face-to-face survey method was used in the collection of data. The number of people that were surveyed and survey information gathered was 205 individuals.

The purpose of this study is investigating the impact of the past experiences of Generation X sample in white goods of VESTEL brand in Bursa on their purchase intentions. And, the other purpose is exploring the probabilistic consequences of the stated relationship. In the context of these objectives, the following *research questions* (RQ) were determined:

RQ1: Does the past experience of Generation X in white goods of VESTEL brand have effect on their purchase intention to white goods of VESTEL brand?

RQ2: Is there a risk in the purchase intention of Generation X in white goods of VESTEL brand?

RQ3: What are the probabilities of not having a purchase intention of the customers who are pleased and who are not pleased with white goods of VESTEL brand?

The binary logistic regression model[3] was used to investigate the proposed relationship between the past experiences of Generation X sample in the purchase of white goods of VESTEL brand in Bursa on their purchase intentions. In this study, the dependent (intention to purchase) and independent (past experience) variable of the binary logistic regression model is dichotomous. Past experience variable is identified as "PAST_EXP", and the intention to purchase is identified as "NEW_INT". Past experience has two categories: "0" represents the customers who are pleased with the purchase of white goods of VESTEL brand and "1" represents the customers who are not pleased with the purchase of white goods of VESTEL brand. Purchase intention has two categories: "0" represents the customers have a purchase intention to buy VESTEL brand white goods and "1" represents the customers don't have a purchase intention to buy VESTEL brand white goods. SPSS package program was used in the analysis of the stated relationship.

3 Research Findings

The following three tables show, respectively, the frequency distributions of qualitative demographic variables, the descriptive statistics of quantitative demographic variable and the cross tabulation of the past experience and intention to purchase variables:

Tab. 2: Frequency Distributions of Qualitative Demographic Variables

Variable	Category	Frequency	Percent
Gender	Female	102	49.8
	Male	103	50.2
	Total	205	100.0
Monthly Income	0–1000 Tl.	16	7.8
	1000–1400 TL.	22	10.7
	1400–4500 TL.	135	65.9
	4500 TL and More	32	15.6
	Total	205	100.0
Education Level	Primary	37	18.0
	Secondary	128	62.4
	Higher	40	19.5
	Total	205	100.0

3 See Hosmer et al. (2013), Hilbe (2015), Pampel (2000), Kleinbaum and Klein (2010), Hilbe (2009).

Tab. 3: Descriptive Statistics of Quantitative Demographic Variable

Statistics Variable	**Mean**	**Mode**	**Minimum**	**Maximum**
Age	45,86	47	39	54

Tab. 4: Cross Tabulation of the Past Experience and the Intention to Purchase Variables

		NEW_INT		**Total**
		Yes	**No**	
PAST_EXP	Yes	64	58	122
	No	27	56	83
Total		91	114	**205**

As is seen in Tab. 2, the sample consists of 205 respondents, of which 49.8 % are female and 50.2 % are male. Most of the respondents' monthly income in the sample is between 1,400 and 4,500 Turkish Liras. And, most of the respondents' education level in the sample is of secondary education level.

As is seen in Tab. 3, the sample mean of age is 45; minimum is 39, maximum is 54.

As is seen in Tab. 4, while 122 respondents are pleased with white goods of VESTEL brand, 83 respondents are not. While 91 respondents declared that they have a purchase intention to buy VESTEL brand white goods in the next six months, 114 respondents do not.

Sixty-four respondents who are pleased with white goods of VESTEL brand declared that they have a purchase intention to buy VESTEL brand white goods in the next six months. Fifty-eight respondents who are pleased with white goods of VESTEL brand declared that they don't have a purchase intention to buy VESTEL brand white goods in the next six months. Twenty-seven respondents who are not pleased with white goods of VESTEL brand declared that they have a purchase intention to buy VESTEL brand white goods in the next six months. Fifty-six respondents who are not pleased with white goods of VESTEL brand declared that they don't have a purchase intention to buy VESTEL brand white goods in the next six months. The rest of the tables below are the results of the binary logistic regression model estimates.

As is seen in Tab. 5, the overall percentage shows that in 55.6 % of the cases are correctly classified when there is no variable in the equation (Block 0: Beginning Block).

Tab. 5: Classification Table (Block 0: Beginning Block)

Observed		**Predicted NEW_INT**		**Total**
		Yes	**No**	
NEW_INT	Yes	0	91	0.0
	No	0	114	100.0
Total				**55.6**

Tab. 6: Omnibus Tests of Model Coefficients

	Chi-Square	**df**	**p-value**
Step 1 Step	8.059	1	0.005
Block	8.059	1	0.005
Model	8.059	1	0.005

Tab. 7: Model Summary

Step	**-2 Log likelihood**	**Cox and Snell R Square**	**Nargelkerke R Square**
1	273.546	0.039	0.052

Tab. 6 represents the Omnibus Test results. The null hypothesis is "H_0: There is no difference between Block 1 and Block 0" tested versus the alternative hypothesis of "H_1: There is a difference between Block 1 and Block 0" in Omnibus Test[4]. Null hypothesis is rejected (p-value=0.005 < α=0.05). There is a difference between Block 1 and Block 0, which means that at least one variable is significant.

Tab. 7 represents the coefficient of determination (R Square) which is interpreted as the proportion of variance in the dependent variable that is predicted from the independent variable. The proportion of variance explained[5] in intention to purchase by past experience is 3 % and 5 %.

4 Block 1 has the meaning for the variable is in the equation in.

5 As is expected, the proportion is low. Because of the stated aim of this research that is to detect the relationship between past experience and purchase intention, the other variables such as demographic, price and so forth that may have effect on purchase intention left out the analysis.

Tab. 8: Hosmer and Lemeshow Test

Step	Chi-Square	df	p-value
1	0.000	0	1

Tab. 9: Classification Table (Block 1)

Observed		Predicted NEW_INT		Percentage Correct
		Yes	**No**	
NEW_INT	Yes	64	27	70.3
	No	58	56	49.1
Overall Percentage				**58.5**

Tab. 10: Binary Logistic Regression Results

							95 % C.I. for EXP(B)	
	B	**S.E.**	**Wald**	**df**	**p-value**	**Exp(B)**	**Lower**	**Upper**
Step 1	0.828	0.296	7.811	1	0.005	2.289	1.281	4.090
PAST_EXP	-0.098	0.181	0.295	1	0.587	0.906		
Constant								

Tab. 8 shows the Hosmer and Lemeshow Test results. The null hypothesis is "H_0: There is no difference between predicted values and observed values" tested versus the alternative hypothesis of "H_1: There is a difference between predicted values and observed values" in Hosmer and Lemeshow Test. Null hypothesis is not rejected (p-value=1 ≥ α=0.05). There is no difference between predicted values and observed values, which means that the data fit the model well.

As is seen in Tab. 9, the overall percentage shows that in 58.5 % of the cases correctly classified while there is a variable in the equation.

Tab. 10 shows the binary logistic regression results. The null hypothesis is "H_0: PAST_EXP variables coefficient is equal to zero" tested versus the alternative hypothesis of "H_1: PAST_EXP variables coefficient is not equal to zero". Because the p-value is less than α value (p-value=0.005 < α=0.05), null hypothesis is rejected, which means that PAST_EXP variable is statistically significant. So, past experience of Generation X in white goods of VESTEL brand have effect on their purchase intention of white goods of VESTEL brand. Odds ratio or Exp (B) in the equation is 2.289. It means the exponentiated value of the coefficient B results in the odds ratio for past experience ($e^B = e^{0.828} = 2.289$) and it can be calculated by using Tab. 3 as well as $\left(\frac{56/27}{58/64} = \frac{2.074}{0.9062} = 2.289\right)$. This implies that the odds being admitted of not having a purchase intention to buy VESTEL brand white goods for the customers who are not pleased with white goods of VESTEL brand is 2.289 times that of the customers who are pleased. The risk of not having a purchase intention for the customers who are not pleased is 2.289 times that of the customers who are pleased.

$$P(Y = 1 \mid X = x) = \frac{1}{1 + e^{-(\beta_0 + \beta_1 x)}}$$

$$P(Y = 1 \mid X = x) = \frac{1}{1 + e^{-(-0.098 + 0.828\ x)}}$$

$$P(Y = 1 \mid X = x) = \frac{1}{1 + e^{-(-0.098 + 0.828\ (1))}} = 0.67470$$

The probability of not having a purchase intention of the customer who is not pleased with white goods of VESTEL brand is 0.67470.

$$P(Y = 1 \mid X = x) = \frac{1}{1 + e^{-(-0.098 + 0.828\ (0))}} = 0.47541$$

The probability of not having a purchase intention of the customer who is pleased with white goods of VESTEL brand is 0.47541.

4 Results

Customer experience is a factor that is directly related to the success of a company. It plays a fundamental role in determining the customers' future purchase behavior. It has been used as a base to predict the customer purchase intention, which affects product sales of companies very much. Depending on the research questions following research results are obtained:

- Past experience of Generation X in white goods of VESTEL brand have effect on their purchase intention of white goods of VESTEL brand.
- The risk of not having a purchase intention for the customers who are not pleased is 2.289 times that of the customers who are pleased.

- The probability of not having a purchase intention of the customer who is not pleased with white goods of VESTEL brand is 0.67470. The probability of not having a purchase intention of the customer who is pleased with white goods of VESTEL brand is 0.47541.

For white goods of VESTEL brand success on a long-term basis, managers of the company should focus on the customer experiences deeply. In this way, as they improve their customer experience, they may use it as a competitive differentiator in the white goods sector.

The independent variables such as demographic variables, price, trust, value and so forth can be used for further studies.

References

Bhasin, H. (2018). What Is Purchase intention? *Marketing Management Articles, Retrieved online March* 5, 2019.

Brakus, J. J., Schmitt, B. H. and Zarantonello, L. (2009). Brand Experience: What Is It? How Is It Measured? Does It Affect Loyalty? *Journal of Marketing*, 73, 52–68.

Gentile, C., Spiller, N. and Noci, G. (2007). How to Sustain the Customer Experience: An Overview of Experience Components that Co-Create Value with the Customer, *European Management Journal*, 25(5), 395–410.

Hilbe, J. M. (2009). *Logistic Regression Models*, New York, USA: CRC Press.

Hilbe, J. M. (2015). *Practical Guide to Logistic Regression*, New York, USA: CRC Press.

Hosmer, D. W., Lemeshow, S. and Sturdivant, R. X. (2013). *Applied Logistic Regression*, New Jersey, USA: John Wiley and Sons.

Kane, S. (2018). The Common Characteristics of Generation X Professionals, *Retrieved online March 15*, 2019.

Kim, H. Y. and Chung, J. E. (2011). Consumer Purchase Intention for Organic Personal Care Products, *Journal of Consumer Marketing*, 28 (1), 40–47.

Kleinbaum, D. G. and Klein, M. (2010). *Logistic Regression a Self-Learning Text*, New York, USA: Springer.

Lee, D., Trail, G. T., Lee, C. and Schoenstedt, L. J. (2013). Exploring Factors That Affect Purchase Intention of Athletic Team Merchandise, *ICHPER-SD Journal of Research*, 8(1), 40–49.

Longman Dictionary of Contemporary English. (1987). Essex. England: Pearson Longman.

Merriam-Webster, Dictionary of English, *Retrieved online March, 5*, 2019.

Mirabi, V., Akbariyeh, H. and Tahmasebifard, H. (2015). A Study of Factors Affecting on Customers Purchase Intention, *Journal of Multidisciplinary Engineering Science and Technology*, 2(1), 267–273.

Mohmed, A. S. I., Azizan, N. B. and Jali, M. Z. (2013). The Impact of Trust and Past Experience on Intention to Purchase in E-Commerce, *International Journal of Engineering Research and Development*, 7(10), 28–35.

Morwitz, V. (2012). Consumers' Purchase Intentions and their Behavior, *Foundations and Trends in Marketing*, 7(3), 181–230.

Nasermoadeli, A., Ling K. C. and Maghnati, F. (2013). Evaluating the Impacts of Customer Experience on Purchase Intention, *International Journal of Business and Management, 8(6),* 128–138.

Pandey, S. and Srivastava, S. (2016). Antecedents of Customer Purchase Intention, *Journal of Business and Management, 18*(10*),* 55–82.

Pampel, F. C. (2000). *Logistic Regression a Primer*, California, USA: Sage Publications.

Rasheed, A., Farhan, M., Zahid, M. Javed, N. and Rizwan M. (2014). Customer's Purchase Intention of Counterfeit Mobile Phones in Pakistan. *Journal of Public Administration and Governance*, 4(3), 39–56.

Richardson, A. (2010). Understanding Customer Experience, *Harvard Business Review, Retrieved online March 10*, 2019.

Rizwan, M., Quayyum, M., Qadeer, W., and Javed, M. (2014). The Impact of Branded Product on Consumer Purchase, *Journal of Public Administration and Governance*, 4(3), 57–74.

Schwager, A. and Meyer, C. (2007). Understanding Customer Experience, *Harvard Business Review, Retrieved online March 10*, 2019.

Song, H., Wang, R. and Hu, Y. (2017). Consumers' Purchase Intentions toward Traceable Beef-Evidence from Beijing China, *American Journal of Industrial and Business Management*, 7, 1128–1135.

Weiers, R. M. (2002). *Introduction to Business Statistics*, USA: Duxbury Press.

Yang, Z. Y. and He, L. Y. (2011). Goal, Customer Experience and Purchase Intention in a Retail Context in China: An Empirical Study, *African Journal of Business Management*, 5(16), 6738–3746.

Younus, S., Rasheed, F. and Zia, A. (2015). Identifying the Factors Affecting Customer Purchase Intention, *Global Journal of Management and Business Research: An Administration and Management*, 15(2), 1–6.

Dilek Kayakiran

Analysis and Comparison of Business Merger and Acquisition Transactions in Turkey and in the World[1]

1 Introduction

The purposes of businesses are to protect their assets, to protect their shareholders, to earn a profit, to minimize the risks of the business, to raise the market value of the business and to grow. Businesses can grow in two ways. One of them is internal growth and the other one is external growth. In internal growth, the business uses its own resources and grows through the investment and financial policies, while in external growth, it grows through mergers. Growth through merger is more effective than internal growth (Gaughan, 2011).

In this study, the concept of merger, the reasons for merger and the types of merger were explained, and it was attempted to analyze merger and acquisition transactions taking place in Turkey and in the world in 2005–2018, to interpret the findings obtained and to determine whether business mergers in Turkey followed a parallel trend with the worldwide.

2 Business Mergers

Merger refers to the fact that more than one businesses come together and continue their existence as a single business (Gaughan, 2011). The fact that businesses are combined with one another or establish another entity with a legal entity or one or several of them join the other business is merger (Ataman, 2000). Business merger is a transaction or event in which an acquirer business takes control of one or more businesses (Gökçen et al., 2011). With general definition, business mergers are transactions in which two businesses are merged within the business that has proposed merger for the agenda, the second business, which is known as the acquired business, is liquidated and all assets and liabilities are incorporated into the balance sheet of the merged business (Sarıkamış, 2003).

---

1 This article is derived from the dissertation "The Effect of Company Mergers on Company's Market Value and a Research"prepared by Dilek Kayakıran under supervision of Prof. Dr. Barış Sipahi.

Business mergers show how growth takes place. Therefore, the reasons causing businesses to grow are also among the reasons for business mergers. Some of the reasons for business mergers are as follows: benefiting from low cost of capital, tax advantages, increased free cash flows (Bühner, 1991), getting get rid of the effect of market stagnation on the business, providing time advantage compared to inward investment projects, gaining advantage by the acquisition of low valued businesses (Koegeler, 1991), strengthening the capital structure of the business, having skillful managers, having the technology of the acquired business (Gropelli and Nikbakht, 2006), meeting the funding need of the business (Nürk, 2009), benefiting from scale economies, rapid and cost-effective growth (Sarıaslan and Erol, 2008), increasing productivity, providing cash by selling inefficient business lines (Ogilvie, 2009), risk reduction and distribution (Bierman, 2010), decreasing stocking expenses, providing a price advantage in purchasing, reducing sales warehouses, saving costs by decreasing sales distribution organization, encouraging quality increase in production, cooperation in research and development and the efficient use of financial resources (Berk, 2010).

Merger transactions take place in three ways. There are mergers through acquisitions, mergers through take-over and mergers through new establishment. Business mergers through acquisition are carried out as the acquisition of some or all of the assets or shares. In mergers through take over, the acquired business is acquired with its all assets and liabilities and consequently loses its own legal entity. The main objective of the take over is to conquer the management of the acquired business (Machiraju, 2003). In take over transactions, the acquirer business has two main expectations. The first of them is the expectation of the acquirer business that it would manage the assets of the acquired business better, and the second one is belief of the acquirer business that it would increase the market value of the acquired business (Buckey and Ghauiri, 2002). Merger through new establishment is defined as the fact that two or more businesses terminate their existence and establish a new business (Clarkson et al., 2012). After the merger, the newly established business has all assets and liabilities of the merged businesses. The name of the business after merger and its capital structure are shown in the articles of association of the newly formed business, and the articles of association of the businesses before the merger become invalid (Miller and Hollowell, 2010).

In the literature, mergers are classified in four ways: horizontal mergers, vertical mergers, conglomerate mergers and concentric mergers. Horizontal mergers are defined as the merger of businesses operating in the same geographical region, producing or providing the same or similar products. Such mergers have a cost-reducing effect by making inefficient resources efficient (Megginson and Smart, 2009). Vertical mergers are defined as the merger transactions taking place between complementary stages (Arnold, 2013). Conglomerate mergers are defined as the merger transaction performed by two or more noncompeting businesses that operate in different sectors and do not have a trading relationship between them (Moyer et al., 2012). Managers support merger with the businesses that grow fast in this way as long as they have a command of the field of activity of the business (Megginson and Smart, 2009). Concentric merger is the establishment of a new business by noncompeting businesses operating complementary activities through merger or the merger transactions of the businesses in the same industry that have no customer and supplier relationship. The purpose of such mergers is not to reduce rival businesses but to obtain operational and financial benefits by taking advantage of scale economies (Gurusamy, 2009). The advantages of concentric merger can be listed as low transaction costs and solid material supply, their disadvantages as increasing coordination are excess capital requirement, decrease in flexibility and decline in specialization (Machiraju, 2003).

3 Analysis of Business Merger and Acquisition Data

The business merger and acquisition transactions in Turkey do not date back a long time. Due to the blockage of industrialization, that became intense in the 1970s in Turkey, at the end of the 1970s, the foreign expansion process started in the 1980s. In 1989, international capital movements were liberalized. Thus, merger transactions started from the beginning of the 1990s along with the foreign capital that paved the way for a convenient environment, and they gained momentum at the beginning of the 2000s along with the formation of an active merger market.

Business mergers that occurred after 2001 developed as a strategy formed by the businesses to survive the crisis experienced. The negotiations initiated with the European Union (EU) had an effect on business mergers that increased after 2004. In the graphic below, the merger transactions between 2005 and 2018 were analyzed.

When merger and acquisition transactions that took place in Turkey in 2005–2018 years are analyzed, it is remarkable that merger and acquisition transactions did not progress on a certain course and fluctuated. High transaction volume in 2005 was due to the reasons such as intensity of privatization transactions and the initiation of full membership negotiations with the EU. The decline in transaction volume in 2009 was due to the fact that the financial crisis, which started as a housing finance abroad, turned into a global crisis and deeply affected all

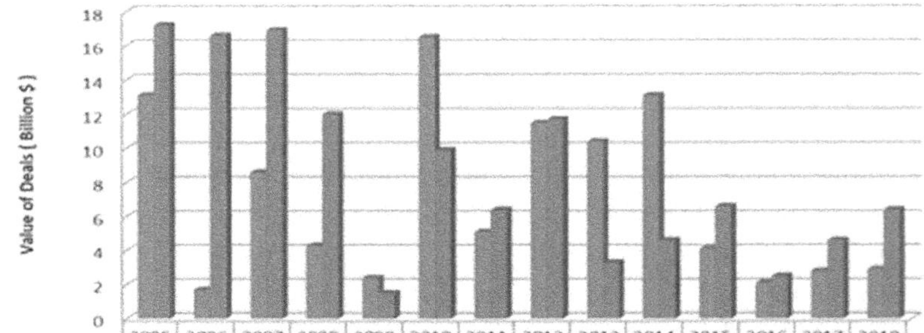

	2005	2006	2007	2008	2009	2010	2011	2012	2013	2014	2015	2016	2017	2018
Local Investors	13,1	1,7	8,6	4,3	2,4	16,5	5,1	11,5	10,4	13,1	4,1	2,1	2,8	2,9
Foreign Investors	17,2	16,6	16,9	12	1,5	9,9	6,4	11,7	3,3	4,6	6,6	2,5	4,6	6,4

Graphic 1: Domestic and Foreign Investors by Transaction Volume. Source: Reviewed from ErnstandYoung, “Mergers and Acquisition Transactions Annual Reports”, 2005–2018 reports.

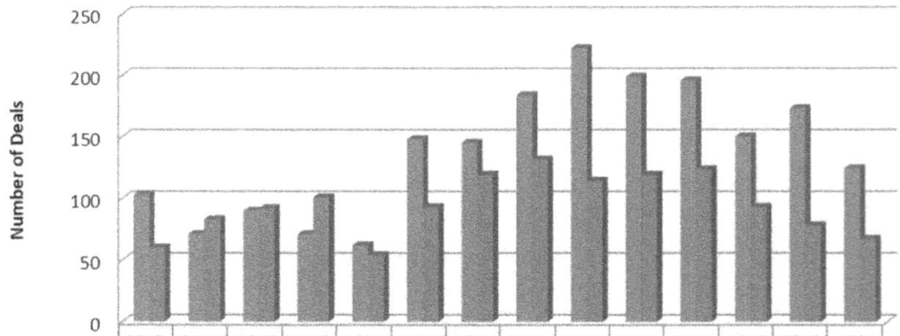

	2005	2006	2007	2008	2009	2010	2011	2012	2013	2014	2015	2016	2017	2018
Local Investors	103	71	90	71	62	148	145	184	222	199	196	150	173	124
Foreign Investors	60	83	92	101	54	93	119	131	114	119	123	93	78	67

Graphic 2: Domestic and Foreign Investors According to Number of Transactions. Source: Reviewed from ErnstandYoung, “ Mergers and Acquisition Transactions Annual Reports”, 2005–2018 reports.

markets in 2009. In the graphic, it is seen that foreign investors are ahead in grand total on the basis of transaction volume.

In the merger and acquisition transactions that took place in Turkey in 2005–2018 years, domestic investors were ahead in grand total.

When the distribution of target businesses by sectors in Turkey in 2018 is analyzed, financial services, logistics and transportation, and media sectors stands out as three sectors with the highest share of merger transactions in 2018.

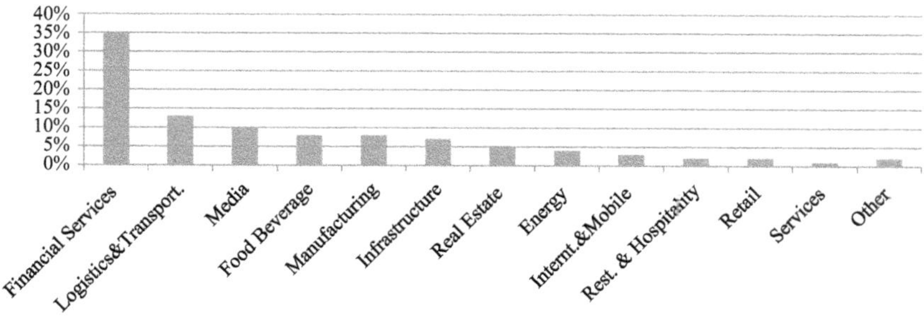

Graphic 3: Turkey Announced MandA by Target Industries. Source: Deloitte "Annual Turkish MandA Review 2018"

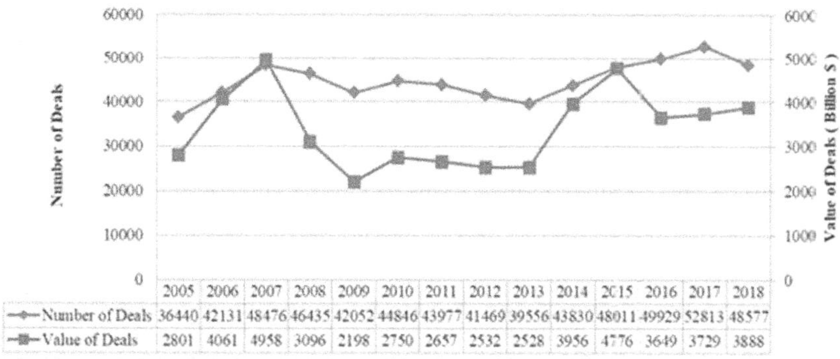

Graphic 4: Number and Value of MandA Worldwide. Source: Imaa, MandA Statistics.

Since 2005, more than 620.000 transactions have been announced worldwide with a known value of over 47 trillion USD. In 2018, the number of deals has decreased to 48.577 transactions, while their value has increased to 3.8 trillion USD.

Energy and power, high technology, healthcare sectors are the three most demanded sectors in merger acquisition transactions in 2018 by 18 %, 13 % and 11 %.

When the numbers of merger and acquisition transactions that took place in Turkey are analyzed, it is seen that it followed a parallel trend with the world in 2007, 2008, 2009, 2010, 2017 and 2018.

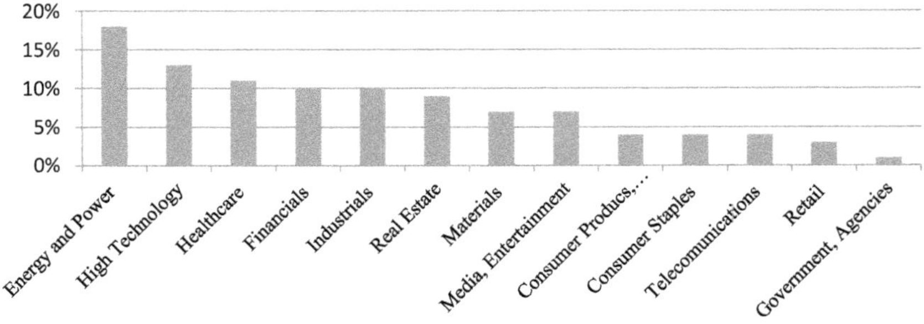

Graphic 5: Worldwide Announced MandA by Target Industry. Source: Thomson Reuters "Mergers and Acquisitions Review Full Year 2018 Report"

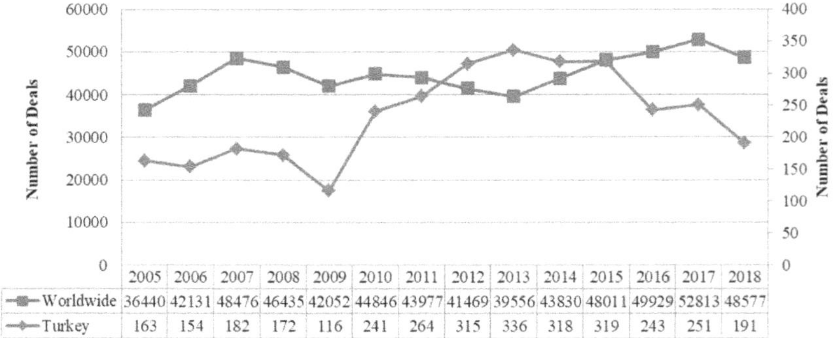

	2005	2006	2007	2008	2009	2010	2011	2012	2013	2014	2015	2016	2017	2018
Worldwide	36440	42131	48476	46435	42052	44846	43977	41469	39556	43830	48011	49929	52813	48577
Turkey	163	154	182	172	116	241	264	315	336	318	319	243	251	191

Graphic 6: Number of Comparative Merger and Acquisition Transactions by Years in the World and in Turkey

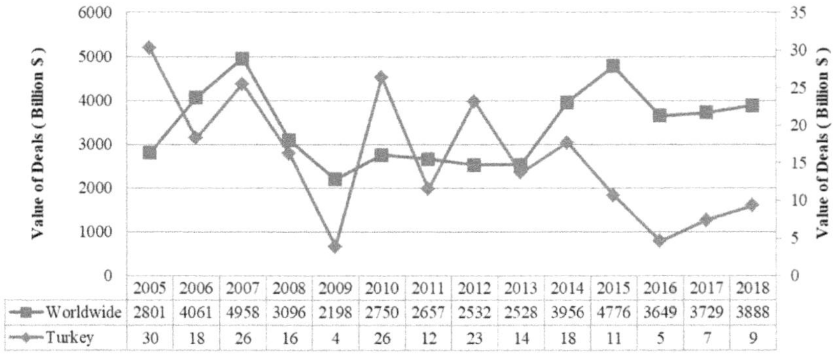

	2005	2006	2007	2008	2009	2010	2011	2012	2013	2014	2015	2016	2017	2018
Worldwide	2801	4061	4958	3096	2198	2750	2657	2532	2528	3956	4776	3649	3729	3888
Turkey	30	18	26	16	4	26	12	23	14	18	11	5	7	9

Graphic 7: Value of Comparative Mergers and Acquisitions by Years in the World and in Turkey

When merger and acquisition transactions that took place in the world and in Turkey are analyzed in terms of total amount, it is seen that the trend was similar in 2007, 2008, 2009, 2010, 2011, 2014, 2016, 2017 and 2018.

4 Conclusion and Evaluation

In the study, the business mergers in Turkey and in the World between 2005 and 2018 were comparatively discussed from various perspectives. When business mergers are considered, remarkable circumstances can be listed as the following:

In general, in business mergers in Turkey, it is seen that domestic investors are ahead in terms of the number of transactions while foreign investors come to the forefront in terms of transaction volume.

The business mergers in the world and in Turkey are very diverse on sectoral basis. In 2018, merger transactions were most intense in the financial services, logistics and transportation, media, food beverage, manufacturing, infrastructure sectors in Turkey and in the energy and power, high technology, healthcare, financials, industrials and real estate sectors in the world.

The numbers of business mergers and the transaction values of these mergers follow a similar trend, except for minor differences, around the world and in Turkey. There are decreases in the numbers of mergers during the crisis periods; however, these decreases do not last long and then increase again by recovering rapidly.

References

Arnold, A. R. (2013), *Microeconomics*, Eleventh Edition, USA, Cengage Learning.

Ataman, Ü. (2000), *Şirketler Muhasebesi*, 4. Baskı, İstanbul, Türkmen Kitabevi.

Bamberger, B. (1994), *Der Erfolg von Unternehmensaqusitionen in Deutshland: Eine theoretische und empirische Untersuchung*, Dissertation, Köln,Universitat Bamberg.

Berk, N. (2010), *Finansal Yönetim*, İstanbul, Türkmen Kitabevi, 2010.

Bierman, H. (2010), *An Introduction to Accounting and Managerial Finance, a Merger of Equals*, USA, World Scientific Publishing.

Buckey, P., P. N. Ghauiri (2002), *International Mergers and Acquisitions*, Singapore, Thomson Learning.

Bühner, R. (1991), The Success of Mergers in Germany, *International Journal of Industrial Organization*, 9(4), s. 513–532.

Clarkson, W. K, Miller, L. R., Cross, B. F. (2012), *Business Law, Text and Cases*, Twelfth Edition, Canada, South Western Cengage Learning.

Deloitte *"Annual Turkish MandA Review 2018"*, https://www2.deloitte.com/content/dam/Deloitte/tr/Documents/mergers-acqisitions/annual-turkish-ma-review-2018.pdf, Erişim:18.01.2019.

Ernst and Young, "*Birleşme ve Satınalma İşlemleri Raporu*", 2005–2018.

Gaughan, P. (2011), *Mergers, Acquisitions, and Corporate Restructurings*, Fifth Edition, USA, John WileyandSons.

Gökçen, G., Ataman, B., Çakıcı, C. (2011), *Türkiye Finansal Raporlama Standartları Uygulamaları*, İstanbul, Türkmen Kitabevi.

Gropelli, A.A, Nikbakht, E. (2006), *Finance*, 5th Edition, New York, Baron's Business Review Books.

Gurusamy, S. (2009), *Financial Services*, Second Edition, New Delhi, Tata Mc Graw-Hill.

Imaa, *MandA Statistics*, https://imaa-institute.org/mergers-and-acquisitions-statistics/ Erişim: 22.01.2019.

Koegeler, R. (1991), *Synergiemanagement im Akquisitions- und Integrationsprozess von Unternehmungen*, Dissertation, Universität Basel.

Machiraju, H. R. (2003), *Mergers, Acquisitions and Takeovers*, New Delhi, New Age International Ltd. Publishers.

Megginson, L. William; Smart, B. S. (2009), *Introduction to Corporate Finance*, USA, South Western Learning.

Miller, L. R., Hollowell, E. W. (2010), *Business Law, Text and Exercises*, Sixth Edition, Canada, Cengage Learning.

Moyer, R. C., McGuigan, R. J., Ramesh, R. P. (2012), *Contemporary Financial Management*, Twelve Edition, USA, South Western Cengage Learning.

Nürk, A. W. (2009), *Drafting Purchase Price Adjustment Clauses in MandA, Guarantees, Retrospective and Future Oriented Purchase Price Adjustment Tools*, Hamburg, Diplomica Verlag Gmbh.

Ogilvie, J. (2009), *Financial Strategy*, Chartered Institute of Management Accountants Edition, Oxford, Elsevier, CIMA Publishing.

Sarıaslan,H., Erol, C. (2008), *Finansal Yönetim Kavramlar, Kurumlar ve İlkeler*, Ankara, Siyasal Basın Yayın Dağıtım.

Sarıkamış, C. (2003), *Şirket Birleşmeleri*, İstanbul, Avcıol Basım Yayın.

Thomson Reuters, "*Mergers and Acquisitions Review Full Year 2018 Report* "http://dmi.thomsonreuters.com/Content/Files/4Q2018_Global_MNA_Legal_Advisory_Review.pdf?utm_source=Eloquaandutm_medium=emailandutm_campaign=00014FJ_NewsletterDQRLegalAdvisory_Otherandutm_content=Newsletter_MandA%20Legal%20Advisory%20Review_2019Jan03, Erişim: 21.01.2019.

Derya Ozturk

Assessment of Service Quality in Logistics Sector Using AHP and TOPSIS Methods

1 Introduction

In today's competitive environment, companies face challenges in keeping up with technological innovations and rapid changes in customer expectations. Sustainable competitive advantage depends, therefore, on developing long-term relationships with customers (Öztürk and Onurlubaş, 2018:551). Providing efficient and high quality services, making customers feel special and achieving high customer satisfaction result in long-term customer relationship (Tekin and Zerenler, 2012:282). Companies operating in the logistics sector can achieve high customer satisfaction and gain competitive advantage by providing efficient services. Logistics is defined as daily planning and utilization of individual resources to deliver individual and corporate customers' packages to recipients as quickly and safely as possible (Akbulut, 2016: 31). In other words, the basic principle of logistics is to meet customer demands on time and to ensure safe and undamaged shipment of goods to recipients. In logistics, the delivery of shipments is important in many ways; therefore, the quality of service of logistics companies plays a key role in customer decisions. The aim of this study is to determine the importance of factors affecting service quality in the logistics sector using AHP method and to assess the service quality of three logistics companies using AHP and TOPSIS methods based on the determined levels of importance and to compare the results of both methods.

There are some studies using AHP and TOPSIS methods together to assess the quality of service at airports (Tsaur et al., 2002), to develop a performance measurement model for manufacturing companies (Yurdakul and İç, 2005), to determine the best maintenance technology in the textile industry (Shyjith et al., 2008), to analyze the process of customer-oriented product design (Lin et al., 2008), to choose the ideal service provider in the logistics industry (Unal, 2008), to determine suppliers for a company that produces corrugated cardboard boxes (Supçiller and Çapraz, 2011), to assess the quality of service in the logistics industry (Uzun, 2013), to select suppliers in a telecommunications industry (Günay and Ünal, 2016), to select an echocardiography device for healthcare providers (Ayan et al., 2016), to choose a specialty in medicine (Ömürbek et al., 2016), a printing house (Geyik et al., 2016) and a third party logistics (3PL) firm on an online shopping site (Eren and Gür, 2017), to measure the quality of service of city bus lines Güner (2017) and to assess the quality of service in the banking sector (Ustasüleyman, 2009; Bağcı et al., 2017). Using AHP, TOPSIS and PROMETHEE methods, Asoğlu and Eren (2018) conducted a study in which firms assessed the quality of services of the logistics companies with which they worked. The importance of this study lies in the fact that there is almost no research on individual customers' assessment of the quality of services of logistics companies.

2 Method

2.1 Analytical Hierarchy Process (AHP)

The Analytical Hierarchy Process (AHP) is a multi-criteria decision-making method developed by Thomas L. Saaty (1977) for the solution of complex problems. AHP makes pairwise comparisons and determines how important, preferable or dominant options and criteria are compared to each other (Özgörmüş et al., 2005:112). It is a powerful and easy-to-understand method that allow groups and people to combine quantitative and qualitative factors in decision-making (Terzi et al., 2006:44). The step-by-step solution hierarchy of a problem in AHP is as follows:

Step 1: The complex problem should be clearly stated and decomposed into a hierarchical structure for ease of application. The main objective of decision problems is, therefore, to establish criteria, sub-criteria and alternatives within a hierarchical structure (Asoğlu and Eren, 2018:105).

Step 2: Pairwise comparisons are made. Based on the assessment scores of decision makers, i.e., experts, criteria are compared with each other and alternatives are compared among themselves based on the criteria. Saaty's 1–9 scale (1980) is used in the pairwise comparisons. Once pairwise comparison matrices are obtained, normalized matrices are generated, and relative priorities are determined. The relative importance of criteria and alternatives is determined according to relative priorities (Küçük and Ecer, 2008:439).

Tab. 1: Scale of Preference. Source: Saaty, 1980: 843.

Intensity of Importance	Definition	Explanation
1	Equally preferred	Two elements contribute equally to the object
3	Moderately preferred	One *element* is moderately preferred over another element
5	Strongly preferred	One element is strongly preferred over another element
7	Very strongly preferred	One element is very strongly preferred over another element
9	Extremely preferred	One element is extremely preferred over another element
2,4,6,8	Intermediate values	1–3, 3–5, 5–7, 7–9 intermediate values
Pairwise	Pairwise comparisons	

Step 3: It is determined whether or not the matrices are consistent to assess how much the relative priorities reflect the truth. In order for a comparison matrix to be consistent, its largest eigenvalue λ_{max} must be equal to its matrix size (n) (Küçük and Ecer, 2008:440). A consistency ratio (CR) is calculated using the equations (1) and (2). CI and RI refer to the coherence and random indicators, respectively.

$$CI = (\lambda_{max} - n)/(n - 1) \quad (1)$$

$$CR = CI/RI \quad (2)$$

RIs (Tab. 2) are composed of constant RI values taking different values depending on the alternative amount of the matrix. Where n represents the size of the matrix. CR < 0.1 indicates acceptable consistency (Saaty, 1994:27).

Tab. 2: Random Indicators. Source: Saaty, 1980: 21.

n	1	2	3	4	5	6	7	8	9	10	11	12	13	14	15
Value	0	0	0.58	0.9	1.12	1.24	1.32	1.41	1.45	1.49	1.51	1.53	1.56	1.57	1.59

Step 4: The sum of the multiplications of the sum of the weight of each criterion and the relative importance of alternatives is the priority value (weight) of each alternative (Asoğlu and Eren, 2018:106).

2.2 TOPSIS Method

Developed by Hwang and Yoon (1981), TOPSIS is a multi-criteria decision analysis method to determine positive and negative ideal solutions of decision making problems in order to select alternatives (Özcan et al., 2017:209). TOPSIS consists of 6 steps (Uygurtürk and Korkmaz, 2012:104–105; Asoğlu and Eren, 2018:106–108).

Step 1: Constructing the decision matrix (A): Alternatives and criteria are listed on the rows and columns, respectively. Matrix A is an initial matrix generated by experts.

Step 2: Constructing the standard decision matrix (R): It is calculated using the elements of matrix A and the following formula.

$$r_{ij} = \frac{a_{ij}}{\sqrt{\sum_{k=1}^{m} a_{kj}^2}} \tag{3}$$

Step 3: Constructing the weighted standard decision matrix (V): First, values (W_i) indicating weights associated with evaluation criteria are calculated ($\sum_{i=1}^{n} w_i = 1$). Then, the values in each column of the matrix R are multiplied by w_i and the weighted standard matrix V is generated.

Step 4: Determining the positive (A^*) and negative (A^-) ideal solutions: TOPSIS assumes that each criterion has a steadily increasing or decreasing trend. The positive ideal solution set is formed by selecting the weighted evaluation factors of the matrix V, that is, the maximum values of the column if they are maximum likelihood criteria while the minimum values of the column are selected if they are minimum likelihood criteria. Equation (4) is used to determine the positive ideal solution set $A^* = \{v_1^*, v_2^*, ..., v_n^*\}$. The negative ideal solution set is formed by selecting the weighted evaluation factors of the matrix V, that is, the minimum values of the column (maximum values of the assessment factor is a maximum likelihood criteria). Equation (5) is used to determine the negative ideal solution set.

$$A^* = \left\{(\max_i v_{ij} \middle| j \in J), \ (\min_i v_{ij} | j \in J' \right\} \tag{4}$$

$$A^- = \left\{(\min_i v_{ij} \middle| j \in J), \ (\max_i v_{ij} | j \in J^{'} \right\} \quad (5)$$

$$A^- = \{v_1^-, v_2^-, \ldots, v_n^-\} \quad \text{denotesthesetcalculatedusingequation} \quad (3)$$

In both equations, j is associated with benefit (maximization) criteria and J' is associated with cost (minimization) criteria. Both the ideal and negative ideal solution sets consist of the number of evaluation factors, that is, the m number of elements.

Step 5: Calculating the relative closeness to the ideal solution: Euclidean distances of the evaluation factor value of each decision point from the positive and negative ideal solutions are calculated. Deviations are referred to as Ideal Separation (S_i^*) and Negative Ideal Separation

(S_i^-). Equation (6) and (7) are used to calculate the Ideal Separation (S_i^*) and Negative Ideal Separation (S_i^-), respectively.

$$S_i^* = \sqrt{\sum_{j=1}^{n} (v_{ij} - v_j^*)^2} \quad (6)$$

$$S_i^- = \sqrt{\sum_{j=1}^{n} (v_{ij} - v_j^-)^2} \quad (7)$$

Where the number of S_i^* and S_i^- is equal to the number of alternatives.

Step 6: Selecting the closest option to the ideal solution: Ideal and negative ideal separation measures are used to calculate the relative proximity (C_i^*) of each decision point to the ideal solution. The criterion here is the ratio of the negative ideal separation measure to the total separation measure. The relative proximity to the ideal solution is calculated using the following formula.

$$C_i^* = \frac{S_i^-}{S_i^- + S_i^*} \quad (8)$$

Where $0 \leq C_i^* \leq 1$ and $C_i^* = 1$ is the proximity of the decision point to the ideal solution and $C_i^* = 0$ is the absolute proximity of the decision point to the negative ideal solution.

3 Procedure

The study population consisted of customers of logistics companies in the city of Ordu. The total number of customers of the companies, hence, the main mass, could not be numerically determined. The sample size was limited to 100 customers based on the implementation and time-cost constraints of AHP. Participants were randomly selected from the customers. The sample included the customers of all three companies for validity and reliability reasons. A survey was conducted to determine the top three logistics companies operating in Ordu. The names of the other companies (alternatives) were kept confidential so that the survey results would not damage their reputation. While their real names were used in the survey, they were referred to as Cargo A, Cargo B and Cargo C in the study. The service quality dimensions of the logistics companies were physical appearance (facilities, equipment, staff and communication facilities), reliability (fulfilling customer services timely and fully), responsiveness (providing services quickly and fully and being willing to help customers), assurance (staff's level of knowledge and ability to win customer confidence) and empathy (staff's ability to communicate with customers closely and effectively and to put themselves in customers' shoes) (Büyükkeklik et al., 2014: 38). The Scale of Quality of Service in Cargo Sector developed by Uzun (2004) was used in this study. The scale consists of three subscales: Corporate credibility, sensitivity to customer needs and service accessibility. Data were collected using face-to-face survey method. Data were analyzed using Microsoft Excel 2013.

3.1 Analytical Hierarchy Process (AHP) Procedure

In the first step of AHP, the main objective, criteria, sub-criteria and alternatives of the decision problem were constructed within a hierarchical structure (Fig. 1).

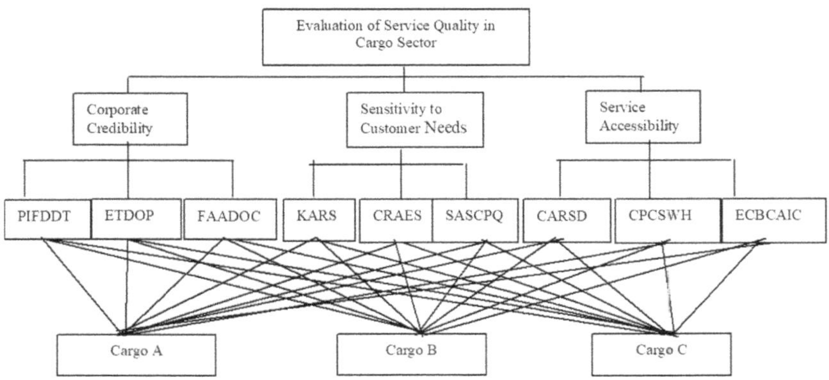

Fig. 1: Hierarchical Structure of Problem

The main criteria were "corporate credibility," "sensitivity to customer needs" and "service accessibility". The subcriteria of corporate credibility were "providing insurance for damages during transportation (PIFDDT)", "ensuring timely delivery of packages (ETDOP)" and "fast and accurate acceptance and delivery of cargo (FAADOC)". The subcriteria of sensitivity to customer needs were "knowledgeable and resourceful staff (KARS)", "courteous, respectful and enthusiastic staff (CRAES)" and "staff's ability to solve customer problems quickly (SASCPQ)". The subcriteria of service accessibility were "company's ability to respond to service demands (CARSD)", "company's proximity to customers and suitability of working hours (CPCSWH)" and "effective communication between company and its customers (ECBCAIC)".

In the second and third steps of AHP, pairwise comparison matrices were constructed, relative priorities were determined and the consistency ratios of the matrices were calculated. The pairwise comparison results of the participants were combined by taking a geometric mean. Pairwise comparison of the main criteria showed that "corporate credibility" (0.540) was more important than "service accessibility" (0.285) and "sensitivity to customer needs" (0.026). The consistency ratio of the pairwise comparison matrix was 0.00, indicating highly reliable evaluation (Tab. 3).

Tab. 3: Pairwise Comparison of Main Criteria.

	Corporate Credibility	Sensitivity to Customer Needs	Service Accessibility	Relative Importance
Corporate Credibility	1.00	2.98	1.97	0.540
Sensitivity to Customer Needs	0.34	1.00	0.59	0.175
Service Accessibility	0.51	1.70	1.00	0.285

CR: 0.00
CR: Consistency Ratio

Tabs. 4, 5 and 6 show the paired comparisons, relative importance levels and consistency ratios of the sub-criteria, respectively. FAADOC (0.472), SASCPQ (0.426) and ECBCAIC (0.426) were the most important subcriteria of corporate credibility, sensitivity to customer needs and service accessibility, respectively. The consistency ratio of all matrices was below 0.10.

Tab. 4: Pairwise Comparison of Subcriteria of Corporate Credibility.

	PIFDDT	ETDOP	FAADOC	Relative Importance
PIFDDT	1.00	1.29	0.55	0.286
ETDOP	0.78	1.00	0.56	0.243
FAADOC	1.81	1.78	1.00	0.472

CR: 0.00
CR: Consistency Ratio

Tab. 5: Pairwise Comparison of Subcriteria of Sensitivity to Customer Needs.

	KARS	CRAES	SASCPQ	Relative Importance
KARS	1.00	0.97	0.54	0.265
CRAES	1.03	1.00	0.83	0.310
SASCPQ	1.84	1.21	1.00	0.426

CR: 0.01
CR: Consistency Ratio

Tab. 6: Pairwise Comparison of Subcriteria of Service Accessibility.

	CARSD	CPCSWH	ECBCAIC	Relative Importance
CARSD	1.00	0.70	0.67	0.254
CPCSWH	1.43	1.00	0.66	0.319
ECBCAIC	1.48	1.52	1.00	0.426

CR: 0.01
CR: Consistency Ratio

In the last step of AHP, the weights of alternatives for each sub-criterion were calculated. Then, the general weights of the alternatives were obtained by multiplying the elements of the matrix by the weights of the sub-criteria (Tab. 7).

Tab. 7: Company Priorities and Consistency Ratios by Main and Sub-Criteria.

	Corporate Credibility (0.540)			Sensitivity to Customer Needs (0.175)			Service Accessibility (0.285)			Relative Importance
	PIFDDT (0,286)	ETDOP (0,243)	FAADOC (0,472)	KARS (0,265)	CRAES (0,310)	SASCPQ (0,426)	CARSD (0,254)	CPCSWH (0,319)	ECBCAIC (0,426)	
Cargo A	0.387	0.409	0.384	0.408	0.409	0.377	0.366	0.407	0.404	0.393
Cargo B	0.262	0.242	0.247	0.268	0.316	0.312	0.289	0.284	0.290	0.270
Cargo C	0.352	0.349	0.369	0.324	0.275	0.310	0.345	0.309	0.306	0.337
CR	0.01	0.01	0.00	0.01	0.00	0.00	0.00	0.00	0.02	

CR: Consistency Ratio

3.2 TOPSIS Procedure

TOPSIS was performed in six steps as follows:

Step 1: Constructing the decision matrix: Tab. 8 shows the decision matrix based on the geometric mean of the scores (1 to 5) given by the decision makers for the alternatives.

Tab. 8: Decision Matrix

	PIFDDT	ETDOP	FAADOC	KARS	CRAES	SASCPQ	CARSD	CPCSWH	ECBCAIC
Cargo A	3.40	3.31	3.40	2.89	2.87	3.36	3.20	2.91	3.27
Cargo B	3.20	3.06	3.29	3.28	3.22	3.14	3.10	3.12	3.12
Cargo C	3.27	3.20	3.34	3.03	3.05	3.13	3.15	3.02	3.25

Step 2: Constructing the normalized decision matrix: Each value in the columns was divided by the square root of the sum of the squares of all values in the column and reduced to a single denominator (Tab. 9).

Tab. 9: Normalized Decision Matrix

	PIFDDT	ETDOP	FAADOC	KARS	CRAES	SASCPQ	CARSD	CPCSWH	ECBCAIC
Cargo A	0.60	0.60	0.59	0.54	0.54	0.60	0.59	0.56	0.59
Cargo B	0.56	0.55	0.57	0.62	0.61	0.56	0.57	0.60	0.56
Cargo C	0.57	0.58	0.58	0.57	0.58	0.56	0.58	0.58	0.58

Step 3: Constructing the weighted decision matrix: The weighted decision matrix (Tab. 11) was constructed by multiplying the normalized decision matrix values by the weight coefficients (W) (Tab. 10) of AHP criteria.

Tab. 10: Criteria Weight Values

	PIFDDT	ETDOP	FAADOC	KARS	CRAES	SASCPQ	CARSD	CPCSWH	ECBCAIC
W	0.154	0.131	0.255	0.046	0.054	0.074	0.072	0.091	0.122

Tab. 11: Weighted Decision Matrix

	PIFDDT	ETDOP	FAADOC	KARS	CRAES	SASCPQ	CARSD	CPCSWH	ECBCAIC
Cargo A	0.092	0.078	0.150	0.025	0.029	0.045	0.042	0.051	0.071
Cargo B	0.087	0.073	0.145	0.028	0.033	0.042	0.041	0.054	0.068
Cargo C	0.088	0.076	0.147	0.026	0.031	0.042	0.042	0.053	0.071

Step 4: Determining the positive and negative ideal solutions: For the ideal solution from the relevant column of each criterion in the weighted decision matrix, negative ideal values for positive ideal and negative ideal solutions were selected and ideal and negative ideal solution values were determined. Tab. 12 shows the positive and negative ideal solution sets for each criterion.

Tab. 12: Positive and Negative Ideal Solution Sets

	PIFDDT	ETDOP	FAADOC	KARS	CRAES	SASCPQ	CARSD	CPCSWH	ECBCAIC
S^*	0.092	0.078	0.150	0.028	0.033	0.045	0.042	0.054	0.071
S^-	0.087	0.073	0.145	0.025	0.029	0.042	0.041	0.051	0.068

Step 5: Calculating the separation measures: Positive ideal and negative ideal values were subtracted from the values in the column of each criterion, and distances from the positive and negative ideal solutions were determined. The criterion values in each column were subtracted from the maximum value, and the result was squared to calculate the distances to the positive ideal solution (Tab. 13).

Tab. 13: Distances to Positive Ideal Solution

	PIFDDT	ETDOP	FAADOC	KARS	CRAES	SASCPQ
Cargo A	0.000000000	0.000000000	0.000000000	0.000011090	0.000012505	0.000000000
Cargo B	0.000030284	0.000034347	0.000024872	0.000000000	0.000000000	0.000008289
Cargo C	0.000012907	0.000005870	0.000007617	0.000004761	0.000002985	0.000009071

	CARSD	CPCSWH	ECBCAIC	TOTAL	SQUARE ROOT	S^*
Cargo A	0.000000000	0.000013192	0.000000000	0.000036788	0.006065295	S1
Cargo B	0.000001841	0.000000000	0.000010732	0.000110366	0.010505507	S2
Cargo C	0.000000367	0.000002964	0.000000355	0.000046897	0.006848115	S3

The distances to the negative ideal solution were calculated by subtracting the criterion values in each column from the smallest value and squaring the result (Tab. 14).

Tab. 14: Distances to Negative Ideal Solution

	PIFDDT	ETDOP	FAADOC	KARS	CRAES	SASCPQ
Cargo A	0.000030284	0.000034347	0.000024872	0.000000000	0.000000000	0.000009071
Cargo B	0.000000000	0.000000000	0.000000000	0.000011090	0.000012505	0.000000018
Cargo C	0.000003650	0.000011819	0.000004961	0.000001319	0.000003271	0.000000000

	CARSD	CPCSWH	ECBCAIC	TOTAL	SQUARE ROOT	S-
Cargo A	0.000001841	0.000000000	0.000010732	0.000111147	0.010542644	S1
Cargo B	0.000000000	0.000013192	0.000000000	0.000036805	0.006066746	S2
Cargo C	0.000000564	0.000003650	0.000007186	0.000036418	0.006034734	S3

Step 6: Selecting the closest option to the ideal solution: For each alternative value, the negative ideal solution value was divided by the sum of its own value and the positive ideal solution value of the same alternative (Tab. 15).

Tab. 15: Proximity to Ideal Solution

C^*	
C^*_1	0.634795
C^*_2	0.366079
C^*_3	0.468432

3.3 Comparison of AHP and TOPSIS Results

This section compared the AHP and TOPSIS results of the companies (Tab. 16).

Tab. 16: Comparative Table of AHP and TOPSIS Results

Company	Weights		Rank	
	AHP	TOPSİS	AHP	TOPSİS
Cargo A	0.393	0.635	1	1
Cargo B	0.270	0.366	3	3
Cargo C	0.337	0.468	2	2

According to AHP weights, Cargos A, C and B ranked first, second and third, respectively. According to TOPSIS weights, Cargo A had the best service quality, followed by Cargos C and B. Both methods ranked the companies the same, indicating that participants assessed the companies consistently in the survey.

4 Conclusion

The services of logistics companies are sought for different reasons and greatly utilized by almost everyone. This study assessed the service quality of logistics companies by using AHP and TOPSIS methods. The greatest limitation of the study was that only three companies could be included in the study because AHP and TOPSIS analyses require that customers purchase services of each company (alternatives as well) at least once. It is recommended that future studies include more companies in their samples and use other multi-criteria decision-making methods as well as AHP and TOPSIS. Another limitation was that only three service quality dimensions were analyzed. Future studies should, therefore, take into account other service quality factors to provide more insight into the sector. The most important criterion was found to corporate credibility, followed by service accessibility and sensitivity to customer needs. The most important subcriteria in terms of corporate reliability, sensitivity to customer needs and service accessibility were FAADOC, ECBCAIC and SASCPQ, respectively. Companies should focus on main components while developing competitive strategies to increase their chances of success. Logistics sector is a human-oriented sector; therefore, logistics companies should give importance to their employees. Companies with polite, attentive and helpful staff gain a great competitive advantage. Today, quality has become an essential part of organizational success in highly competitive service sectors. According to AHP and TOPSIS results, Cargo A has the best service quality, followed by Cargos C and B, suggesting that logistics companies should take the criteria addressed in this study into consideration in order to provide better service and achieve a competitive advantage. We, therefore, believe that the results of this study will be useful for logistics companies.

References

Akbulut, D. (2016). "Türkiye'de Karayoluyla Yapılan Kargo Taşımacılığının Yapısı ve Sektörel Değerlendirmeler", Ulaştırma ve Haberleşme Uzmanlığı Tezi, Ulaştırma Denizcilik ve Haberleşme Bakanlığı, Ankara.

Asoğlu, İ. and Eren, T. (2018). AHS, TOPSIS, PROMETHEE Yöntemleri ile Bir İşletme için Kargo Şirketi Seçimi, *Yalova Sosyal Bilimler Dergisi*, 8(16):102–122.

Ayan, E., Cihan, Ş., Eren, T., Topal, T. and Yildirim, E. K. (2016). AHP ve TOPSIS Yöntemleri ile Ekokardiografi Cihazı Seçimi, *Sağlık Bilimleri ve Meslekleri Dergisi*, 4(1): 41–49.

Bağcı, B., Hoş, S. and Demirer, Ö. (2017). Bankacılıkta Hizmet Kalitesinin AHS ve TOPSIS Teknikleriyle Değerlendirilmesi: Çorum Örneği. *Hitit Üniversitesi Sosyal Bilimler Enstitüsü Dergisi*, 10(2): 1617–1638.

Büyükkeklik, A., Özoğlu, B. and Bülbül, H. (2014). Kargo Hizmet Sağlayıcılarında Kalitenin Tüketici Davranışına Etkisi: Bireysel Tüketici

Araştırması, *Selçuk Üniversitesi Sosyal Bilimler Enstitüsü Dergisi*, 27(1): 33–43.

Eren, T. and Gür, S. (2017). Online Alışveriş Siteleri İçin AHP ve TOPSİS Yöntemleri İle 3PL Firma Seçimi. *Hitit Üniversitesi Sosyal Bilimler Enstitüsü Dergisi*, 10(2): 819–834.

Geyik, O., Tosun, M., Ünlüsoy, S., Hamurcu, M. and Eren, T. (2016). Kitap Basımevi Seçiminde AHP Ve TOPSIS Yöntemlerinin Kullanımı, *Uluslararası Sosyal ve Eğitim Bilimleri Dergisi*, 3(6):106–126.

Günay, Z. and Ünal Ö.F. (2016). AHP-TOPSIS Yöntemi ile Tedarikçi Seçimi (Bir Telekomünikasyon Şirketi Örneği), *PESA Uluslararası Sosyal Araştırmalar Dergisi*, 2(1): 37–53.

Güner, S. (2017). Operational Efficiency and Service Quality Analysis in Public Transportation Systems, *Journal of Transportation and Logistics*, 2(2): 33–47.

Küçük, O. and Ecer, F. (2008). İmalatçı İşletmelerde Uygun Tedarikçi Seçimi: Analitik Hiyerarşi Yöntemi ile Bir Kobi Uygulaması, *Atatürk Üniversitesi İktisadi ve İdari Bilimler Dergisi*, 22(2): 435–450.

Lin, M.C., Wang, C.C., Chen, M.S. and Alec Chang, C. (2008). Using AHP and TOPSIS Approaches in Customer-Driven Product Design Process, *Computers in Industry*, 59, 17–31.

Ömürbek, N., Tunca, M.Z., Özcan, A., Yildiz, E. and Karataş T. (2016). AHP TOPSIS Yönteminin Tipta Uzmanlik Alan Seçiminde Kullanımı, *Akdeniz Üniversitesi İktisadi ve İdari Bilimler Fakültesi Dergisi*, 16 (33): 201–219.

Özcan, E.C., Ünlüsoy, S. and Eren, T. (2017). ANP ve TOPSIS Yöntemleriyle Türkiye'de Yenilenebilir Enerji Yatırım Alternatiflerinin Değerlendirilmesi, *Selcuk University Journal of Engineering, Science and Technology*, 5 (2): 204–219.

Özgörmüş, E. Mutlu, Ö. and Güner, H. (2005). "Bulanık AHP İle Personel Seçimi", V. Ulusal Üretim Araştırmaları Sempozyumu, İstanbul Ticaret Üniversitesi, 25–27 Kasım 2005, ss 111–115.

Öztürk, D. and Onurlubaş, E. (2018). Gıda Sektöründe Yeni Ürün Geliştirme: Konya'da Bisküvi, Çikolatalı ve Şekerli Mamuller Alt Sektörü Üzerine Bir Uygulama. *Uluslararası İktisadi ve İdari İncelemeler Dergisi*. 17. UİK Özel Sayısı: 551–568.

Saaty, T.L. (1977). "A Scaling Method for Priorities in Hierarchical Structures", *Journal of Mathematical Psychology*, 15(3): 234–281

Saaty, T.L. (1980). *The Analytic Hierarchy Process*, McGraw-Hill, New York

Saaty, T.L. (1994). "How to Make a Decision: The Analytic Hierarchy Process", *Interfaces*, 24(6): 19–43.

Shyjith, K., Ilangkumaran, M. and Kumanan, S. (2008). Multi-Criteria Decision-Making Approach to Evaluate Optimum Maintenance Strategy in Textile Industry, *Journal of Quality in Maintenance Engineering*, 14(4): 375–386.

Supçiller, A.A. and Çapraz, O. (2011). AHP-TOPSIS Yöntemine Dayalı Tedarikçi Seçimi Uygulaması, *Ekonometri ve İstatistik e-Dergisi*, 13:1–22.

Tekin, M. and Zerenler, M. (2012). *Pazarlama*, Günay Ofset, Konya.

Terzi, Ü., Hacaloğlu, S.E. and Aladağ, Z. (2006). Otomobil Satın Alma Problemi İçin Bir Karar Destek Modeli, *İstanbul Ticaret Üniversitesi Fen Bilimleri Dergisi*, 5(10): 43–49.

Tsaur, S.H., Chang, T.Y. and Yen, C.H. (2002). The Evaluation of Airline Service Quality by Fuzzy MCDM, *Tourism Management*, 23(2): 107–115.

Ustasüleyman, T. (2009). "Bankacılık Sektöründe Hizmet Kalitesinin Değerlendirilmesi: AHS-TOPSIS Yöntemi", *Bankacılar Dergisi*, 69, 33–43.

Uygurtürk, H. and Korkmaz, T. (2012). Finansal Performansın TOPSIS Çok Kriterli Karar Verme Yöntemi İle Belirlenmesi: Ana Metal Sanayi İşletmeleri Üzerine Bir Uygulama. *Eskişehir Osmangazi Üniversitesi İİBF Dergisi*, 7(2): 95–115.

Uzun, H. (2013). Kargo Taşmacılık Sektöründe Hizmet Kalitesinin Değerlendirilmesi: AHS ve TOPSIS Yöntemi, İşletme Yüksek Lisans Tezi, Gazi Üniversitesi, Sosyal Bilimler Enstitüsü, Ankara.

Ünal, G. (2008). Lojistikte Hizmet Sağlayıcısı Seçiminde AHP ve TOPSIS Yöntemlerinin Uygulanması, Yayınlanmamış Yüksek Lisans Tezi, Kocaeli Üniversitesi Fen Bilimleri Enstitüsü, Kocaeli.

Yurdakul, M. and İç, Y.T. (2005). Development of a Performance Measurement Model for Manufacturing Companies Using the AHP and TOPSIS Approaches, *International Journal of Production Research*, 43(21): 4609–4641.

Gulsah Sezen Akar

Sustainable Production: Evaluation of Turkish Automotive Sector

1 Introduction

Along with the industrial revolution, the transition to mechanization in the production processes allowed for further production. Along with the increasing production, the accumulation of capital became an important factor for businesses. The increasing level of welfare of consumers and increasing population also directed businesses to only produce without considering the natural resources and environment.

By the end of the 20th century, the damage to the environment became noticeable. The necessity of governments to take measures emerged with the pressures of consumers and non-governmental organizations. With the Brundtland Report (WCED, 1987) sustainability and sustainable development terms become to agenda. In first time, sustainable development was defined as "development that meets the needs of the present without compromising the ability of future generations to meet their own needs."

Then, in the "Environment and Development" conference held in Brazil in 1992, sustainable production in relation to sustainable development was first mentioned, and it was concluded that unsustainable production and consumption were the main reasons of global degradation (UN, 1992). In this report while sustainable consumption targets consumers, sustainable production is related to companies and organizations that make products or offer services (Veleva and Ellenbecker, 2001).

Today, sustainable production has become a critical issue that cannot be ignored. The reports published reveal the extent of the damages to the environment in particular. In the Climate change report published in 2014, the IPCC reported that 95 % of current global warming was human-induced. The greenhouse gas emission, which is the cause of climate change, increased by 78 % between the years 1970 and 2010 due to energy consumption and industrialization, and it is predicted that the temperature in the world will increase by 2 degrees if this increase continues. In the "Global Warming of 1.5 °C" report which was also published by the IPCC in 2018, it was expressed that an increase of 2 degrees should be reduced 1.5 degrees and that even the difference of 0.5 degrees would cause that more areas in the world would be affected by temperature, the countries such as Africa and Asia would become poor due to climate change, and many species would be extinct.

In this case, governments as well as manufacturing businesses have major tasks on sustainability. It is important to increase and control the efforts regarding the fact that production should be sustainable not only environmentally but also socially and economically.

In this study, the sustainable production performance of the businesses in the Turkish automotive sector was evaluated. In the sector, the increase in production due to the increasing demand is considered positive for the countries in terms of economy. However, the sector has a strategic importance due to its effects on the environment during and after production. In this respect, production activities should be monitored, controlled and inspected continuously.

2 Sustainable Production and Indicators of Sustainable Production

Sustainable Production is defined by the Lowell Center for Sustainable Production (LCSP) as "the creation of goods and services using processes and systems; non-polluting, conserving of energy and natural resources, economically viable, safe and healthful for employees, communities and consumers, socially and creatively rewarding for all working people" (LCSP, 1998). In Fig. 1, the questions are given to ensure sustainable products. As a result of the positive answers to the questions, it can be said that the product is sustainable.

The LCSP principles include the energy and material use, the natural environment, social justice and community development, economic performance,

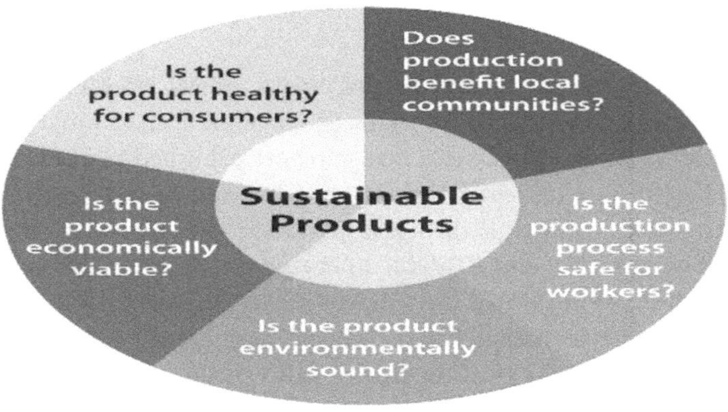

Fig. 1: Sustainable Products. Source: (LCSP, 2019)

Tab. 1: Principles of Sustainable Production (Veleva and Ellenbecker, 2001)

No.	Principle	Main Aspect
1	Products and packaging/services are designed to be safe and ecologically sound throughout their life cycles.	Products
2	Wastes and ecologically incompatiable byproducts are continuously reduced, eliminated or recycled.	Natural Environment
3	Energy and materials are conserved, and forms of energy and materials used are most appropriate for the desire ends.	Energy and Material Use
4	Chemical substances, physical agents, technologies, and work practices that present hazards to human health or the environment are continuously reduced or eliminated	Natural Environment
5	Workplaces are designed to minimize or eliminate physical, chemical, biological, and ergonomic hazards.	Workers
6	Management is committed to an open, participatory process of continuous evaluation and improvement, focused on the long-term economic performance of the firm.	Economic Performance
7	Work is organized to conserve and enhance the efficiency and creativity of employees.	Workers
8	The security and well-being of all employes is a priority, as is the continuous development of their talents and capacities.	Workers
9	The communities around workplaces are respected and enhaced economically, socially, culturally and physically; equity and fairness are promoted.	Social Justice and Community Development

workers and products of sustainable production. There are nine principles of sustainable production which are shown in the Tab. 1. (Veleva and Ellenbecker, 2001).

Various indicators have been developed by many different organizations and non-governmental organizations to evaluate sustainable production. In their study, Veleva and Ellenbecker (2001) analyzed four best-known indicators presented by International Organization for Standardization ISO 14031, Global Reporting Initiative (GRI), World Business Council for Sustainable Development (WBCSD) and Center for Waste Reduction Technologies (CWRT) and stated that they were insufficient to evaluate sustainable production in terms of economic, social and environmental systems.

Ortiz, Castells and Sonnemann (2009) analyzed the construction sector and evaluated sustainable production by the life cycle analysis (LCA). Andersson et al. (1998) performed the feasibility studies of incorporating sustainable production into the product development phase with LCA. Life cycle analysis is quite inadequate in evaluating sustainable production since it only considers the environmental dimension.

In their study, Krajnc and Glavic (2003) proposed 89 different indicators for the evaluation of sustainable production in social, environmental and economic dimensions. The study revealed a new approach in the systematization of indicators, symbols and units.

Sustainable production indicators that are part of continuous improvement are leveled by the Lowell Center. It is recommendable that an organization first begins with simple, easy to implement measures of compliance and resource efficiency and then moves toward more complex indicators, addressing supply-chain, social effects and lifecycle impacts (Veleva and Ellenbecker, 2001).

Facility compliance/conformance indicators (Level 1) evaluate the extent to which a facility is in compliance with regulations or in conformance to some industry/association standards. Examples of Level 1 indicators include number of reportable spills and number of notices of non-compliance. Facility material use and performance indicators (Level 2) include measures of facility/company inputs, outputs and performance, such as resource use efficiency, byproducts, emissions or waste. Facility effects indicators (Level 3) are developed to measure effects of the internal production processes on the external environment (e.g., global warming potential, percent of workers with work-related disease, population growth in the local area as result of facility operations). Supply chain and product life-cycle indicators (Level 4) evaluate that the measurement focus goes

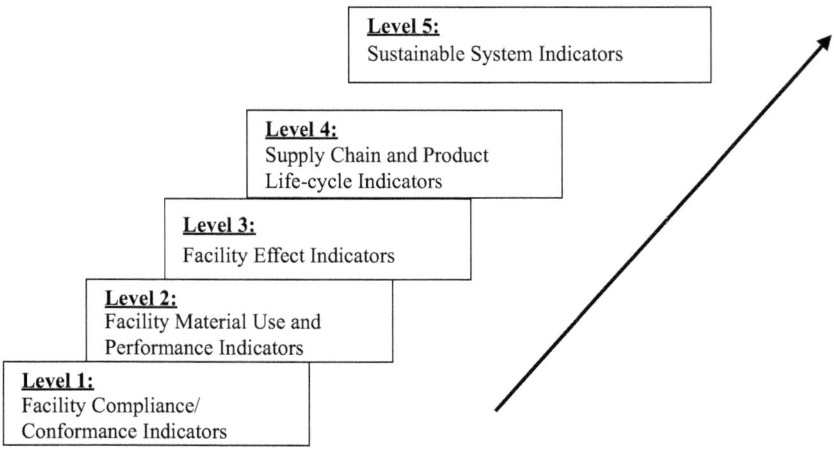

Fig. 2: Framework of Sustainable Production Indicator. Source: (Greiner, 2001)

beyond the boundary of the company/facility to look at the supply chain as well as product distribution, use and ultimate disposal (e.g., percentage of products designed to be easily reused or recycled, percentage of suppliers receiving safety training per year, embodied energy in key raw materials and packaging, tons of GHG emissions generated during product transportation).

Sustainable systems indicators (Level 5) show how an individual company's production processes fit into the larger picture of a sustainable society. Level 5 indicators measure the effects of production on the long-term quality of life and human development within the ecological carrying capacity (e.g., percent of water from local sources used at average local, recharge rate; percent of energy from renewable sources, harvested sustainably and incidence of a specific disease, in the local community compared to the national average).

3 Evaluation of Sustainable Production in Turkish Automotive Sector

Sustainable production performance of the businesses in the automotive sector and included in the BIST Sustainability Index was examined. Although there are 5 businesses from the automotive sector in the BIST Sustainability Index, Ford Otosan, Otokar and Tofaş businesses that announced their Sustainability Reports in 2017 were evaluated to make the comparison in a healthy way. While Otokar business produces bus, minibus, truck, van, trailer and defense industry vehicles, Ford Otosan and Tofaş produces passenger cars and spare parts. The indicators used in the study of Veleva and Ellenbecker (2001) were used to evaluate sustainable production in the automotive sector.

The main aspect, indicators and indications of businesses are presented in Tab. 2. The indicator value of the businesses that did not provide information on the relevant indicator in the sustainability report is represented with (---).

When the indicator values related to businesses' sustainable productions are examined,

- Main aspect of natural environment, energy and material use: Otokar, which differs significantly in terms of water and energy use and CO2 emission values, produces larger vehicles unlike other businesses. The number of vehicles produced is less compared to others. Businesses did not provide information on PBT although they used PBT in production. The reports also do not include content about acidification potential and the material used.
- Main aspect of economic performance: The sustainability report of Otokar has no data on its economic performance. Businesses generally do not provide

Tab. 2: Sustainable Production Indicators Data of Businesses

Main Aspect	Indicators	Firms		
		Ford Otosan	**Tofaş**	**Otokar**
Natural Environment, Energy and material use	Fresh water consumption per unit (m^3)	2,41	3,15	21,7
	Materials used (per unit of product)	---	---	---
	Energy use (per unit of product)	5,9	3,76	24
	Percent energy from renewables	0,009	0	0,002
	Global warming potential (Total Tons of CO2)	196.959	137.603	13.570
	Acidification potential	---	---	---
	kg of PBT chemicals used	---	---	---
Economic Performance	Costs associated with EHS compliance	---	---	---
	Rate of customer complaints and returns	---	---	---
	Organization's openness to stakeholder review and participation in decision-making process (Scale 1–5)	5	5	5
Community Development and Social Justice	Community spending and charitable contributions as percent of revenues (Total Community Investments/ Revenue)	0.0010	0.0004	---
	Number of employees per unit of product or dollar sales	---	---	---
	Number of community–company partnerships *	5	7	3
Workers	Lost workday injury and illness case rate (LWDII)	0,51	0,08	1,74
	Rate of employees' suggested improvements in quality, social and EHS performance	---	---	---
	Turnover rate of employees (%)	11	---	---
	Average number of hours of employee training per year (OHS+Env./number of employee)	6,97	7,22	7,67
	Percent of workers, who report complete job satisfaction (based on questionnaire)	---	---	---

Tab. 2: (continued)

Main Aspect	Indicators	Firms		
		Ford Otosan	Tofaş	Otokar
Products	Percent of products designed for disassembly, reuse or recycling**	---	----	---
	Percent of biodegradable packaging	100	100	100
	Percent of products with take-back policies in place	---	---	---

* The number related to this indicator was not provided in the sustainability reports of businesses. The number was obtained by counting the community-company partnerships mentioned in the report.
** Businesses declared that they used recyclable materials but did not indicate any percentage.

negative data such as customer complaints in their reports. When the openness levels of businesses were evaluated, since sustainability reports were prepared and published on annual basis and shared with all stakeholders, they were rated as "completely open", in other words level 5.

- Main aspect of community development and social justice: Otokar did not include community expenditures in its report. When community expenditures are evaluated according to income, it can be said that Ford Otosan displayed a better performance than Tofaş.
- Main aspect of workers: Lost workday injury and illness case rate value is expected to be low when it is evaluated in terms of employee health and safety. According to Otokar's 2017 sustainability report, it is seen that it needs to make more efforts although it decreased this indicator value compared to previous years. Only Ford Otosan provided information on labor turnover. This also makes it impossible to compare the sector in terms of this indicator
- Main aspect of products: No information was given on the product return processes of businesses. It is a positive application that 100 % of packaging wastes of all three companies are recyclable. In their sustainability reports published, businesses declared that they used recyclable materials in the vehicles produced but did not indicate any percentage.

4 Conclusion

In this study, three businesses operating in the automotive sector were evaluated by considering sustainability reports data. The fact that Otokar did not publish economic sustainability indicator values among the businesses evaluated does not allow the evaluation of sustainability in terms of its three dimensions.

High number of empty cells encountered when Table 4 is evaluated leads to the conclusion that businesses are not sufficiently open in sustainability reports. The fact that the concept of sustainability has become quite popular in recent years is considered as a marketing tool not only for the automotive sector but also for the businesses in many sectors. Businesses only mention sustainability efforts in which they are successful. This does not allow the evaluation of sustainability with all its dimensions and decreases the possibility of comparison.

Indicators of sustainable production should be calculated by more businesses even at different levels and they should be supervised by the authorities. This will ensure that especially social and environmental damages will be revealed and measures will be taken. It is observed that the indicators of sustainable production are difficult to compare even in businesses in the same sector. There appears the need for the standardization of indicators.

References

Andersson K., Eide M. H., Lundqvist U. and Mattsson B. (1998). The Feasibility of Including Sustainability in LCA for Product Development. *Journal of Cleaner Production* 6, 289–298.

Ford Otosan (2017). Sürdürülebilirlik Raporu 2017. Accessed on January 14th, 2019. https://www.fordotosan.com.tr/documents/Documents/Surd_Raporlari/Ford_Otosan_Surdurulebilirlik_Raporu.pdf

Greiner T. J. (2001). Indicators of Sustainable Production – Tracking Progress: A Case Study on Measuring Eco-Sustainability at Guilford of Maine, Inc. Accessed on January 5th, 2019. https://www.uml.edu/docs/Indicators%20of%20Sust%20Prod%20A%20Case%20Study%20on%20Measuring%20Eco_tcm18-229909.pdf

IPCC (2014). Climate Change 2014: Synthesis Report. Contribution of Working Groups I, II and III to the Fifth Assessment Report of the Intergovernmental Panel on Climate Change. IPCC, Geneva, Switzerland.

IPCC (2018). Global Warming on 1.5 °C. Intergovermental Panel on Climate Change. IPCC, Switzerland.

Krajnc, D. and Glavic P. (2003). Indicators of Sustainable Production. Clean Technologies and Environmental Policy (5). 279–288.

LCSP (1998). Sustainable Production: A Working Definition. Lowell Center for Sustainable Production Informal Meeting of the Committee Members.

LCSP (2019). *Sustainable Products*. Accessed on February 2th. 2019. https://www.uml.edu/research/lowell-center/chemicals-materials-products/sustainable-products/sustainableproducts.aspx

Ortiz, O., Castells F. and Sonnemann G. (2009). Sustainability in the Construction Industry: A Review of Recent Developments Based on LCA. *Construction and Building Materials*. 23 (1): 28–39.

OTOKAR (2017). Sürdürülebilirlik Raporu 2017. Accessed on January 14th, 2019. https://www.otokar.com.tr/tr-tr/kurumsal/otokar-hakkinda/Documents/Otokar_Surdurulebilirlik_Raporu_2017.pdf

TOFAŞ (2017). Sürdürülebilirlik Raporu 2017. Accessed on January 14th, 2019. http://irsustainability.tofas.com.tr/files/tr-tofas.pdf

UN (1992). United Nations Sustainable Development. United Nations Conference on Environment and Development- Agenda 21. Accessed on December 14th, 2018. https://sustainabledevelopment.un.org/content/documents/Agenda21.pdf

Veleva, V. and Ellenbecker M. (2001). Indicators of Sustainable Production: Framework and Methodology. *Journal of Cleaner Production*. 9: 519–549.

WCED (1987). *Our Common Future. World Commission on Environment and Development*. Oxford University Press, Oxford.

Metin Bas, Niyazi Kurnaz and Ali Kestane

Statistical Analysis of Corporate Sustainability in the TRNC Banking Sector after the Crisis

1 Introduction

In this study, the corporate sustainability of the banks, which *are operating in Turkish Republic of Northern Cyprus (TRNC) and lack of an organized market, was aimed to be evaluated from economic, social and environmental aspects, by the years 2009, and 2016 in 2008 post-financial crisis. The universe of the study has consisted of the banks operating in the Turkish Republic of Northern Cyprus (TRNC). In order to make more realistic comments and issue more reliable information about the sustainability of the banks operating in the industry, the study was restricted to "**private capital banks**". Since the majority of the banking industry is consisted of private capital banks, according to the data of TRNC Central bank and North Cyprus Banks Association, in order to make their sustainability performances from the year 2009 to today a current issue, **12 analysable private capital banks** in TRNC banking industry were selected as the sample of the study. In order to make easier analyses and more reliable comments of the information of the banks, they were evaluated **through social, environmental and economic** indicators.*

The study consists of two parts. In the first part, the basic explanations of sustainability concept and approaches are made, and in the second part, a practice of the social, environmental and economic evaluations of corporate sustainabilities of the banks are given.

2 Sustainability Concept and Its Importance

The fact that the sustainability concept has been involved in many fields, used together with various issues and corresponds too many means, which have made it disputable. Accordingly, to express its widely accepted definition has become difficult (Yavuz, 2010: 65); that is, *Sustainability is defined as economically, legally and morally assessment of the current resources used by human, in such a way to allow next generations to sustain their vital activities at an optimum level (Kestane, 2016: 6).*In this context, it is estimated that sustainable development with a competitive advantage will be ensured with their continuation of sustainable activities (Eccles and Michael, 2010: 133).

3 Sustainability Approaches

Three main approaches guiding to sustainability are stated to be social sustainability, environmental sustainability and economic sustainability (Bansal, 2005: 198).

Social Sustainability: Refers to the responsibilities of enterprises against the environment (Epstein, 2008: 37), and defined as survivability and having best living conditions of people through the studies conducted to create a sustainable environment (Liverman et.al., 1988: 143).

Environmental Sustainability: Refers to sustaining life in accordance with the limitations of nature, and contributes to the creation of a healthy economy with sustainable environmental activities (Hitchcock and Williard, 2009: 9).

Economic Sustainability: Economic Sustainability, which refers to provide for enterprises to sustain their performances and keep their position in the market for making their profit maximum, aims to create long term asset for shareholders by taking advantage of opportunities issued by economic, social and environmental activities, for providing social benefit (Nemli, 2004: 81). Financial performance is regarded as the main indicator in the assurance of economic sustainability (Tuna, 2014: 11).

4 Sustainability Studies

In the context of economic developments provided with globalized trading, world wide exchange markets have taken various decisions in order to inform the public about sustainability studies and risk elements that will likely to be encountered and raise awareness to increase transparency. For example, the integration of sustainability-related conditions to those related to listing on the stock exchange; actualizing sustainability indexes through published guides are some of the main decisions. Accordingly, the first created sustainability index in the world is the Domini 400 Social Index, calculated by "KLD Research and Analytics", which was established in 1990 and is making studies for institutional investors. The sustainability studies accelerated in 1990 with the establishment of Dow Jones index, and leading companies on sustainability indexes are listed as London, Nasdaq and Euronext. When the studies from the past to the present time are reviewed, it is seen that South Africa initiated sustainability studies in 2004, Brasil in 2005, Germany in 2007, Spain, Austria, Denmark, Sweden, Norway in 2008, China, Indonesia and Korea in 2010, and Turkey in 2014 (ISC, 2011: 9–10; Kestane, 2016: 38).

5 Data and Methodology

In this part of the study, the Corporate Sustainability of the banks by the years of 2009 and 2016 in the post-crisis period, which are operating in TRNC and lack of an organized market, are evaluated in terms of social, environmental and economic. In addition, the purpose and importance of the study were discussed and its scope was identified, and the content of the study was explained as well.

Aim and Importance of the Study

In this study, it is aimed to evaluate social, environmental and economical sustainabilities of the banks by years of 2009 and 2016 in the post-crisis period, which are operating in TRNC and lack of an organized market. This study has a distinctive importance in respect to revealing the sustainability performances of the banks through social, environmental and economic data from 2009 to the present time; planning sustainability studies to be done in TRNC in the future; creating an organized market with clarifying the importance of TRNC in banking industry among Mediterranean island countries and making banking industry transparent.

Hypotheses

The objective of the study was addressed by testing following hypotheses.

Null hypothesis H0: The rankings of the data formed from the social, environmental and economic sustainability variables of the banks by years of 2009–2016 are similar. In other words, the social, environmental and economic sustainability variables of the banks do not significantly differ by years. The social, environmental and economic sustainability variables of each bank are those randomly distributed and not different from each other.

Alternative hypothesis H1: The rankings of the data formed from the social, environmental and economic sustainability variables of the banks by years of 2009–2016 are different from each other. In other words, the social, environmental and economic sustainability variables of the banks significantly differ by years. These differences are due to the discrepancy of the social, environmental and economic sustainability variable of each bank, and they are significant.

Scope and Limitations of the Study

The scope of the study consists of the banks operating in the TRNC. The limitations of the study were defined with "***private capital banks***", with the aim of making more realistic comments and submitting more reliable information about the sustainabilities of the banks operating in the industry. Since an important part of the banking industry consisted of private capital banks according to the data of TRNC Central bank and Northern Cyprus Banking Association, analyzable ***12 private capital banks*** were considered as the sample of the study to bring up sustainability performance of TRNC banking industry from 2009 to today to the agenda.

Private banks with operating capital in TRNC are as follows: ***Akfinans Bank, Asbank, Creditwest Bank, Kıbrıs İktisat Bankası, Kıbrısfaisal, Kooperatif Bank, Limasol Bank, Şeker Bank, Türk Bankası, Universal Bank, Viyabank, Yakındoğu Bank***.

Collection and Classification of the Data

The required information of the banks was obtained from "official web sites, North Cyprus Central Bank (NCCB) and North Cyprus Banking Association (NCBA)". In order to make easier analyses and more reliable comments of the information of the banks, they were evaluated through social, environmental and economic indicators. The criteria based on the classification of these indicators shown in Tab. 1 below (Aktaş ve Kargın, 2007: 40; Kestane, 2016:92):

Tab. 1: Sustainability Variables Used in the Study

Social Sustainability Variables Used in the Study
S1: Number of Staff
S2: Number of Educations
S3: Number of Personnel Attending Trainings
S4: Amount of Investment in Trainings
S5: Investment in Projects
S6: Representation/Promotion Investments
Environmental Sustainability Variables Used in the Study
C1: Number of Banks
C2: Number of Branches
C3: Number of Staff
C4: Change in Asset Investments

Tab. 1: (continued)

Social Sustainability Variables Used in the Study
C5: Stationery
C6: Energy
C7: Water
C8: Communication/Communication
C9: Cleaning Agent Usage
C10: Maintenance - Repair Expenses
Economic Sustainability Variables Used in the Study
E1: Asset Profitability = Net Profit/Average Asset
*E2: Equity Profit = Net Profit/Equity * 100*
E3: Net Interest Margin = Net Interest Income/Total Assets
E4: Net Profit Margin = Period Net Profit/Interest Income + Non-Interest Income
E5: Asset Cycle = Interest Income + Non-Interest Income/Average Asset
E6: Loan Growth Rate = Period End Loan-Term Loan/Loan Per Period
E7: Active Growth Rate = End-of-Term Active-Term Active/Per Period Active
E8: Equity Growth Rate = End of Period Equity - Equity at the Beginning of Period/Equity at the Beginning of the Period
E9: Interest Growth Rate = End-of-Period Net Interest.
E10: Current Ratio = Liquid Assets/Short Term Liabilities
E11: Liquid Ratio = Liquid Assets/Total Assets
E12: Net Loans/Total Assets
E13: Total Revenues/Total Expenses
E14: Interest Income/Interest Expenses
E15: Interest Income/Total Revenues
E16: Interest Expenses/Total Expenses

Analysis of the Data

"*Microsoft Excel*" and "*SPSS*" package program was used in the analysis of the obtained data concerning the years 2009–2016. The statistical significance of sustainabilities of 12 private capital banks in Cyprus between 2009 and 2016 was tested by years from social, environmental and economic perspective using above coded variables. The variables used were discussed in three dimensions, including ***social, environmental and economic sustainability,*** and a total of 32 variables were benefited from. Since the number of banks is statistically inadequate, nonparametric the Friedman two-way Aalysis of variance by ranks was used. The effect of the developments in post-crisis on 32 various variables of the 12 banks for 2009–2016 was examined by this test.

The two-way analysis of variance can be used when the effects of two different variables, at two or more levels, on one continuous dependent variable are intended to be examined (Oğuzlar, 2007:119). Thus, it may be possible to see the effects of these two independent variables on the dependent variable separately and commonly. But, it requires some assumptions to be tested (Seçer, 2015: 44). If all assumptions become valid as a result of the test, two-way analysis of variance can be made. If tested assumptions don't become valid, then the Friedman two-way analysis of Varivnce by ranks can be used (Canküyer and Aşan, 2005: 226). The key feature of this test is to relieve normality and homogeneous variance assumption from being an obligation. A data table with n block and k industries, created for this purpose, is arranged.

The observation values in the table created for making the test should be gradable. The test, by assigning sequence numbers to observation values, can be conducted over the scores (Canküyer and Aşan, 2005:227). Since the number of banks is statistically inadequate, 32 variables that were let as dependent variables didn't exhibit a normal distribution, the Friedman two-way analysis of variance by ranks was used in the study. In the analysis, 2009–2016 years in the post-crisis period, 12 banks were considered as independent variables; 6 variables for social sustainability, 10 variables for environmental sustainability, and 16 variables for economic sustainability as dependent variables. The dependent variables are those measured with a permanent scale. The banks were arranged as blocks by years and variables as industries by sustainability groups. There was no interaction between the banks and variables, according to the identified years. Accordingly, these assumptions assured the requirements of the test.

Findings and Evaluation

This part includes the analysis of social, environmental and economic data of the banking industry of TRNC in post 2008 crisis period and socially, environmentally and economically evaluation of the findings obtained from the analysis, and graphical drawings were utilized so as to make comments after the statistical analyses, in an easier and more realistic way, and they were explained below in headings.

Social Sustainability Related Analysis Results

The results of the analysis on social sustainability are given in Tab. 2 below:

Tab. 2: Descriptive Statistics of Social Sustainability

Var	Mean	Std. Deviation	Minimum	Maximum	Percentiles 25th	Percentiles 75th	Friedman Test Mean Rank
S1	1665,00	197,682	1433	1934	1442,50	1815,50	3,50
S2	21,00	4,840	11	24	17,75	24,00	1,00
S3	496,00	131,953	225	677	460,50	586,50	2,25
S4	57975,25	18361,993	24200	84546	50501,25	73291,00	6,00
S5	20000,00	,000	20000	20000	20000,00	20000,00	5,00
S6	4518,50	6937,787	99	19989	337,75	7680,00	3,25
Friedman Test Statistics			**Chi-Square:37,429**		**Asymp. Sig.: 0,000**		**Statistical decision:H_0 unacceptable**

According to the result of the analysis, since Chi-Square:37,429 value was randomly created, and Asymp.Sig:0,000 value is less than α:0,05, H_0 hypothesis was rejected. Accordingly, it is seen that social sustainability variables of the banks are so different from each other in the post-crisis period that cannot be explained with coincidence. Since the social sustainability variables of the banks were seen to differ by years, in order for the effects of social sustainability in the post-crisis period to be commented in a better way, the graphs of these values by years were drawn and stated below.

Graph 1 shows that the staff of the banks have a permanent increase tendency especially from the year 2011, number of training held have an increasing tendency except for the years 2011 and 2014; number of staff participated in the training and investments made in training have an increasing tendency except for the year 2010; the investments made in projects have the same tendency by years and representation-introduction investments have an increasing tendency especially from the year 2015.

When social sustainability components of the banks are examined as a whole, it is seen that there is an important decline in the number of personnel, and education, number of staff participated in training and amount of investments made immediately after the crisis, and the severity of the crisis was obviously felt. More clearly, it is seen from Graph 1 that the number of training was reduced since the banks went downsizing in the number of staff in the post-crisis period, and accordingly, the budget allocated for training was reduced. Moreover, it is seen that the banks tended to representation-introduction investments as of the year 2012 thereby providing the effects of the crisis to be decreased, staff were recruited, the number of training arranged, and that of staff participated in

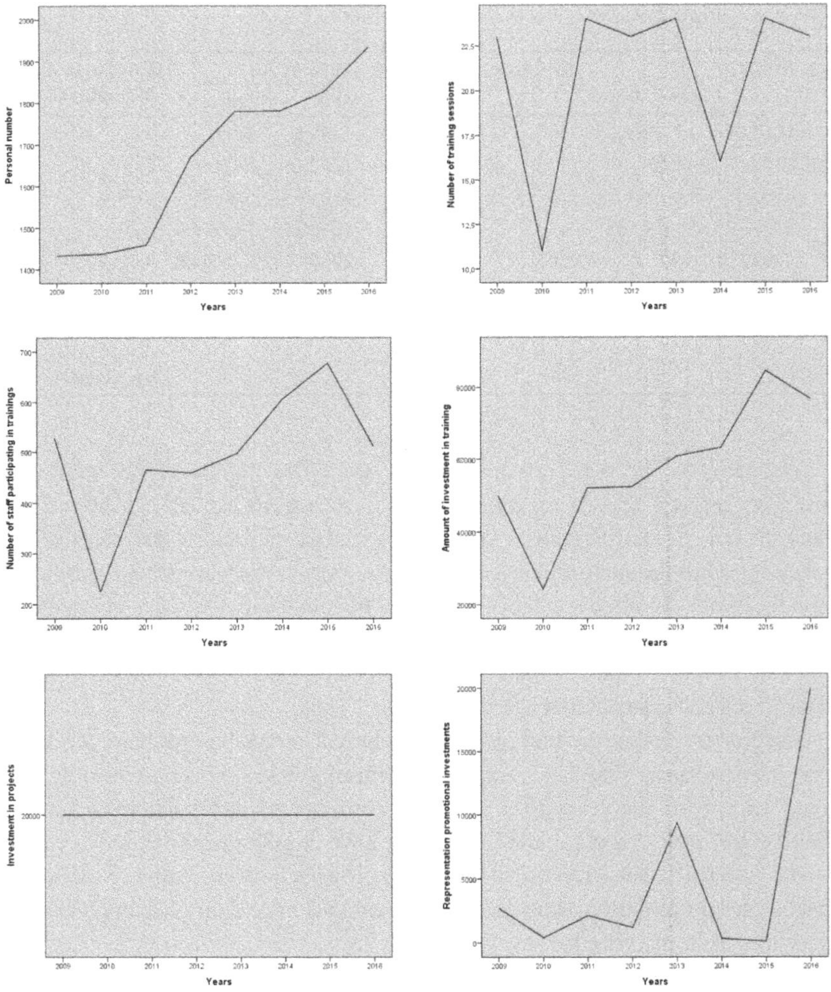

Graph 1: Components of Social Sustainability

those increased, by means of which staff quality was increased, and the quality of training was increased and return from investments was provided. It can be said that project investments had no effect on the mentioned process.

Environmental Sustainability Related Analysis Results

The results of the analysis on environmental sustainability are identified as in Tab. 3 below:

Tab. 3: Descriptive Statistics of Environmental Sustainability

Var	Mean	Std. Deviation	Min.	Max	Percentiles		Friedman Test Mean Rank
					25th	75th	
C1	14,13	,991	13	16	13,25	14,75	1,00
C2	132,25	13,101	117	151	118,50	143,50	2,00
C3	1665,38	198,267	1433	1937	1442,50	1815,50	4,25
C4	4361309,50	1768974,122	2317000	7364874	2855875,5	5903141,75	10,00
C5	4664,63	1357,129	2774	6296	3191,00	5998,50	5,75
C6	9180,38	1610,269	6587	11040	7490,25	10351,25	7,38
C7	1444,25	818,419	560	3315	962,00	1478,25	3,38
C8	10886,50	4505,600	3212	17349	9589,25	15315,50	7,38
C9	4564,88	3625,412	758	9912	1354,75	8201,50	4,88
C10	29217,38	7107,987	20736	41613	24531,25	35974,50	9,00
Friedman Test Statistics			**Chi-Square:68,564**		**Asymp. Sig.: 0,000**		**Statistical decision:H_0 unacceptable**

According to the result of the analysis, since Chi-Square:68,564 value was randomly created, and Asymp.Sig:0,000 value is less than α:0,05, H_0 hypothesis was rejected. Accordingly, it is seen that environmental sustainability variables of the banks are so different from each other in the post-crisis period that cannot be explained with coincidence. Since the environmental sustainability variables of the banks were seen to differ by years, in order for the effects of environmental sustainability in the post-crisis period to be commented in a better way, the graphs of these values by years were drawn and stated below.

When Graph 2 is examined, it is seen that the number of the banks and departments had a tendency to relatively increase in the post-crisis period in the years of 2009–2016 especially as of the year 2011, and accordingly, the number of staff was positively affected from this situation. Besides, it is seen that the asset investments of the banks had a permanently increased tendency, stationery expenses increased especially except the years of 2012 and 2014, the use of energy had a tendency to increase as of the year 2010, but water consumption decreased. On the other hand, although correspondence/communication

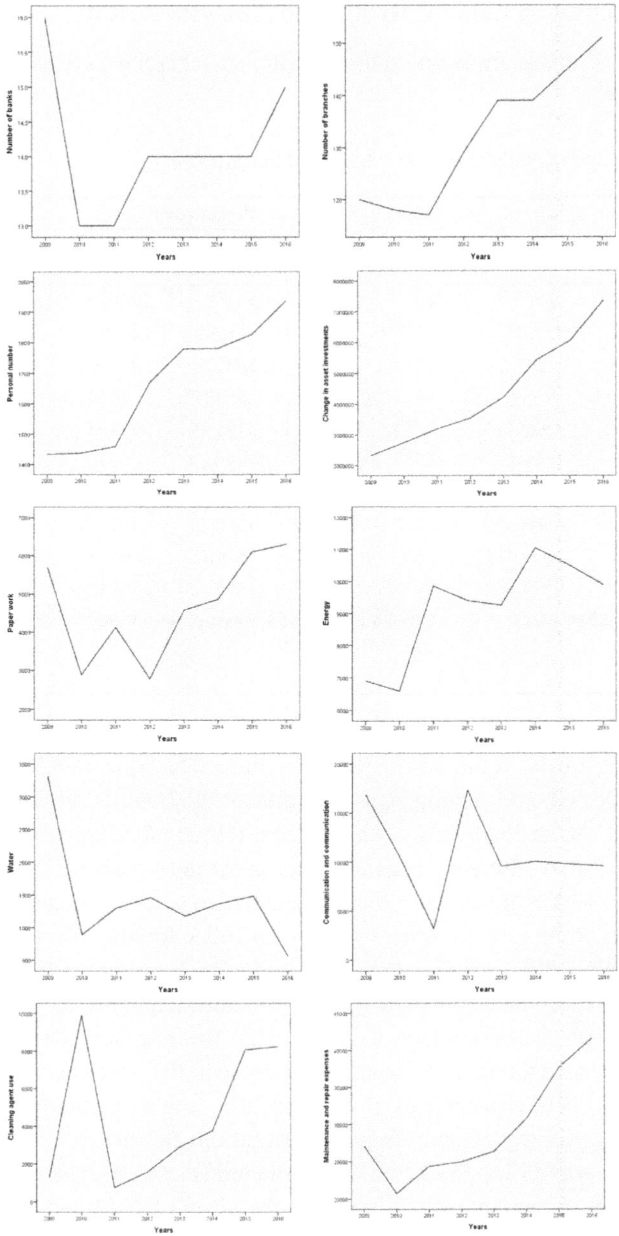

Graph 2: Components of Environmental Sustainability

expenses decreased immediately after the crisis, they had a stable increase tendency as of the year 2015, the use of the cleanser realized at the minimum level especially in 2011, but began to increase from 2013, repair-maintenance expenses had a permanent increase tendency as of the year 2010.

When environmental sustainability components of the banks are examined as a whole, it is seen that the increase in the number of the banks immediately after the crisis triggered the increase in the number of departments and accordingly that of staff. It is understood from the changes in investments that the banks weren't affected significantly by the crisis especially in terms of asset investments, and turned the crisis into the opportunity. It is seen clearly from the graph that stationery expenses changed depending on the number of the banks in the post-crisis period, and energy usage also increased depending on the increase in the number of bank and department. On the other hand, it can be said that the banks derived correct lessons from the adverse consumption of water resources in the world, and the staff's awareness was raised about the water usage, or economical devices were placed into the banks and thus, unnecessarily water consumption was prevented. The decrease in the correspondence/communication expenses can be said to result from the internet economy, e-transactions, and intensely usage of data processing technologies. Besides, the reason why an increase occurred in clear usage and repair and maintenance expenses is thought because of the increase in the number of bank and department, but, staff is needed to have correct training on the cleanser usage, and it is obvious that the training to be provided for the technical usage of devices used in the banks will reduce the technical expenses.

Economic Sustainability Related Analysis Results

The results of economic sustainability analysis for 2009 are as in Tab. 4 below:

Tab. 4: Descriptive Statistics of 2009

Var	Mean	Std. Deviation	Minimum	Maximum	Percentiles 25th	Percentiles 75th	Friedman Test Mean Rank
E1	,0123083	,02277512	-,02390	,07380	,0034250	,0142500	2,00
E2	,1722833	,25344623	-,33370	,69550	,0310000	,3144750	6,42
E3	,0484583	,03915585	,00130	,16040	,0307500	,0585750	3,92
E4	,0691000	,11670391	-,14160	,36450	,0170000	,1043000	3,92
E5	,1680250	,05667809	,10560	,31770	,1311000	,1941500	6,58
E6	,2882833	,51933036	-,11830	1,84070	,0480500	,3197000	7,08
E7	,3224083	,29090566	,06680	1,16290	,1400500	,3763750	8,83
E8	,2206500	,37842330	,00000	1,35720	,0208750	,2327250	6,25
E9	,6555167	2,15156705	-,36950	7,43600	-,2496750	,3177000	5,58
E10	,3686333	,12294116	,22080	,58970	,2741000	,4987750	10,75
E11	,2918750	,11451183	,11970	,50740	,2089000	,3492250	8,67
E12	,4976417	,16567343	,14530	,83920	,4529250	,5832750	11,67
E13	1,0426750	,39734709	,09210	1,91330	,9936500	1,1478750	14,17
E14	2,7706917	4,42430743	,46320	16,75310	1,2542750	1,9566000	15,67
E15	,6765417	,24205814	,15010	,88240	,6574000	,8278500	13,25
E16	,4526083	,23859351	,09630	,88410	,2055000	,5743500	11,25
Friedman Test Statistics			**Chi-Square:125,301**		**Asymp. Sig.: 0,000**		**Statistical decision:H_0 unacceptable**

According to the result of the analysis, since Chi-Square:125,301 value was randomly created, and Asymp.Sig:0,000 value is less than α:0,05, H_0 hypothesis was rejected. Accordingly, it is seen that economic sustainability variables of the banks are so different from each other in the year 2009 in the post-crisis period that cannot be explained with coincidence.

Analyses in 2010 **as in Tab. 5 below:**

Tab. 5: Descriptive Statistics of 2010

Var	Mean	Std. Deviation	Min.	Max.	Percentiles 25th	Percentiles 75th	Friedman Test Mean Rank
E1	,0146500	,02081239	-,03410	,05490	,0049500	,0241500	2,00
E2	,2277750	,22238793	-,16640	,73020	,1058500	,3536750	7,83
E3	,0522333	,04244407	-,01430	,15980	,0321750	,0648000	3,83
E4	,0811917	,20143380	-,47890	,33940	,0347750	,1698500	5,17
E5	,1542167	,07651152	,07140	,38030	,1131000	,1603500	6,17
E6	,2283833	,18657568	-,02410	,59980	,1090000	,3452750	7,75
E7	,1257250	,11351896	-,04000	,33180	,0247750	,1340000	5,50
E8	,1312833	,16277907	-,14270	,47510	,0228500	,2070250	5,58
E9	-,8716417	3,95772134	-13,38290	1,37610	,0085250	,3153500	6,17
E10	,3105667	,11200198	,14690	,55580	,2154500	,3581000	10,58
E11	,2553667	,11521577	,06960	,48790	,1646000	,3203500	8,25
E12	,5422833	,18117286	,14780	,89210	,4651000	,6434500	12,42
E13	1,1480083	,20504275	,67580	1,48890	1,0412000	1,2795500	15,08
E14	2,6623250	3,18266757	,31630	12,54320	1,5498250	2,2583000	15,75
E15	,6619250	,26148874	,09260	,87580	,6407000	,7975250	13,08
E16	,3842333	,18025123	,06670	,59520	,2378500	,5577000	10,83
Friedman Test Statistics			**Chi-Square:130,574**		**Asymp. Sig.: 0,000**		**Statistical decision:H_0 unacceptable**

According to the result of the analysis, since Chi-Square:130,574 value was randomly created, and Asymp.Sig:0,000 value is less than α:0,05, H_0 hypothesis was rejected. Accordingly, it is seen that economic sustainability variables of the banks are so different from each other in the year 2010 in the post-crisis period that cannot be explained with coincidence.

Analyses in 2011 **as in Tab. 6 below:**

Tab. 6: Descriptive Statistics of 2011

Var	Mean	Std. Deviation	Minimum	Maximum	Percentiles 25th	Percentiles 75th	Friedman Test Mean Rank
E1	,0185750	,01863185	,00010	,07270	,0072500	,0229500	1,63
E2	,2578250	,17915169	,00410	,61290	,0724000	,3687000	8,42
E3	,0476583	,03596034	-,00270	,15060	,0337500	,0495750	3,25
E4	,1152417	,06866386	,00010	,27190	,0781000	,1607000	5,04
E5	,1689333	,12750387	,04060	,52950	,0987000	,1941250	6,50
E6	,4189333	,50465314	,07650	1,96020	,1393750	,4149000	9,54
E7	,1753333	,07003820	,07660	,28490	,1044750	,2368750	7,00
E8	,1699500	,26269927	,00000	,94660	,0183750	,2365500	5,08
E9	,0865167	,21319529	-,37670	,37370	,0244500	,2199250	5,04
E10	,3009750	,16246449	,16240	,74760	,2034500	,3270750	9,75
E11	,2502333	,14924280	,05890	,63730	,1614250	,2890000	8,08
E12	,5892167	,15192429	,20880	,84530	,5604750	,6703000	12,75
E13	1,2577500	,33720759	1,00240	2,22970	1,0883250	1,2485250	15,08
E14	2,3913083	2,08618089	,71580	8,87950	1,7216000	2,0599250	15,83
E15	,6117583	,25977430	,07490	,85320	,5181500	,7756750	12,58
E16	,3683417	,18333513	,04380	,56110	,1557500	,5000000	10,42
Friedman Test Statistics			**Chi-Square:135,048**		**Asymp. Sig.: 0,000**		**Statistical decision:H_0 unacceptable**

According to the result of the analysis, since Chi-Square:135,048 value was randomly created, and Asymp.Sig:0,000 value is less than α:0,05, H_0 hypothesis was rejected. Accordingly, it is seen that economic sustainability variables of the banks are so different from each other in the year 2011 in the post-crisis period that cannot be explained with coincidence.

Analyses in 2012 **as in Tab. 7 below:**

Tab. 7: Descriptive Statistics of 2012

Var	Mean	Std. Deviation	Minimum	Maxi-mum	Percentiles		Friedman Test Mean Rank
					25th	75th	
E1	,0126083	,01499494	-,00320	,05650	,0052000	,0144000	2,83
E2	,1668250	,11813170	-,01510	,35260	,0564750	,2646250	7,92
E3	,0442083	,03997543	-,00690	,16190	,0306000	,0481500	4,25
E4	,0738917	,06817820	-,05480	,21740	,0442250	,1088750	5,00
E5	,1514667	,07176343	,05820	,31870	,1080750	,1652750	7,50
E6	,1603750	,25274329	-,10250	,82180	-,0408750	,2419000	6,25
E7	,1092417	,10190245	-,02910	,28610	,0120000	,1462000	5,83
E8	,1279583	,11870414	,00010	,32860	,0224000	,2411500	6,00
E9	-,1159583	,45678173	-1,53940	,20750	-,0574250	,0339250	2,75
E10	,3063500	,15172998	,18670	,72490	,2004500	,3420500	10,67
E11	,2561417	,13888794	,06070	,61220	,1743250	,2953000	9,17
E12	,5867750	,16076030	,21810	,89910	,5155000	,6520250	13,00
E13	1,1131917	,11560291	,94790	1,39810	1,0567750	1,1596500	15,08
E14	2,3402750	2,72017484	,26690	10,85770	1,5384750	1,7982250	15,83
E15	,6316333	,25573475	,04330	,84330	,5950500	,7978500	12,92
E16	,4015167	,19139157	,08260	,63040	,2070500	,5373500	11,00
Friedman Test Statistics			**Chi-Square:139,507**		**Asymp. Sig.: 0,001**		**Statistical decision: H_0 unacceptable**

According to the result of the analysis, since Chi-Square:139,507 value was randomly created, and Asymp.Sig:0,000 value is less than α:0,05, H_0 hypothesis was rejected. Accordingly, it is seen that economic sustainability variables of the banks are so different from each other in the year 2012 in the post-crisis period that cannot be explained with coincidence.

Analyses in 2013 **as in Tab. 8 below:**

Tab. 8: Descriptive Statistics of 2013

Var	**Mean**	**Std. Deviation**	**Minimum**	**Maximum**	**Percentiles**		**Friedman Test Mean Rank**
					25th	**75th**	
E1	,0123000	,01957025	-,00340	,07230	,0047500	,0109750	2,00
E2	,1591250	,13395657	-,01520	,41060	,0721000	,2812000	6,75
E3	,0333833	,02552047	-,00720	,10230	,0227500	,0368000	3,50
E4	,0826917	,12186168	-,06040	,42990	,0291250	,0850750	4,33
E5	,1455583	,07929528	,05640	,35980	,1009750	,1636750	6,67
E6	,2667000	,23977781	,01020	,91830	,1062000	,3412250	8,58
E7	,2903833	,20862534	,10790	,89990	,1613750	,3307500	9,67
E8	,1876000	,23574262	,00650	,74630	,0149500	,3038000	6,33
E9	-,0108917	,19898970	-,32870	,31160	-,1496750	,1456000	3,42
E10	,2815833	,08086704	,07540	,39260	,2456500	,3266750	9,58
E11	,2461583	,08017591	,04330	,37540	,2178500	,2907750	8,25
E12	,5926083	,12719424	,37320	,90770	,5307750	,6266750	13,25
E13	1,1735750	,35926213	,94300	2,28670	1,0368500	1,1072500	15,08
E14	1,9368750	1,48088637	,15560	6,38490	1,5016000	1,9405750	15,50
E15	,5592167	,25087899	,02350	,78140	,4169750	,7331750	12,42
E16	,3775250	,16933752	,06650	,58020	,2223250	,4981250	10,67
Friedman Test Statistics			**Chi-Square:137,176**		**Asymp. Sig.: 0,004**		**Statistical decision:** H_0 **unacceptable**

According to the result of the analysis, since Chi-Square:137,176 value was randomly created, and Asymp.Sig:0,000 value is less than α:0,05, H_0 hypothesis was rejected. Accordingly, it is seen that economic sustainability variables of the banks are so different from each other in the year 2013 in the post-crisis period that cannot be explained with coincidence.

Analyses in 2014 **as in Tab. 9 below:**

Tab. 9: Descriptive Statistics of 2014

Var	Mean	Std. Deviation	Minimum	Maximum	Percentiles 25th	Percentiles 75th	Friedman Test Mean Rank
E1	,0132917	,02388858	,00010	,08780	,0032250	,0102250	1,83
E2	,1291750	,10581040	,00010	,28480	,0224250	,2335500	6,33
E3	,0356417	,03248500	,00910	,13410	,0221750	,0392000	3,33
E4	,0816000	,09286528	,00010	,32640	,0178000	,1286750	4,50
E5	,1861667	,15211800	,09430	,63270	,1098750	,2340750	7,50
E6	,0961417	,14724338	-,26910	,26230	,0408750	,2338500	5,92
E7	,1079167	,14460972	-,14160	,45660	,0465000	,1695250	5,83
E8	,2029083	,24002218	,00940	,89030	,0565750	,2848000	7,42
E9	,3070417	,80725102	-,24830	2,82030	-,0102500	,2114500	6,42
E10	,3281250	,11799998	,15920	,55580	,2550750	,4346250	11,08
E11	,2775750	,09128502	,13990	,44280	,2032500	,3596250	9,67
E12	,5817500	,10671247	,36640	,74430	,4903500	,6614750	12,67
E13	1,1235500	,20724421	1,00290	1,74480	1,0192500	1,1217000	14,83
E14	1,8361250	,80815729	1,26440	4,28560	1,4806500	1,8857750	15,92
E15	,6393083	,37272122	,13060	1,54940	,3546250	,7327000	12,58
E16	,3711583	,18455271	,06440	,58530	,2057250	,5191750	10,17
Friedman Test Statistics			**Chi-Square:133,529**		**Asymp. Sig.: 0,000**		**Statistical decision: H_0 unacceptable**

According to the result of the analysis, since Chi-Square:133,529 value was randomly created, and Asymp.Sig:0,000 value is less than α:0,05, H_0 hypothesis was rejected. Accordingly, it is seen that economic sustainability variables of the banks are so different from each other in the year 2014 in the post-crisis period that cannot be explained with coincidence.

Analyses in 2015 **as in Tab. 10 below:**

Tab. 10: Descriptive Statistics of 2015

Var	Mean	Std. Deviation	Mini-mum	Maxi-mum	Percentiles		Friedman Test Mean Rank
					25th	75th	
E1	,0104667	,01430520	,00010	,05460	,0045750	,0100750	1,67
E2	,1337583	,11416710	,00390	,39480	,0569750	,1943000	6,08
E3	,0400000	,03952576	,01310	,16210	,0201250	,0406000	3,67
E4	,0846750	,10258348	,00180	,37810	,0163500	,1041250	4,00
E5	,2537083	,33210526	,09240	1,26240	,1019750	,3141250	7,67
E6	,1625167	,13448014	-,20620	,30180	,1203000	,2516500	7,25
E7	,1951250	,15172582	-,04210	,56610	,0989500	,2433250	7,25
E8	,1873667	,26600098	,01370	,95480	,0308250	,2519000	6,08
E9	,5483750	1,43550847	-,15650	5,06650	-,0324000	,3500000	7,17
E10	,3400500	,11659221	,19670	,58320	,2400000	,4359000	10,83
E11	,2722167	,08461184	,16050	,42260	,1874000	,3343750	9,25
E12	,5784333	,11998463	,34910	,77950	,5296750	,6469500	12,50
E13	1,0982417	,09415784	1,00260	1,29180	1,0137750	1,1565000	14,83
E14	2,1552250	1,53314685	1,21070	6,86560	1,4581250	1,9511500	15,92
E15	,5502583	,25271613	,02260	,76020	,5041750	,7375000	12,17
E16	,3536167	,21372010	,01140	,57810	,1283750	,5290500	9,67
Friedman Test Statistics			**Chi-Square:126,801**		**Asymp. Sig.: 0,001**		**Statistical decision:H_0 unacceptable**

According to the result of the analysis, since Chi-Square:126,801 value was randomly created, and Asymp.Sig:0,000 value is less than α:0,05, H_0 hypothesis was rejected. Accordingly, it is seen that economic sustainability variables of the banks are so different from each other in the year 2015 in the post-crisis period that cannot be explained with coincidence.

Analyses in 2016 **as in Tab. 11 below:**

Tab. 11: Descriptive Statistics of 2016

Var	Mean	Std. Deviation	Mini-mum	Maxi-mum	Percentiles 25th	75th	Friedman Test Mean Rank
E1	,0211000	,04038940	,00200	,14780	,0049750	,0144500	1,75
E2	,2376167	,23648910	,00810	,85480	,0571750	,3635000	8,17
E3	,0380583	,02796067	,01370	,12130	,0226250	,0403250	3,33
E4	,1007833	,11154744	,00890	,39120	,0205250	,1371750	4,58
E5	,2201417	,21729504	,08240	,82220	,1028250	,3346500	7,58
E6	,1408917	,09461423	-,00530	,27730	,0498250	,2100250	5,83
E7	,1517333	,14492625	-,20200	,43820	,1039750	,2119500	6,58
E8	,0996333	,09158818	,01060	,32450	,0169500	,1372500	5,08
E9	,1866250	,20141192	-,09550	,64270	,0244000	,2898000	6,92
E10	,3423333	,09734549	,19710	,53450	,3008500	,4167000	10,83
E11	,2740000	,09704315	,08090	,44240	,1934250	,3412250	9,17
E12	,5747667	,12343647	,30910	,81980	,4971250	,6443000	12,92
E13	1,1079250	,12205405	,96860	1,43140	1,0302250	1,1314250	15,00
E14	2,3704000	2,00282550	1,23860	8,62180	1,5241750	2,2024500	16,00
E15	,5478750	,25269668	,05210	,78970	,3795500	,7305250	12,33
E16	,3447333	,20822137	,03050	,56120	,1052500	,5176500	9,92
Friedman Test Statistics			**Chi-Square:134,529**		**Asymp. Sig.: 0,001**		**Statistical decision:H_0 unacceptable**

According to the result of the analysis, since Chi-Square:134,529 value was randomly created, and Asymp.Sig:0,000 value is less than α:0,05, H_0 hypothesis was rejected. Accordingly, it is seen that economic sustainability variables of the banks are so different from each other in the year 2016 in the post-crisis period that cannot be explained with coincidence.

Since the economic sustainability variables of the banks were seen to differ by years, in order for the effects of economic sustainability in the post-crisis period to be commented in a better way, the volatility graph of these values by years was drawn and stated below.

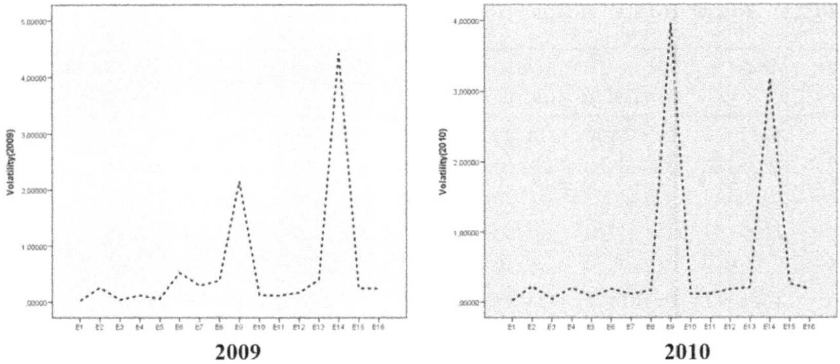

Graph 3: Volatility of 2009–2010

When Graph 3 (2009) is examined, it is seen that growth of the equity capitals of the banks (E9) and their interest incomes and expenses (E:14) fluctuated at the maximum level by the year of 2009 in the post-crisis period. But, said fluctuation shows that the crisis quite adversely affected the capital structure and growth levels of the banks, and since a stable interest rate couldn't be charged due to the economic cyclical environment, fluctuations appeared in interest rates. On the other hand, it is striking that a stable fluctuation didn't exist in (E3) net interest margin and (E5) asset turnover rate. In the light of outstanding indicators, it is obvious that the crisis caused important problems for the banks to obtain interest income in 2009, and resources and assets were also affected by this situation. In other words, it is possible to say that asset turnover rates of the banks weakened and accordingly, the timely return of credits couldn't be assured. It is apparent that since credit collection became difficult, and stability could not be assured in interest rates.

When Graph 3 (2010) is examined, it is seen that growth of the equity capitals of the banks (E9) and their interest incomes and expenses (E:14) fluctuated at the maximum level by the year 2010 in the post-crisis period. But, said fluctuation shows that the crisis quite adversely affected the capital structure and growth levels of the banks, and since a stable interest rate couldn't be charged due to the economic cyclical environment, fluctuations appeared in interest rates. On the other hand, it is striking that a stable fluctuation doesn't exist in (E3) net interest margin and (E5) asset turnover rate. In the light of outstanding indicators, it is obvious that the crisis caused important problems for banks to obtain interest income in the years 2009–2010, and resources and assets were also affected by this situation. In other words, it is possible to say that the occurrence of the fluctuations in active growth of the banks weakened turnover rates of assets and accordingly, timely return of credits couldn't be assured. It is clear that since credit collection became difficult, and stability could not be assured in interest rates, and there is a negative fluctuation in interest expenses in the years 2009–2010.

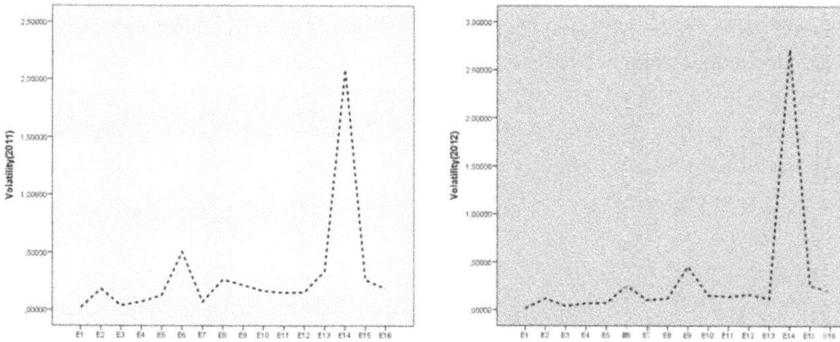

2011 **2012**

Graph 4: Volatility of 2011–2012

When Graph 4 (2011) is examined, it is seen that by year of 2011 in the post-crisis period; equity capital profitability (E2), credit growth rate (E6), especially total income/total expenses (E13), interest incomes (E14) of the banks showed maximum fluctuation in the satisfaction of interest expenses.

It is clear that the mentioned situation, and major fluctuations in credit growth rate, included in asset groups of banks, directly affects interest incomes, and indirectly affects total income. But, it is seen that problems have been encountered in banking activities, especially in credit and interest incomes in the period starting from the year 2009. No fluctuation is seen in the solvency (E10) of the banks in the crisis period starting from the year 2009, which raises the doubt whether debts have been paid with income from the main activities. Moreover, relative active growth levels of the banks in comparison to the previous year (E7) yields an unstable image, which justifies above-mentioned suspicions, and it is possible to say that the crisis continued to affect income-expense and capital structure of the banks by the year of 2011.

When Graph 4 (2012) is examined, it is seen that by the year of 2012 in the post-crisis period, equity capital profitability (E2), credit growth rate (E6),interest growth (E9) especially interest incomes (E14) of the banks showed maximum fluctuation in the satisfaction of interest expenses, but, the interest incomes (E15) rate in total income showed a little fluctuation. The mentioned situation means that major fluctuations especially in the credit growth rate, included in asset groups of banks, affect interest income and total income. Nominated, that banks encounter problems in terms of credit growth and fail to sell credit to their customers can cause positive developments in the growth of interests, and that can cause constant changes in the rate of interest incomes in total income.. In other words, it can be said that there is not a stable tendency in the main incomes of the banks and this is because of the crisis. Accordingly, it is clear that the fluctuations occurred in capital profitabilities of the banks can betray investors' trust, which is shown in the graphs as well. It will not be false to say that the banks failed to follow an effective credit and interest policy in the crisis period and in the first two years.

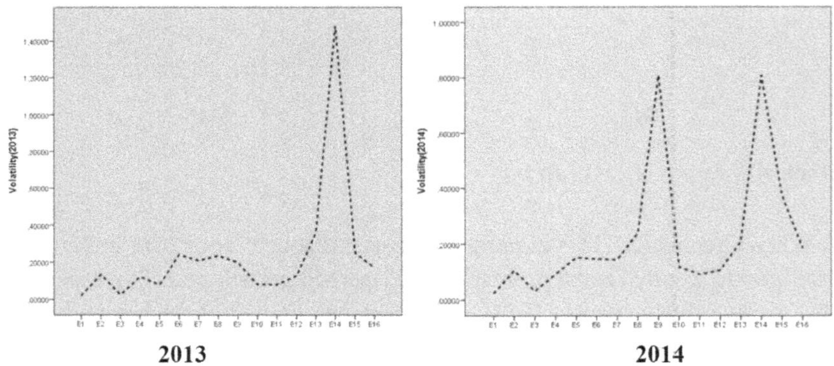

Graph 5: Volatility of 2013–2014

When Graph 5 (2013) is examined, it is seen that by the year of 2013 in the post-crisis period, equity capital profitability (E2), net profit margin (E4), credit growth rate (E6), active growth level E7), equity capital growth level (E8), interest growth (E9) and especially interest incomes (E14) of the banks showed maximum fluctuation in the satisfaction of interest expenses, but the interest incomes (E15) rate in total income showed a little fluctuation, and there is fluctuation in the rate of interest incomes (E16) in total incomes and in the rate of interest expenses (E15) in total expense. The mentioned situation reflects the intention of the creation of significant changes in the asset and resource groups of the banks, and the decisions taken have a permanent important effect on this issue. The aforementioned said change in the banking activities by the year of 2013 in comparison to previous years is understood from the graphical images of profitability, growth, continuity and income-expense structure rates, and simply means that all cogs in a wheel will almost come away, and how important is to get especially interest incomes under control in the banking activities is seen from Graph 6. The mentioned situation is thought to create important fluctuations in decisions that information users will take in the overall of the banks and is regarded as a sign on taking positive steps in the provision of credit and interest incomes.

When Graph 5 (2014) is examined, it is seen that by year of 2014 in the post-crisis period, equity capital profitability (E2), net profit margin(E4), asset turnover rate (E5), credit growth rate (E6), active growth level (E7), equity capital growth level (E8), interest growth (E9),especially total incomes/total expenses (E13) of the banks, and satisfaction of interest expenses by interest incomes(E14), and the rate of interest incomes (E15) in total income showed maximum fluctuation; there is fluctuation in the rate of interest incomes (E15) in total incomes and in the rate of interest expenses (E16) in total expenses. It is thought that the mentioned situation reflects the intention of the creation of significant changes in the asset and resource groups of the banks in 2013, and the decisions taken in 2014 have a positive effect on this issue. The graphical images of the mentioned profitability, growth, continuity and income-expense structure rates, aforementioned for the banks by year of 2014 in comparison to previous years, point out that in case of that especially interest incomes is correctly gotten under control and debt paying plans (E10) are made correctly, then equity capital (E8), and interest incomes (E9) increase. That the mentioned situation positively contributes to asset profitability can be said when compared with the data of the previous years. The above-mentioned developments are very important for potential investors, in terms of the formation of a more reliable point of view for the banks.

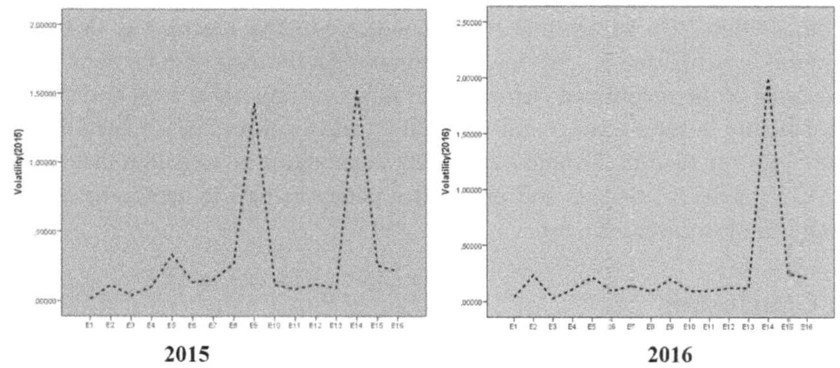

Graph 6: Volatility of 2015–2016

When Graph 6 (2015) is examined, it is seen that by year of 2015 in the post-crisis period, equity capital profitability (E2), net profit margin(E4), asset turnover rate (E5), equity capital growth rate (E8), interest growth level (E9), especially satisfaction of interest expenses by interest incomes(E14) showed maximum fluctuation, and there is fluctuation in the rate of interest incomes (E15) in total incomes and in the rate of interest expenses (E16) in total expenses. The mentioned situation clearly shows the reflections of the steps taken for making significant changes in the asset and resource groups of the banks in the process from 2012 to 2015. But, it is seen that the fluctuations in the interest growth and interest income dimensions of the banks didn't create any significant fluctuation on the asset growth and profitability levels. Accordingly, it means that credit and interest policies followed in actualizing the decisions taken as of the year 2012 were insufficient, and in the years that followed, the banks are required especially to get their solvency levels under control, and form predictable cost tables so as to keep their capitals and increase their assets.

When Graph 6 (2016) is examined, it is seen that by year of 2016 in the post-crisis period, equity capital profitability (E2), net profit margin(E4),asset turnover rate (E5), credit growth rate (E6), active capital growth rate (E7), equity capital growth level (E8), interest growth (E9), especially satisfaction of interest expenses by interest incomes (E14) of the banks showed maximum fluctuation, and the analysis results and graphs show that there is not any significant fluctuation in the rate of interest incomes (E15) in total incomes and in the rate of interest expenses (E16) in total expenses, compared to previous year. The aforementioned said change in the banking activities by the year of 2016 in comparison to previous years is understood from the graphical images of profitability, growth, continuity, and income-expense structure rates, and the stability in getting interest incomes under control, in the banking industry in the period from 2009 to 2016, means that effective and productive practices in this issue couldn't be actualized. It is obvious that in case that the banks put forward stable practices of the mentioned elements and focus on important asset and capital profitability in future, and it will establish a trust for investors – missed due to the crisis – to tend to the banks again. But, it shouldn't be forgotten that banks should pursue a balanced and productive policy in paying debts, which will establish the mentioned trust.

6 Conclusion

This study has a special importance in respect to revealing sustainability performances of the banks in the period from 2009 to the present time, through social, environmental and economic data; planning of sustainability studies to be carried out in TRNC; understanding the importance of TRNC among Mediterranean island countries in terms of banking industry and making banking industry transparent and creation of an organized market. The universe of the study consisted of the banks operating in the TRNC. In the study, the statistical significance of social, environmental and economic sustainabilities of 12 private capital banks in North Cyprus was analyzed for the period of 2009–2016 using above-mentioned variables. Since the number of banks is statistically inadequate, nonparametric the Friedman two-way analysis of variance by ranks was used. The effects of the developments in post-crisis on 32 various variables of the 12 banks for the years 2009–2016 were examined by this test, and below results have been obtained.

In Terms of Social Sustainability: The results obtained are as follows:

- Since the banks went downsizing in the number of staff in the post-crisis period, the number of training decreased and accordingly the budget allocated for training decreased.
- The banks tended to representation-introduction investments as of the year 2012, and the effect of the crisis was reduced in this way, personnel recruitment was done, the number of arranged training was increased, participation in training increased, and accordingly, both the quality of staff and training were increased, and return of investments could be assured.• The project investments didn't have any effect in the mentioned period.

In Terms of Environmental Sustainability: The results obtained are as follows:

- The increase in the number of banks following the crisis triggered the increase in the number of department and accordingly that of staff.
- The crisis didn't have any important effect on the banks, especially in terms of asset investments and they could turn it into the opportunity.
- Stationary expenses changed depending on the number of banks in the crisis period.
- Energy usage increased depending on the increase in the number of the bank and department.
- The banks derived correct lessons from adverse consumption of the water resources in the world, the awareness of the staff was raised, or economical devices were placed into the banks thereby preventing unnecessary water consumption.

- Correspondence/communication expenses decreased due to the intensive use of the internet economy in communication, e-transactions, and data processing technologies.
- The increase in cleanser usage and repair-maintenance expenses might be due to the increase in the number of bank and department, and adequate training on the usage of cleansers and used devices were thought to be provided to staff.

In Terms of Environmental Sustainability: The results obtained are as follows:

By the year of 2009: The crisis caused major problems in earning interest income; the asset turnover rates of the banks weakened, and accordingly, timely return of credits couldn't be provided; stability couldn't be assured in interest incomes due to having difficulty in collecting credits.

By the year of 2010: The results obtained are similar to those in 2009; the asset turnover rates of the banks weakened, timely return of credits couldn't be provided, interest expenses yielded a negative fluctuation.

By the year of 2011: The major fluctuations especially in credit growth rate directly affected interest incomes and indirectly total income; banks faced with problems as of 2009 in respect to paying debts; the mentioned fluctuation continued to negatively affect income-expense structure by the year of 2011.

By the year of 2012: The incomes that the banks obtained from their main activities didn't show a stable tendency; the fluctuations in capital incomes betrayed investors' trust; the banks couldn't follow a correct and effective credit and interest policy in first two years of the post-crisis period.

By the year of 2013: The rates of profitability, growth, continuity and income-expense structure changed a little in comparison to previous years, which was regarded as an indicator of that positive steps could be taken in credit and interest collection policies.

By the year of 2014: That, especially, interest incomes in banking activities were gotten under control, which was regarded as an indicator of that debt paying plans were made correctly, and equity capital and interest growth were assured.

By the year of 2015: The pursued credit and interest policies were insufficient, especially getting debt paying levels under control became necessary for banks to increase their assets by keeping their capitals,

By the year of 2016: The stable fluctuation showed by the banks in respect to getting interest incomes under control correctly in the period from 2009 to 2016 suggests that an efficient and productive practice could not be actualized on that issue and that a balanced and efficient policy was needed to follow and assure debt paying issue.

When above-mentioned results are evaluated from a general perspective, it is seen that banks' assurance to sustain their economic performances, required to assure a sustainable development, can guarantee the finance needed for social and environmental sustainability studies, and show that banks having economic power can make quality studies in respect to social and environmental in future.

When the banks' profitability, growth, income/expense structures are evaluated from a general perspective, it is seen that the mentioned banks should make important progress in their asset growth, increase interest incomes obtained from credits, for managing their assets, and they should correctly manage their interest incomes, which is one of their main activities, for making positive contribution to their capital profitabilities, along with increasing equity capital usage with actualization of collecting policy. It becomes necessary for the banks to correctly structure their credit and interest policies especially in 2009–2016 years in the post-crisis period, and the results showed that this situation has a direct effect on staff's education, quality, up to the correct usage of banking interactive devices. In the light of these facts, in case of that the banks' economic performances increase for making a sustainable growth in the future, it will likely reflect on their social and environmental performances. Besides, the place and importance of TRNC in banking industry among Mediterranean island countries increase the importance of the study, and the studies to make in the mentioned industry from different perspectives by various researchers will provide to obtain more reliable and correct results with more detailed analyses, and can assure users information about the banking industry in TRNC.

References

Bansal, Pratima, (2005). "Evolving Sustainably: A Longitudinal Study of Corporate Sustainable Development", *Strategic Management Journal*, 2: 197–218.

Canküyer, Ersoy ve Aşan Zerrin, (2005). "Parametrik Olmayan İstatistiksel Teknikler"Anadolu Üniversitesi YayınlarıNo:1613, Eskişehir.

Eccles, Robert G. and P. Krzus Michael, (2010), One Report: Integrated Reporting for Sustainable Strategy, John Wiley and Sons Inc, https://books.google.com.tr /books?id=mEBe9MBOWn4C&printsec=frontcover&dq=One+Report:+Integrated+Reporting+for+Sustainable+Strategy&hl=tr&sa=X&ved=0ahUKEwjk3_vFn9PJAhWBnhQKHckeAr8Q6AEIJDAA#v=onepage&q=One%20Report%3A%20Integrated%20Reporting%20for%20Sustainable%20Strategy&f=false, (Erişim: 22.09.2018).

Epstein, Marc J., (2008), "Making Sustainability Work; Best Practices in Managing and Measuring Corporate Social, Environmental and Economic Impacts", Greenleaf Publishing, USA.

Hitchcock, Darcy and Marsha Williard, (2009), *The Business Guide to Sustainability: Practical Strategies and Tools for Organizations*, Second Edition, Axis Performance Advisors, London • Sterling, VA.

Kestane, Ali, (2016), *Kurumsal Sürdürülebilirlik Perspektifinde İşletmelerin Finansal Performansının Analizi ve Yatırımcı Davranışları Üzerine Bir Araştırma: BIST Sürdürülebilirlik Endeksinde Bir Uygulama*, Yüksek Lisans Tezi, Sosyal Bilimler Enstitüsü, Dumlupınar Üniversitesi, Kütahya.

Liverman, Diana M., Hanson, Mark E., Brown, Becky J. and Robert W. Merideth, (1988), "Global Sustainability: Toward Measurement", *Environmental Management*, 12/2, pp: 133–143, https://books.google.com.tr/books?hl=tr&id=hoTtAA AAMAAJ&dq=Global+Sustainability%3A+Toward+Measurement&focus=searchwithinvolume&q=Global+Sustainability%3A+Toward+Measurement (E.T: 01.09.2018)

Nemli, Esra, (2004), *Sürdürülebilir Kalkınma: Şirketlerin Çevresel ve Sosyal Yaklaşımları, Birinci* Baskı, Filiz Kitabevi, Ankara.

Oğuzlar, Ayşe (2007), *İstatistisel Veri Analizi 1 SPSS ve MINITAB Uygulamalı*, Ezgi Kitabevi, Bursa.

Seçer, İsmail (2015). *SPSS ve LISREL ile Pratik Veri Analizi-Analiz ve Raporlaştırma*, Genişletilmiş İkinci Baskı, Anı Yayıncılık, Ankara.

Tuna, Özlem, (2014). *Kurumsal Sürdürülebilirlik Yaklaşım ve Uygulamaları: KOBİ'lere Yönelik Bir Araştırma*, Doktora Tezi, Sosyal Bilimler Enstitüsü, Afyon Kocatepe Üniversitesi, Afyon.

Yavuz, V. Alpagut, (2010). "Sürdürülebilirlik Kavramı ve İşletmeler Açısından Sürdürülebilir Üretim Stratejileri", *Mustafa Kemal Üniversitesi Sosyal Bilimler Enstitüsü Dergisi*, Cilt/Volume: 7, Sayı/Issue: 14, s. 63–86.

Tansel Cetinoglu

A New Concept in Accounting Profession: Cloud Accounting

1 Introduction

Nowadays, it has become a necessity for enterprises to adapt quickly to new technologies and to benefit from these technologies, to maintain competition and to prevent their competitors. In addition, a constant need for technology is created in order to achieve global accounting standards and practices. This situation affects the development of the companies, the accounting department and the future of the accountants. In this context, cloud computing has created new business models. Cloud computing applications offer alternative solutions to basic business functions and offer advantages in terms of cost and speed. The reflection of cloud computing applications to accounting, which is a basic business function, has revealed the concept of cloud accounting. Compared to traditional accounting practices, cloud accounting provides businesses with significant facilities and benefits. Cloud accounting is a new technology that is used to deliver the data stored in the desired format to decision makers and other interested parties very quickly. In our study, general information about cloud computing and cloud accounting concepts are given, traditional accounting and cloud accounting are compared, the benefits and disadvantages of cloud accounting application are expressed. In addition, the issues that need to be considered in the transition to the cloud system are explained and it is aimed to explain the subject of cloud accounting, which is a new concept in accounting profession.

2 Cloud Computing and Cloud Accounting

Aksu (2017) has defined the concept of cloud as a kind of parallel and distributed system consisting of interconnected independent computers that work together as a single integrated computer resource. Aksu (2017) cloud computing, data or information is stored on the Internet, not on your computer, and the need to be used over the network to provide access as defined. Kizil, Yilmaz and Aslan (2018) stated that cloud computing has emerged as an indispensable solution tool for the rapidly increasing data collection, classification and processing requirements of enterprises In addition, the most well-known and heavily used cloud computing business models are specified as SaaS (Software-as-a-Service),

PaaS (Platform-as-a-Service) and IaaS (Infrastructure-as-a-Service). Aksu (2017) stated that the success of the enterprises depends on many other factors as well as the harmonization of these two worlds (business and technology) and that the support of information technology and especially the accounting information system contributes to the performance and efficiency of the enterprises. According to Dimitriu and Matei (2015), the large volume of information needed and the time required to process the information have made accounting software an indispensable tool for accountants to do their jobs more quickly and effectively. Nowadays, cloud accounting is a new business reality supported by cloud computing. Also known as cloud accounting or online accounting, this software is like accounting applications installed on users' computers. However, the software is running on servers that provide online services that users can access from their web browser. The key feature is the use of the accounting service without the need to install any software to invest in the computer infrastructure, hence the naming of the service. The app is accessed via the web browser over the internet. The customer's data is securely stored and processed on the servers of the provider (in the cloud). The customer is only able to use the application. All you need is an internet connection, and companies can access their financial data from any device and location. A cloud-based accounting solution reduces the amount of labor required by the accounting department, allowing for a variety of complex demands and activities to be addressed through an integrated online system. According to Aksu (2017), the activities carried out by cloud accounting services are:

- Creating automatic accounting notes for different operations,
- Ensuring the relationship between financial accounting and management accounting for relevant accounts by automatic review,
- Preparing required periodic tables or synthetic financial reports and dashboards,
- Using alternative accounting plans to prepare accounting reports with different financial reporting standards,
- Calculating various financial ratios and formulas and provide the opportunity to create accounting reports and documents when necessary.

Öz (2016) stated that a significant measure of the use of cloud computing in accounting is the variety of software provided to users. Nowadays, it is seen that domestic software (LUCA, t360, Patrofin, Dia, 1TÇ, Reeleezee, LOGO Cloud, MEP etc.) is more than 10. In addition to this, foreign software (SAP, ZoHo) is less but it is an option. According to Oz (2016), LUCA Project launched in 2005, developed by Union of Chambers of Certified Public Accountants of

Turkey – TÜRMOB and Basic Education and Internship Center – TESMER is Turkey's first Internet-based central accounting system. Because the LUCA system is a web-based central system, it has managed the business processes successfully and has provided significant advantages, thanks to technology. The efficiency and productivity to be achieved through the use of the system makes a significant contribution to the business processes of the companies.

3 Comparison of Traditional Accounting and Cloud Accounting

In recent years, Öz (2016) has analyzed the trend toward web-based systems to manage financial data from the platform (pc, telephone, terminal, etc.) and from place to place (inside and outside the business). In addition, the reasons for this are the significant differences between the classical accounting software used for this purpose and cloud computing based software. According to Elitaş and Özdemir (2014), these differences are as follows.

In traditional accounting programs, data are entered manually; there is no remote access to the system. The installation and updating is carried out manually, and there is no possibility to work out of the workplace; the backup takes place at the local terminal. The legislative changes are tracked individually. The declarations are filled and sent manually. There are time losses in the transactions, invoices and other official documents manually filled in and sent. Administrators cannot access the financial data at any time, and there is no constant communication with the client organizations in the financial advisors.

In cloud computing-based accounting programs, data is entered automatically. There is remote access to the system. Installation and update is done by remote access; work is possible outside the workplace. Backup takes place in cloud computing system and local terminal; legislative changes are monitored from the cloud information system, and declarations are automatically filled and sent. In transactions when the time losses are not experienced, invoices and other official documents are filled and sent to the web-based, and it is possible for administrators to access the financial data remotely at any time. Financial advisors are a continuous web-based communication with the client businesses.

4 Benefits of Cloud Accounting

Kırlı, Ersöz, Kulu and Tokmak (2017) stated that the accounting software has been moved to a whole new dimension via cloud computing. According to Kırlı, Ersöz, Kulu and Tokmak (2017), accounting in the cloud means that everyone in the client company can access the same financial data at the same real time through a number of applications provided via internet connection from different locations.

According to Kırlı, Ersöz, Kulu and Tokmak (2017), the benefits of using cloud accounting are:

- In cloud computing-based accounting software, the client business always has the right to use the latest version of the software. There is no charge for access to the latest features of the software. In addition, legal changes concerning accounting are adapted to the software as soon as it is realized and submitted to the service of the customer.
- Cloud computing-based accounting software offers unlimited data storage capacity and automatic backup without any loss of data and without any additional cost to the customer.
- Cloud computing-based accounting software allows the client business to work independently without time and space limits. There is unlimited geographic access through remote network access.
- Businesses using cloud computing-based accounting software provide significant savings in costs compared to businesses using traditional accounting software. There are two main reasons for this cost savings. First, the software license is not purchased in cloud computing. Secondly, cloud computing-based accounting software is web-based, so there is no need for high-cost hardware systems for information technology within the enterprise. The significant reduction of fixed costs (hardware, software licensing and maintenance costs) related to information technologies in enterprises by cloud computing accounting software is an important advantage especially for small and medium enterprises. The rents paid for cloud computing-based accounting software and the fixed costs to be incurred for traditional accounting software will turn into variable costs; in this way customer enterprises will be able to optimize their costs.
- The flexible nature of cloud computing-based accounting software offers businesses the ability to react quickly to changing conditions and thus positively impacts business performance. Fast data transfer and real-time interaction between customer business and cloud computing-based accounting software service company, facilitating compliance with changing conditions.
- In the case of cloud computing-based accounting software, the security of the customer business data is the responsibility of the company that provides the cloud computing-based accounting software service and the service provider keeps the security at the highest level by using the special cloud deployment

model described in the previous section so that the data cannot be received by malicious third parties. Thus, the financial data and information of the client business are protected from malicious people.

- Cloud computing-based accounting software are user-friendly software and offer easy and quick solutions to their users. This facilitates the work of accountants and prevents the loss of time in the accounting process. Moreover, the communication between the service provider company and the client business is real-time, because communication and collaboration are possible at an advanced level.
- In the use of cloud computing-based accounting software, it is not necessary that there is a harmony between the version of the installed operating system and the accounting software on the devices where the customer enterprises access the cloud. Accounting software applications can be accessed with the help of an internet browser; all users of the software can use the same version software program, regardless of their operating system.

5 Disadvantages of Cloud Accounting

Öz (2016) found that the risks to be exposed to businesses using cloud accounting and the disadvantages that may arise due to these risks are generally caused by some infrastructure and technology deficiencies or problems that are inherent in cloud technology, and it is also impossible to prevent the disadvantages that may arise by not using cloud accounting. According to Öz (2016), the fact that they have not completed their development yet and that the weaknesses that cannot be solved bring about the use risks. According to Kırlı, Ersöz, Kulu and Tokmak (2017), the risks and disadvantages that prevent the increase in the number of users are as follows:

- Possible downtime in internet connection or possible slowdowns in internet connection speed can prevent enterprises using cloud computing-based accounting software from accessing their data in the cloud, performing accounting records and making backups.
- When using cloud computing-based accounting software, customer businesses may become dependent on the software provider by losing control over system maintenance, system update and management.
- When a client wants to use a new cloud-based accounting software program, the client may not be able to access financial data in the cloud-based legacy accounting software program; may not transfer the data in the old software

to the new software. This shows the dependence on the software program being used.

- Customer businesses are concerned about data privacy and data security in terms of their financial data, bank accounts and cash flow information.
- For direct access to data in the cloud, an internet connection is required. A powerful and fast internet connection is constantly needed to manage business activities in a healthy manner and to back up their data.
- Considering that cloud computing services are distributed globally, users from different countries operate with different business cultures and legal regulations. The fact that cloud computing service providers have data centers in different countries and regions may require that they comply with legal regulations in the country where they are located. The fact that countries have different legal regulations on data confidentiality and control may cause problems in compliance with different legal regulations while performing the services of Cloud Computing service providers.

6 Factors to Be Considered in Transition to Cloud Accounting in Enterprises

Aksu (2017) stated that the factors that should be considered in the transition to Cloud Accounting can be discussed in two groups as technical and financial issues.

Technical Issues: Öz (2016) stated that cloud accounting offers a wide range of solutions to businesses. Therefore, practitioners need to determine which system or vehicle is better suited to the purposes of the entity. The most important step in choosing the most appropriate cloud accounting service for enterprises is to analyze the specific characteristics of the enterprise. The information of many different businesses in cloud technology is stored together on the same service provider's equipment. He stated that the system should be designed in such a way as to prevent the access of shared users to each other's information. Choosing the right cloud solution will enhance the competitiveness of the enterprise by improving the level of adaptation to the market. When switching to a cloud-based system, there are three important factors that businesses should consider carefully. They are data quality and storage of data, business-specific information requests and determination of the most appropriate time for transition to cloud accounting. According to Oz (2016), businesses should consider the complexity of their financial reporting requirements before deciding to switch to a new accounting system, and should even consider the reporting components that may be needed in the future. The new accounting system must be fully integrated with other operating systems and allow the enterprise to adapt and develop according to the changing conditions. In addition to simple book keeping, each accounting service has its own set of solutions. Therefore, practitioners should review each option carefully. Businesses should choose a supplier that is safe, feasible and experienced in the field and can meet the needs of the user.

According to Dimitriu and Matei (2014), the cloud solution to be selected should be the most appropriate service to the business profile. Security needs vary depending on the type of service received. For this reason, it is mandatory to determine whether the company receiving the service meets the desired level of security before signing the contract of use.

Price and Financial Issues: According to Aksu (2017), the main financial issues to be considered in relation to cloud accounting are cost of application, cost of personalization, staffing cost and periodic membership fee. In traditional accounting models, businesses buy computer equipment and pay for it. When using the accounting software, businesses have to pay separate fees (such as a license fee) to receive different services. In cloud accounting, because the enterprise can get what they need from the technology and software resources required for it, they can only take their needs from the cloud service providers and at a lower cost. In some cases, these services may cost the cost of existing accounting solutions, so businesses should understand and evaluate the benefits and possibilities offered by cloud accounting. According to Öz (2016), it should be taken into consideration how adequate the service provider is in maintaining this service. The possibility of revealing a negativity such as complete loss of data in the long term should be evaluated in terms of the infrastructure, experience, financial situation and functioning of a weak and problematic company.

7 Conclusion

According to Allahverdi (2017), the internet and information technologies, which have developed in recent years, provide many opportunities to facilitate transactions in the state, citizen and business world. One of these opportunities is cloud information systems. While the term cloud is used instead of the word internet, information systems refer to the use of technology. Cloud computing systems offer services, applications and data over the Internet. Therefore, cloud systems give users the opportunity to carry the flexibility and data to work. Accounting information systems with addiction, such as working in a specific area, endeavor to create their own flexibility by taking advantage of the latest opportunities offered by technology. Cloud computing, which is expected to guide the future of the business world, is the provision of information technologies required by external sources. In the business world, where the Internet is brought closer to each other, the competition has also increased and the businesses have led to more efficient, flexible, fast and low cost work. It has become possible to acquire the information infrastructure required for both large and medium and small enterprises to work in this way.

Service sector is one of the sectors in which the developments in the IT sector find its application area in the fastest way. Software and accounting, which is one of the leading areas of the service sector, provides important opportunities for businesses with cloud computing. The use of cloud computing-based accounting systems allows businesses to record financial data from anywhere and in a continuous, even partially automated manner, while offering the opportunity to perform this cost effectively compared to older systems. One of the most valuable information for businesses is to save financial data, convert them to accounting information, store them and access them all the time. In spite of these advantages provided by cloud computing, the security, access problems and lack of legal regulations brought about by a new technology adversely affect the current and potential users' view of this technology and slow the spread of them. Therefore, it is necessary to carry out studies to eliminate the problems that decrease the rate of use. Cloud accounting applications bring many advantages of cloud technology systems. Software licensing and hardware acquisition, data backup, system maintenance and updates, especially to save many cost has been made. Cloud accounting brings various advantages such as security, adaptation and synchronization, ease of access, flexible capacity and low cost. At the same time, researches have shown that small- and medium-sized enterprises can gain significant advantages through the use of cloud accounting systems. There are some concerns and risks caused by cloud accounting. They focus more on the security and confidentiality of data, loss of connection, dependency on the system service provider, auditing and legal arrangements. Khanom (2017) stated that although cloud accounting has become more common day by day, many business owners and experts are not sure about what it is, what benefits it will or how it will shape the future accounting method. In our study, the advantages and disadvantages of cloud technology and cloud accounting are specified, and compared with traditional accounting practices, the factors that businesses should pay attention to in the transition to cloud accounting, thus providing a theoretical overview to the topic of cloud accounting which is a new concept in the accounting profession. While there are many concerns and risks, the accounting data and the fast and easy access to financial reports, which play an important role in the assessment of financial position and correct management decisions, increase the attractiveness of cloud accounting. Finally, given the advancements in technology and the progress of the business world, it is thought that cloud accounting applications will be even more popular in the coming years.

References

Aksu İ. (2017). Bilişim Teknolojisinden Muhasebeye Açılan Pencere: Bulut Muhasebesi. *Birey ve Toplum Dergisi*, 7(13): 79–102.

Allahverdi M. (2017). Bulut Muhasebe Sistemleri ve Bir SWOT Analizi. *Muhasebe ve Finansman Dergisi*, Özel Sayı, 92–105.

Aytekin A., Erdoğan Y. and Kavalcı K. (2016). Yeni Bir İş Modeli: Muhasebe Alanında Bulut Bilişim. *Uluslararası Yönetim İktisat ve İşletme Dergisi Özel Sayısı*, (ICAFR 16), 46–62.

Dimitriu O. and Matei M. (2014). A New Paradigm for Accounting through Cloud Computing. *Procedia Economics and Finance*, 15: 840–846.

Dimitriu O. and Matei M. (2015). Cloud Accounting: A New Business Model in a Challenging Context. *Procedia Economics and Finance*, 32: 665–671.

Elitaş C. and Özdemir S. (2014). Bulut Bilişim ve Muhasebede Kullanımı. *Muhasebe Bilim Dünyası Dergisi*, 6(2): 93–108.

Khanom T. (2017). Cloud Accounting: A Theoretical Overview. *IOSR Journal of Business and Management*, 6(19): 31–38.

Kırlı M., Ersöz Ş.Ö, Kulu T. and Tokmak S. (2017). Bulut Bilişim Temelinde Bulut Muhasebesi: Kavramsal Bir Çerçeve. *International Journal of Human Sciences*, 14(4): 4642–4657.

Kızıl C., Yılmaz E. and Aslan T. (2018). Bulut Teknolojisi Muhasebe Üzerine Etkileri. *Cemil Meriç 10. Uluslararası Sosyal Bilimler ve Spor Kongresi Özet Metinler Kitabı*, Saybilder Yayıncılık, Rize.

Öz Y. (2016). Bulut Bilişim (Cloud Computing) ve Muhasebe. *Bartın Üniversitesi İ.İ.B.F Dergisi*, 7(13), 63–79.

Mehmet Utku and Yusuf Kaya

IFRS Adoption in Europe: The Case of Industrial Sectors

1 Introduction

International Financial Reporting Standards (IFRS) are accounting standards prepared by the International Accounting Standards Board (IASB) in order to create a common accounting system and eliminate differences (Ball, 2006: 6). The main starting point for the formation of this common accounting system is that, with the development of international trade, global users of accounting information face difficulties in interpreting and analyzing the financial statements of different countries as a result of different accounting practices. The universalization of financial markets and the increasing volume of international capital movements have led to the creation of these international standards and regulations.

Standardization in accounting and financial reporting with IFRS creates a common financial language, thus minimizing investment risks caused by regional implementation differences in international markets. Standards improve the quality, comprehensibility and comparability of financial information, so that investors and other market participants make decisions in the capital markets by increasing the efficiency. In addition, own accounting practices of countries lead to difficulties in the entry of multinational enterprises into the national economy. Therefore, the increasing capital requirement in emerging markets requires compliance with these standards.

For the first time, works were started in the 1960s for purposes such as providing comparability, eliminating multiple reporting requirements and eliminating costs and evaluating health. The International Federation of Accountants (IFAC), the International Securities Organization (IOSCO) and the United Nations Organization for Economic Cooperation and Development (OECD) established the International Accounting Standards Committee (IASC) in 1973 for the purpose of achieving compliance in accounting. Until 2000, it published 39 standards (Kocamaz, 2012, 107). In 2001, the IASC assigned its accounting standard to IASB.

Since the beginning of 2005, thousands of enterprises have started to use international accounting and financial reporting standards instead of national accounting policies. This year was the year of the beginning of a very significant change in the international capital markets that increased efficiency. The main objective of this study is to examine the effects of the change in the financial performance of the companies on the transition to IFRS in 2005. For this purpose, the financial statements of the industrial enterprises in the industrial indices of Europe, which can be accessed, are analyzed between the years 1995 and 2014. The analysis was performed at 10 different financial ratios before and after 2005, at 3-year and 10-year intervals. The significance of the change in financial ratios was measured by t test.

2 IFRS and IFRS Adoption in Europe

The global economy and developing capital markets have also affected the accounting information system closely. Investors should be able to make investments in any country in the world and financial statements should be comparable in financial markets. The differentiation of accounting information systems has adversely affected the users of the financial statements due to various reasons such as the legal structure of the countries, differences in taxation and differences due to the development of the accounting profession. Different accounting systems in countries have lead to the following:

- Impossible to compare financial information
- Difficulty in fund collection through global investors in financial markets
- Difficulties in international mergers and trading

Similar negativity has made it necessary to apply common accounting standards worldwide. The purposes of creating accounting standards can be considered as follows (Usta, 2007):

- Eliminating application differences between countries
- Ensure that the financial statements are clear, understandable and comparable
- Ensuring full and complete access to financial table users' information
- Creating a common language in the use of financial information in the international arena
- Solve the problems arising from the different accounting standards faced by multinational companies

In this context, a study on the development of a common financial language and accounting system and the resulting International Financial Reporting Standards are as follows (https://www.ifrs.org/about-us/who-we-are/ #history):

- First, in 1973, Australia, France, Canada, Germany, Japan, Mexico, the Netherlands, the United Kingdom and the United States professional accounting organizations came together and formed the Accounting Standards Board (IASC).

- In 1989, the IASC published the first International Conceptual Framework.
- In 1990, the IASC introduced 31 sets of International Accounting Standards for the first time and in the same year the IASC issued a similarity table of the Financial Statements that intend to reduce the number of alternative accounting procedures permitted under the International Accounting Standards.
- In 1999, the G7 countries urged the IASC to conclude a broad range of internationally accepted accounting standards to strengthen the international financial system.
- In 2000, the IFRS Foundation was established.
- In 2001, the International Accounting Standards Board (IASB) made its first meeting and adopted IASC standards.
- In 2002, Europe adopted a law requiring public companies to prepare consolidated financial statements in accordance with IFRS Standards with regulated securities markets, including banks and insurance companies.
- In 2003, IASB published IFRS 1, the first standard.
- In 2004, the IFRS issued 2 to 6 standards and launched a separate accounting framework for SMEs.
- In 2005, 25 countries and 7000 companies in Europe switched from national accounting standards to IFRS. In addition, countries such as Australia, New Zealand, Hong-Kong and South Africa have passed IFRS.
- In 2007, more than 100 countries have made the transition to IFRS compulsory for their companies, or have enabled their use. The US has allowed the use of IRFS standards in non-US companies in the country.
- In 2009, IFRS for SMEs was prepared and a roadmap was also prepared for Japan.
- In 2014, IFRS 9 Financial Instruments standard was published.
- As of 2019, in a total of 166 countries, local and international companies are required to prepare or issue financial statements in accordance with IFRS.

3 Literature Review

The drastic change in 2005 in terms of accounting policies in the world and the transition of thousands of enterprises in many countries around the world, especially in the EU countries, have been the subject of many studies examining the effects of this transition in both national and international literature. With the transition to IFRS, the format and content of the financial statements have changed in many countries and the reflection of this change on financial analysis has been examined by many researchers. Some of these studies are summarized in this section.

Susana Callao et al. (2007) examined the impact of transition to IFRS in Spain on the comparability of financial reports. In the study, 9 financial ratios were used for 26 companies and cash ratio, total foreign resources/own funds and ROE ratios, total assets/total foreign resources and ROA ratios decreased compared to the prior period.

Mingyi Hung and K.R. Subramanyam (2007), in their analysis on 80 German companies between 1998 and 2002, concluded that the financial statements were affected by the transition to international accounting standards. With the transition to IAS, they determined significant increases in total assets and equity amounts.

Ahmet Ağca and Rafet Aktaş (2007) analyzed the impact of IFRS applied for the first time in the transition period between 2004 and 2005 on financial ratios of 147 enterprises operating in various sectors in BIST. As a result of the study, especially in the textile, apparel and leather sector, they determined that the financial ratios have changed in this process.

In 2004–2005, Anna-Maija Lantto and Petri Sahlström (2009) analyzed the impact of the transition to IFRS on financial ratios in the studies involving data from 91 enterprises in Finland. In this process, while the profitability ratios increased, debt and liquidity ratios decreased.

Francisco José Ferreira Silva et al. (2009) aimed to measure the impact of the transition to IFRS on the financial data of Portuguese firms. Thirty nine companies were investigated and it was determined that the transition to IFRS resulted in a significant change on the balance sheet and income statement.

George Iatridis and Sotiris Rouvolis (2010), in their study on 254 companies traded on the Greek stock exchange, analyzed the differences in financial reports with the transition to IFRS. As a result of the study, there was a decrease in the rates of profitability, liquidity and growth in the first year of transition to IFRS.

Karol Marek Klımczak (2011), in her study on the effects of the transition to IFRS in Poland, aimed to determine how market participants reacted to new accounting standards. As a result of the study conducted on the Polish stock exchange, it was determined that the transition to IFRS did not have an unexpected effect on the annual financial reports.

Michail Pazarskis et al. (2011) investigated the possible effects of the transition to IFRS on the financial statements of 20 enterprises in the Greek IT sector. In the study, financial statements of the enterprises, 3 years before and 3 years after the transition to IFRS, were analyzed by using 12 financial ratios, and statistically significant differences were determined only in the ratio of interest rate and tax before profitability and financial leverage ratio.

Gönül İpek Alkan and Onur Doğan (2012) examined the short- and long-term effects of the transition to IFRS on financial ratios in the studies involving 148 companies traded in Borsa Istanbul between 2000 and 2009. In the analysis carried out at 12 rates, they concluded that long-term effects are different from the results in the transition period.

Serkan Terzi et al. (2013) used the data of 140 enterprises in the manufacturing sector in BIST between 2003 and 2005. They have concluded that the financial statements prepared in accordance with IFRS and the financial statements prepared in accordance with national legislation are statistically different.

Mehmet Aygün et al. in their study conducted in 2016 examined the impact of the transition to IFRS on financial ratios and datas of 158 companies from different sectors registered to Borsa İstanbul were utilized. In the study covering the years 1995–2013, an increase in the liquidity and activity rates of enterprises in the post-IFRS period, profitability, debt, growth and market rates decreased significantly.

Yusuf Gör et al. (2016) examined the possible effects of IFRS on financial ratios over a 10-year period between 2000 and 2009. According to the results of the analyses conducted on 85 enterprises, which are traded continuously in BIST, there are statistically significant differences between financial ratios obtained before and after IFRS.

4 Research Design

4.1 Purpose and Method of Research

The aim of the study was to determine whether the transition to IFRS had an impact on the financial performance of publicly traded companies operating in the industrial sector in Europe. Compliance with IFRS in accounting policies has become mandatory in the member states of the European Union since 2005. In this study, it was analyzed whether the effect of the transition to IFRS on financial ratios was significant in 2 different periods 3 years before 2005 and 3 years after 2005 and 10 years before 2005 and 10 years after 2005.

In this direction, t test was used for difference tests. T test is the statistical analysis method used to determine whether the averages of 2 independent groups are different (Durmuş et al., 2016: 118)

$$t = \frac{\bar{X}_1 - \bar{X}_2}{\sqrt{\frac{s_1^2}{n_1} + \frac{s_2^2}{n_2}}}$$

n = number of examined ratios
$\bar{X}_1$ = mean of Pre-IFRS ratios
$\bar{X}_2$ = mean of Post-IFRS ratios
s = standard deviation
1 = group of Pre-IFRS ratios
2 = group of Post-IFRS ratios

The hypothesis of measuring the 3-year effect of transition to IFRS on financial ratios is as follows:

H_0: $\mu_{(2002\text{-}2004)} = \mu_{(2005\text{-}2007)}$
H_1: $\mu_{(2002\text{-}2004)} \neq \mu_{(2005\text{-}2007)}$

The hypothesis of measuring the 10-year effect of transition to IFRS on financial ratios is as follows:

H_0: $\mu_{(1995\text{-}2004)} = \mu_{(2005\text{-}2014)}$
H_1: $\mu_{(1995\text{-}2004)} \neq \mu_{(2005\text{-}2014)}$

4.2 Population and Sample

In this study, public companies in Europe, which have been able to access their financial data in the 20-year period between 1995 and 2014, are examined. The distribution of these companies by country is shown in Tab. 1. The data were obtained from Bloomberg database and analyzed in SPSS 16 program.

Tab. 1: Distribution of Companies by Country According to Research Subjects

Countries	Number of Companies
Germany	36
Belgium	15
Denmark	34
Finland	34
France	60
Netherlands	20
Spain	24
Swedish	46
Portugal	8
Greece	4
Turkey	103
Total	**384**

A total of 10 financial ratios, including 4 structure ratios, 2 profitability ratios and 4 operational ratios, were tested in the study. These ratios and how they are calculated are shown in Tab. 2.

Tab. 2: Financial Ratios and Calculation Methods in Research

Ratios	Definitions
Structure Ratios	
Current Ratio	Current Assets/Current Liabilities
Quick_Ratio	(Cash and Near Cash + Short Term Investments + Account Receivables)/Current Liabilities
Cash_Ratio	[(Cash and Near Cash Items + Mrktable Sec and Other ST Invts)/Current Liabilities]
Financial Leverage	Total Assets/Total Common Equity
Profitability ratios	
Return On Asset	(Trailing 12M Net Income/Average Total Assets) * 100
Return_On_Equity	(T12 Net Income Available for Common Shareholders/Average Total Common Equity) * 100
Operational ratios	
Net Fixed Assets Turnover	Trailing 12M Net Sales/((Net Fixed Assets - Current Period + Net Fixed Assets - Prior Year Period)/2)
Asset Turnover	Trailing 12M Net Sales/((Total Assets - Current Period + Total Assets - Prior Year Period)/2)
Inventory Turnover	Trailing 12 Month Cost of Goods Sold or Trailing 12 month Cost of Materials/Average Inventory
Accounts Receivable Turnover	Trailing 12 Month Sales/Average Account Receivable

4.3 Research Results

In this part of the study, the results of SPSS program were tabulated and the results were interpreted. Before and after IFRS 3 and 10-year data were subjected to t-test and the following results were achieved. Firstly, Tab. 1 shows the results of the analysis of the companies whose data can be accessed in the 3-year industrial index before and after the IFRS.

Tab. 3: The Change in the Structure Ratios of Industrial Index Companies 3-Year before and after the IFRS, and Significance Levels According to the T Test

Countries	Current Ratio			Quick Ratio			Cash Ratio			Financial Leverage		
	Mean Pre-IFRS	Mean Post-IFRS	P Value	Mean Pre-IFRS	Mean Post-IFRS	P Value	Mean Pre-IFRS	Mean Post-IFRS	P Value	Mean Pre-IFRS	Mean Post-IFRS	P Value
Germany	1,76	1,81	0,46	0,97	1,03	0,21	0,40	0,42	0,66	0,39	0,34	0,10
Belgium	1,44	1,31	0,08	0,76	0,77	0,87	0,25	0,26	0,34	1,13	4,45	0,08
Denmark	1,70	1,82	0,18	1,00	1,15	**0,04**	0,35	0,54	**0,03**	2,56	2,46	0,16
Finland	1,67	2,24	0,45	0,99	1,60	0,43	0,41	1,00	0,45	2,64	2,59	0,76
France	1,62	1,56	0,20	1,06	1,02	0,19	0,93	0,36	**0,04**	4,25	6,66	**0,03**
Netherlands	1,58	1,48	0,21	0,95	0,73	0,21	0,27	0,17	0,26	1,01	3,24	0,07
Spain	1,28	1,29	0,44	0,75	0,84	**0,03**	0,48	0,28	**0,00**	4,66	4,75	0,88
Swedish	2,18	2,00	0,23	1,31	1,25	0,67	0,73	0,67	0,69	2,99	2,74	0,07
Portugal	0,68	0,75	0,43	0,32	0,44	**0,00**	0,13	0,30	**0,00**	7,53	4,58	0,06
Greece	2,18	1,56	**0,02**	1,66	0,99	**0,00**	1,00	0,25	**0,00**	2,31	2,31	0,99
Turkey	2,08	2,71	**0,03**	1,26	1,58	0,09	0,50	0,83	**0,02**	0,10	0,20	0,27

* The results were interpreted according to 5 % significance level.

When Tab. 2 and Tab. 3 are examined, it is observed that the changes in the structure ratios in Germany, Belgium, Finland, the Netherlands and Sweden in the 3-year period before and after 2005, when the transition to IFRS was achieved, was not significant. When the analysis was performed for 10 years, significant changes were observed in the structure ratios in all countries except Finland.

In terms of the ratio, the number of countries in which the change in current ratio is significant is only 2 in the 3-year period, whereas 6 in the 10-year period. When examined in the cash ratio, both 10-year period required for 3 years in the transition to IFRS has led to significant changes in France, Portugal, Greece and Turkey. While the cash ratio decreased in Greece, it has increased in France, Portugal and Turkey. Likewise, in the 10-year period, the number of countries with a significant change in the financial leverage ratio increased. It can be said that the transition to IFRS significantly increased the share of foreign funds in total resources in companies in Denmark, France and Spain.

In Tab. 5 and Tab. 6, where changes in profitability ratios are examined, the number of countries with significant changes in profitability ratios in the short term is higher than in the long term. In the short term, it was observed that all the countries in the industrial sectors increased the profitability of their companies. When the 10-year period is examined, the transition to IFRS has changed

Tab. 4: The Change in Construction Ratios of Industry Index Companies 10 Years before/after IFRS and Significance Levels According to T Test

Countries	Current Ratio			Quick Ratio			Cash Ratio			Financial Leverage		
	Mean Pre-IFRS	Mean Post-IFRS	P Value	Mean Pre-IFRS	Mean Post-IFRS	P Value	Mean Pre-IFRS	Mean Post-IFRS	P Value	Mean Pre-IFRS	Mean Post-IFRS	P Value
Germany	1,63	1,80	**0,03**	0,93	1,13	**0,05**	0,38	0,47	**0,03**	0,40	0,37	0,11
Belgium	1,46	1,45	0,83	0,80	0,85	0,40	0,28	0,36	0,22	6,60	3,45	**0,02**
Denmark	1,70	1,91	0,19	1,00	1,24	0,14	1,95	0,69	0,10	2,51	2,79	**0,04**
Finland	1,70	1,66	0,86	1,01	1,00	0,95	0,40	0,51	0,52	2,83	2,96	0,51
France	1,56	1,53	0,32	1,00	0,95	**0,04**	0,59	0,35	**0,02**	4,18	7,55	**0,00**
Netherlands	1,57	1,42	**0,02**	1,01	0,57	**0,00**	0,29	0,11	0,27	5,31	3,18	0,11
Spain	1,70	1,20	0,09	1,08	0,75	0,22	0,67	0,28	0,14	4,04	6,00	**0,00**
Swedish	2,34	1,95	**0,00**	1,53	1,17	**0,00**	0,93	0,57	**0,00**	2,81	2,76	0,43
Portugal	0,73	0,59	**0,01**	0,34	0,34	0,97	0,15	0,21	**0,01**	5,47	6,94	0,10
Greece	2,74	1,54	**0,05**	2,10	0,99	**0,03**	1,40	0,34	**0,02**	2,36	2,40	0,73
Turkey	1,89	2,51	**0,00**	1,13	1,52	**0,00**	0,43	0,68	**0,00**	0,60	0,27	0,17

* The results were interpreted according to 5 % significance level.

Tab. 5: The Change between Profitability Ratios of Industrial Index Companies 3 Years before/after IFRS and Significance Levels According to T Test

Countries	Return On Asset			Return on Equity		
	Mean Pre-IFRS	Mean Post-IFRS	P Value	Mean Pre-IFRS	Mean Post-IFRS	P Value
Germany	0,0235	0,0552	**0,05**	0,0484	0,1395	**0,03**
Belgium	0,0403	0,0451	**0,10**	-0,0497	0,1017	**0,02**
Denmark	0,0372	0,0711	0,06	0,0774	0,0152	**0,05**
Finland	0,0387	0,0949	**0,03**	0,0512	0,0255	**0,02**
France	0,0139	0,0474	**0,02**	0,0320	0,0343	0,98
Netherlands	0,0187	0,0657	0,08	0,0397	0,0195	**0,05**
Spain	0,0496	0,0582	0,16	0,0275	0,0236	0,22
Swedish	-0,0332	0,0314	**0,01**	-0,0478	0,0103	**0,02**
Portugal	0,0189	0,0482	0,16	0,0847	0,0205	0,41
Greece	0,0437	0,0870	0,07	0,0983	0,0216	0,08
Turkey	0,0411	0,0705	**0,03**	0,0751	0,0932	**0,05**

* The results were interpreted according to 5 % significance level.

Tab. 6: The Change between Profitability Ratios of Industrial Index Companies 10 Years before/after IFRS and Significance Levels According to T Test

Countries	Return On Asset			Return on Equity		
	Mean Pre-IFRS	Mean Post-IFRS	P Value	Mean Pre-IFRS	Mean Post-IFRS	P Value
Germany	0,03	0,04	0,42	0,12	0,10	0,46
Belgium	0,02	0,02	0,72	0,03	0,06	0,38
Denmark	0,05	0,02	**0,04**	0,10	0,30	**0,02**
Finland	0,05	0,03	0,23	0,01	0,03	**0,04**
France	0,02	0,03	0,16	0,08	0,06	0,64
Netherlands	0,05	0,04	0,32	0,01	0,01	0,35
Spain	0,04	0,02	**0,03**	0,01	0,08	0,28
Swedish	0,01	0,02	**0,02**	0,02	0,08	0,06
Portugal	0,01	0,02	0,50	0,10	0,10	0,94
Greece	0,08	0,03	**0,00**	0,02	0,08	**0,01**
Turkey	0,07	0,05	0,27	0,09	0,06	0,55

* The results were interpreted according to 5 % significance level.

significantly in Denmark and Greece in terms of both profitability ratios. In these two countries in long term, while their return on assets ratios decreased, their return on equity ratios increased.

Tab. 7 and Tab. 8 show the change in the ratios of operational in companies. Accordingly, the number of countries with significant changes in activity rates in the long run has increased significantly. The change in inventory turnover has become meaningful in all countries. However, generalization cannot be made about the direction of change. There were also significant changes in asset turnover and MDV turnover in many countries in the long term. When countries with significant changes in asset turnover rates are analyzed in the long term, decreases are observed in countries other than Belgium. The receivables turnover showed only significant change in the short term and in Turkey decreased. However, in the long term, this ratio decreased in Belgium, France and Turkey and increased in Greece and Denmark.

Tab. 7: The Change between Operational Ratios of Industrial Index Companies 3 Years before/after IFRS and Significance Levels According to T Test

Countries	**Net Fixed Assets Turnover**			**Asset Turnover**			**Inventory Turnover**			**Accountants Receivable Turnover**		
	Mean Pre-IFRS	**Mean Post-IFRS**	**P Value**	**Mean Pre-IFRS**	**Mean Post-IFRS**	**P Value**	**Mean Pre-IFRS**	**Mean Post-IFRS**	**P Value**	**Mean Pre-IFRS**	**Mean Post-IFRS**	**P Value**
Germany	7,12	8,93	**0,04**	1,20	1,21	0,79	4,50	5,34	0,16	5,26	5,32	0,34
Belgium	6,31	5,95	0,67	0,99	1,06	0,19	4,94	7,90	0,30	0,21	0,20	0,54
Denmark	4,85	6,48	**0,00**	1,35	1,44	**0,03**	3,05	1,07	**0,00**	0,15	4,18	0,18
Finland	9,51	1,47	**0,01**	1,37	1,43	0,23	1,50	2,61	**0,04**	0,20	0,21	0,45
France	1,21	1,24	0,53	1,11	1,09	**0,03**	6,62	1,20	**0,00**	0,25	0,25	0,45
Netherlands	1,52	2,23	0,19	1,72	1,64	0,41	2,89	1,32	**0,00**	0,17	0,17	0,81
Spain	6,85	6,22	0,42	0,09	0,08	0,06	4,00	6,96	**0,00**	0,29	0,29	0,88
Swedish	9,73	1,86	**0,02**	1,20	1,30	**0,04**	9,04	2,09	0,11	0,18	0,17	0,15
Portugal	2,41	4,19	**0,03**	0,86	0,84	0,54	1,25	1,53	0,46	0,11	0,09	0,06
Greece	4,83	3,11	0,08	2,31	0,93	0,72	7,97	5,28	**0,00**	0,26	0,26	0,94
Turkey	3,85	3,40	0,30	1,11	1,06	0,19	7,73	8,11	0,47	8,90	6,20	**0,00**

* The results were interpreted according to 5 % significance level.

Tab. 8: The Change between Operational Ratios of Industrial Index Companies 10 Years before/after IFRS and Significance Levels According to T Test

Countries	Net Fixed Assets Turnover			Asset Turnover			Inventory Turnover			Accountants Receivable Turnover		
	Mean Pre-IFRS	Mean Post-IFRS	P Value	Mean Pre-IFRS	Mean Post-IFRS	P Value	Mean Pre-IFRS	Mean Post-IFRS	P Value	Mean Pre-IFRS	Mean Post-IFRS	P Value
Germany	2,22	0,05	0,15	1,44	1,19	**0,00**	4,59	5,06	**0,00**	5,70	5,70	0,99
Belgium	7,04	6,74	0,54	0,94	1,02	**0,01**	3,93	1,09	**0,00**	0,22	0,19	**0,00**
Denmark	5,43	5,79	0,31	1,31	1,27	0,41	1,93	9,48	**0,00**	0,15	2,08	**0,04**
Finland	7,18	2,26	**0,00**	1,40	1,30	**0,03**	1,02	3,02	**0,00**	0,20	0,20	0,57
France	1,19	1,18	0,87	1,16	1,06	**0,00**	5,16	1,12	**0,00**	0,25	0,23	**0,00**
Netherlands	1,36	2,13	**0,00**	1,91	1,46	**0,00**	1,00	1,49	**0,00**	0,16	0,16	0,31
Spain	6,34	4,69	**0,00**	0,92	0,71	**0,00**	3,52	7,06	**0,00**	0,37	0,29	0,27
Swedish	7,88	2,27	**0,00**	1,24	1,22	0,55	8,08	3,05	**0,00**	0,18	0,18	0,77
Portugal	3,10	4,23	**0,00**	1,07	0,88	**0,01**	1,94	1,44	**0,01**	0,08	0,08	0,67
Greece	1,08	2,28	**0,00**	1,42	0,72	**0,00**	7,99	5,26	**0,00**	0,20	0,29	**0,00**
Turkey	4,56	3,66	**0,01**	1,19	0,99	**0,00**	6,38	8,00	**0,00**	7,98	4,89	**0,00**

* The results were interpreted according to 5 % significance level.

5 Conclusions

With globalization, the need for understandable and comparable accounting standards and regulations in financial markets have increased. Standardization in accounting and the creation of common financial language started in the 1960s, until the year 2000 published 39 standard. Since the beginning of 2005, financial statements have started to be prepared in accordance with IFRS in many countries, especially in the EU member countries. It is thought that this change in 2005 may affect the financial results of the enterprises. In this respect, many studies in the literature focused on measuring the effects of the transition to IFRS on financial ratios. Studies generally cover a specific country or sector, and short periods in 2005 and beyond, where the adoption took place.

In this study, the industrial sectors of 11 countries in Europe have been analyzed in order to measure the impact of the transition to IFRS on the financial ratios of enterprises. The analyses carried out on 10 different financial ratios of 384 companies cover a long period of 20 years between 1995 and 2014. Financial ratios are classified into 3 different categories: structure ratios, profitability ratios and activity rates. The analyses were applied before and after 2005 at 3- and 10-year periods.

As a result, with the adoption to IFRS, differences in structure ratios and operational ratios, which are statistically significant in the long term, have occurred. In terms of profitability ratios, there was a significant change in more countries in the short-term rather than in the long-term. However, the results obtained in both short-term and long-term analyses show that there is no generalization covering all countries on the direction of change of financial ratios. This may be due to the fact that many European companies, primarily German companies, have voluntarily adoption to IFRS before 2005. As financial markets develop, there will be constant change and improvement in IFRS. It is inevitable that new updates will affect the financial ratios of firms. As IFRS practices become widespread in companies and countries, the comparability of companies and investment decisions in financial markets will become reliable.

References

Ağca, A. and Aktaş, R. (2007). First Time Application of IFRS and Its Impact on Financial Ratios: A Study on Turkish Listed Firms. *Ukraine: Problems and Perspectives in Management*, 5(2), 99–112.

Alkan, G.İ. and Doğan, O. (2012). Uluslararası Finansal Raporlama Standartları'nın Finansal Rasyolara Kısa ve Uzun Dönemli Etkileri: İMKB'de Bir Araştırma. *Muhasebe ve Finansman Dergisi*, 54(2): 87–100.

Aygün, M., Alpaslan, A., Aslan, Y. and Çalık, A. (2016). Uluslararası Finansal Raporlama Standartlarının Finansal Oranlar Üzerindeki Etkisi: Borsa İstanbul Üzerine Bir İnceleme. *Yüzüncü Yıl Üniversitesi İktisadi ve İdari Bilimler Fakültesi Dergisi*, 1: 126–139.

Ball R. (2006). International Financial Reporting Standards (IFRS): Pros and Cons for Investors. *Accounting and Business Research*, 36(1): 5–27.

Bayazıtlı E., Çelik O. and Üstündağ S. (2006). *Meslek Mensupları için Türkiye Muhasebe Standartlarına Genel Bakış*. Ankara: TURMOB Temel Eğitim ve Staj Merkezi Yayınları, No: 67.

Callao, S., Jarne J.I. and Lainez J.A. (2007). Adoption of IFRS in Spain: Effect on the Comparability and Relevance of Financial Reporting. *Journal of International Accounting. Auditing and Taxation*, 16: 148–178.

Durmuş B., Yurtkoru E.S. and Çinko, M. (2016). *Sosyal Bilimlerde SPPS'le Veri Analizi*. İstanbul: Beta Yayınları. 6. Baskı.

Gör Y., Cengiz S. and Dilsiz, M.Ş. (2016). Uluslararası Finansal Raporlama Standartlarının (UFRS) Finansal Oranlar Üzerindeki Etkisi: Bist'de Bir Araştırma. *Çukurova Üniversitesi İİBF Dergisi*, 20(2): 53–64.

Güvemli, O. and Güvemli B. (2015). Türk Ticaret Kanunlarının Türk Muhasebe Düşüncesinin Gelişmesindeki Etkileri. *Muhasebe ve Finans Tarihi Araştırmaları* Dergisi, Sayı 8, 26–50.

Hale Usta (2007). Muhasebe Mesleği ile İlgili Uluslararası Muhasebe Standartları Ve Türkiye'deki Düzenlemeler ile Karşılaştırılması. Ankara: Yüksek Lisans Tezi, Gazi Üniversitesi Sosyal Bilimler Enstitüsü, s. 15–16.

Hung, M. and Subramanyam, K. (2007). Financial Statement Effects of Adopting International Accounting Standards: The Case of Germany. *Review of Accounting Studies*, 12(4): 623–657.

Iatridis, G. and Rouvolıs, S. (2010). The Post- Adoption Effects of the Implementation of International Financial Reporting Standards in Greece. *Journal of International Accounting, Auditing and Taxation*, 19(1): 55–65.

Klimczak, K. M. (2011). Market Reaction to Mandatory IFRS Adoption: Evidence from Poland. *Accounting and Management Information Systems*, 10(2): 228–248.

Kocamaz, H. (2012). Uluslararası Muhasebe Standartlarının Dünyada ve Türkiye'de Oluşum ve Gelişim Süreci. *Kahramanmaraş Sütçü İmam Üniversitesi İktisadi ve İdari Bilimler Dergisi*, 2(2): 105–120.

Lantto, A. M. and Sahlstrom, P. (2009). Impact of International Financial Reporting Standard Adoption on Key Financial Ratios. *Accounting and Finance*, 49: 341–361.

Pazarskis, Michail et al. (2011), IFRS aAdoption eEffects in Greece: Evidence from the IT sSector. *MIBES Transactions-International Journal*, 5(2): 101–111.

Silva, F.J.F., Do Couto, G.M.M. and Corderio, R.M. (2009). Measuring the Impact of International Financial Reporting Strandards (Ifrs) to Financial Information of Portuguese Companies. *Revista Universo Contabil Blumenau*, 5(1): 129–144.

Terzi, S. and Şen, İ.K. (2013). Uluslararası Finansal Raporlama Standartlarına Geçişin Özkaynak Üzerine Etkileri: Borsa İstanbul Örneği. *Muhasebe Bilim Dünyası Dergisi*, 2013(4): 1–19.

Zencirkıran, S. (2015). Uluslararası Muhasebe Ve Denetim Standartlarının Ulusal Düzeydeki Mevzuat İle İlişkisi: Türkiye Örneği. *Sayıştay Dergisi*, 98(1): 61–74.

https://www.ifrs.org/about-us/who-we-are/#history (E.T: 10.02.2019)

Yavuz Selim Düger

Impact of HRM Practices and Leadership on Internal Branding

1 Introduction

In today's modern World, the brand is seen as a means of self-expression and directing habits and behaviors of people and becomes a marketing concept with increasing value day by day. Companies try to create brand with marketing activities such as advertising, personal sales, promotion and public relations. All these practices approach to the brand externally or customer oriented. In today's competitive environment, external brand activities alone are insufficient to create the brand and ensure its sustainability. A more powerful brand could be created with an employee-oriented approach. In the literature, employee-oriented branding approach is defined as internal branding. Internal branding focuses on the promotion of the brand to employees before customers and plays a significant role in fulfilling the promises of the product or service. The ultimate goal to be achieved through internal branding is to create brand ambassador employees with behaviors compatible with brand values. Certainly, marketing alone will be very insufficient to achieve this goal. It is clear that the most important task in the process of aligning employees' behaviors with brand value is human resources management and leadership.

2 Definition of Internal Branding

Internal branding starts with the fulfillment of brand promises, which are delivered to customers as a result of marketing activities (Burmann and Zeplin, 2005, pp. 279–280). Employees' attitudes and behaviors in the process of fulfilling the brand promises affect the success of the brand. Hence, the internal branding aims to align the employees' attitudes and behaviors with brand value (Punjaisri, Evanschitzky and Wilson, 2008, p. 408). In this direction, in order for the brand to be properly understood and to support the brand more by the employees, a common understanding and terminology of the brand within the organization should be developed (de Chernatony and Segal-Horn, 2003, pp. 1104–1106).

There are many different definitions of the concept of internal branding emerging from internal marketing in the literature. Some of these are given below:

Punjaisri and Wilson (2011) describe internal branding as "*the activities undertaken by an organization to ensure that the brand promise reflecting the espoused brand values that set customers' expectations is enacted and delivered by employees."*

According to Aurand, Gorchels and Bishop (2005) internal branding is "*the introduction of the brand to employees and training in line with brand values.*"

Miles and Mangold (2004) define internal branding as "*the process by which employees internalize the desired brand image and are motivated to project the image to customers and other organizational constituents.*"

Internal branding can be defined as the total of joint activities of marketing, human resources management and leadership in order to the recognition of the brand within the organization, internalization of brand values of employees and creating a brand ambassador behaviors.

All these definitions provide some basic assumptions about internal branding, promotion of the brand within the organization, alignment employees' behaviors in line with the brand promises, training of employees in line with the brand values, internalizing the brand values and exhibiting brand ambassador behaviors.

3 Importance of Internal Branding

A strong brand is needed for sustainable competition and profitability, especially in the service sector. However, the creation of a strong brand can be achieved through internal branding. The most important role of internal branding in creating a successful brand is to bring a spirit to the brand within the organization. This brand spirit differentiates the company from its competitors and provides a superiority that cannot be imitated. Internal branding activities play an important role in building trust and positive image, as it ensures aligning employees' attitudes and behaviors with brand value. It also plays a critical role in reflecting the brand quality and providing unique experiences to customers.

An effective internal branding strategy will strengthen the company from the inside to outside. On the contrary, if internal branding and employees' behavior toward the brand are ignored, all marketing efforts may be at risk of failing to succeed. Moreover, an effective internal branding not only strengthens the corporate brand image but also creates brand ambassadors who live the brand.

Internal branding has many significance and advantage for employees, brands and companies. Some of these are given below (Kahraman, 2011, pp. 89–90; King and Grace, 2008, p. 360; Vallaster and de Chernatony, 2005, p. 183; Burmann and Zeplin, 2005, pp. 279–280; Berry and Lampo, 2004, p. 20; Jacobs, 2003, p. 23):

- Recognition and adoption of the brand by employees,
- The sense of high brand loyalty of employees and internalization of brand values,
- Exhibiting an extra role for brand success by employees,
- Fulfillment of brand promises and providing unique experiences to customers,
- High customer satisfaction and loyalty,
- Creating a strong brand and corporate image,
- An inimitable differentiation for companies,
- And ensuring a sustainable competitive advantage.

4 The Impact of Leadership on Internal Branding

Internal branding is not a once-only done activity, but rather a continuous process. Such activities with continuity should be managed within the organization under leadership responsibility. Furthermore, in order to achieve the success of internal branding, leadership has an important responsibility and role in ensuring the active participation of employees in this process. Burmann and Zeplin (2005) stated that leadership could positively influence employees' attitudes toward the brand and persuade employees to support the brand. In other words, leadership effectively spreads brand value within the organization; thus, leadership can enable employees to reach the level of a brand embassy from the point of a representation of the brand (Vallaster and de Chernatony, 2006, pp. 762–763).

Leadership has many duties and responsibilities as an impressive element in the internal branding process. As an incentive, the leader should support the morale and motivation of employees in line with brand success. As an agent of change, the leadership should be an inspiring and pioneer at the point of internal branding. At the same time, the leader needs to be a role model for all other employees with the attitudes and behaviors that he or she exhibits (Vallaster and de Chernatony, 2006, pp. 762–763). Leadership should create a brand-focused vision and mission and spreads it within the organization (King and Grace, 2005, pp. 278–281). Leadership should encourage employees to work with team spirit for the success of the brand (Morhart, Herzog and Tomczak, 2009, p. 123).

There are many things that leadership can do within the organization for the success of internal branding. Some of these are (Baileygp, 2016):

- Creating a brand success story and internalizing the brand by employees,
- Holding brief information meetings in small groups to explain the value and significance of the brand,

- Giving weight to visual information materials and keeping written information materials to a minimum,
- Providing less but clearly understandable messages instead of too many messages for the brand,
- Building an effective communication network within the company and keeping track of the employees' feedback on the brand,
- Creating a corporate culture that includes brand value.

5 The Impact of HRM Practices on Internal Branding

Although the concept of internal branding has emerged as an extension of marketing and branding, the importance of human resources management, which is the only factor that brings the process of internal branding to life, needs to be well understood. In particular, the interest in the concept of internal branding is increasing day by day in terms of human resources management, due to the great impact of human resource management practices on internal branding process.

Although there is a marketing approach in internal branding strategies, human resource management practices are in place at the application point (Aurand et al. 2005, p. 169). As a result of the participation of human resources practices in the internal branding process, many acts can be done for employee and brand value; shaping employees' attitudes and behaviors in a brand-oriented value (Kahraman, 2011, p. 107), recognizing the brand and understanding of brand values, ensuring brand-employee fit (Burmann and Zeplin, 2005, p. 287), ensuring the voluntary participation of employees in the internal branding process (Nardalı, 2011, p. 135), delivering the brand promise and expectations to the employees (Punjaisri and Wilson, 2007, p. 58–59). HRM practices, such as recruitment, selection, training, development, internal communication, performance assessment, rewarding, have important implications in the internal branding process. These are briefly mentioned below:

Recruitment and Selection: Selection of the most suitable candidate for the brand value at the recruitment point is the beginning of the internal branding process in terms of human resources management. In order to achieve this, first of all, it should be given clear messages to potential candidates about the brand values by human resources management and so that candidates who are eligible for brand value can apply for job advertisements.

According to Alshuaibi and Shamsudin (2016), hiring candidates suitable in line with brand value and organizational purposes will make a significant contribution to business and brand performance. In addition, it is much easier to achieve a successful branding in case of person-brand compliance. However, the selection and recruitment of the appropriate candidate can reduce the costs of internal branding in the long run.

Training and Development: Employees who act compatible with brand value can be created by providing training in line with brand-oriented (Aurand et al. 2005, p. 165). In other words, training has a great importance in terms of exhibiting employees' attitudes and behaviors compatible with the brand values. In addition, thanks to brand-oriented training, it is ensured that employees get to know the brand, learn brand values and understand brand promises. According to Punjaisri and Wilson (2007), training is the most significant human resource management practice to reinforce employees' brand supportive behavior. Training could be given to employees either inside or outside of the company and it could also be given using the e-learning system. Furthermore, transferring the brand value to new followers and the continuity of the internal branding process could be ensured by having a brand-based coaching and mentoring approach.

Internal Communication: Internal communication is an important practice of human resources management in the development of a common mentality of the brand and in the formation of a common terminology of the brand in the organization (de Chernatony, Drury and Segal-Horn, 2003, p. 1096). The brand value, which is initially delivered to employees through training, is continuously reminded to employees through internal communication channels. Internal communication system ensures the instant sharing of any information related to the brand as well as the mutual communication of the employees. Thus, employees' emotional commitment to the brand is also increased day by day (Miles and Mangold, 2004, p. 74). Internal communication system should work effectively in order to prevent employees from losing faith in the brand and also do not encounter job dissatisfaction. Moreover, an environment could be created where employees can freely express their thoughts and opinions about the brand if internal communication is supported by the feedback system.

Performance Assessment and Reward: Employees are encouraged to develop brand supportive attitudes and behaviors by adopting a brand-oriented approach in the performance assessment system. In addition, the motivation of employees could be increased by integrating brand-oriented rewarding and career development into the performance assessment system. The reward, which depends on the performance, given may also be like giving honor to employees and making them feel valuable as it is material. In fact, making employees feel valued can be a much more effective rewarding tool. According to Aurand et al. (2005), employees' loyalty to the brand could be increased and the ultimate performance could be achieved, thanks to the brand-oriented performance assessment and reward system.

6 Conclusion

In today's competitive environment, it is seen that companies are made competition and differentiation with promises of brands and brands. It is better understood that a brand has an internal dimension as well as the external dimension in an environment where brands are so important. The two dimensions of the brand must also be coordinated to achieve a successful branding. Moreover, some researchers argue that internal branding should be done before external branding activities. The internal dimension of the brand is internal branding. Internal branding is an ongoing approach, as in external branding and it is not done and completed at once.

At the same time, internal branding process is an approach carried out under the common responsibility of human resources management, marketing and leadership. In other words, internal branding is a process in which marketing techniques are adopted, human resources practices are used and under control of the leadership.

Leadership plays an important role in ensuring the continuity of internal branding and employee participation. On the other hand, human resources management plays a key role in aligning employees' attitudes and behaviors with brand values. An internal branding strategy only with a marketing perspective is not enough without leadership and human resource management practices. Certainly, in this case, a successful branding result is unthinkable. Branding process, supported by internal branding, is more likely to be successful as a result. A successful branding will lead to demonstrating high performance of the company and the brand. A successful branding also will directly or indirectly contribute to profitability, sustainability and growth, which are the three main objectives of the companies.

References

Alshuaibi, A. S. and Shamsudin, F. M. (2016). The Role of Human Resource Management Practices in Enhancing Internal Branding. *International Soft Science Conference, Research and Innovation Management*, Centre Universiti Utara Malaysia, 11–13 April 2016, 599–605.

Aurand, T. W., Gorchels, L. and Bishop, T. R. (2005). Human Resource Management's Role in Internal Branding: An Opportunity for Cross-Functional Brand Message Synergy. *Journal of Product and Brand Management, 14* (3), 163–169.

Baileygp, (2016). The importance of Internal Branding, 2016 Summer Foresight: https://baileygp.com/article/importance-of-internal-branding/ Access: 10.03.2019.

Berry, L. L. and Lampo, S. S. (2004). Branding Labor-Intensive Services. *Business Strategy Review, 15* (1), 18–25.

Burmann, C. and Zeplin, S. (2005). Building Brand Commitment: A Behavioral Approach to Internal Brand Management. *Journal of Brand Management, 12* (4), 279–300.

De Chernatony, L. and Segal-Horn, S. (2003). The Criteria for Successful Services Brands, *European Journal of Marketing*, 37 (7/8), 1095–1118.

De Chernatony, L., Drury, S. and Segal-Horn, S. (2003). Building a Services Brand: Stages, People and Orientations. *The Services Industries Journal, 23* (3), 1–21.

Jacobs, R. (2003). Turn Employees into Brand Ambassadors. *ABA Bank Marketing, 35* (3), 22–26.

Kahraman, A. (2011). *Marka Vaadinin Çalışanlara İletilmesi: İçsel Markalaşma.* (Yayınlanmış Yüksek Lisans Tezi), Celal Bayar Üniversitesi, Sosyal Bilimleri Enstitüsü, Manisa.

King, C. and Grace, D. (2005). Exploring the Role of Employees in the Delivery of the Brand: A Case Study Approach. *Qualitative Market Research: An International Journal, 8* (3), 277–295.

King, C. and Grace, D. (2008). Internal Branding: Exploring the Employees' Perspective. *Journal of Brand Management, 15* (5), 358–372.

Miles, S., J. and Mangold, G. (2004). A Conceptualization of the Employee Branding Process. *Journal of Relationship Marketing, 3* (2–3), 65–87, DOI: 10.1300/J366v03n02_05

Morhart, F., M., Herzog, W. and Tomczak, T. (2009). Brand-Specific Leadership: Turning Employees into Brand Champions. *Journal of Marketing, 73* (5), 122–142.

Nardalı, S., (2011). *Yükseköğretimde Markalaşma*, Ankara: Detay Yayıncılık

Punjaisri, K. and Wilson, A. (2007). The Role of Internal Branding in the Delivery of Employee Brand Promise. *The Journal of Brand Management, 15* (1), 57–70.

Punjaisri, K. and Wilson, A., (2011). Internal Branding Process: Key Mechanisms, Outcomes and Moderating Factors. *European Journal of Marketing, 45* (9/10), 1521–1537.

Punjaisri, K., Evanschıtzky, H. and Wilson, A. (2008). Exploring the Influences of Internal Branding on Employees' Brand Promise Delivery: Implications for Strengthening Customer-Brand Relationships. *Journal of Relationship Marketing, 7* (4), 407–418.

Vallaster, C. and De Chernatony, L, (2005). Internationalisation of Services Brands: The Role of Leadership during the Internal Brand Building Process. *Journal of Marketing Management, 21* (1–2), 181–203.

Vallaster, C. and De Chernatony, L. (2006). Internal Brand Building Structuration: The Role of Leadership. *European Journal of Marketing, 40* (7/8). 761–784.

Selami Erdogan and Abdulbaki Bilgin

ISIS as a Terrorist Organization: Its Effort of Statehood[1]

1 Introduction

ISIS (Islamic State Iraq and Syria) has become the most fundamentalist terrorist organization since the rise of fundamentalist terrorism. Terrorist organizations like ISIS and similar (counterparts) are fed by global imbalances, power gaps and collapsing state systems. Global imbalances and unfair system assessments are made through central-periphery, oppressive-oppressed and exploitative-exploited dilemmas (Sandıklı, 2015: 27). ISIS gained the opportunity to improve its organization by taking advantage of the complex structure and situation in the Middle East geography, which is the region where ISIS is active. In an increasingly complex structure, ISIS has expanded its activities to expand and diversify its active potential pool across the world, particularly in the Western World.

In the heart of the Western World, finding marginalized, young and feverish young people to participate in the organization has gained great importance for the organization. But he realized that he needed to change and develop the means of propaganda in order to find a place in this geography. ISIS, which has an incredible capacity for military conquest in Iraqi and Syrian territories, ruthless custody and hostage torture, ruthless treatment for local minorities and foreign jihadists, has attracted attention in the news media since June 2014. The existence of ISIS with the killing and displacement of thousands of people poses a significant threat to the stability and security of the Middle East (Gonchar, 2014: 1–3).

2 The Ideological Structure of ISIS

The traditionalist-conservative approach reflects the religious resistance of religious experiences and acquisitions in the religious context (Kutlu, 2016: 209). The ideology of ISIS, which resisted the change and innovation in religion, consists of religious fanaticism, Salafist Islamic approach, anti-Westernism and terrorism (Sandıklı, 2015: 15). There is no distinction between religion and the

---

1 This study is derived from the master's thesis prepared and presented by Abdulbaki Bilgin under the supervision of Selami Erdogan at Kutahya Dumlupinar University, Institute of Socail Sciences, Department of Public Administration Thesis was name as "The Use of Soft Power Concept by States and Terrorist Organisations: ISIS Example".

state in this approach. All decisions are based on a harsh interpretation of the Sharia (Islamic law), which is brutally practiced in the territories controlled by the Islamic State (Freidland, 2015: 13). But non-Islamic practices under the name of Islam are criticized by other states. Barack Obama's "ISIS certainly does not represent Islam. Also, Turkish President Erdoğan has said so many times. Similarly, the presidents of Muslim countries have said this" (www.sabah.com.tr, 2015) words confirm this.

The ideology of other groups such as al-Qaeda and Taliban is almost the same. There are differences in their approach to the timing and conditions required to establish a caliphate. Groups such as Jabhat Al-Nusra (al-Qaeda's official extension in the Syrian Civil War) believed that while there was an Islamic caliphate which was a long-term target, time was still inadequate for such a move (Freidland, 2015: 10).

The Salafist ideology, which sharply blames those who do not think like their followers, is based on the idea of returning to the so-called pure form of Islam that is applied by the prophet Muhammed and his first followers. They reject the later additions to religion as bidat and anti-Islam. The doctrine of the organization allows those who have deviated from the strictly defined interpretation of Islam to declare themselves as unfaithful Muslims. The punishment for perversion is death (Freidland, 2015: 13).

3 The Purpose of ISIS

In April 2013, Abu Bakr al-Baghdadi (the leader of ISIS) issued a statement on behalf of a group known as ISIS. He noted that they don't recognize the existent borders and their aim was "progress". The progress of ISIS appears to be aimed at the establishment of an Islamic caliphate. This current geographical gap is not entirely clear, but the discourse at this point suggests that its final target is far beyond the existing territory in Iraq and Syria (al-Ubaydi vd., 2014: 27). It aims to dominate a wide geography in order to achieve the ultimate goal and to achieve improvement.

ISIS has short, medium and long-term plans for its purpose in short term, it aimed to gain land in the region where it is located. In the medium term, he aimed to attack the Shiites and establish a great caliphate (Freidland, 2015: 13). Although the target of ISIS is (encompasses) Iraq-Syria and Lebanon, it is understood (it is revealed by the ISIS-guided media) that the primary targets of the organization is to reach Abbasid dynasty borders at first stage and then to expand it worldwide (Ağar, 2015: 261).

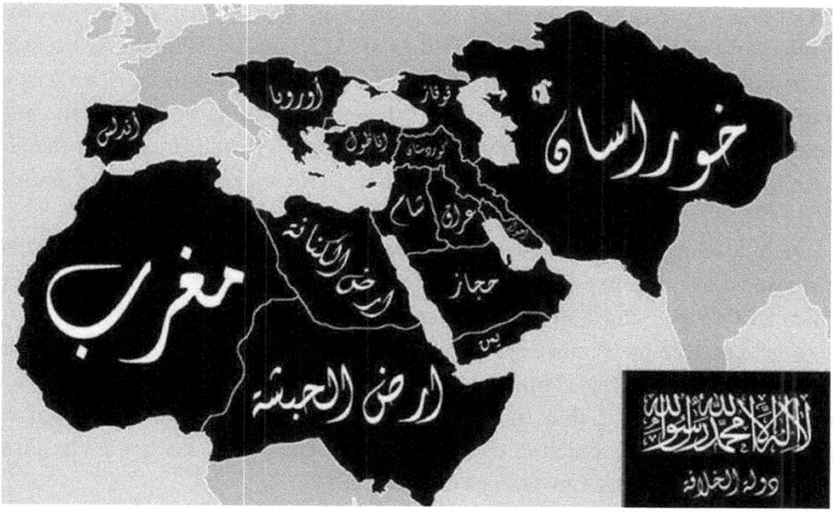

Fig. 1: Possible Caliphate Borders of ISIS (al-Ubaydi et.al., 2014)

One of the leaders of the organization, Zarqawi's strategic goal, was to trigger the Sunni-Shia Islam war from the start and to mobilize and coordinate its Sunni vision. Zarqawi clearly repeated the priority of action against the Shiites and promised to brutally attack civilian and religious targets and thus encouraged Shiites to retaliate against the Sunnis (Fawaz, 2016: 98).

In the long term, it is understood from Fig. 1. that the "Caliphate State", which is wanted to be established by ISIS, has aimed to progress from Africa to Middle Asia from the Hejaz to Europe. On the map, there are Shiite and Christian regions as well as Sunni regions.

At present, there have been many conflicts of identity between Sunni Muslims and Shiite Muslims in the Middle East and beyond. Although ISIS is a Salafi Jihadist organization, it is mainly directed toward a Shiite campaign against genocide in the name of romantic idea of reviving the caliphate (Fawaz, 2016: 40).

4 Development of ISIS

ISIS emerged from the US invasion of Iraq in 2003. When it was first established, it was just one of a number of Sunni extremist groups who fought against US forces and attacked Shiite civilians to provoke a sectarian civil war (Cronin, 2016: 374). The Fallujah revolt against the US occupation began just after the collapse of Saddam Hussein's regime on April 9, 2003. Two hundred resident of Fallujah protested the activities of US troops in Fallujah. As a result, 17 demonstrators were killed and 30 demonstrators were wounded. The armed Iraqis shot down the American military helicopter, killing 16 Americans and injuring 26 soldiers (http://www.aljazeera.com, 2016). In addition, many people from Mosul, Ramadi, Najaf and Kirkuk supported these demonstrations (Gerges, 2016: 122).

Such developments continued by retaliating of parties. Therefore, the parties increased their violence against each other. Four Blackwater mercenaries were killed in Fallujah, and their bodies were burned on the streets and then hung on a bridge over the Euphrates. In April 2004, the US forces responded to the Blackwater incident by intensively bombing the city with the help of the Iraqi army. It was reported that the American military offensive was planned to destroy al-Qaeda; but failed to check the status. This war is known as the First Battle of Fallujah (http://www.aljazeera.com, 2016).

In January 2014, Fallujah and Ramadi were seized with predecessor (pioneer) groups. However, ISIS preferred to remain in Fallujah (Stern ve Berger, 2015: 14). On June 29, 2014, on the first day of Ramadan, ISIS spokesman Muhammad al-Adnani stated that the victories he had won against all his enemies were the glory of God and a shura was established by them. This shura is discussed and the decision of the Caliphate is also a shura where the design is made (This Shura has a feature in which the Caliphate is discussed, decided and also designed.) (Dyer, 2015: 119). ISIS, which became the dominant power in the region after these developments, has declared the announcement of the "Islamic State" (Duman, 2013).

ISIS is not just a terrorist group. It is a political and military organization that aims to make a radical interpretation of Islam as a political philosophy and to impose this world view on Muslims and non-Muslims. ISIS, who was excluded from al-Qaeda on the grounds that it was excessive, argues that he is the legitimate ruler of all Sunni Muslims. They established a structure ruled from Raqqa in Syria, which they saw as a state with large areas in Syria and Iraq (http://www.bbc.com, 2015). The current Islamic State, founded by Abu Musab al-Zarqawi, known as the Al-Qaeda of Iraq (AQI), fought against American forces and has joined the Iraq war after the fall of Saddam Hussein. In 2013, they participated in the Syrian civil war, but they focused not on defeating Bashar al-Assad's regime but on establishing the Islamic State (Zelin, 2014: 6).

Abu Musab al-Zarqawi and Al-Qaeda leader Osama bin Laden, who founded the Tawheed and Jihad Congregation (JTWJ) in 1999, aged in the Afghan jihad against the Soviet Union in the 1980s; however, their own organizations had different genetic materials that could in part be attributed to their different background, leadership styles and objectives. Although two groups formed an agreement in 2004, there were differences (Zelin, 2014: 1). This structural situation led to ideological and operational differences between the two organizations.

Al-Qaeda came out of anti-Soviet jihad in Afghanistan in the 1980s. While the Soviets were preparing to retreat, Osama bin Laden and some of his close associates cemented his victory over the powerful Soviet Union; they decided to take advantage of their network for global jihad. Bin Laden's vision was to create the pioneers of the elite warriors who could lead the global jihad project, and to assemble under a single structure, struggling closely with hundreds of small jihad groups' own regimes (Byman, 2015: 2). However, the Iraqi al-Qaeda adopted different methods from the very beginning. Although Bin Laden financed Zarqawi to establish his organization, Zarqawi did not take the oath of loyalty and loyalty to Al-Qaeda because he initially shared some of bin Laden's aims and wanted to remain independent. However, after months of negotiations, Zarqawa took an oath of loyalty and in 2004 the group received the name of the Al-Qaeda in Iraq and stated this connection.

In a period when al-Qaeda was weak, bin Laden established a partnership in the most important field of jihad, and Zarqawi seized al-Qaeda's respect and contacts to strengthen its legitimacy. Even in the early periods of the group, Al-Qaeda leadership and bin Laden when highlihted to focus on US targets, Zarqawi emphasized the sectarian war. Zarqawi and his followers, with the help of a tactic they used to create shock and create publicity in Iraqi al-Qaeda's successor organizations, made their name known with their terrible beheading videos and incredible atrocities. Despite Zevahiri's doubts, in the light of Zarqawi's strategy, the Iraqi Al-Qaeda launched a large uprising and seemed to work well for a number of years since it controlled part of the Sunni population in Iraq. Zawahiri in public and Bin Laden continued to embrace their loyalty in Iraq (Byman and Williams, 2015: 317).

Bin Laden and his staff grew up in the upper middle class at least, and while studying at the University, Zerkawi and his closest ones came from poor, less educated backgrounds. Zarqawi's past and extreme views of tekfir (accusing another Muslim of perversion and thus justifying his massacre) have led to significant disagreements between the two founding leaders (Zelin, 2014: 1). As a result of many years of disagreements, the separation of the group from Al-Qaeda took place as a natural process. In addition, during this period, the organization continued its ideological and operational activities under different names. These organizations, in turn, are as follows;

- The JAMA'at Tawhid wal jiad-JTWJ
- Al-Qaeda (al-Qaeda in Iraq-AQI)
- Iraq Islamic State (ISI)
- Islamic State of Iraq and Syria-ISIS
- The Islamic State (is): 2013-…: since 2013, but, many media sources continue to use ISIS (http://web.stanford.edu, 2017).

The leaders of the organization since its foundation are as follows:

Tab. 1: ISIS Leaders in History (http://web.stanford.edu, 2017)

Leader	Years
Abu Musab ez-Zarqawi	2002-2006
Abu Omar al-Baghdadi	2006-2010
Ebu Eyyup el-Mısri	2006-2010
Abu Bakr al-Baghdadi	2010-…

Today, ISIS appears to be more of a state than an organization. Jürgen Todenhöfer, a German journalist who visited Iraq and Syria, a part of its territory controlled by ISIS, said in 2014 that "We must understand that ISIS is a state now" (Walt, 2015: 42). This shows that the methods used may have been transferred from states.

5 State Building of ISIS

ISIS, who declared himself as the first Salafi state in history, reveals its new structure in many areas. Although there are no ministries in the usual sense, it has a functional division of work and specialized administrative units (Luizard, 2016: 102).

The terrorist organization ISIS, which emerged with the claim of being a state, made its structure similar to the states in terms of administrative units. The provision of services provided by States to their citizens through organization is vital importance for sustainability. One of the most important conditions for proving sub-departments that ISIS is a state on its state organization and another is coin money. ISIS has carried out this organization and it has followed a holistic state structure by seizing the coinage part.

It aims to dominate the people in the region and to increase its social attractiveness. For this reason, in the organization structure, organizations related to

Tab. 2: ISIS Organization Structure (http://news.bbc.co.uk, 2014)

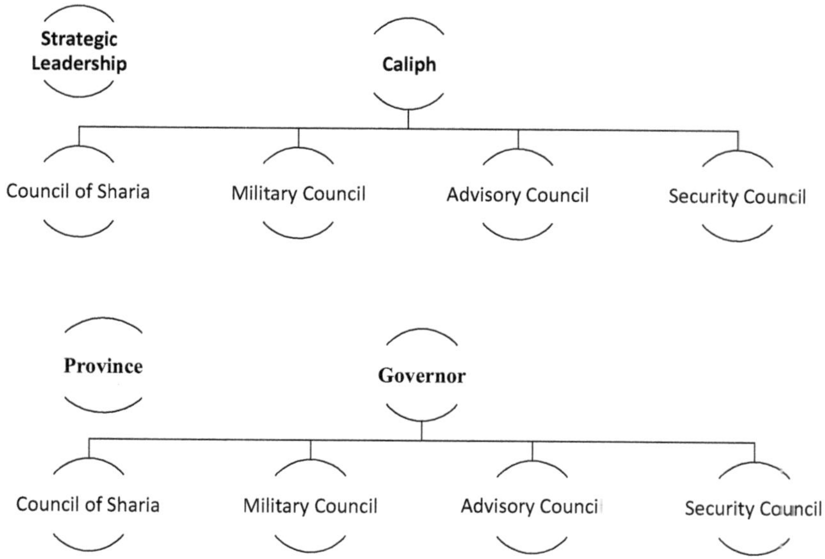

religious affairs and security works are important. A society that feels secure makes it even easier to be influenced.

ISIS organization structure is structured as Strategic Leadership, Province and Kitahat (Districts). In the Strategic Leadership level, the highest authority is the Caliph. There are Sharia, Military, Consultation and Security Council depending on the Caliph. In the province level, there is the Sharia, Military, Advisory and Security Council, which is attached to the Governor. Kitahat (Districts) also organized in the same way.

In order to complete the state organization, an appropriate profile is tried to be drawn by the organization to the image of the social state. Through this image, efforts to prove the claim that there is a state rather than an organization are among the considerable efforts.

The services in Fig. 2. correspond to the state organization structure when the social state concept is taken into consideration. It is important that the services expected to be provided to the citizens by an ordinary state are provided by the organization. The provision of health and infrastructure services are examples of organized state structure.

Fig. 2: Social State Services of ISIS (https://clarionproject.org, 2014)

6 Reasons for Participation and Support to ISIS

The ISIS organization followed a relatively good intelligent policy when it declared the Caliphate as state regime. In order to ensure that the members of the organization and the people of the region have obeyed, the thesis that the leader of the organization, Abu Bakr al-Baghdadi, came from the line of Prophet Mohammad.

Abu Bakr al-Baghdadi is a member of El Bu Bedri line of El Bu Abbas tribe settled in Salahaddin-Samarra which is known efficient and respectable one. The most important feature of this tribe is that he claims to be a descendant of Imam Hasan bin Ali. In this case, the ISIS leader claims that he was a descendant of the prophet and has many arguments to support his claim (Ağar, 2015: 262). However, this evidence alone is not sufficient for participation in the organization, but there are many factors in the context of the factors affecting participation.

Syrian-born and trained in the Muslim world of the Islamic world, Lebanon Nabeel Jabbour gathered the reasons for Muslims' participation in ISIS under 10 headings. These are success and persistence, up-to-date and attractive social media, the purpose of life, America's support to Israel, the moral structure of western societies, kneeling through shock and fear, the influence of intermediaries, the inflating and exploitation of Shiites in power, the strong financial support. The attractiveness of its structure is listed as the hope for the restoration of the caliphate (http://www.nabeeljabbour.com, 2017).

Explaining the reasons for participation in ISIS only with the mechanical structure of the organization is insufficient to reach the root of the problem. Within the scope of the opportunities provided by the organization, participants should be eager to reach these opportunities.

ISIS carried out propaganda activities in order to get behind Sunni support. As a classical technique, he aimed to take the support of the people. Abu Ghraib prison was transformed into a azaphan where the Sunnis gathered for the Iraqi Sunnis and was referred as the center of torture, rape and bribery (Ağar, 2015: 299–300). ISIS has used abuses in Abu Ghraib and the detainees in order to embrace its propaganda to recruit more militants and get popular support.

The torture in Abu Ghraib prison has been reproduced in newspapers and magazines all over the world and has been seen by almost all people who have access to television and the Internet. Here, people were treated with despair and oppression, stripped naked, tied up, sexually abused, beaten with sticks and punched into the body, attacked with dogs (Eisenman, 2007: 7). These practices, which have a great impact on the Sunni community, will create the "The Lucifer Effect" (Zimbardo, 2008) even on the most moderate people.

When Saddam Hussein's regime was destroyed, his army was liquidated. The former members of the army were both a well-trained warrior and this constituted a great source of recruitment for ISIS because these members were Sunnis. In addition, the rifts that arise as a result of the differences between the rebel groups in Syria are another source. These groups have joined the organization and used as a major force against the Bashar al-Assad regime in Syria. Such party substitutions occur continuously between organizations.

Many people living in Iraq and Syria put the blame on to the western world for backwardness and oppression. Therefore, they are sympathetic to ISIS, which is based on a sharp western opposition. In addition, the economic opportunities, social facilities and services provided by the organization cause an increase in sympathy. Some were eager to support the organization to restore the great Islamic state and to recover what the West had taken from them (Graham, 2017).

The search for adrenalin for young people living in socially backward and underdeveloped regions leads to the strengthening of global terrorist organizations. They want to experience their adventures in computer games in real life. These requests of young people also reveal social disorders. From movies to comics, from television shows to computer games, there are fantastic media.

Single-player and multi-player online computer games are the most effective games for the fantasy world, because in such games, one can behave in real life (Bainbridge, 2013: 5).

One of the factors that triggered participation is the desire to defend the Sunnis. At this point, ISIS's goal of getting Sunni support is quite a pragmatist effort. What has been done by the US in Abu Ghraib allows ISIS to gain a reputation in the Sunni community.

7 Financing Sources of ISIS

As with any terrorist organization, ISIS has to support the structure it established with financial support. It is of vital importance to meet and maintain the vital and tactical needs of the organization. Here, oil, gas and historical artifacts constitute the most important financial resources in order to strengthen the organization and provide operational sustainability (http://www.aljazeera.com.tr, 2017). Between July 2014 and December 2014, ISIS had obtained 56,000 barrels of oil a day from 42 oil production sites under its control. By 2016, this amount is estimated to be as low as 16,000 barrels (https://www.statista.com, 2017). As of 2014, ISIS received more than $ 60 million monthly through the sale of oil (http://www.aljazeera.com.tr, 2017). The sale of the obtained oil is only possible if there is a group of buyers.

The most important buyer in sale of the oil is the Assad regime. The Syrian administration finances ISIS terrorists as the biggest buyer (http://fortune.com, 2017). To agents, Damascus administration transported oil through tankers from Deyr Ez Zor and no further treatment was available (http://www.aljazeera.com.tr, 2017). In addition to the oil and gas trade, the smuggling of historical artifacts constitutes another source of financing. 100,000 historical artifacts of global significance were under ISIS's control in 4500 archaeological sites, nine of which were included in the UNESCO World Heritage List (http://www.businessinsider.com, 2017). The magnitude of the financial income obtained is estimated to be 150–200 million dollars per year, although it is not known exactly due to the fact that these works are sold on the black market (FATF, 2015: 16).

In addition, it is estimated that the sales of agricultural products (wheat, barley, etc.) obtained from the fertile agricultural regions acquired by ISIS reaches $ 200 million annually (Bisard ve Martinez, 2014: 9). However, one of the most notable financial sources is the tax revenues. Rakka Credit Bank has worked as a tax authority and has collected 20 dollars every two months for security, electricity and water from store owners. They also stated that the taxes

Fig. 3: ISIS Bitcoin Donation Address (Zenko, 2017)

received with ISIS logo and stamped official receipts were less than the bribes given to the Assad regime (https://www.nytimes.com, 2017).

The money to be obtained from the sources of belief seems to be quite difficult to be transferred through official channels. In terms of traceability and security, it poses a great risk for ISIS. Therefore, the use of money transfer systems that are difficult to follow up reinforces the organization's access to financial resources. In this context, Bitcoin and other Crypto (virtual) currencies come to the fore as a means of providing financial resources for terrorist organizations. ISIS has also discovered the use of crypto currencies. Crypto currencies are increasing due to the availability of anonymity (anonymity) to both the sender and the recipient. In recent years, companies such as Samurai, BitcoinFog and DarkWallet are focused on producing a Bitcoin wallet that provides an anonymity and these are almost completely untraceable in transactions. This system, which can be called "Dark Wallet", is seen as an important tool of financal transactions (Zenko, 2017).

Fig. 3. shows the Bitcoin address for ISIS in the Dark Web. The organization uses this way in order to provide financing due to its anonymity and is engaged in how to make donations.

8 Conclusion

The problem of terrorism and the fight against terrorism posed an ever-present danger. It increases the authority of states against terrorist organizations and the protection of citizens. There is a change in the organization, techniques and uses of terrorist organizations in the extent of terrorism. It has become difficult to study the existing ones by ignoring the methods of global terrorism, which are evolving instead of the regional terror that has been the main trend since the ages. However, the western states, the English Middle East policies, strengthen the globalization of terrorism.

ISIS has chosen to act as a state rather than a stateless organization and this identifies the status of organization by differentiating it from organizations of the past. It's like reviving the Taliban and al-Qaeda. In the form of the history of states rather than the methods used by classical terrorist organizations to ISIS supporters have acted with the state identity.

Those who advance with their ideologies based on a deviant interpretation of Islam are doing classic team work to combat this organization. First, a common and internationally accepted definition of terrorism should be introduced by the international community. The different nomenclature of different groups and organizations, such as the president of various states, the terrorist organization and the newspaper warrior, will not serve the purpose other than to deepen the problem.

There is a need that the international oil trade should be strictly followed. There is a need to form special international commission list. Besides, it can follow up the global arms trade. Also, it is possible to keep track of payment systems using virtual money such as Bitcoin which cannot be tracked.

It should be aimed to construct institutions that provide original interpretation of Islamic Religion against the preverse interpretation. The institutions that will correct the image of the evil Islam in the Western states should be organized and the existing institutions need to go through structural reforms. Turkey might help West through the appointment of clergy that will operate in these institutions. In Western societies, the exclusion of Muslim youths who have been marginalized and deprived of poverty can fall into the network of perverse ideologies.

With the use of social media reaching more than half of the world's population, account ban is no longer a method to fight against terrorism. Psychological and sociological development should be provided for individuals who cannot reach opportunities of education. The individuals affected by the virtual world should be reminded by experts that their acts will cause serious consequences.

References

Ağar, A. (2015). *IŞİD ve Irak*. İstanbul: Remzi Kitabevi.

Al-Ubaydi, M. Lahoud, N. Milton, D. and Price, B. (2014). *The Group That Calls Itself a State: Understanding the Evolution and Challenges of the Islamic State.* The Combating Terrorism Center at West Point, New York.

Bainbridge, W. S. (2013). *eGods: Faith Versus Fantasy in Computer Gaming.* New York: Oxford University Press.

Brisard, J. C. and Martinez, D. (2014). *Islamic State: The Economy-Based Terrorist Funding.* New York.

Byman, D. (2015). Terrorism in Africa: The Imminent Threat to the United States. https://www.brookings.edu/wp-content/uploads/2016/06/Byman-AQ-v-IS-HSC-042315-2.pdf 16 Haziran 2017.

Byman, D. L. Williams, Jennifer R. (2015). ISIS vs. Al Qaeda: Jihadism's Global Civil War. https://www.brookings.edu/articles/isis-vs-al-qaeda-jihadisms-global-civil-war/ 03 Eylül 2017.

Cronin, A. K. (2016). "ISIS Is Not a Terrorist Group: Why Counter Terrorism Won't Stop the Latest Jihadist Threat". *Foreign Affairs: The Arab Spring at Five.* March, Vol:94(2), pp. 382–397.

Duman, B. (2013). Irak İslam Devleti ve El-Nusra Cephesi Birleşiyor mu? http://orsam.org.tr/orsam/DPAnaliz/13463?dil=tr25 Ağustos 2017.

Dyer, G. (2015). *Don't Panic: ISIS, Terror and Today's Middle East.* Toronto.

Eisenman, S. F. (2007). *The Abu Ghraib Effect.* London: Reaktion Books.

Fatf. (2015). *Financing of the Terrorist Organisation Islamic State in Iraq and the Levant (ISIL)*, The Financial Action Task Force, Paris.

Gerges, F. A, (2016). *A History-ISIS.* New Jersey: Princeton University Press.

Freidland, E. (2015). *Special Social Report: The Islamic State.* http://clarionproject.org/wp-content/uploads/islamic-state-isis-isil-factsheet-1.pdf 10 Haziran 2017.

Gonchar, M. (2014). The ISIS Threat: Teaching About the Complex War Raging in Iraq and Syria. *New York Times.* (17 Eylül, 2014).

Graham, J. (2017). Who Joins ISIS and Why? https://www.huffingtonpost.com/john-graham/who-joins-isis-and-why_b_8881810.html 10 Eylül 2017.

Kutlu, S. (2016). *Selefiliğin Fikri Arka Planı-İslam Düşüncesinde İlk Gelenekçiler.* Ankara: Otto Yayınları.

Sandikli, A. (2015). *Terörün Geldiği Yeni Boyut: IŞİD Örneği.* İstanbul: Bilgesam Yayınları.

Stern, J. and Berger, J. M. (2015). *ISIS: The State of Terror.* New York.

Luizard, P.J. (2016). *IŞİD Tuzağı. Charles. (Y. ÖZDEN, Çev.). (2.b.).* İstanbul: İletişim Yayınları.

Walt, S. M. (2015). "ISIS as Revolutionary State: New Twist on an Old Story". *Foreign Affairs.* 94 (6), pp. 42–51.

Zelin, A. Y. (2014). "The War between ISIS and al-Qaeda for Supremacy of the Global Jihadist Movement". Washington: The Washington Institute for Near East Policy. Volume: 20.

Zimbardo, P. (2008). *The Lucifer Effect: Understanding How Good People Turn Evil*. Random New York: House Trade Paper backs.

Zenko, M. (2017). Bitcoin for Bombs. https://www.cfr.org/blog/bitcoin-bombs 25 Kasım 2017.

http://www.bbc.com/news/world-middle-east-2905214403 Eylül 2017.

https://www.sabah.com.tr/gundem/2015/11/16/obama-askerlerin-sahaya-inmesi-dusuncesi-yanlistir 25 Haziran 2017.

http://www.aljazeera.com/indepth/interactive/2016/05/timeline-battle-fallujah-160531111034135.html 03 Eylül 2017.

http://web.stanford.edu/group/mappingmilitants/cgi-bin/groups/view/110 Ekim 2017.

http://news.bbc.co.uk/2/shared/bsp/hi/pdfs/03_09_14_is_governance.pdf 03 Eylül 2017.

https://clarionproject.org/docs/isis-isil-islamic-state-magazine-Issue-1-the-return-of-khilafah.pdf 23 Ağustos 2017.

http://www.nabeeljabbour.com/Blog/February-2015/ISIS-10-Reasons-Muslims-are-Eager-to-Join02 Aralık 2017.

http://www.aljazeera.com.tr/haber/isid-petrolunu-kime-nasil-satiyor 24 Kasım 2017.

https://www.statista.com/statistics/272014/global-social-networks-ranked-by-number-of-users/ 23 Mayıs 2017.

http://fortune.com/2017/01/20/oil-gas-isis-syria-assad/ 03 Ekim 2017.

http://www.businessinsider.com/r-islamic-state-nets-up-to-200-million-a-year-from-antiquities-russia-2016-413 Eylül 2017.

https://www.nytimes.com/2014/07/24/world/middleeast/islamic-state-controls-raqqa-syria.html?hpandaction=clickandpgtype=Homepageandversion=LedeSumandmodule=first-column-regionandregion=top-newsandWT.nav=top-newsand_r=1 05 Eylül 2017.

İskender Gumus and Ayşe Nur Ciftci

Development of Minimum Wage in Turkey: A Critical Evaluation

1 Introduction

Social policy aims to fight disadvantageousness, whether it is considered in the narrow or broad sense. Within disadvantageousness, struggling against poverty is an extremely important social policy implementation area due to the large masses it covers. Along with the adoption of the minimum wage, the fact that the wage had a base led to a decrease in inequality in income distribution, which also led to an increase in welfare in the general sense. Furthermore, the fact that the marginal consumption tendencies of those in the income group subject to minimum wage are higher than those with high income causes greater part of the additional income obtained to be canalized into consumption. This also supports economic growth since it will lead to a further increase in demand, as well.

There has been a considerable delay in the implementation of minimum wage, which has such an important function, in the modern sense in Turkey. It is seen that amount determination was adopted on a local/regional/national scale since 1951. The aim of this study was to examine the temporal development of minimum wage, which has an important place in social policy implementation tools, in Turkey. Thus, the temporal differentiation experienced in the application of minimum wage will be determined and presented. The subject was examined under three headings to achieve the ultimate aim of the study:

In the first part entitled "Fundamentals of minimum wage and first applications", the basic principles on which minimum wage applications are based, and the transfer of first applications were outlined. In the second part entitled "Legal foundations of minimum wage in Turkey", the legal foundations on which the minimum wage application is based was first discussed with the distinction between international and national resources. While ILO Conventions, Universal Declaration of Human Rights, European Social Charter of International foundations were examined, 1924, 1961 and 1982 constitution acts, labor laws and minimum wage regulations of national foundations were examined. In the last part entitled "Minimum wage in the decisions of the minimum wage determination commission published in the official gazette", all decisions of the minimum wage determination commission that have been published in the official gazette since 1969 were examined, and the relevant developments in commission decisions with innovations were presented.

2 Theoretical Fundamentals of Minimum Wage and First Applications

In the determination of wages, it is generally essential to provide employees with a wage at a level to allow them to achieve minimum standards of living, and this amount may vary depending on being married or single and having child or no child (Isaac, 1949: 50). When it is examined by its structure, since minimum wage can be changed within the mandatory provisions provided that it is in favor of the worker, it is included in relative mandatory provisions (Erdem, 2005: 97). However, public powers both around the world and in Turkey, in particular, abstained from establishing mandatory provisions for the determination of wages for many years. The monopolistic position of any class for the determination of wages in modern businesses developing in western countries since the 18th century was not adopted due to the implementation of the objective that competitive environment would have an absolute command of every stage of the production process in liberalism constituting the adopted economic understanding of the period (Furgaç, 1955: 51). This led to a delay in the initiation of the applications for minimum wage, as well. Nevertheless, it is seen that approaches to the minimum wage at the intellectual level were put forward in the 19th century. For instance, the views that the long-term level of wages would be determined at the base level to meet the minimum needs of society due to Ricardo's natural wages (bronze law of wages) and reserve army of the employed with technology in Marx can be considered as the first determinations and theories for minimum wage in the modern sense (See. Akyüz, 1980: 27).

The minimum wage application was first legally framed in England where the Industrial Revolution also started in 1909, and the method of the determination of the minimum wage by industry committees was introduced. Then, this law reached a scale to include half a million workers in 1913 with the inclusion of some of other business lines. Since 1921, it reached an extent in which determination was made by 63 industry councils and 3 million workers were included. The first legal regulation against the first public interventions for wages in France in 1899 was made for those working in the cottage industries on July 10, 1915. In the United States, the first regulation for determination of minimum wage was adopted in the state of Massachusetts in 1912, the number of states accepting the minimum wage increased to fifteen until 1923, and all workers in the country were covered by federal legal regulation in 1933 (Kutal, 1969: 98–99,

106, 113). As it was emphasized by Zaim (1962: 28–29), minimum wage also led to a decrease in the share of high incomers in the US in total GDP, as one of the elements with an important function in the establishment of a fair distribution of income. This also ensured the effective use of minimum wage as a social policy application since its first applications.

In particular, the distinction between informal and formal employment and "dual labor market structure" in low-income countries bring along the transformation of minimum wage into common wage in formal employment and also cause wage difference between the two labor markets to be at low level contrary to common belief (Türcan Özşuca and Toksöz, 2003: 12). Öney (1980: 8) attributes the transformation of minimum wage into common wage in low-income countries to widespread hidden unemployment in the agricultural sector and the excess of unemployment and mentions that the state also had to determine minimum wage above the common wage in these countries. It is seen that a much more limited sector in high-income countries obtained income at the minimum wage level despite the transformation of minimum wage into common wage in low-income countries; for instance, the weight of minimum wage earners among all wage earners in Ceylon reached up to 80 % in 1949; on the contrary, this ratio was limited to 10 % in high-income countries (Kutal, 1965: 52). Therefore, the effect of minimum wage in high-income countries is far below its effect in low-income countries (Akgül, 2016: 100). From this point of view, it can be concluded that there was a significant differentiation in the effect level of the determination of minimum wage as a social policy implementation tool in country groups according to levels of development. As it is indicated by Dama (2017: 1), minimum wage is among the important components of both economic policy and social policy such as production, employment and unemployment, especially in developing countries. When the transformation of minimum wage into common wage in low- and middle-income countries is taken into account, it is seen that it has come to a much more important social policy tool in these countries compared to developed countries.

When the minimum wage determination is examined, it is concluded that determination is generally made in three ways. Accordingly, 1) it can be determined by the determination of the state, 2) it can be determined by commission/commissions on a local, line of business or national scale, 3) it can be determined as a result of "collective bargaining" by the negotiation of trade unions and employers together (Arndt, 1955: 36). It is seen that any of these methods can be preferred both around the world and periodically in Turkey. Therefore, the methods of the determination of the minimum wage completely vary depending on the preference of political power.

It is very difficult to measure the effectiveness of minimum wage as a social policy tool apart from its effect on the establishment of justice in the distribution of income. However, functional analysis methods come to the forefront in testing the effect of minimum wage as a social policy instrument, under the assumption that its effect on growth, which is one of the prerequisites for the increase in welfare, will lead to both economic policy and an increase in welfare. In this context, the presence of causality relationship between growth and minimum wage in Turkey in particular was determined by testing through the analyses based on statistical methods in various studies (See. Sunal and Sezgin Alp, 2015; Korkmaz and Çoban, 2006).

3 Legal Foundations of Minimum Wage in Turkey

The first application for the determination of minimum wage in Turkey began with the decree issued to be implemented in some areas in 1806, and then, it gained a modern form at the business and local level along with the determination of the level of minimum wage to be paid for the employees in mines in article eleven of the "Law No. 151 on Ereğli Coal Basin Mine Workers". Although municipalities were decreed to determine the minimum wage every 3 months during the first Izmir Economy Congress in 1923, but it could not find a field of application. With the Labor Law No. 3008 dated 1936, the first legal foundation for minimum wage in the modern sense was established at the law level (Yılmaz Eser and Terzi, 2008: 129–130).

In the first minimum wage regulation, which was prepared based on the first labor law no. 3008 and issued in 1951, the determination of minimum wage was left to the initiative of the Ministry of Labor and it was preferred to make determinations at the local level instead of determining a single amount on a national scale, and this type of application brought along a large number of different minimum wage determinations. Although the objections to the amounts determined by the local commissions were attempted to be evaluated by the "Minimum Wage Appeal Commission" of the Ministry of Labor by considering the local conditions and the situation of business lines, the relevant multi-authority significantly damaged the comprehensiveness of the system in the first period between 1951 and 1967, as it was also indicated by Tekin (2007: 90–91).

It will be appropriate to start with the distinction between international and national resources with respect to the systematization of the issue in terms of legal foundations. The binding force of the international conventions based on international legal foundations brings along the formation of legal basis, as well.

These conventions, which are not subject to the supervision of the constitutional court, are mainly framework contracts.

In the Washington Conference, which was the first conference held in 1919 after the First World War, workers' wage levels were emphasized, and the establishment of the ILO was based on the decision taken in the same conference (Bilik, 1949: 82). Thus, ILO, which is among the most important framework contracting institutions for minimum wage to which Turkey is also a party, was then established. It is remarkable that the minimum wage decided by the ILO in the first quarter of the twentieth century and then the framework provisions on determination methods were approved by Turkey for many years. In 1958, in a study carried out by the ILO, it was reported that minimum wage was actually applied by taking advantage of international resources in most of 50 countries that were not parties to minimum wage provisions in which Turkey was also included (Kutal, 1970: 190). On the contrary, these countries did not become parties to international convention and did not prefer the formation of binding supreme decision in their countries.

With the Council of Ministers' Decision No. 9119 dated April 6, 1949, which was published in the Official Gazette No. 7217 on May 27, 1949, the "Universal Declaration of Human Rights" was decided to be taught at schools and broadcast in radio and published in newspapers, though not binding (Council of Ministers' Decision No. 9119, RG. Issue 7217, Date 27.05.1949). Although not legally binding, it can be considered as an important step within the context of international conventions. In paragraph 3 of Article 23 of the relevant declaration, the following provision was included:

> *"3 - Everyone who works has the right to just and favorable remuneration ensuring for himself and his family an existence worthy of human dignity, and supplemented, if necessary, by other means of social protection."*

Although the political power is not put under any legal commitment regarding the determination of minimum wage in this decision, there is an opportunity to accept it as a beginning with respect to considering international resources.

The first international convention, which was legally binding for political power, was for agriculture-dependent workers in 1969 and approved by the Council of Ministers' decision in 1970 (Law No. 1168 of 30.04.1969 on the adoption of the International Labor Convention No. 99 on the Minimum Wage Determination Procedures in Agriculture, RG. no: 13194, Date: 09.05.1969, 7/91 Council of Ministers' decision, RG. No: 13455, Date: 26.03.1970). It is noteworthy that the first binding international convention adopted is limited to employees in the agricultural sector. Although the agricultural sector's weight in both production and labor market was very high under the condition of the period, the fact that the employees in the sector were mainly self-employed and free assistant family workers caused the sector to be covered was very limited. Moreover, since there were also flexible provisions, such as paying a part of the wage in kind, in the provisions of the contract approved, it is impossible to ensure that non-landowner villagers have a standard wage effectively even if they may not be considered a tenant like "tenant farmers". Probably for this reason, it started with the approval of the convention no. 99 adopted in 1951. The convention no. 26, which was adopted on 30.05.1928 by ILO, which is an international convention bringing responsibility mainly on national scale, was put into effect in 1973 and started to be implemented from 1974 (Law no. 1769 and dated 25.06.1973 on the Approval of the International Labor Convention No. 26 on the Execution of Minimum Wage Determination Procedures, RG. No: 14583, Date: 03.07.1973; 7/8685 Council of Ministers' decision, RG. No: 14994, Date: 02.09.1974). When the acceptance dates of these conventions by ILO are considered, the convention no.26 was first adopted while the convention no. 99 was adopted after a quarter century. The fact that the convention no. 26 has a general character means that the convention no. 99 was also created based on the convention no. 26. However, the orders of acceptance of conventions of Turkey are just the opposite.

The unwillingness to be included in international conventions was shaped by the unwillingness to assess the minimum wage, especially on a scale that would meet the basic needs of the workers' family. In this context, ILO's convention no. 131 as an advisory decision for developing countries was not acceded (Uçucu, 2014: 106–107). In Article 4 of the European Social Charter, employees are entitled to receive the right amount of wage required to live well with their families (Koç and Görücü, 2018: 60). This situation was excluded from approval on the grounds that Paragraph 1 of Article 4 would lead to the obligation to employ the minimum wage determination for the minimum subsistence of the worker and his/her family although Turkey has signed the European Social Charter in 1989 (Korkmaz, 2004: 54; Korkmaz and Avsallı, 2012: 152).

The national legal foundations for minimum wage would be listed as 1) Constitution, 2) Law and 3) Regulation according to the hierarchy of law. Accordingly, it would be appropriate to examine three constitutions "1924, 1961, 1982", four Labor Laws no. "3008, 931, 1475, 4857", and four minimum wage regulations no. "1951, 1968. 1972, 2004" created based on the four labor laws.

The adoption of minimum wage in constitutional supreme framework was not possible until 2001, contrary to common belief. The fact that no provision related to wages other than the minimum wage was included in the 1924 constitution act, including the changes to the 1961 constitution, are clearly seen

(See. T.C. 1924 constitution act, RG. No: 5905, Date: 15.01.1945). Therefore, the Article 32 of the first Labor law No. 3008 and the first minimum wage regulation dated 1951 have no legal basis. So, minimum wage also does not have an internationally binding legal basis since the ILO Convention No. 26 was adopted later.

Although 1961 constitution act had no clear provision for minimum wage, the provisions of the Article 45 were considered as the basis for minimum wage. In this article, it is stated that

> *"The State shall take necessary measures to ensure that employees receive a fair wage that is appropriate for the work performed and provides a level of wage that is worthy of human dignity."*

and this article is very general. The phrase "wage that is worthy of human dignity" in the article is open to comment. The phrase "appropriate for the work performed" is also far from functionality since it would lead to the determination of a large number of different amounts. Likewise, the uncertainty about what the measures in the phrase "take measures" would be leads to uncertainty that would limit the possibilities of the implementation of minimum wage (See. T.C. 1961 constitution act, RG. No: 10859, Date: 20.07.1961).

When the 1982 constitution act, which is still in force, is examined despite the intense changes made, it is seen that the phrase

> *"The State shall take necessary measures to ensure that employees receive a fair wage and benefit from other welfare benefits."*

was included until the amendment to the article 55 on 03.10.2001, just like in the 1961 constitution act. Therefore, the uncertainty in the 1961 constitution act was also preserved in the 1982 constitution act. In the amendment in 2001, the phrase

> *"The economic conditions of the country and the livelihood conditions of the employees are taken into consideration in the determination of minimum wage."*

was added, and it is seen that the constitutional framework of the minimum wage could be established. Therefore, it is clearly seen that the four labor laws and the first three of the four regulations are devoid of constitutional basis (T.C. 1982 constitution act, RG. No: 17863, Date: 09.11.1982).

The first legal basis for minimum wage in national legislation was ensured in Article 32 of the first labor law no. 3008, which entered into force in 1936. However, the clear definition of minimum wage was not made in this article, and the principle of determining the minimum wage level based on social and economic imperatives was adopted. In addition to this, flexibility was ensured in the determination of amount by time, and pricing opportunities based on overtime or piece work/work load were also acknowledged. The provision of the relevant article is as follows:

> *"Article 32 - The minimum limits of workers' wages to be paid per hour or per day or weekly or monthly accounts and per piece and for the work performed in the works to be proposed by the Ministry of Economy due to economic and internal obligations are determined by a regulation."* (See. Labor Law No. 3008, RG. No: 3330, Date: 15.06.1936).

In the labor laws put into force in 1967, 1971 and 2003 after the first labor law, the Article 32 of the first labor law was preserved by simplifying in terms of language. The additional provision for the minimum wage commission was the only addition. In all three laws, the commission members were appointed and formed from the elected; the number of appointed members was kept less than the number of the representatives of social partners, and the representatives of social partners were determined as workers and employers' representatives consisting of five people. The conditions for meeting and decision-making of the commission were also included in the law, and it was ensured that the codes of practice would be determined in the regulation (See. Labor Law No. 931, RG. No: 12672, Date: 12.08.1967 "Article 33"; Labor Law No. 1475, RG. No: 13943, Date: 01.09.1971 "Article 33"; Labor Law No. 4857, RG. No: 25134, Date: 10.06.2003 "Article 39".) The first minimum wage regulation, which entered into force in 1951, consisted of 21 articles. The first labor law no. 3008 was shown as the legal basis in its first article, and it was decided that employers could not pay wages below the amount specified in the fourth article and that there was no discrimination based on gender in the second article. In the third article of the regulation, it was stated that the minimum wage would be determined by the commissions to be established at the level of local and business sectors, but an alternative for determination at national level was not presented. In the fifth article, the structure of the commission members to be formed from the representatives of workers, employers, professional chambers, labor unions and physicians and municipal councilors under the presidency of an official to be appointed by the local authorities of the Ministry of Labor was determined in the establishment of the minimum wage determination commissions. Subsequent articles also include the detailing of the functioning of the local minimum wage commissions (See Minimum Wage Regulation dated 1951, RG. No: 7707, Date: 13.01.1951).

The number of articles of the second minimum wage regulation, which entered into force in 1968, was reduced to fifteen and it differed from the first regulation at five points: 1) It was based on the second labor law no. 931. 2) In the second article, the principle that there cannot be difference by age was added to the decision that there would not be gender-based inequalities in wages. 3) In the third article, it was ensured that minimum wage could be determined at the national level, except for the determination at the local or business lines level. 4) In the sixth article, it was adopted that the commission would be established on a national scale instead of being established on a local scale. 5) In the sixth article, it was decided that minimum wage would come into force with the publication of the commission decision in the official gazette. Apart from the fact that the legal basis for the third minimum wage regulation, which came into force in 1972, consisting of sixteen articles was the Labor Law No. 1475, the only aspect which differs from the previous regulation is the fact that at what level the minimum wage should be and the needs to be met with the wage to be received were limited by concretization in the first article by listing as

> *"…minimum wage is the wage which is paid to workers in return for a normal working day and is sufficient to meet the mandatory requirements of the worker such as food, housing, clothing, health, transportation and culture through the prices of the day at a minimum level."*

Apart from the fact that the fourth and final regulation consisting of nineteen articles, which came into force in 2004 and which is still in force, was based on the last labor law no. 4857, the only aspect which differs from the previous regulation is the provision that minimum wage determination can be made only at the national scale (See Minimum Wage Regulation dated 1968, RG. No: 12867, Date: 05.04.1968; Minimum Wage Regulation dated 1972, RG. No: 14097, Date: 12.02.1972; Minimum Wage Regulation dated 2004, RG. No: 25540, Date: 01.08.2004).

4 Minimum Wage in the Decisions of the Minimum Wage Determination Commission Published in the Official Gazette

In the second minimum wage regulation published in 1968, the principle that the minimum wage commission decisions would come into force after publication in the official gazette was adopted, and this principle was maintained in the next two regulations. Therefore, it is possible to reach the decisions of the minimum wage determination commission since 1969 until today, instead of 1951 during which the first minimum wage regulation came into force. Since there was not a single minimum wage commission on a national scale between 1951 and 1969, and many commissions carried out activities on the local level, the number of decisions taken by them is quite high. When it is considered that there was a separate commission for each local unit, it is possible to find hundreds and maybe thousands of different commissions in eighteen years.

It is remarkable that the minimum wage determination commissions published between 1969 and 1818 in the official gazette were based on the repetition of the decisions made in previous years, in addition to decisions containing significant innovations. Accordingly, the decisions of the committees had distinctive decisions. The important innovations included in the eleven decisions are as follows:

The outstanding issue in the decision of the first minimum wage determination commission consisting of five items in 1969 was the determination of daily wages ranging from 19.50 TL to 15 TL per day for workers aged over 16 years by dividing provinces into six regions according to the level of development. In workers under 16 years of age, minimum wage determination was different in six regions with a reduction of 2 TL. This decision does not contain any information on how minimum wage was determined (Decision of Minimum Wage Determination Commission dated 1969, RG. No: 13216, Date: 13.06.1969).

The decision of the next minimum wage determination commission consisting of four items came into force 3 years after the first decision, and it is seen that the minimum wage determination differentiating according to the level of development was maintained. However, the minimum wage level which was determined by dividing into six regions in the first commission decision in 1969 was calculated by dividing into four regions with daily minimum wage amounts ranging from 25 TL to 22 TL. In those who did not turn 16, this wage range was between 18.50 TL and 21 TL (Decision of Minimum Wage Determination Commission dated 1972, RG. No: 14349, Date: 23.10.1972). In the relevant first two commission decisions, it is remarkable that the minimum wages that were previously determined at the local level and determined by several different local commissions were determined by regions, and the wages were determined at a scale between the local and centric.

In 1974, there was a new break in the commission decisions, and the presentation of determination methods were detailed under the title of the justification of four-item decision. More importantly, it is seen that minimum wage was determined on a national scale instead of multi-part pricing on the local scale, for the first time in this decision. Furthermore, the presentation of the determination method was partly included in the decision by accepting that 3500-calorie daily food consumption would correspond to 48 % of the minimum wage (Decision of Minimum Wage Determination Commission dated 1974, RG. No: 14931, Date: 30.06.1974).

In the decision of the minimum wage determination commission in 1977 during which there was a change in the minimum wage determination, it was decided that food consumption would correspond to 45 % of the minimum wage; in addition to this, one of workers' dependent children aged between 0 and 14 years would be taken into account in determining the minimum wage. Thus, there was a transition from minimum wage determination based on subsistence for a single person to a new determination method as the amount required for himself and a child of him (Decision of Minimum Wage Determination Commission dated 1977, RG. No: 16155, Date: 30.10.1977). The outstanding innovation in the commission's decision in 1979 is the fact that three standard justifications gathered under the title of the principles to be followed in determining the minimum wage, which have been included in every commission decision so far, were listed in the decision text for the first time. Accordingly:

> *"JUSTIFICATION*
> *Principles to be Followed in Determining the Minimum Wage:*
> *1 — Minimum wage is not a matter of negotiation. It is the base pay which is determined by scientific, objective and reliable measures according to the methods in the law and regulation that will provide the daily income of the worker.*
> *2 — Minimum wage should help to improve economic and social conditions in the long term and provide a fair income distribution.*
> *3 — Minimum wage should be determined at the national level by taking into account the differences between the provinces, and even the districts connected to each province, the difficulties in reflecting these differences to the minimum wage, the ease of access and the costs and the integrity of the country."* (See. Decision of Minimum Wage Determination Commission dated 1979, RG. No: 16624, Date: 30.04.1979).

After the 1980 military coup, the first decision of the minimum wage determination commission was established in 1982, and the traces of the fear caused by military coup in society are clearly seen in the decision text. The majority of votes formed due to a minute of dissent reported by employers' representatives on the grounds that high wages were generally expected in previous decision texts this time turned into unanimity of votes. The most remarkable issue is that the fact that worker's representatives stated that

> *"As workers' representatives, we want to express our belief that we are opposed to the Commission Decision on dependency ratio, but because we consider the gentle conditions in our country, we do not find it sufficient, but we believe that we are favorable because we believe in the benefits of the minimum wage."*

although they reported a minute of dissent reveals the severity of the relevant pressure (See Decision of Minimum Wage Determination Commission dated 1982, RG. No: 17908, Date: 24.12.1982).

The difference in the decision of the commission in 1987 compared to previous commission decisions was the inclusion of the determination of two different minimum wages in non-agricultural activities and agricultural activities in a single decision. Accordingly, the calculation that food consumption corresponded to 44 % of the minimum wage was calculated by determining as 50 % for those working in agriculture. The second remarkable issue in the decision is that both workers and employer's representative reported a minute of dissent on the decision (See Decision of Minimum Wage Determination Commission dated 1987, RG. No: 19500, Date: 27.06.1987).

In the commission decision dated 1988, daily as well as monthly minimum wage amounts were also included for the first time in this commission decision despite the inclusion of only daily minimum wage amounts in the decisions taken in previous years (See Decision of Minimum Wage Determination Commission dated 1988, RG. No: 19858, Date: 30.06.1988).

In the commission decision dated 1989, it is seen that the calculation method was changed. Accordingly, the long-term calorie-based minimum wage calculation was abandoned and the calculation method containing updating according to CPI was employed (See Decision of Minimum Wage Determination Commission dated 1989, RG. No: 20234, Date: 27.07.1989).

Finally, in the decision of the minimum wage determination commission in 2018, the calculation method of the minimum wage was changed and this time the calculation method was completely excluded from the commission decision text (See Decision of Minimum Wage Determination Commission dated 2018, RG. No: 30638, Date: 27.12.2018).

5 Conclusion

Turkey is a country with a deep rooted history dating back to the Ottoman period for minimum wage. However, the beginning of the minimum wage determination in the modern sense is quite new. What the amount of minimum wage applied since 1951 would be shaped based on the principle of calculating the amount required for the employee's own livelihood by ignoring the obligation of the worker to support his family. For this reason, the tendency to be a party to the conventions that are binding in terms of political power has decreased. In the national legislation, the feature excluding family oriented view stands out in the regulation and decision adopted in this field until 2001. Although this dominant structure was extended to be calculated on the scale to provide for the livelihood of workers and their only child under 14 in the calculation of minimum wage, so had an increase in the gap between the minimum wages of workers who turned and did not turn 16, the widespread expectation is to increase the minimum wages to a level covering the whole of the worker and his family.

Since 1969, there have been periodic differentiations in the calculation methods of minimum wages. While no detailed calculation method presentation was made in the first commission decisions, the minimum wage determination was later made by calculating the amount that would provide 3500 calorie food intake per day for the worker, "one child of the worker was later added to it", according to the weight of food spending in the spending basket. However, it is remarkable that the calculation method in commission decisions was abandoned in time and CPI-based updates were employed.

The issue of whether the minimum wage will be determined by differing according to regional units and business lines or as a single amount on a national scale is another question of debate. The fact that there was a wide range of local minimum wage determined on the local units scale and with limited members at first, computational complexity and central management control problem caused that the method of application on a local and regional scale was replaced by the determination of a single minimum wage on a national scale. Furthermore, despite the inclusion of the provision that minimum wage could also be determined at the business level in the first three minimum wage regulations, no actual wage diversification has been made in any of the actual realizations since 1951. The effect of determination complexity is likely important in this diversification. Furthermore, the fact that a framework to allow determination at the business level on how to establish commissions was not formed in minimum wage regulations also supports the fact that the administrations are reluctant to make determination based on the line of business although it was decided to make arrangement according to the line of business in the framework decision.

The political structure of the country was also influential in determining the minimum wage. Indeed, the dissenting opinions emerging in the employers' front before 1980 were replaced by the workers' front. The political management aimed at the reduction of input costs for the businesses to increase their competitiveness on a global scale in the implementation of the economic policy, which was transformed from import-substitution industrialization strategy to outward-oriented industrialization strategy after the decisions of January 24, 1980, supported the real reduction of workers' wages, which have an important place in input costs. In this context, it is important to limit the minimum wage increases to prevent an increase in general wages. The dissenting opinions of employers' representatives before the 1980s to the decisions of the minimum wage determination commission after 1980 were turned into dissenting opinions of workers' representatives. As an important indicator of this situation, in the commission decision in 1982 during which military government did not end, the expression that the political/military power was supported to protect its power in the sensitive environment in the country could be included although workers did not find the amount determined in the decision satisfactory and they did not adopt it. Despite the possibility of reporting a minute of dissent in an environment where the harsh measures of military junta made it impossible to express complaints loudly, it is noteworthy that workers' representatives added their support by detailing in the dissenting opinion feature despite all possible sanctions. Moreover, the fact that they expressed that they supported the unanimous decision of the decision due to the sensitivity of the period is also important in terms of going down the threat experienced in history by adding it to the legal text. The dissenting opinions of worker's representatives continued to be included in a significant part of the subsequent commission decisions.

References

1168 sayılı ve 30.04.1969 tarihli Tarımda Asgarî Ücret Tespiti Usulleri Hakkında 99 sayılı Milletlerarası Çalışma Sözleşmesinin Onaylanmasının Uygun Bulunduğuna Dair Kanun, RG. no: 13194, Tarih: 09.05.1969.

1475 Sayılı İş Kanunu, RG. No: 13943, Tarih: 01.09.1971.

1475 Sayılı İş Kanunu, RG. No: 13943, Tarih: 01.09.1971.

1769 sayılı ve 25.06.1973 tarihli Asgarî Ücret Tespit Usulleri İhdası Hakkında 26 Sayılı Milletlerarası Çalışma Sözleşmesinin Onaylanmasının Uygun Bulunduğuna Dair Kanun, RG. No: 14583, Tarih: 03.07.1973.

1951 tarihli Asgari Ücret Yönetmeliği, RG. No: 7707, Tarih: 13.01.1951.

1968 tarihli Asgari Ücret Yönetmeliği, RG. No: 12867, Tarih: 05.04.1968.

1969 tarihli Asgari Ücret Tespit Komisyonu Kararı, RG. No: 13216, Tarih: 13.06.1969.

1972 tarihli Asgari Ücret Tespit Komisyonu Kararı, RG. No: 14349, Tarih: 23.10.1972.

1972 tarihli Asgari Ücret Yönetmeliği, RG. No: 14097, Tarih: 12.02.1972.

1974 tarihli Asgari Ücret Tespit Komisyonu Kararı, RG. No: 14931, Tarih: 30.06.1974.

1977 tarihli Asgari Ücret Tespit Komisyonu Kararı, RG. No: 16155, Tarih: 30.10.1977.

1979 tarihli Asgari Ücret Tespit Komisyonu Kararı, RG. No: 16624, Tarih: 30.04.1979.

1982 tarihli Asgari Ücret Tespit Komisyonu Kararı, RG. No: 17908, Tarih: 24.12.1982.

1987 tarihli Asgari Ücret Tespit Komisyonu Kararı, RG. No: 19500, Tarih: 27.06.1987.

1988 tarihli Asgari Ücret Tespit Komisyonu Kararı, RG. No: 19858, Tarih: 30.06.1988.

1989 tarihli Asgari Ücret Tespit Komisyonu Kararı, RG. No: 20234, Tarih: 27.07.1989.

2004 tarihli Asgari Ücret Yönetmeliği, RG. No: 25540, Tarih: 01.08.2004.

2018 tarihli Asgari Ücret Tespit Komisyonu Kararı, RG. No: 30638, Tarih: 27.12.2018.

3008 Sayılı İş Kanunu, RG. No: 3330, Tarih: 15.06.1936.

4857 Sayılı İş Kanunu, RG. No: 25134, Tarih: 10.06.2003.

7/8685 sayılı Bakanlar Kurulu Kararı, RG. No: 14994, Tarih: 02.09.1974.

7/91 sayılı Bakanlar Kurulu Kararı, RG. No: 13455, Tarih: 26.03.1970.

9119 Sayılı Bakanlar Kurulu Kararı, RG. Sayı 7217, Tarih 27.05.1949.

931 Sayılı İş Kanunu, RG. No: 12672, Tarih: 12.08.1967.

Akgeyik, T. (2007). *Bölgesel Asgari Ücret Yaklaşımı*, İstanbul: İTO Yayınları.

Akgül, O. (2016). "Türkiye'de Asgari Ücretin Mahzurlu Alanları ve Öneriler", *Hak İş Uluslararası Emek ve Toplum Dergisi*, 5 (12), 96–127.

Akyüz, Y. (1980). *Emek Deper Teorisi ve Nitelikli İşgücü Sorunu*, Ankara: AÜSBF Yayınları.

Arndt, H. (1955). "Asgari Ücret", *Sosyal Siyaset Konferansları Dergisi*, 7, 33–40.

Bilik, E. (1949). "Devletlerarası Çalışma Teşkilatı", *AÜ Hukuk Fakültesi Dergisi*, 6 (2), 62–94.

Dama, N. (2017). *Sosyal Politika Perspektifinde Asgari Ücret*, Ankara: SETA Perspektif,

Furgaç, H. (1955). "Hayat Pahalılığı ve Ücretlerin Tayini", *Sosyal Siyaset Konferansları Dergisi*, 7, 51–60.

Isaac, A. (1949). "Ücret Sistemleri", *Sosyal Siyaset Konferansları Dergisi*, 2, 49–64.

Koç, M. and Görücü, İ. (2018). "Türkiye'de Asgari Ücretin Uygulanması", *Social Sciences Studies Journal*, 4 (13), 58–73.

Korkmaz, A. (2004). "Bir Sosyal Politika Aracı Olarak Türkiye'de Asgari Ücret: 1951–2003", *Kocaeli Üniversitesi Sosyal Bilimler Enstitüsü Dergisi*, 7, 53–69.

Korkmaz, A. and Avsallı, H. (2012). "Türkiye'de Asgari Ücretin Hukuksal Yönü", *Uluslar arası Alanya İşletme Fakültesi Dergisi*, 4 (2), 151–162.

Korkmaz, A. and Çoban, O. (2006) "Emek Piyasasında Asgari Ücret, İşsizlik ve Enflasyon Arasındaki İlişkilerin Ekonometrik Bir Analizi, Türkiye Örneği, 1969-2006", *Maliye Dergisi*, 151, 16–22.

Kutal, M. (1965). "Türkiye'de Asgari Ücret Mevzuatı ve Tatbikatının Tahlili", *İktisat Fakültesi Mecmuası*, 24 (3–4), 52–108.

Kutal, M. (1969). *Teorik Esasları ve Tatbikatı Açısından Asgari Ücret*, İstanbul: İÜ İktisat Fakültesi Yayınları.

Kutal, M. (1970). "Uluslararası Çalışma Teşkilatının Yasama Faaliyeti ve Türkiye Cumhuriyetinin Durumu (1919–1969)", *Sosyal Siyaset Konferansları*, 21, 169–198.

Öney, E. (1980). *İktisadi Planlama*, 2. Baskı, Ankara: AÜSBF Yayınları.

Özdemir, E. (2005). "İş Hukukunda Mutlak Emredici Hükümlerin Yeri", *Ankara Üniversitesi Hukuk Fakültesi Dergisi*, 54 (3), 95–120.

Sunal, O. and ve Sezgin Alp, Ö. (2015). "Türkiye'de Reel Asgari Ücretler ve Reel GSYİH Değişmeleri Arasındaki Nedensellik İlişkisi: Enflasyon Oranına Endekslenmiş Bir Nominal Asgari Ücret Politikası", *Ankara Üniversitesi SBF Dergisi*, 70 (1), 111–129.

T.C. 1924 Anayasası, RG. No: 5905, Tarih: 15.01.1945.

T.C. 1961 Anayasası, RG. No: 10859, Tarih: 20.07.1961.

T.C. 1982 Anayasası, RG. No: 17863, Tarih: 09.11.1982.

Türcan Özşuca, Ş. and Toksöz, G. (2003). *Sosyal Koruma Yoksunluğu Enformel Sektör ve Küçük İşletmeler*, Ankara: AÜSBF Yayınları.

Uçucu, M. (2014). "Çalışma Hayatında Asgari Ücretlerinin Sosyal Güvenliklerini Destekleme Fonu Projesi ve Fransa Örneği", *Çalışma Dünyası Dergisi*, 2 (1), 101–117.

Yılmaz Eser, B. and Terzi, H. (2008). "Türkiye'de Asgari Ücret: Sorunlar Öneriler", *Atatürk Üniversitesi İktisadi ve İdari Bilimler Dergisi*, 22 (1), 129–143.

Zaim, S. (1962). "Sendikaların Milli Gelirin Dağılışına ve İşçi-Gelir Payına Tesiri", *Sosyal Siyaset Konferansları Dergisi*, 13, 15–34.

List of Figures

List of Tables